HARD

IDNIGHTER

WRITTEN BY
STEVE ORLANDO
BRIAN K. VAUGHAN
CHRISTOS GAGE
PETER MILLIGAN

ART BY
ACO
HUGO PETRUS
DAVID MESSINA
GAETANO CARLUCCI
DARICK ROBERTSON
KARL STORY
JOHN PAUL LEON
SIMON BISLEY

COLOR BY
ROMULO FAJARDO, JR.
JEROMY COX
RANDY MAYOR
JONNY RENCH
BRIAN BUCCELLATO

LETTERS BY
TOM NAPOLITANO
PHIL BALSMAN
SAL CIPRIANO

COVER ART BY
ACO & ROMULO FAJARDO, JR.

ORIGINAL SERIES COVERS BY
ACO & ROMULO FAJARDO, JR.
CHRIS SPROUSE & KARL STORY

CHRIS CONROY ALEX ANTONE SCOTT DUNBIER SHELLY BOND Editors – Original Series
BRITTANY HOLZHERR KRISTY QUINN GREGORY LOCKARD Assistant Editors – Original Series
JEB WOODARD Group Editor – Collected Editions
SCOTT NYBAKKEN Editor – Collected Edition
STEVE COOK Design Director – Books
DAMIAN RYLAND Publication Design

BOB HARRAS Senior VP – Editor-in-Chief, DC Comics

DIANE NELSON President
DAN DIDIO AND JIM LEE Co-Publishers
GEOFF JOHNS Chief Creative Officer
AMIT DESAI Senior VP – Marketing & Global Franchise Management
NAIRI GARDINER Senior VP – Finance
SAM ADES VP – Digital Marketing
BOBBIE CHASE VP – Talent Development
MARK CHIARELLO Senior VP – Art, Design & Collected Editions
JOHN CUNNINGHAM VP – Content Strategy
ANNE DEPIES VP – Strategy Planning & Reporting
DON FALLETTI VP – Manufacturing Operations
LAWRENCE GANEM VP – Editorial Administration & Talent Relations
ALISON GILL Senior VP – Manufacturing & Operations
HANK KANALZ Senior VP – Editorial Strategy & Administration
JAY KOGAN VP – Legal Affairs
DEREK MADDALENA Senior VP – Sales & Business Development
JACK MAHAN VP – Business Affairs
DAN MIRON VP – Sales Planning & Trade Development
NICK NAPOLITANO VP – Manufacturing Administration
CAROL ROEDER VP – Marketing
EDDIE SCANNELL VP – Mass Account & Digital Sales
COURTNEY SIMMONS Senior VP – Publicity & Communications
JIM (SKI) SOKOLOWSKI VP – Comic Book Specialty & Newsstand Sales
SANDY YI Senior VP – Global Franchise Management

MIDNIGHTER VOL. 2: HARD

DC Comics. 2900 West Alameda Ave. Burbank, CA 91505
Printed by RR Donnelley, Salem, VA, USA. 9/16/16. First Printing.
ISBN: 978-1-4012-6493-2

Library of Congress Cataloging-in-Publication data is available.

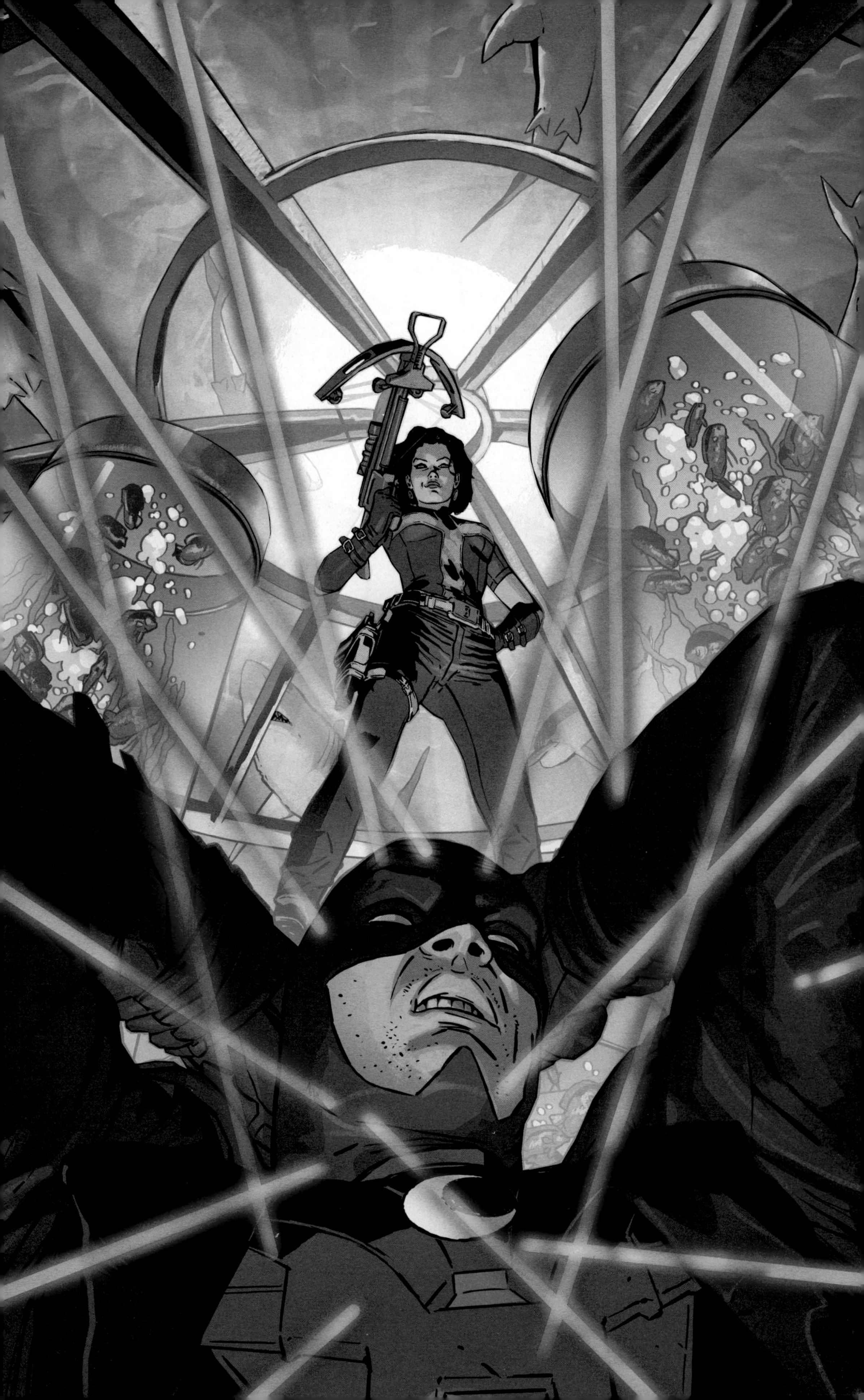

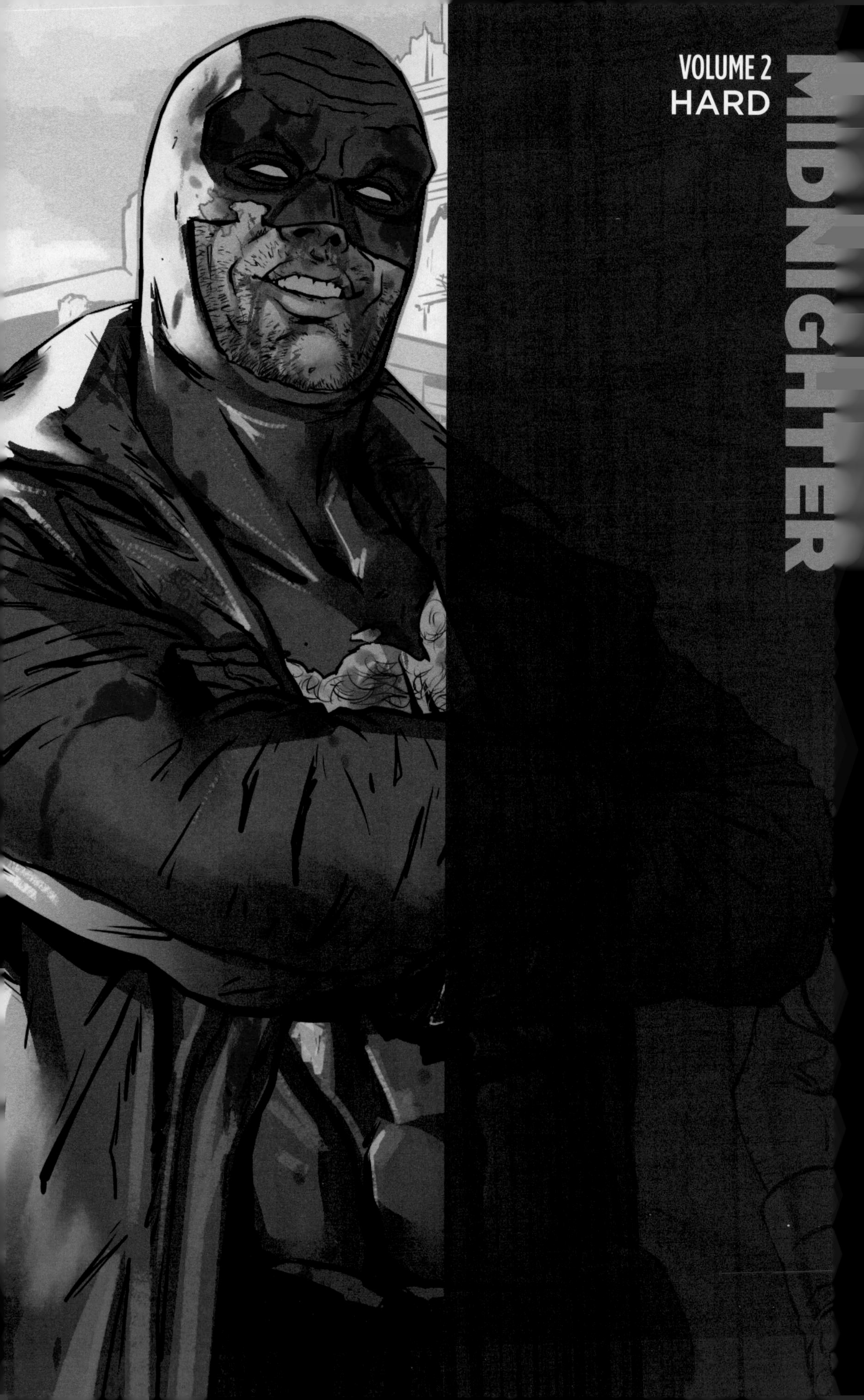
VOLUME 2
HARD
MIDNIGHTER

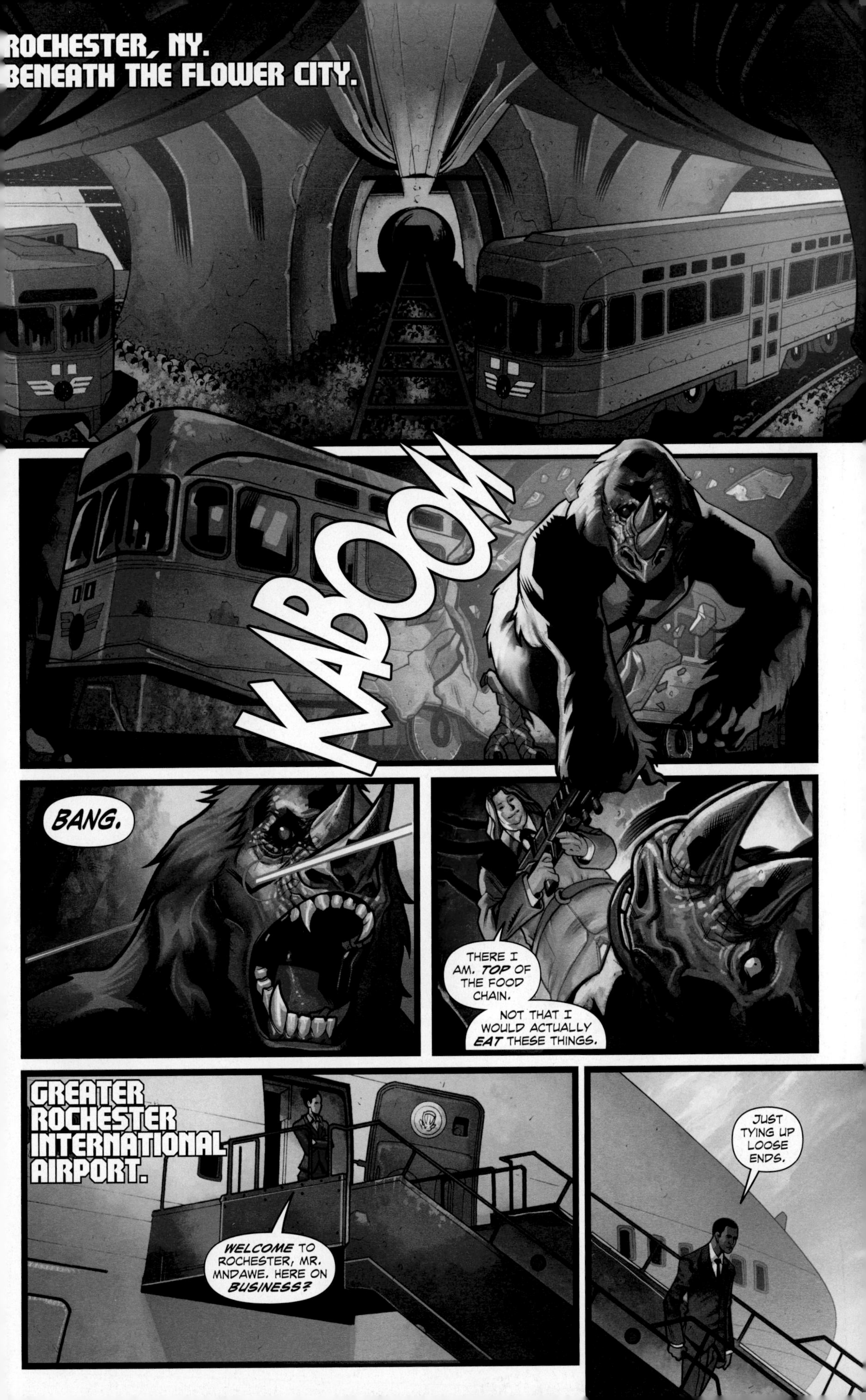

ROCHESTER, NY.
BENEATH THE FLOWER CITY.
KABOOM
BANG.
THERE I AM. TOP OF THE FOOD CHAIN.
NOT THAT I WOULD ACTUALLY EAT THESE THINGS.
GREATER ROCHESTER INTERNATIONAL AIRPORT.
WELCOME TO ROCHESTER, MR. MNDAWE. HERE ON BUSINESS?
JUST TYING UP LOOSE ENDS.

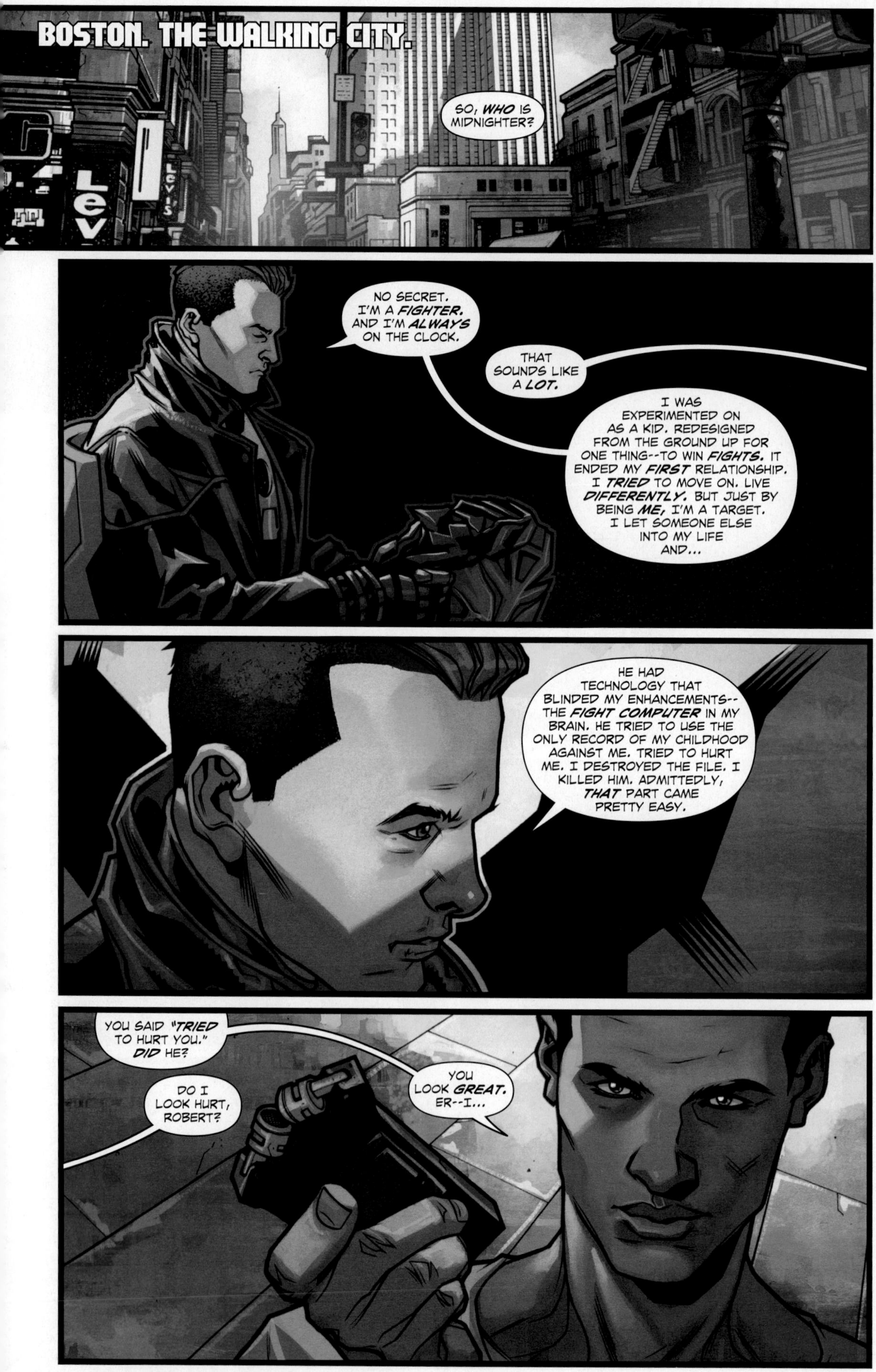
BOSTON. THE WALKING CITY.
SO, WHO IS MIDNIGHTER?
NO SECRET. I'M A FIGHTER. AND I'M ALWAYS ON THE CLOCK.
THAT SOUNDS LIKE A LOT.
I WAS EXPERIMENTED ON AS A KID. REDESIGNED FROM THE GROUND UP FOR ONE THING--TO WIN FIGHTS. IT ENDED MY FIRST RELATIONSHIP. I TRIED TO MOVE ON. LIVE DIFFERENTLY. BUT JUST BY BEING ME, I'M A TARGET. I LET SOMEONE ELSE INTO MY LIFE AND...
HE HAD TECHNOLOGY THAT BLINDED MY ENHANCEMENTS-- THE FIGHT COMPUTER IN MY BRAIN. HE TRIED TO USE THE ONLY RECORD OF MY CHILDHOOD AGAINST ME. TRIED TO HURT ME. I DESTROYED THE FILE. I KILLED HIM. ADMITTEDLY, THAT PART CAME PRETTY EASY.
YOU SAID "TRIED TO HURT YOU." DID HE?
DO I LOOK HURT, ROBERT?
YOU LOOK GREAT. ER--I...

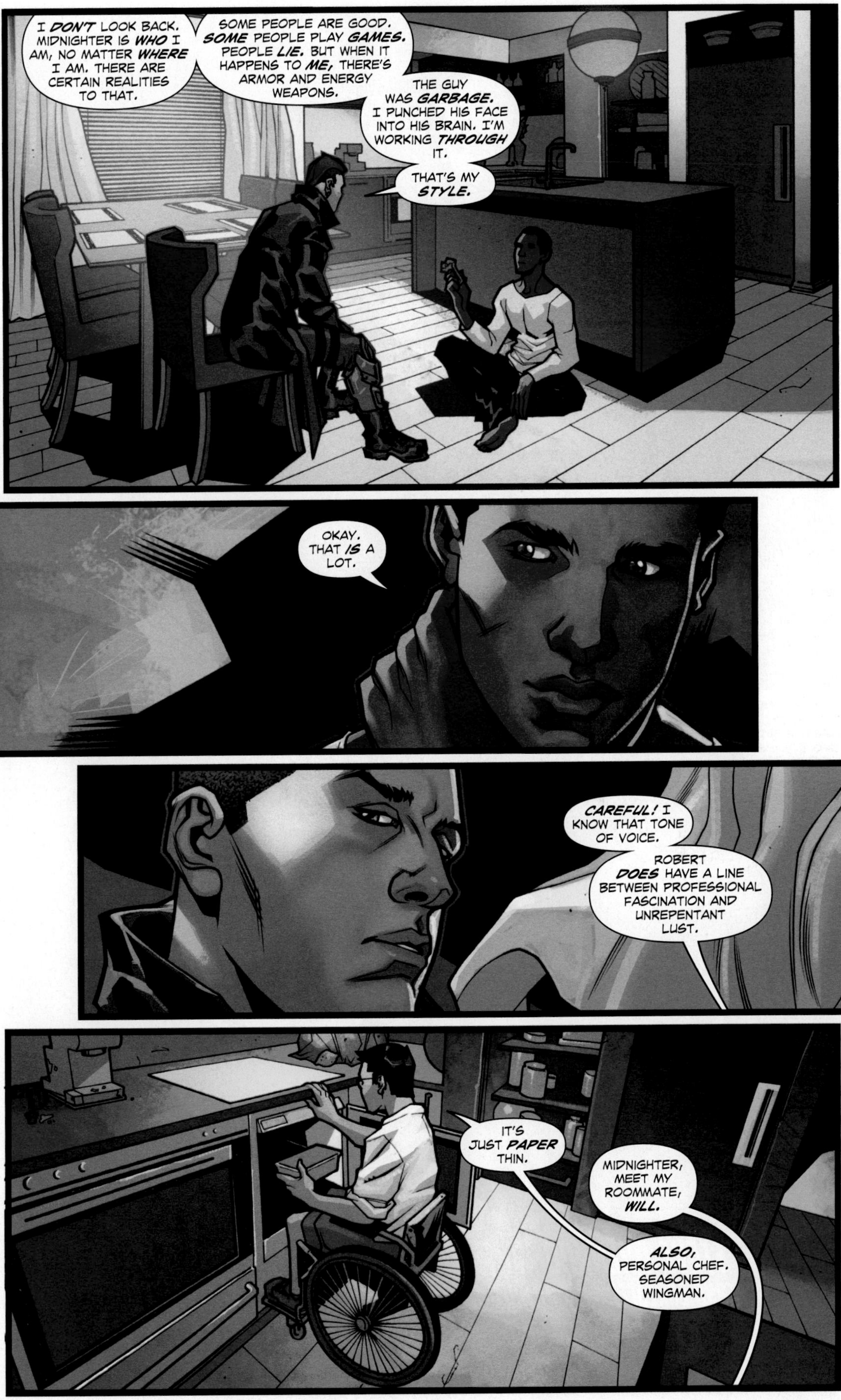
I DON'T LOOK BACK. MIDNIGHTER IS WHO I AM, NO MATTER WHERE I AM. THERE ARE CERTAIN REALITIES TO THAT.
SOME PEOPLE ARE GOOD. SOME PEOPLE PLAY GAMES. PEOPLE LIE. BUT WHEN IT HAPPENS TO ME, THERE'S ARMOR AND ENERGY WEAPONS.
THE GUY WAS GARBAGE. I PUNCHED HIS FACE INTO HIS BRAIN. I'M WORKING THROUGH IT.
THAT'S MY STYLE.
OKAY. THAT IS A LOT.
CAREFUL! I KNOW THAT TONE OF VOICE.
ROBERT DOES HAVE A LINE BETWEEN PROFESSIONAL FASCINATION AND UNREPENTANT LUST.
IT'S JUST PAPER THIN.
MIDNIGHTER, MEET MY ROOMMATE, WILL.
ALSO, PERSONAL CHEF. SEASONED WINGMAN.

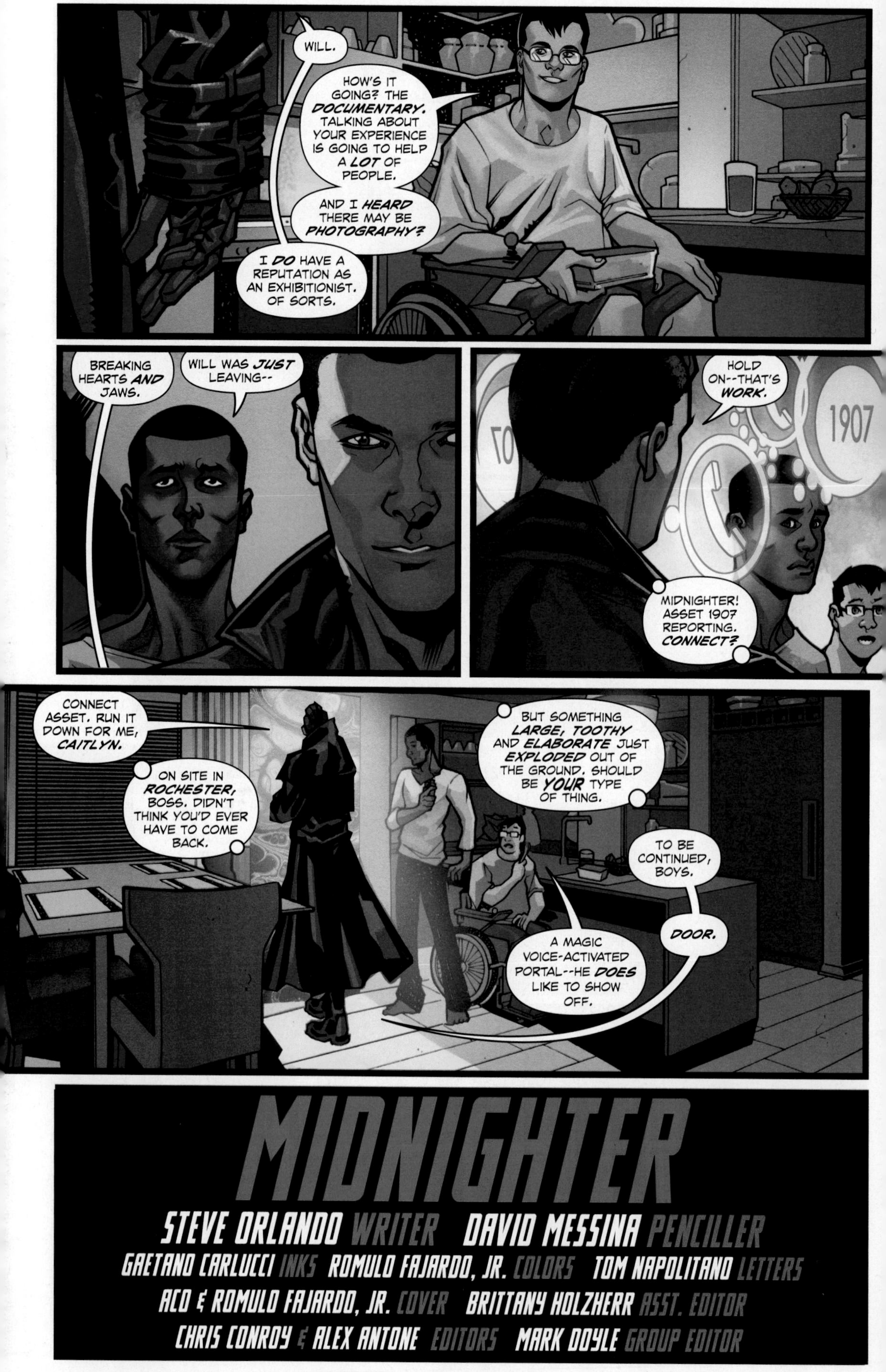
WILL.
HOW'S IT GOING? THE *DOCUMENTARY.* TALKING ABOUT YOUR EXPERIENCE IS GOING TO HELP A *LOT* OF PEOPLE.
AND I *HEARD* THERE MAY BE *PHOTOGRAPHY?*
I *DO* HAVE A REPUTATION AS AN EXHIBITIONIST. OF SORTS.
BREAKING HEARTS *AND* JAWS.
WILL WAS *JUST* LEAVING--
HOLD ON--THAT'S *WORK.*
1907
MIDNIGHTER! ASSET 1907 REPORTING. *CONNECT?*
CONNECT ASSET. RUN IT DOWN FOR ME, *CAITLYN.*
ON SITE IN *ROCHESTER,* BOSS. DIDN'T THINK YOU'D EVER HAVE TO COME BACK.
BUT SOMETHING *LARGE, TOOTHY* AND *ELABORATE* JUST *EXPLODED* OUT OF THE GROUND. SHOULD BE *YOUR* TYPE OF THING.
TO BE CONTINUED, BOYS.
DOOR.
A MAGIC VOICE-ACTIVATED PORTAL--HE *DOES* LIKE TO SHOW OFF.

MIDNIGHTER

STEVE ORLANDO WRITER DAVID MESSINA PENCILLER
GAETANO CARLUCCI INKS ROMULO FAJARDO, JR. COLORS TOM NAPOLITANO LETTERS
ACO & ROMULO FAJARDO, JR. COVER BRITTANY HOLZHERR ASST. EDITOR
CHRIS CONROY & ALEX ANTONE EDITORS MARK DOYLE GROUP EDITOR

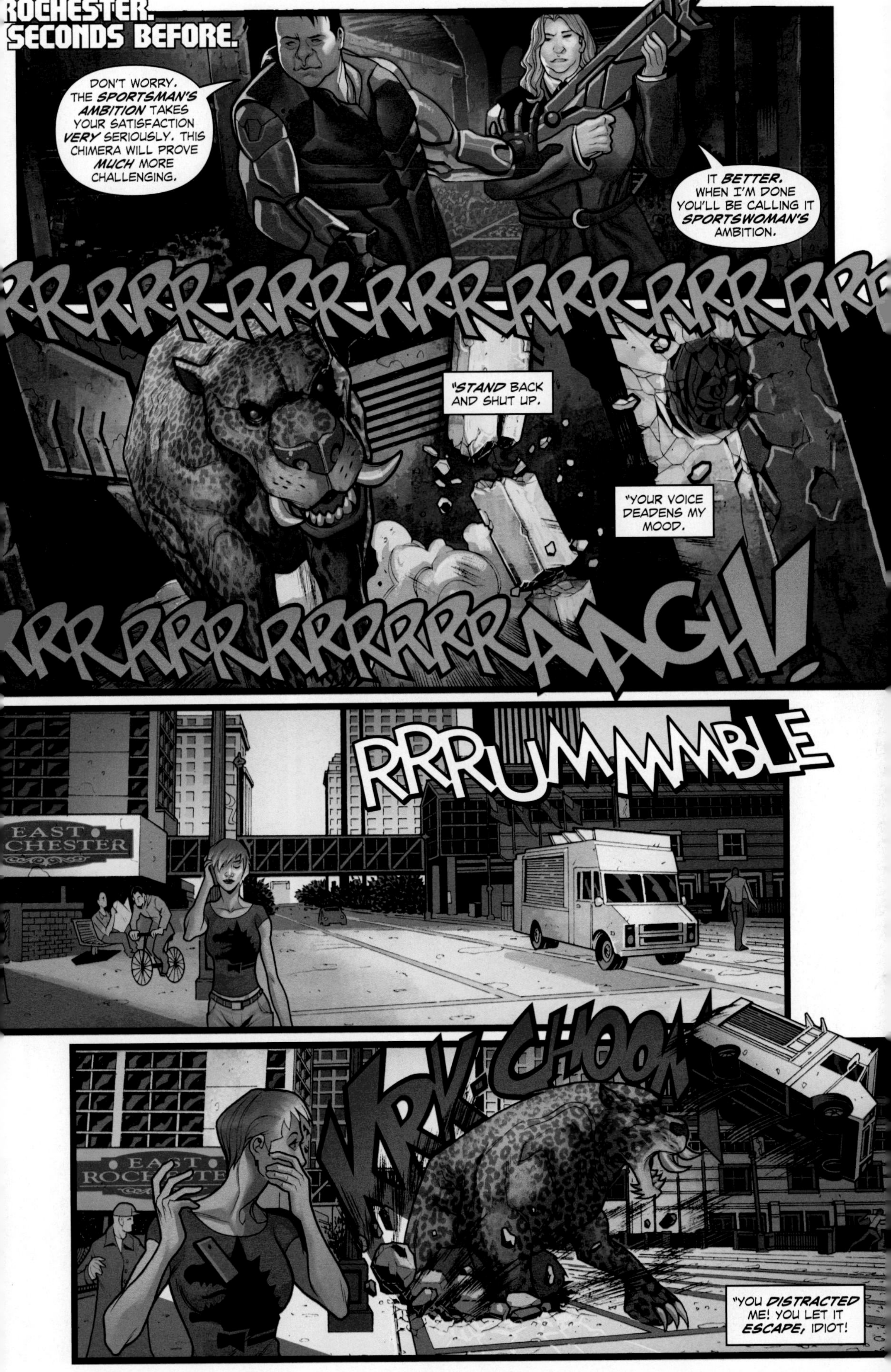
ROCHESTER.
SECONDS BEFORE.
DON'T WORRY. THE SPORTSMAN'S AMBITION TAKES YOUR SATISFACTION VERY SERIOUSLY. THIS CHIMERA WILL PROVE MUCH MORE CHALLENGING.
IT BETTER. WHEN I'M DONE YOU'LL BE CALLING IT SPORTSWOMAN'S AMBITION.
RRRRRRRRRRRRRRRRRRRRRRRR
"STAND BACK AND SHUT UP.
"YOUR VOICE DEADENS MY MOOD.
RRRRRRRRRRRRRAAGH!
RRRUMMMBLE
EAST
CHESTER
KRAK-CHOO
"YOU DISTRACTED ME! YOU LET IT ESCAPE, IDIOT!

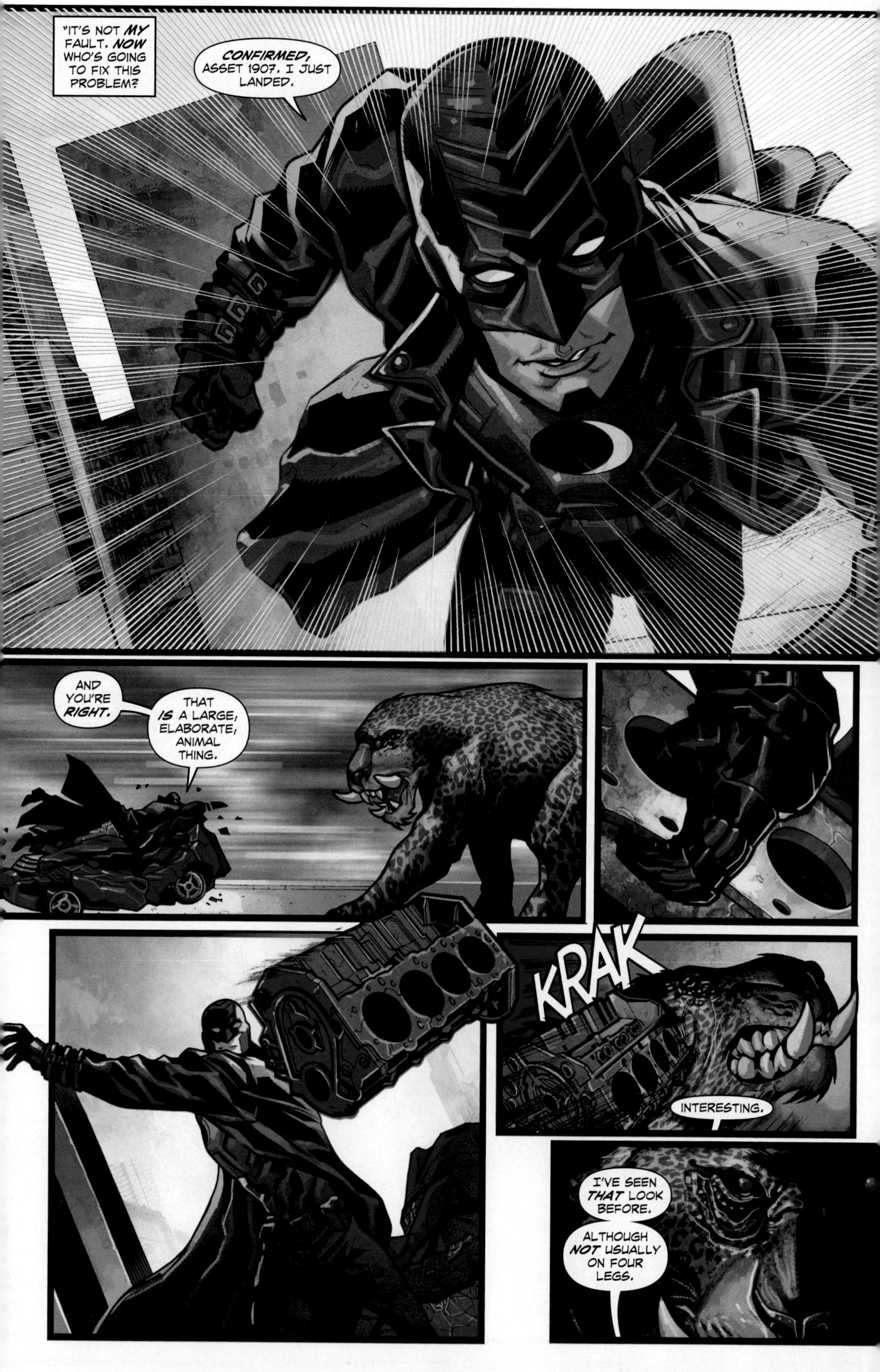
"IT'S NOT MY FAULT. NOW WHO'S GOING TO FIX THIS PROBLEM?
CONFIRMED, ASSET 1907. I JUST LANDED.
AND YOU'RE RIGHT.
THAT IS A LARGE, ELABORATE, ANIMAL THING.
KRAK
INTERESTING.
I'VE SEEN THAT LOOK BEFORE.
ALTHOUGH NOT USUALLY ON FOUR LEGS.

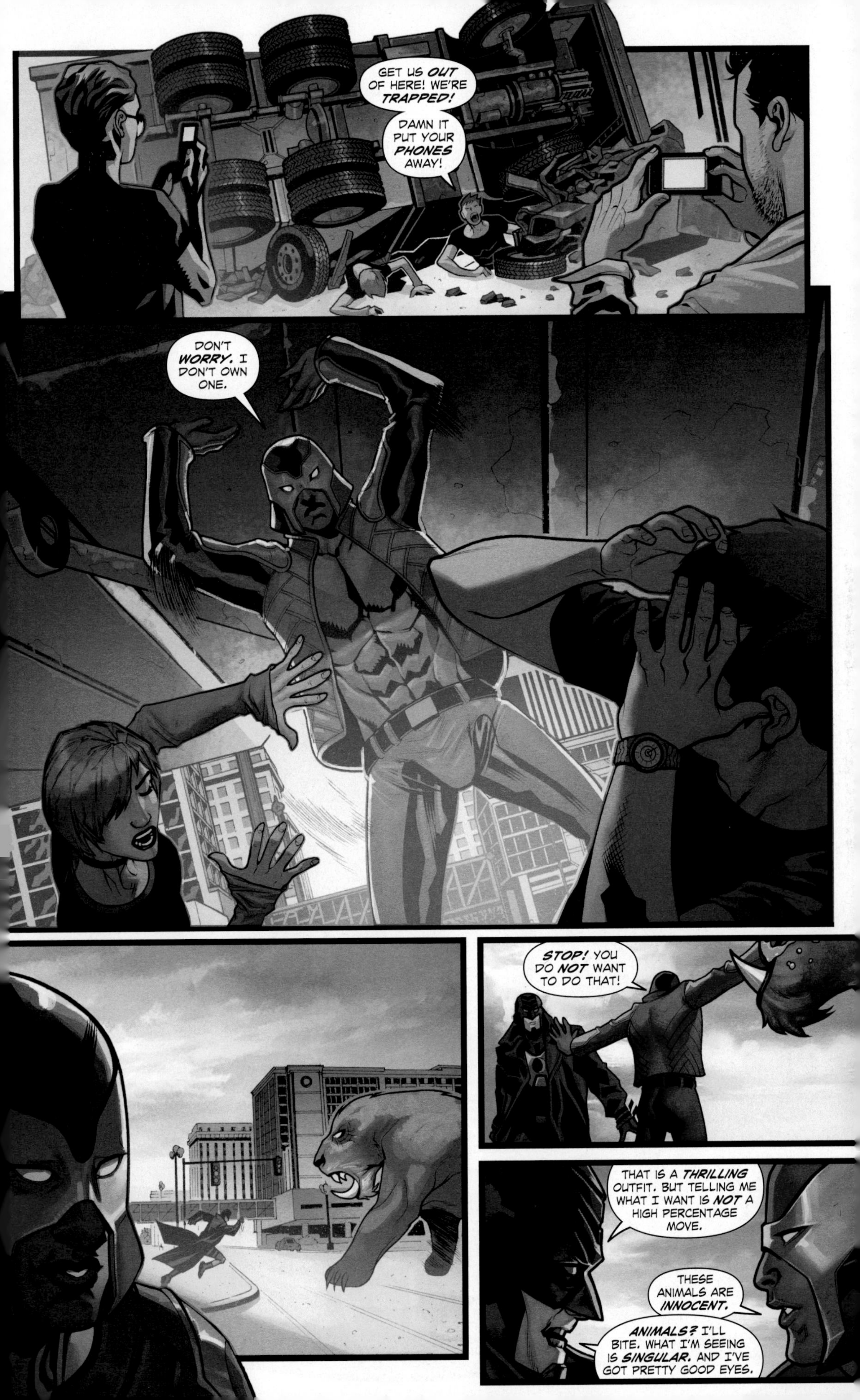
GET US *OUT* OF HERE! WE'RE *TRAPPED!*
DAMN IT PUT YOUR *PHONES* AWAY!
DON'T *WORRY.* I DON'T OWN ONE.
STOP! YOU DO *NOT* WANT TO DO THAT!
THAT IS A *THRILLING* OUTFIT. BUT TELLING ME WHAT I WANT IS *NOT* A HIGH PERCENTAGE MOVE.
THESE ANIMALS ARE *INNOCENT.*
ANIMALS? I'LL BITE. WHAT I'M SEEING IS *SINGULAR.* AND I'VE GOT PRETTY GOOD EYES.

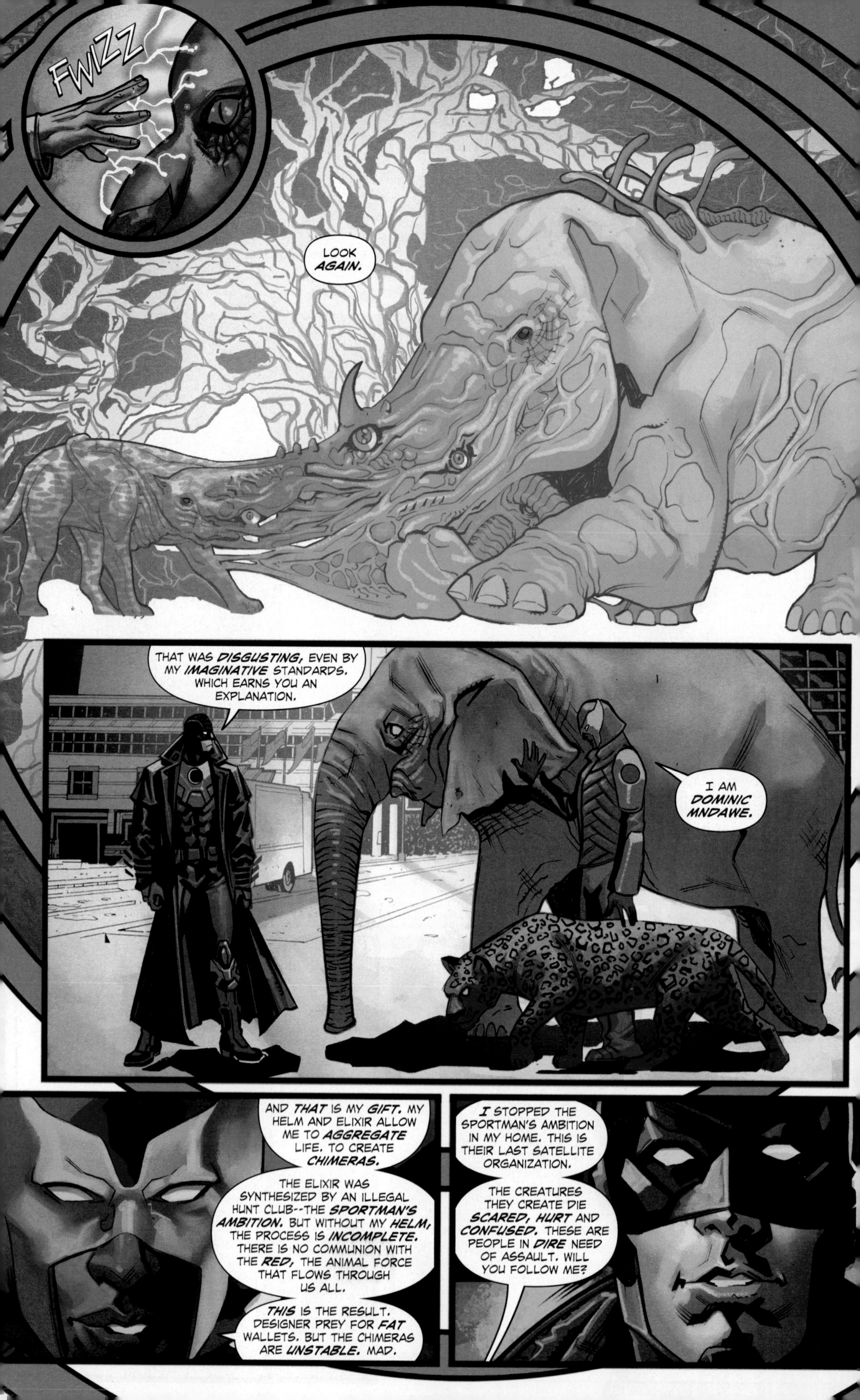
FWIZZ
LOOK AGAIN.
THAT WAS DISGUSTING, EVEN BY MY IMAGINATIVE STANDARDS. WHICH EARNS YOU AN EXPLANATION.
I AM DOMINIC MNDAWE.
AND THAT IS MY GIFT. MY HELM AND ELIXIR ALLOW ME TO AGGREGATE LIFE. TO CREATE CHIMERAS.
THE ELIXIR WAS SYNTHESIZED BY AN ILLEGAL HUNT CLUB--THE SPORTMAN'S AMBITION. BUT WITHOUT MY HELM, THE PROCESS IS INCOMPLETE. THERE IS NO COMMUNION WITH THE RED, THE ANIMAL FORCE THAT FLOWS THROUGH US ALL.
THIS IS THE RESULT. DESIGNER PREY FOR FAT WALLETS. BUT THE CHIMERAS ARE UNSTABLE. MAD.
I STOPPED THE SPORTMAN'S AMBITION IN MY HOME. THIS IS THEIR LAST SATELLITE ORGANIZATION.
THE CREATURES THEY CREATE DIE SCARED, HURT AND CONFUSED. THESE ARE PEOPLE IN DIRE NEED OF ASSAULT. WILL YOU FOLLOW ME?

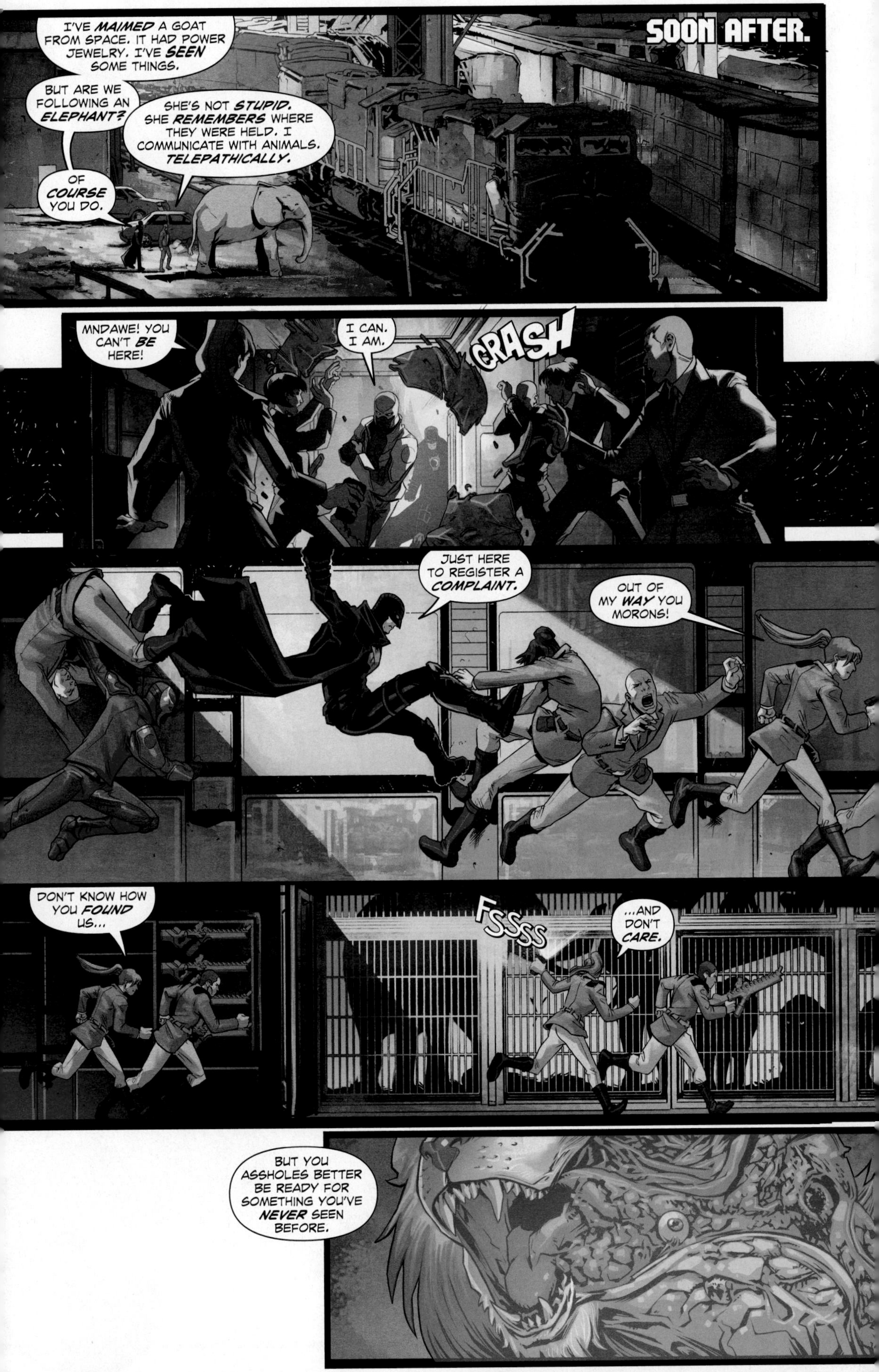
SOON AFTER.
I'VE MAIMED A GOAT FROM SPACE. IT HAD POWER JEWELRY. I'VE SEEN SOME THINGS.
BUT ARE WE FOLLOWING AN ELEPHANT?
SHE'S NOT STUPID. SHE REMEMBERS WHERE THEY WERE HELD. I COMMUNICATE WITH ANIMALS. TELEPATHICALLY.
OF COURSE YOU DO.
MNDAWE! YOU CAN'T BE HERE!
I CAN. I AM.
CRASH
JUST HERE TO REGISTER A COMPLAINT.
OUT OF MY WAY YOU MORONS!
DON'T KNOW HOW YOU FOUND US...
FSSSS
...AND DON'T CARE.
BUT YOU ASSHOLES BETTER BE READY FOR SOMETHING YOU'VE NEVER SEEN BEFORE.

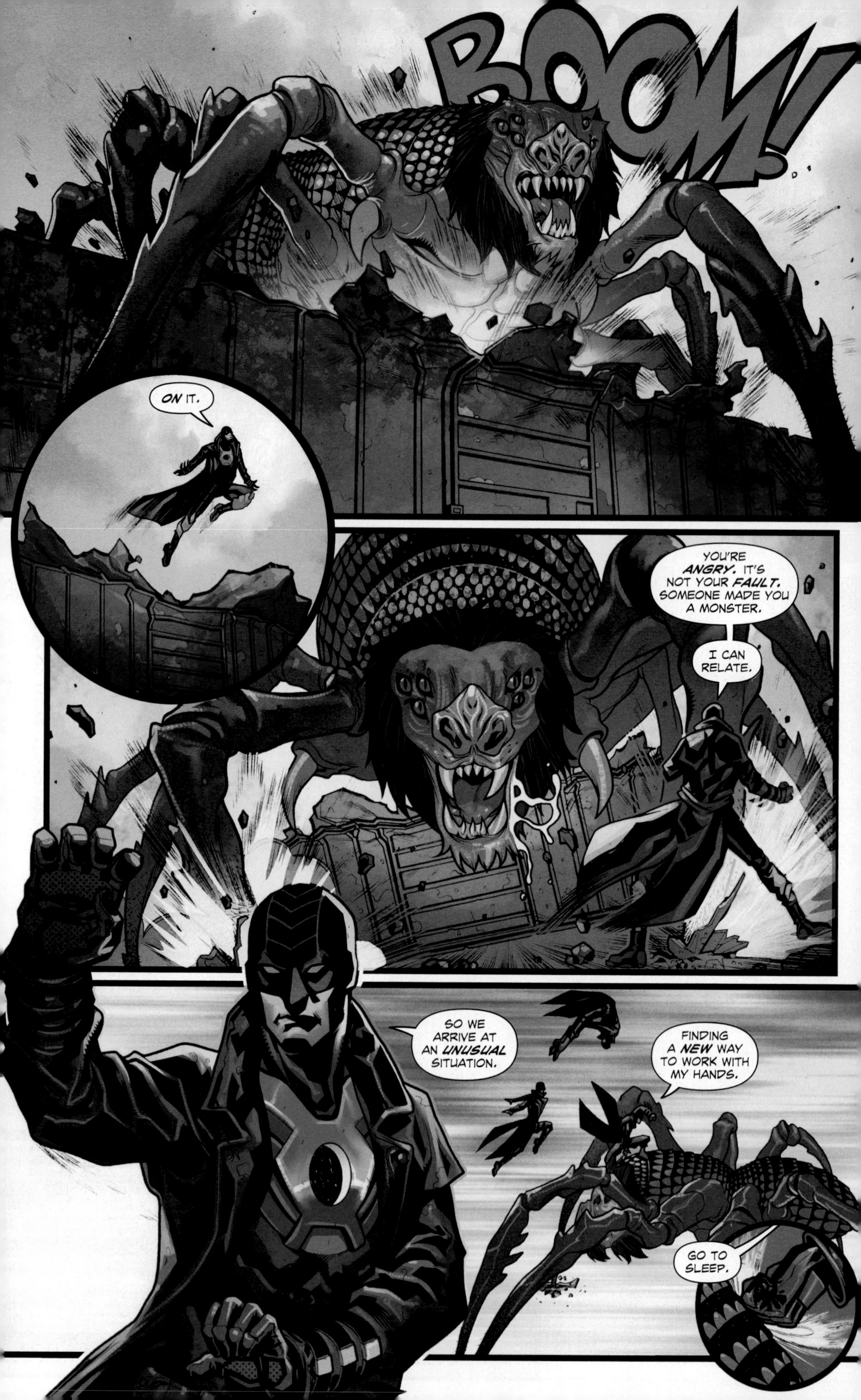
BOOM!
ON IT.
YOU'RE ANGRY. IT'S NOT YOUR FAULT. SOMEONE MADE YOU A MONSTER.
I CAN RELATE.
SO WE ARRIVE AT AN UNUSUAL SITUATION.
FINDING A NEW WAY TO WORK WITH MY HANDS.
GO TO SLEEP.

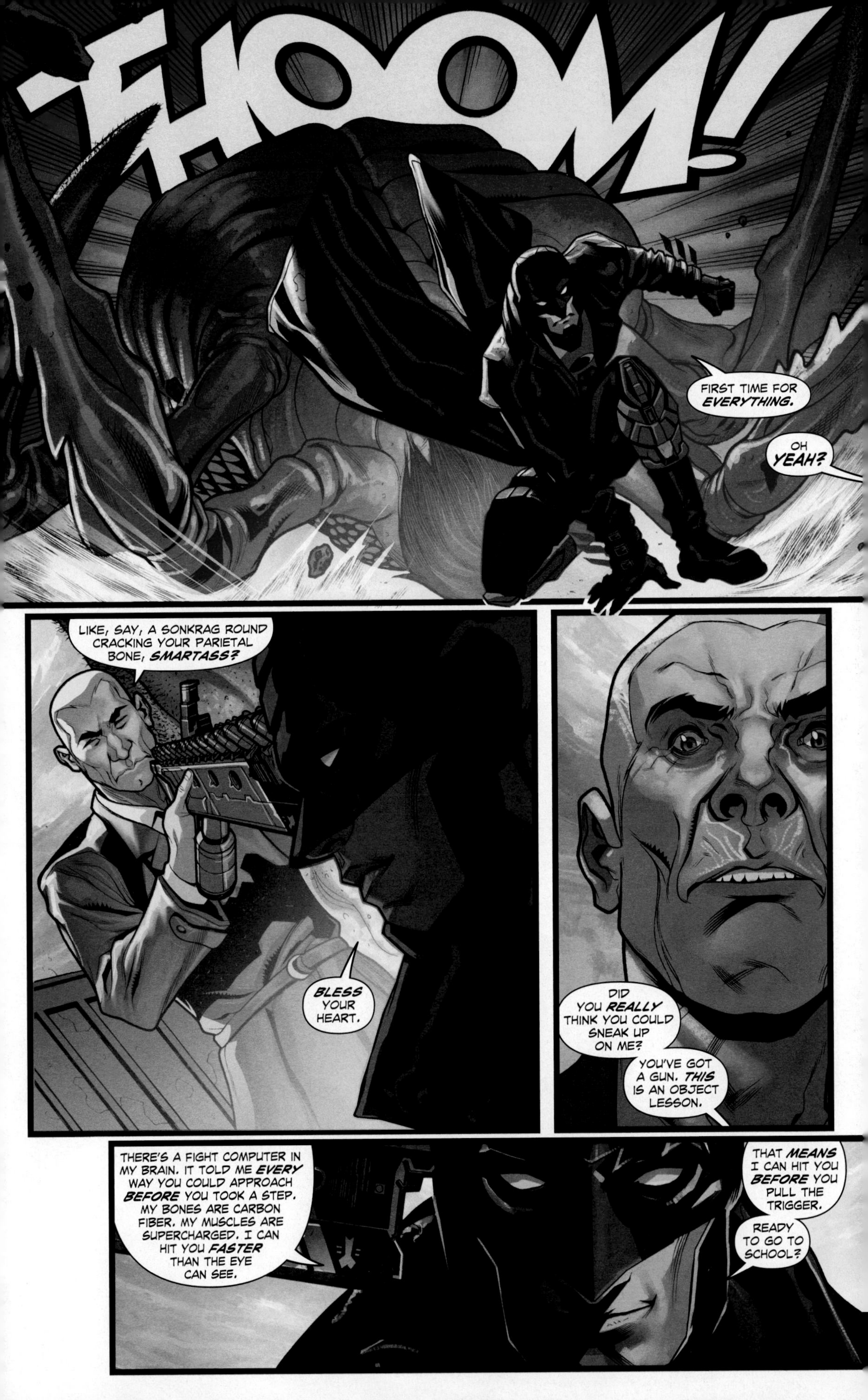
FHOOM!
FIRST TIME FOR EVERYTHING.
OH YEAH?
LIKE, SAY, A SONKRAG ROUND CRACKING YOUR PARIETAL BONE, SMARTASS?
BLESS YOUR HEART.
DID YOU REALLY THINK YOU COULD SNEAK UP ON ME?
YOU'VE GOT A GUN. THIS IS AN OBJECT LESSON.
THERE'S A FIGHT COMPUTER IN MY BRAIN. IT TOLD ME EVERY WAY YOU COULD APPROACH BEFORE YOU TOOK A STEP. MY BONES ARE CARBON FIBER. MY MUSCLES ARE SUPERCHARGED. I CAN HIT YOU FASTER THAN THE EYE CAN SEE.
THAT MEANS I CAN HIT YOU BEFORE YOU PULL THE TRIGGER.
READY TO GO TO SCHOOL?

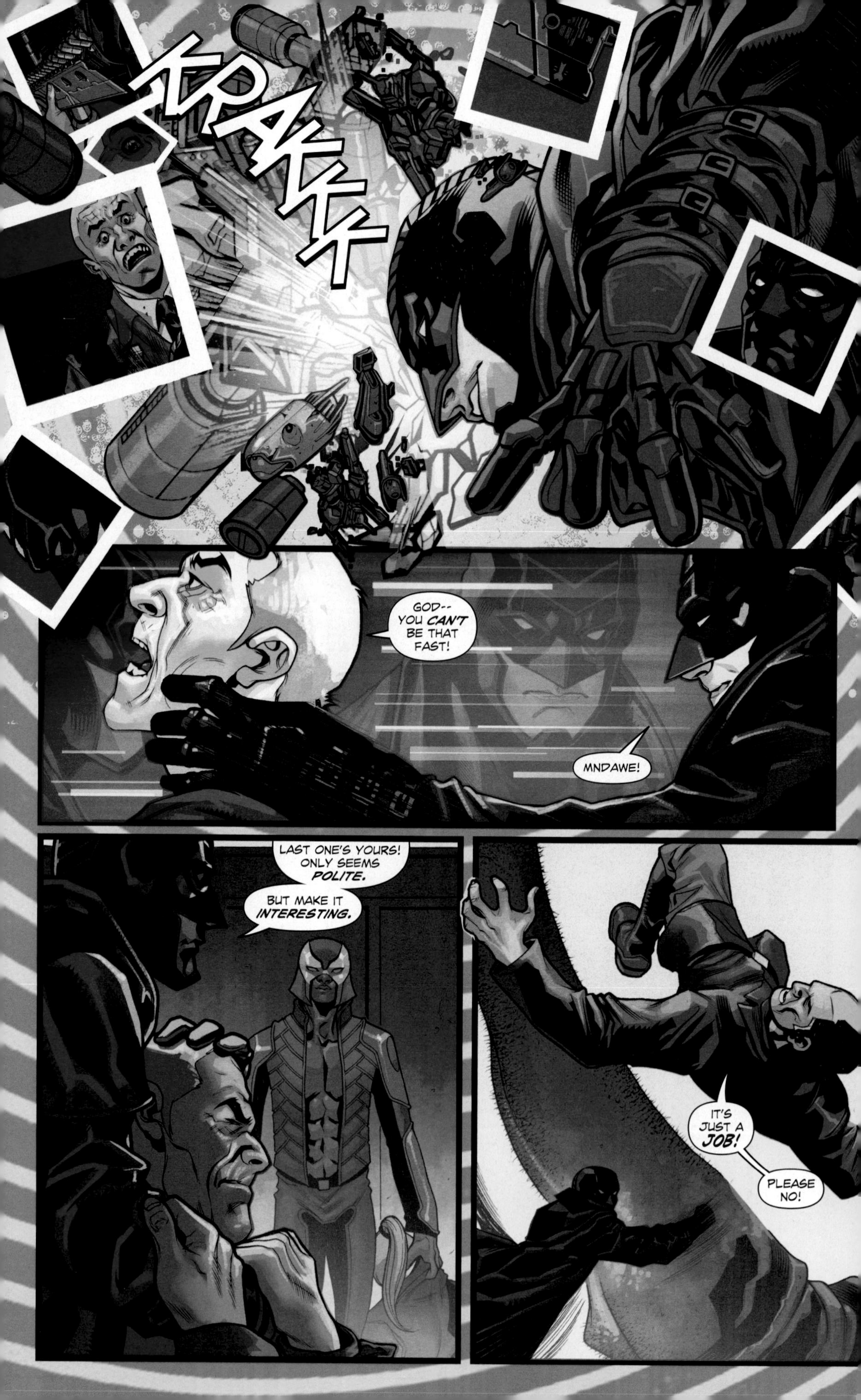
KRAKKK
GOD-- YOU CAN'T BE THAT FAST!
MNDAWE!
LAST ONE'S YOURS! ONLY SEEMS POLITE.
BUT MAKE IT INTERESTING.
IT'S JUST A JOB!
PLEASE NO!

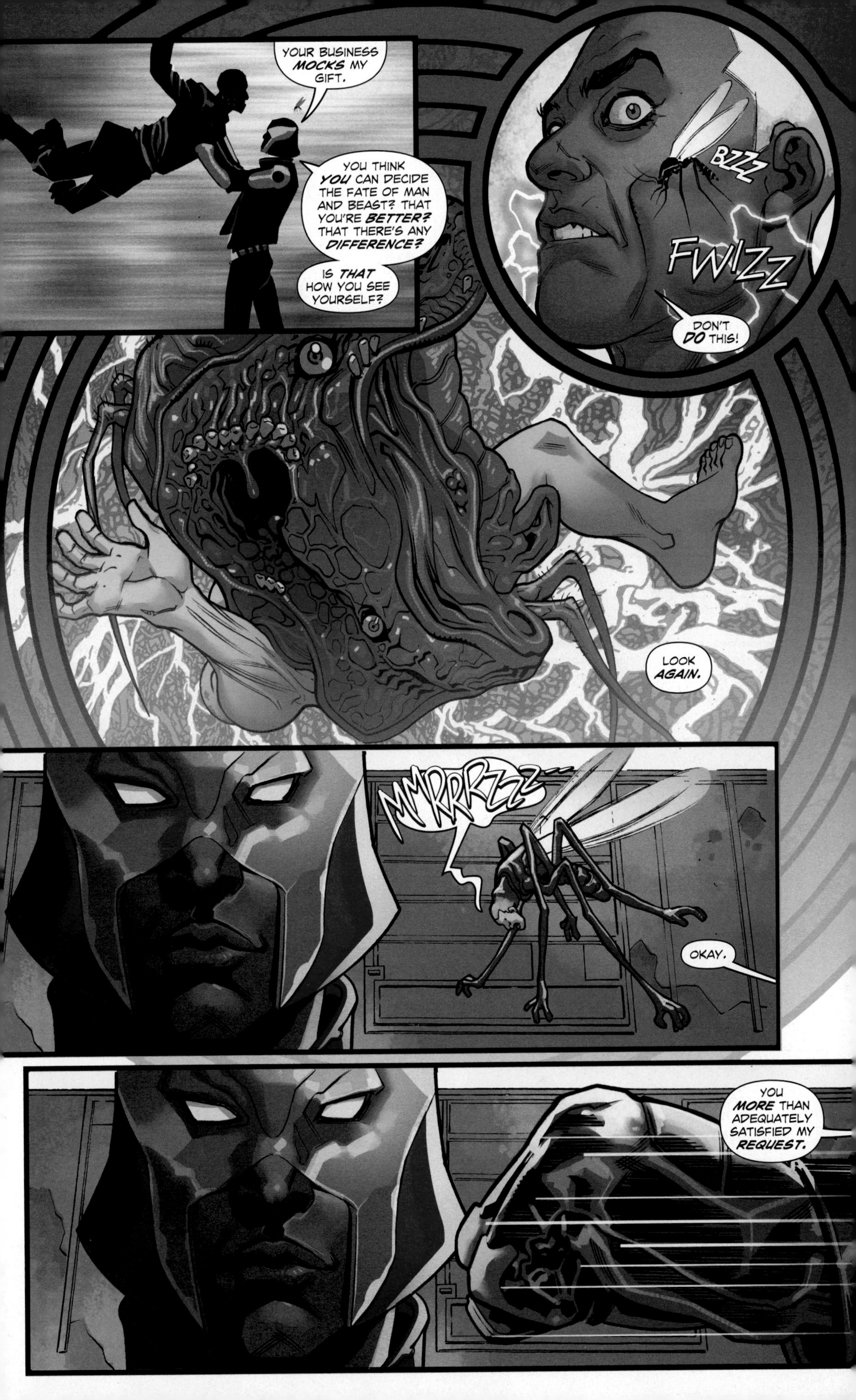
YOUR BUSINESS MOCKS MY GIFT.
YOU THINK YOU CAN DECIDE THE FATE OF MAN AND BEAST? THAT YOU'RE BETTER? THAT THERE'S ANY DIFFERENCE?
IS THAT HOW YOU SEE YOURSELF?
BZZZ
FWIZZ
DON'T DO THIS!
LOOK AGAIN.
MMRRRZZZ--
OKAY.
YOU MORE THAN ADEQUATELY SATISFIED MY REQUEST.

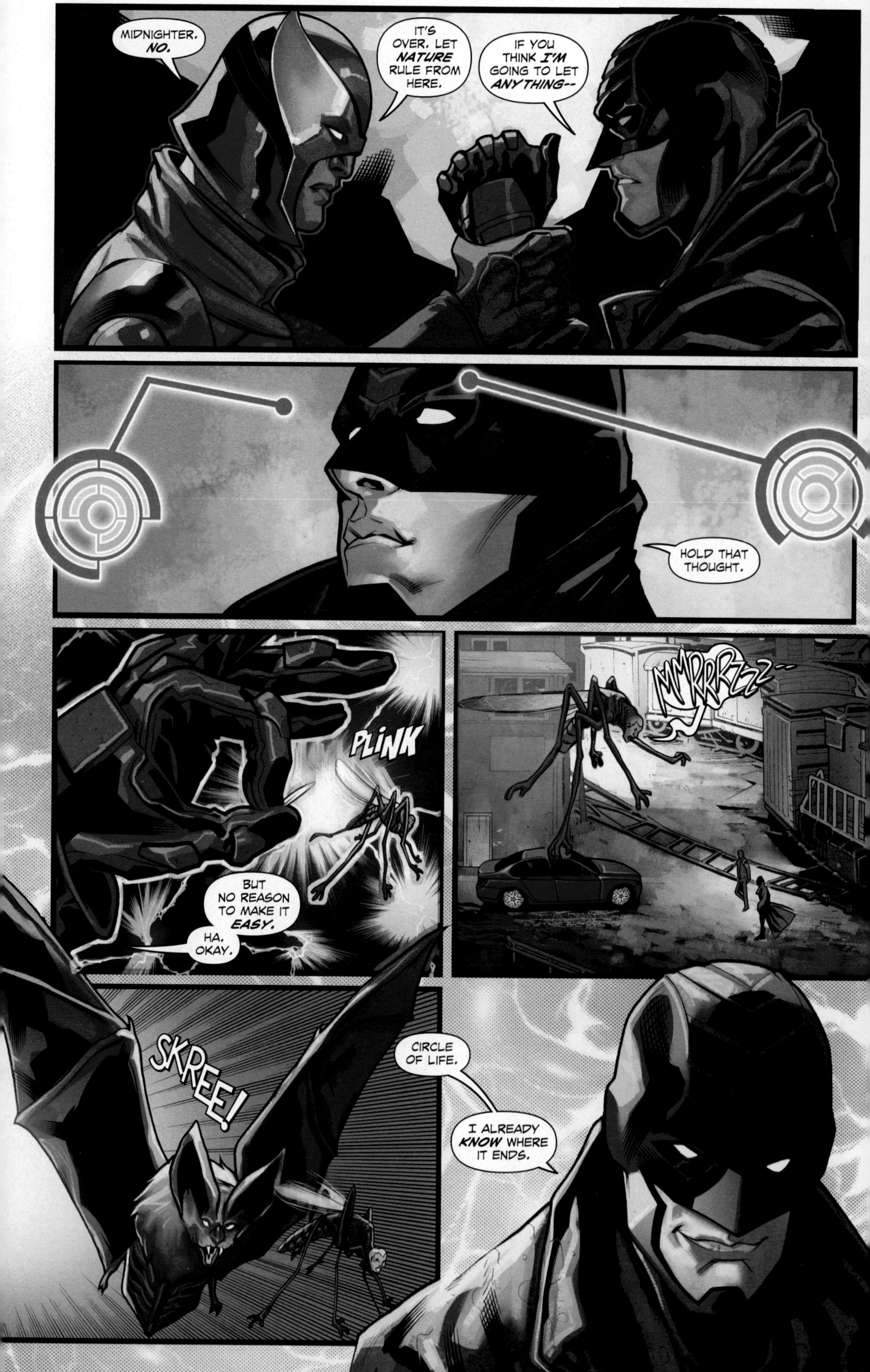
MIDNIGHTER. NO.
IT'S OVER. LET NATURE RULE FROM HERE.
IF YOU THINK I'M GOING TO LET ANYTHING--
HOLD THAT THOUGHT.
PLINK
BUT NO REASON TO MAKE IT EASY.
HA. OKAY.
MMRRRZZZ--
SKREE!
CIRCLE OF LIFE.
I ALREADY KNOW WHERE IT ENDS.

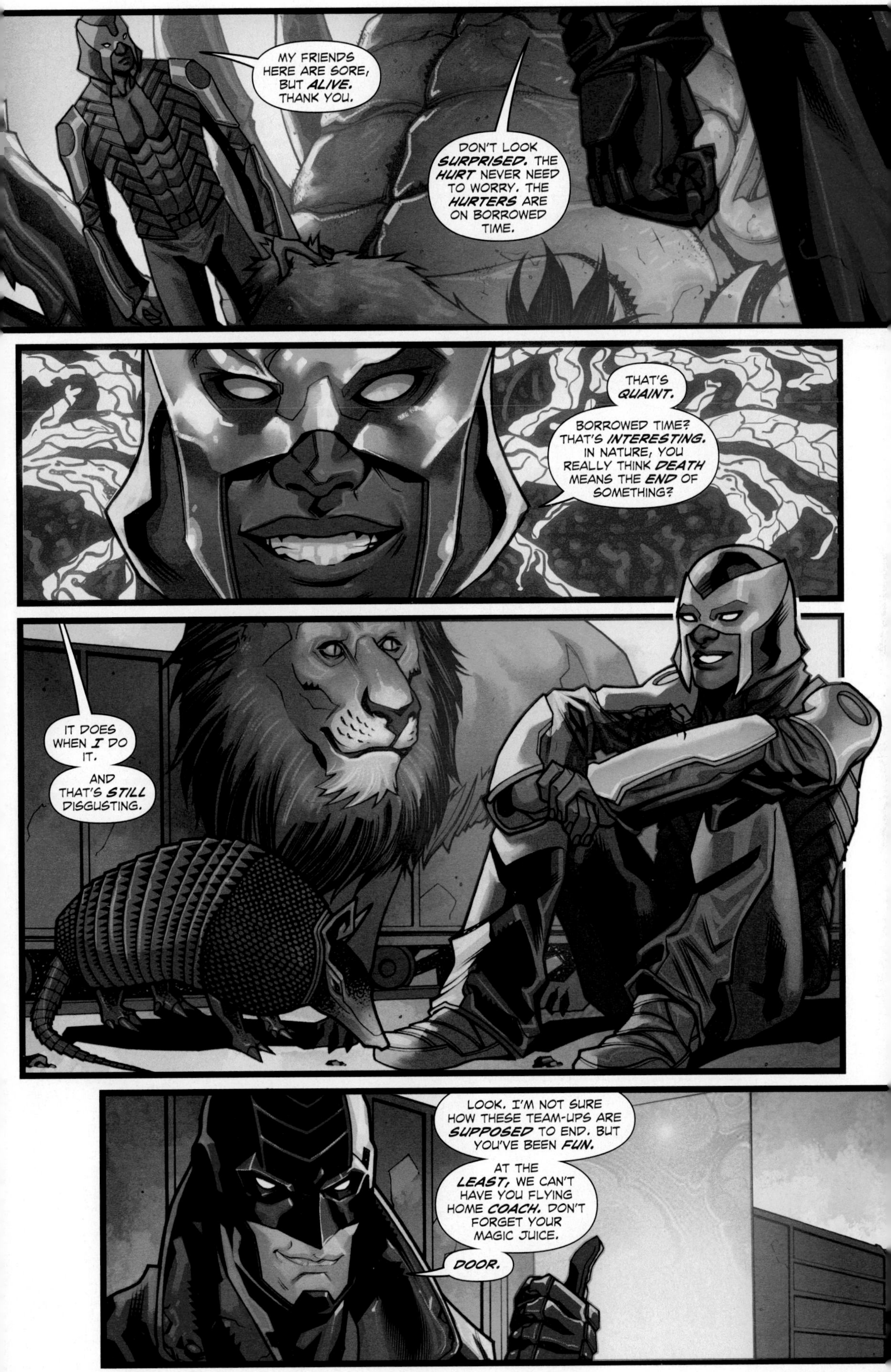
MY FRIENDS HERE ARE SORE, BUT ALIVE. THANK YOU.
DON'T LOOK SURPRISED. THE HURT NEVER NEED TO WORRY. THE HURTERS ARE ON BORROWED TIME.
THAT'S QUAINT.
BORROWED TIME? THAT'S INTERESTING. IN NATURE, YOU REALLY THINK DEATH MEANS THE END OF SOMETHING?
IT DOES WHEN I DO IT.
AND THAT'S STILL DISGUSTING.
LOOK. I'M NOT SURE HOW THESE TEAM-UPS ARE SUPPOSED TO END. BUT YOU'VE BEEN FUN.
AT THE LEAST, WE CAN'T HAVE YOU FLYING HOME COACH. DON'T FORGET YOUR MAGIC JUICE.
DOOR.

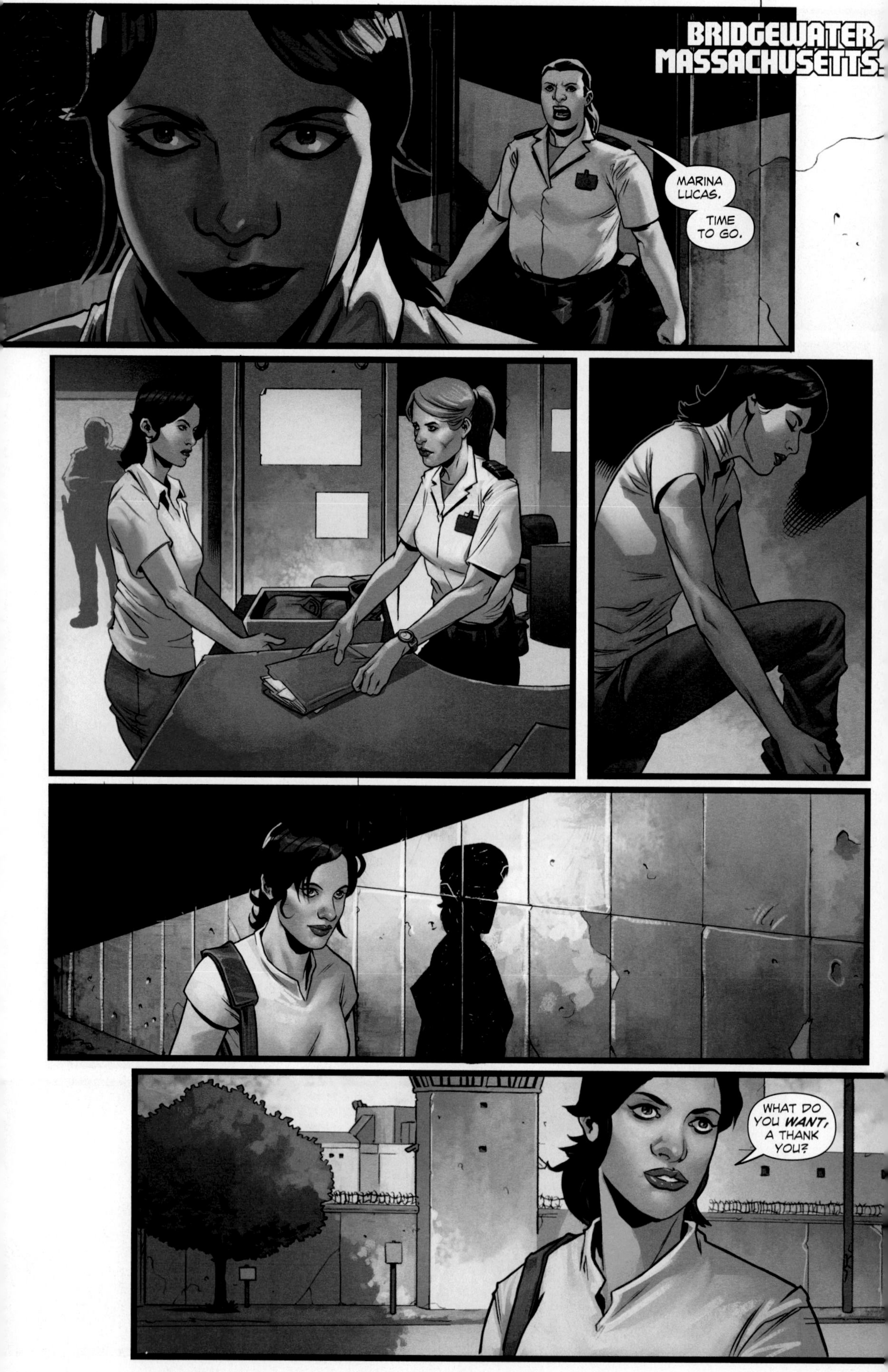
BRIDGEWATER, MASSACHUSETTS.
MARINA LUCAS.
TIME TO GO.
WHAT DO YOU *WANT*, A THANK YOU?

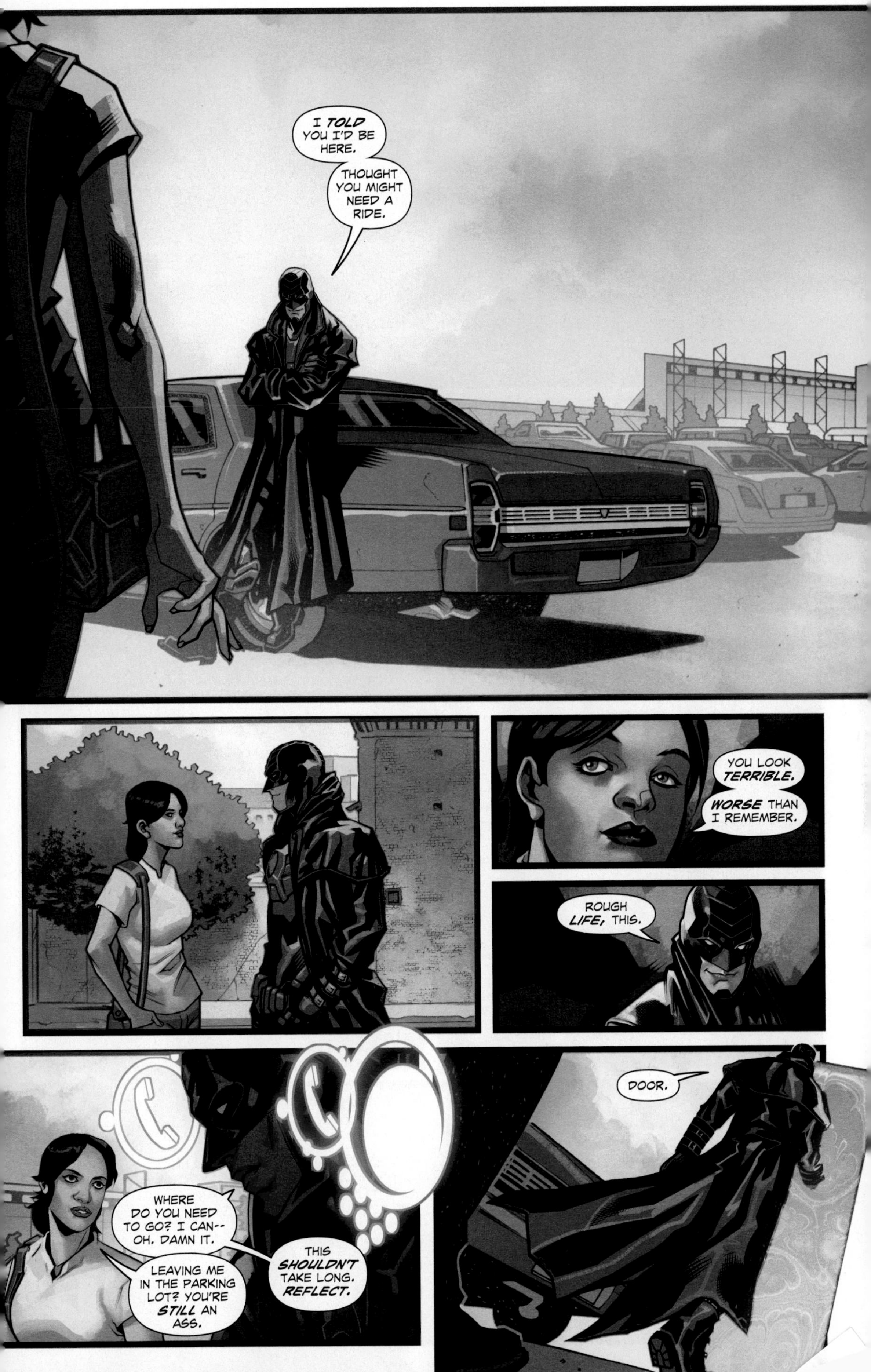
I TOLD YOU I'D BE HERE.
THOUGHT YOU MIGHT NEED A RIDE.
YOU LOOK TERRIBLE.
WORSE THAN I REMEMBER.
ROUGH LIFE, THIS.
WHERE DO YOU NEED TO GO? I CAN-- OH. DAMN IT.
THIS SHOULDN'T TAKE LONG. REFLECT.
LEAVING ME IN THE PARKING LOT? YOU'RE STILL AN ASS.
DOOR.

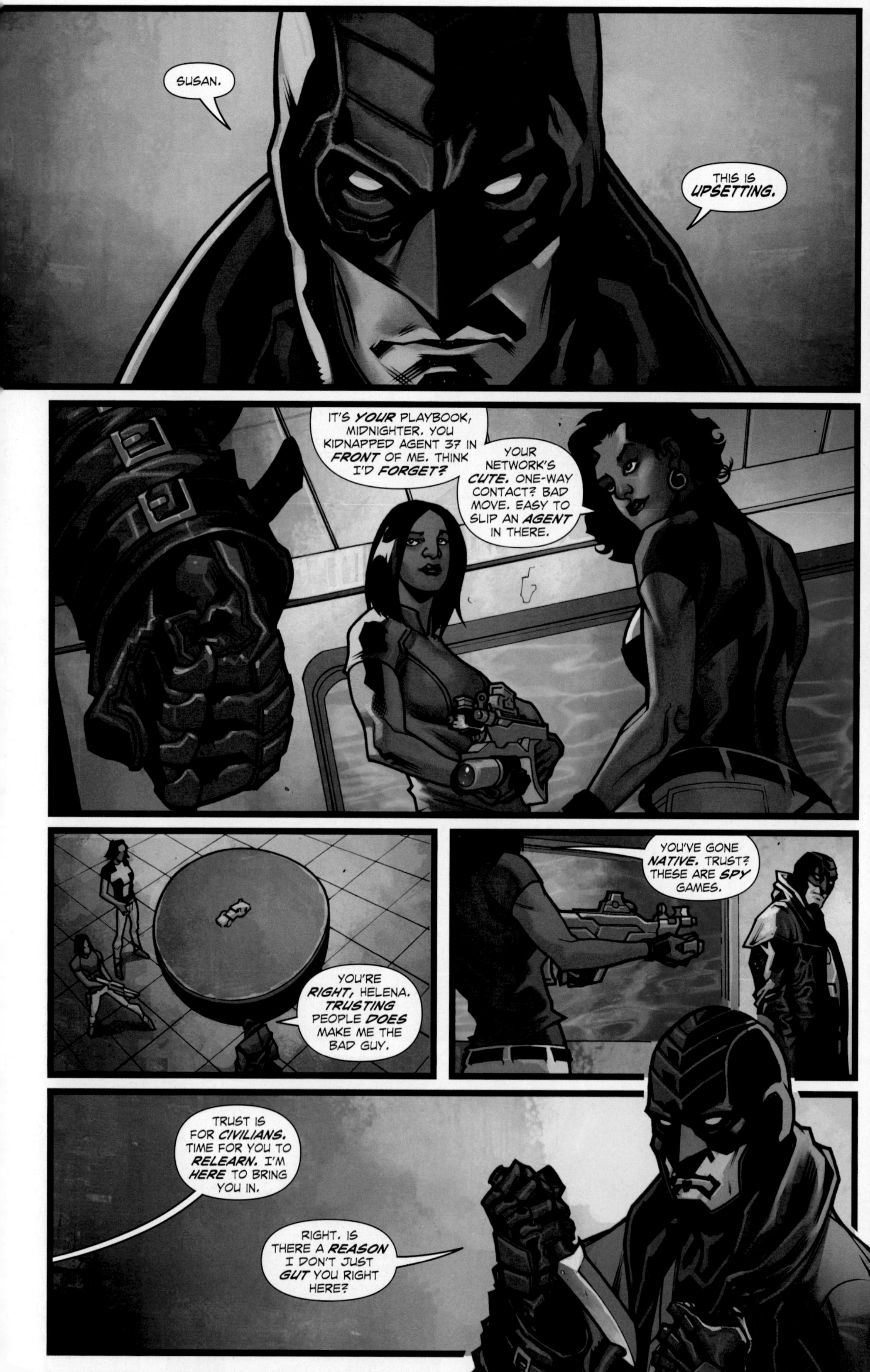
SUSAN.
THIS IS UPSETTING.
IT'S YOUR PLAYBOOK, MIDNIGHTER. YOU KIDNAPPED AGENT 37 IN FRONT OF ME. THINK I'D FORGET?
YOUR NETWORK'S CUTE. ONE-WAY CONTACT? BAD MOVE. EASY TO SLIP AN AGENT IN THERE.
YOU'RE RIGHT, HELENA. TRUSTING PEOPLE DOES MAKE ME THE BAD GUY.
YOU'VE GONE NATIVE. TRUST? THESE ARE SPY GAMES.
TRUST IS FOR CIVILIANS. TIME FOR YOU TO RELEARN. I'M HERE TO BRING YOU IN.
RIGHT. IS THERE A REASON I DON'T JUST GUT YOU RIGHT HERE?

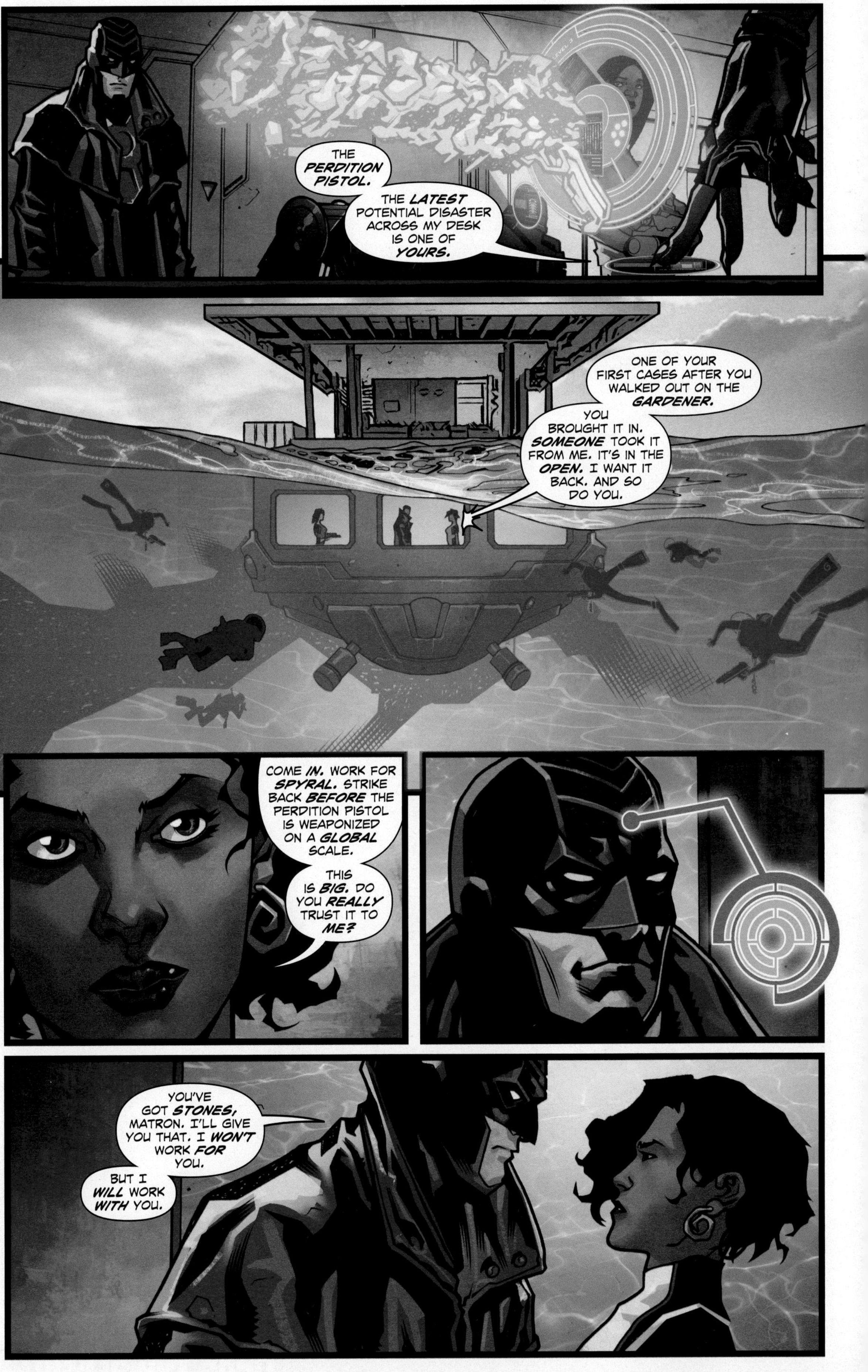
THE PERDITION PISTOL.
THE LATEST POTENTIAL DISASTER ACROSS MY DESK IS ONE OF YOURS.
ONE OF YOUR FIRST CASES AFTER YOU WALKED OUT ON THE GARDENER.
YOU BROUGHT IT IN. SOMEONE TOOK IT FROM ME. IT'S IN THE OPEN. I WANT IT BACK. AND SO DO YOU.
COME IN. WORK FOR SPYRAL. STRIKE BACK BEFORE THE PERDITION PISTOL IS WEAPONIZED ON A GLOBAL SCALE.
THIS IS BIG. DO YOU REALLY TRUST IT TO ME?
YOU'VE GOT STONES, MATRON. I'LL GIVE YOU THAT. I WON'T WORK FOR YOU.
BUT I WILL WORK WITH YOU.

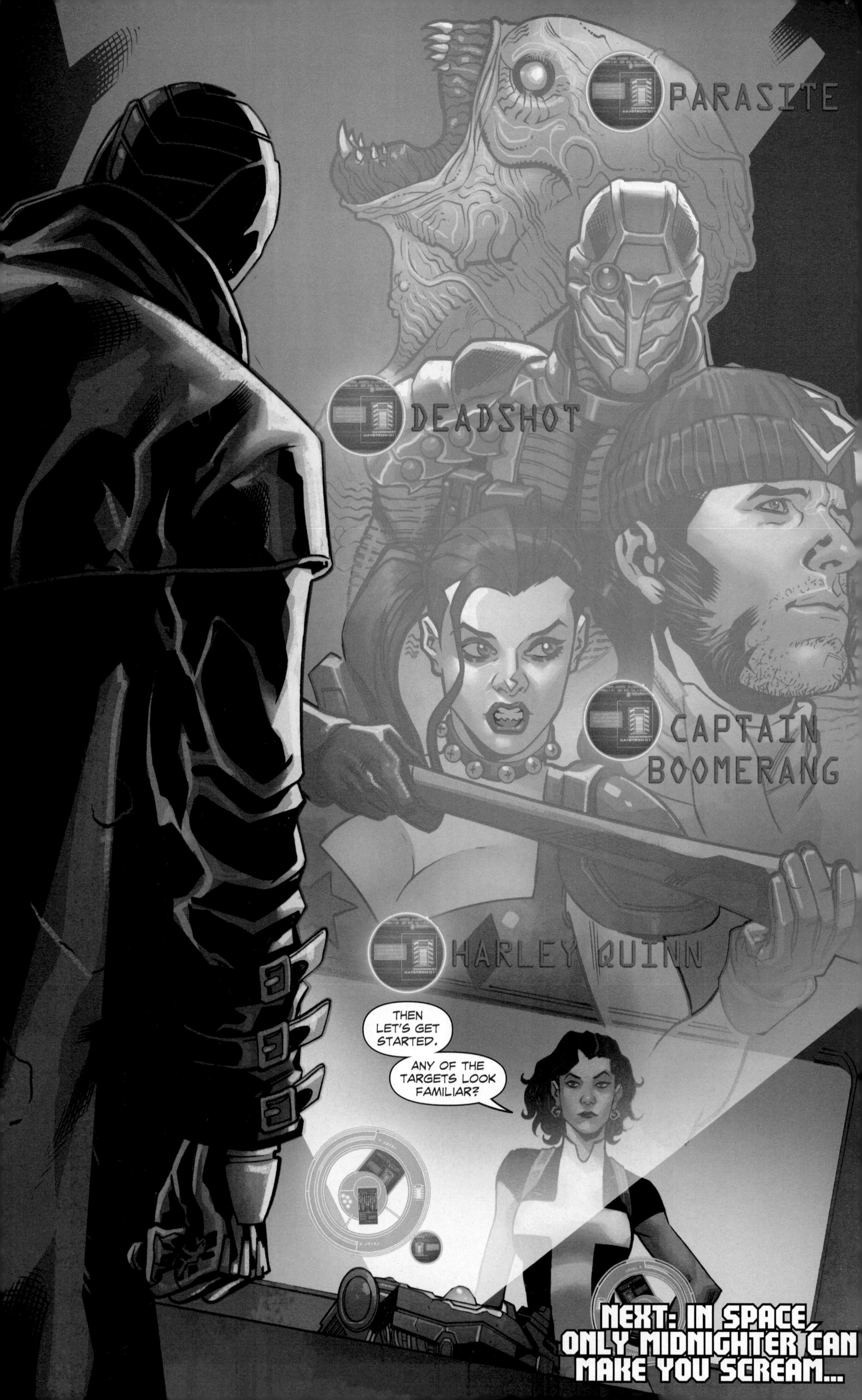
PARASITE
DEADSHOT
CAPTAIN BOOMERANG
HARLEY QUINN
THEN LET'S GET STARTED.
ANY OF THE TARGETS LOOK FAMILIAR?
NEXT: IN SPACE, ONLY MIDNIGHTER CAN MAKE YOU SCREAM...

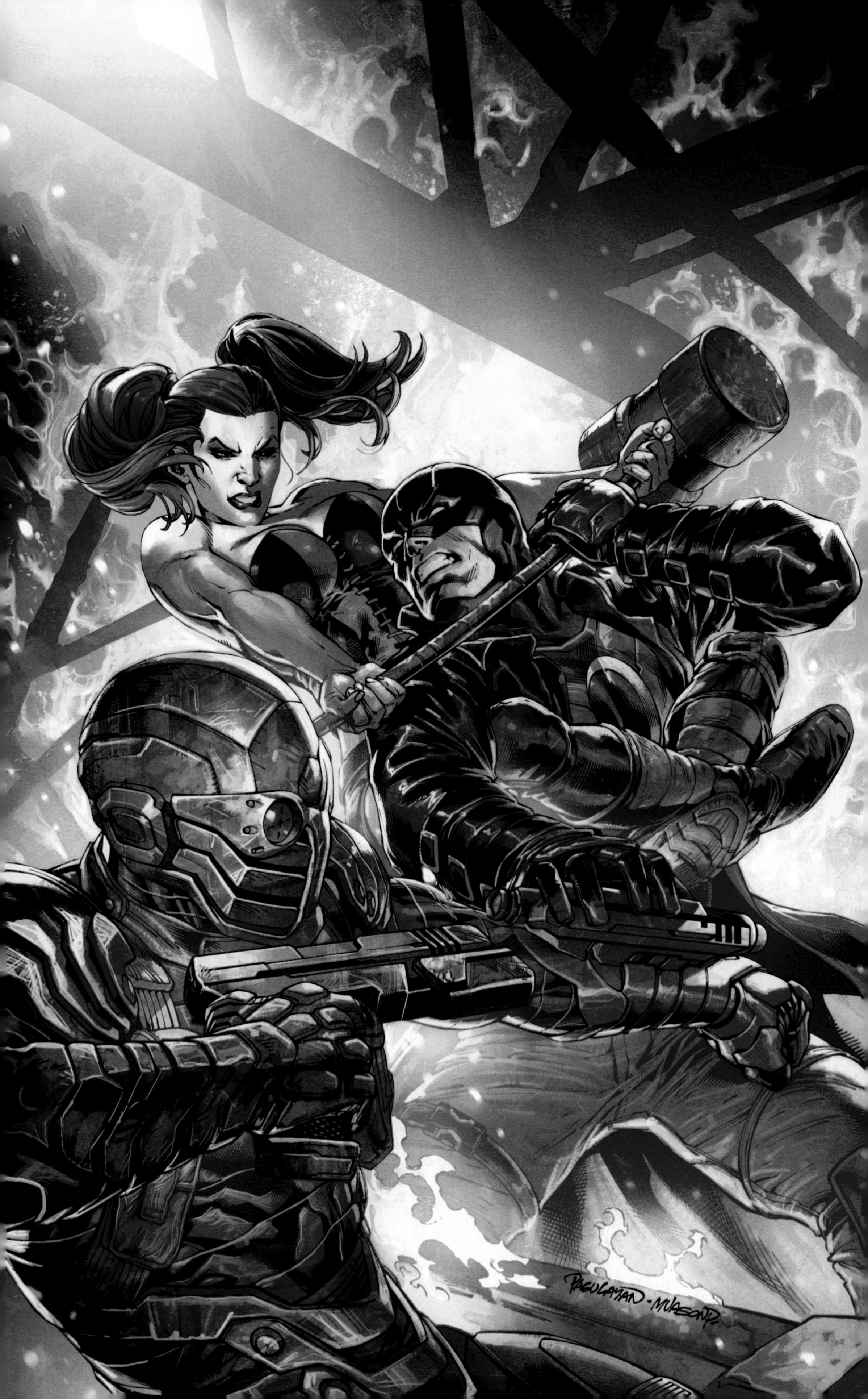

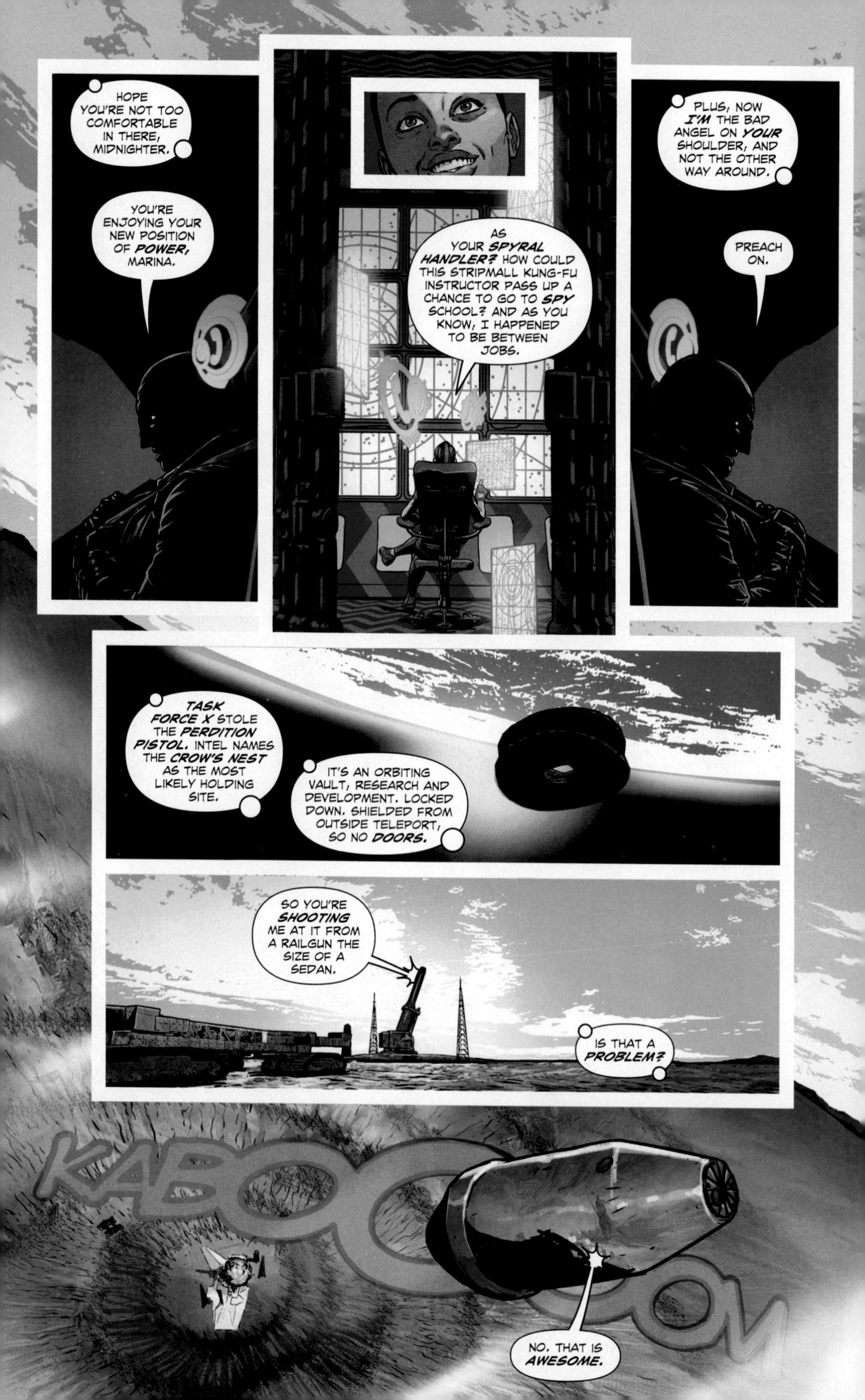
HOPE YOU'RE NOT TOO COMFORTABLE IN THERE, MIDNIGHTER.
YOU'RE ENJOYING YOUR NEW POSITION OF POWER, MARINA.
AS YOUR SPYRAL HANDLER? HOW COULD THIS STRIPMALL KUNG-FU INSTRUCTOR PASS UP A CHANCE TO GO TO SPY SCHOOL? AND AS YOU KNOW, I HAPPENED TO BE BETWEEN JOBS.
PLUS, NOW I'M THE BAD ANGEL ON YOUR SHOULDER, AND NOT THE OTHER WAY AROUND.
PREACH ON.
TASK FORCE X STOLE THE PERDITION PISTOL. INTEL NAMES THE CROW'S NEST AS THE MOST LIKELY HOLDING SITE.
IT'S AN ORBITING VAULT, RESEARCH AND DEVELOPMENT. LOCKED DOWN. SHIELDED FROM OUTSIDE TELEPORT, SO NO DOORS.
SO YOU'RE SHOOTING ME AT IT FROM A RAILGUN THE SIZE OF A SEDAN.
IS THAT A PROBLEM?
KABOOOOM
NO. THAT IS AWESOME.

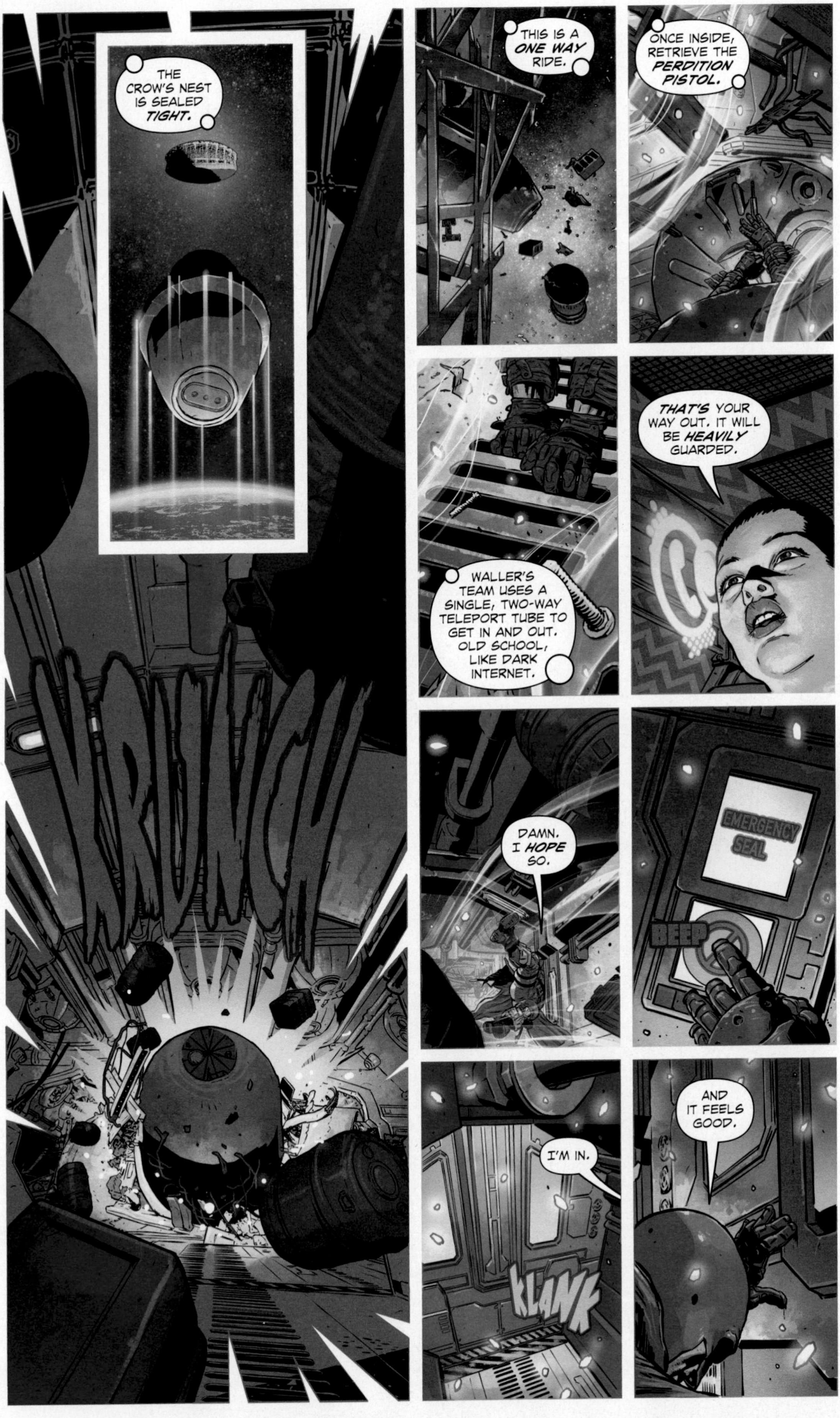
THE CROW'S NEST IS SEALED *TIGHT.*
THIS IS A *ONE WAY* RIDE.
ONCE INSIDE, RETRIEVE THE *PERDITION PISTOL.*
WALLER'S TEAM USES A SINGLE, TWO-WAY TELEPORT TUBE TO GET IN AND OUT. OLD SCHOOL, LIKE DARK INTERNET.
THAT'S YOUR WAY OUT. IT WILL BE *HEAVILY* GUARDED.
DAMN. I *HOPE* SO.
EMERGENCY SEAL
BEEP
I'M IN.
KLANK
AND IT FEELS GOOD.

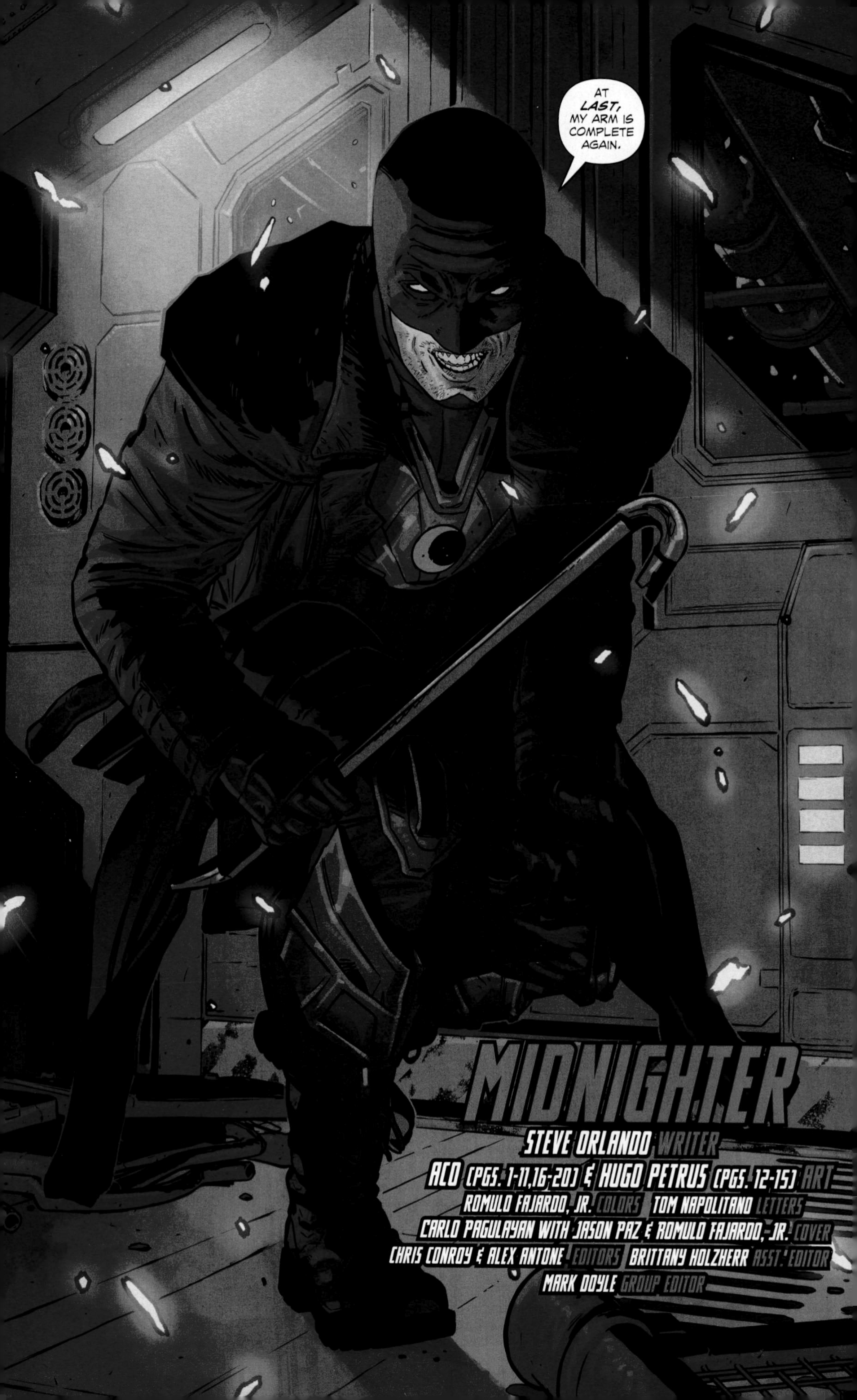
AT LAST, MY ARM IS COMPLETE AGAIN.
MIDNIGHTER
STEVE ORLANDO WRITER
ACO (PGS. 1-11,16-20) & HUGO PETRUS (PGS. 12-15) ART
ROMULO FAJARDO, JR. COLORS TOM NAPOLITANO LETTERS
CARLO PAGULAYAN WITH JASON PAZ & ROMULO FAJARDO, JR. COVER
CHRIS CONROY & ALEX ANTONE EDITORS BRITTANY HOLZHERR ASST. EDITOR
MARK DOYLE GROUP EDITOR

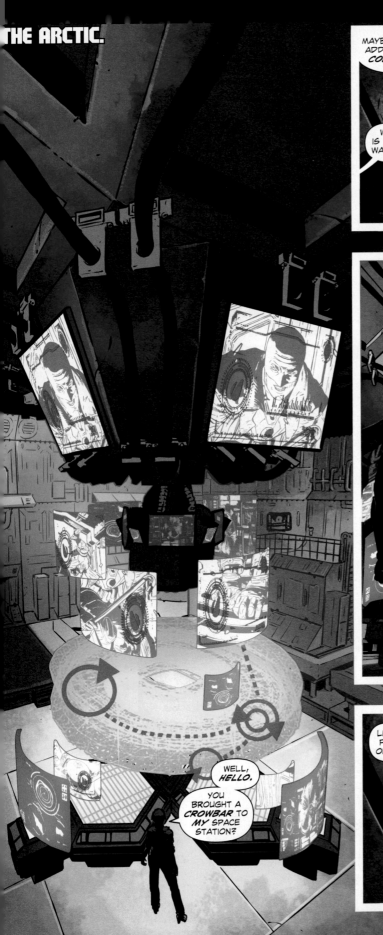

WELL, *HELLO.*

YOU BROUGHT A *CROWBAR* TO MY SPACE STATION?

MAYBE I SHOULD ADD YOU TO MY *COLLECTION.*

WHAT IS *THAT,* WALLER?

YOU DON'T ALREADY SEE WHAT I'LL SAY, *AFA?*

SURE. IF I ASK THE QUESTION.

THAT UP THERE IS ONE OF TWO THINGS.

YOUR *REPLACEMENT,* OR THE NEXT *NOTCH* IN YOUR UNDEFEATED STREAK.

WHAT DOES IT *DO?*

LET'S FIND OUT...

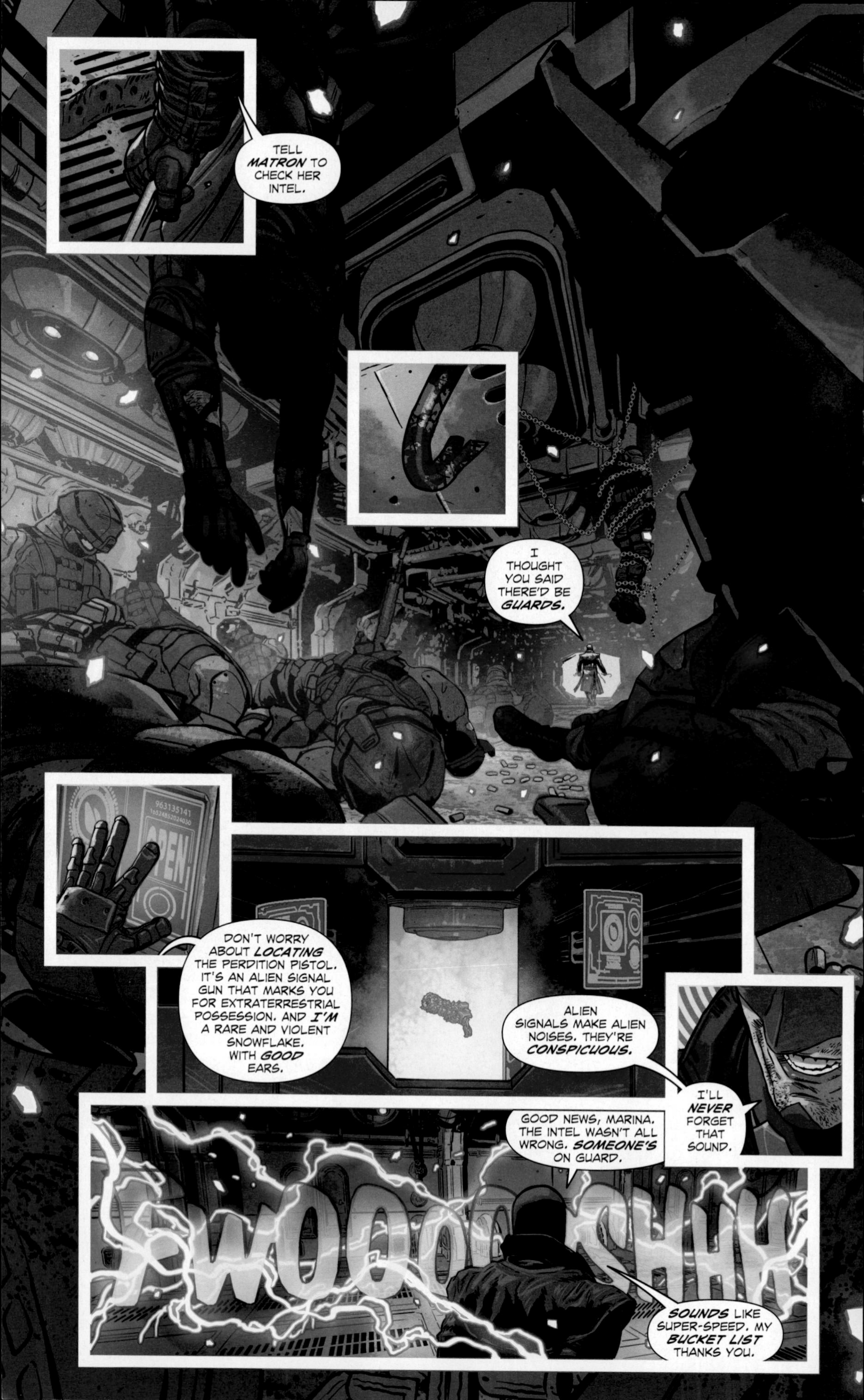
TELL MATRON TO CHECK HER INTEL.
I THOUGHT YOU SAID THERE'D BE GUARDS.
OPEN
DON'T WORRY ABOUT LOCATING THE PERDITION PISTOL. IT'S AN ALIEN SIGNAL GUN THAT MARKS YOU FOR EXTRATERRESTRIAL POSSESSION. AND I'M A RARE AND VIOLENT SNOWFLAKE. WITH GOOD EARS.
ALIEN SIGNALS MAKE ALIEN NOISES. THEY'RE CONSPICUOUS.
I'LL NEVER FORGET THAT SOUND.
GOOD NEWS, MARINA. THE INTEL WASN'T ALL WRONG. SOMEONE'S ON GUARD.
SOUNDS LIKE SUPER-SPEED. MY BUCKET LIST THANKS YOU.

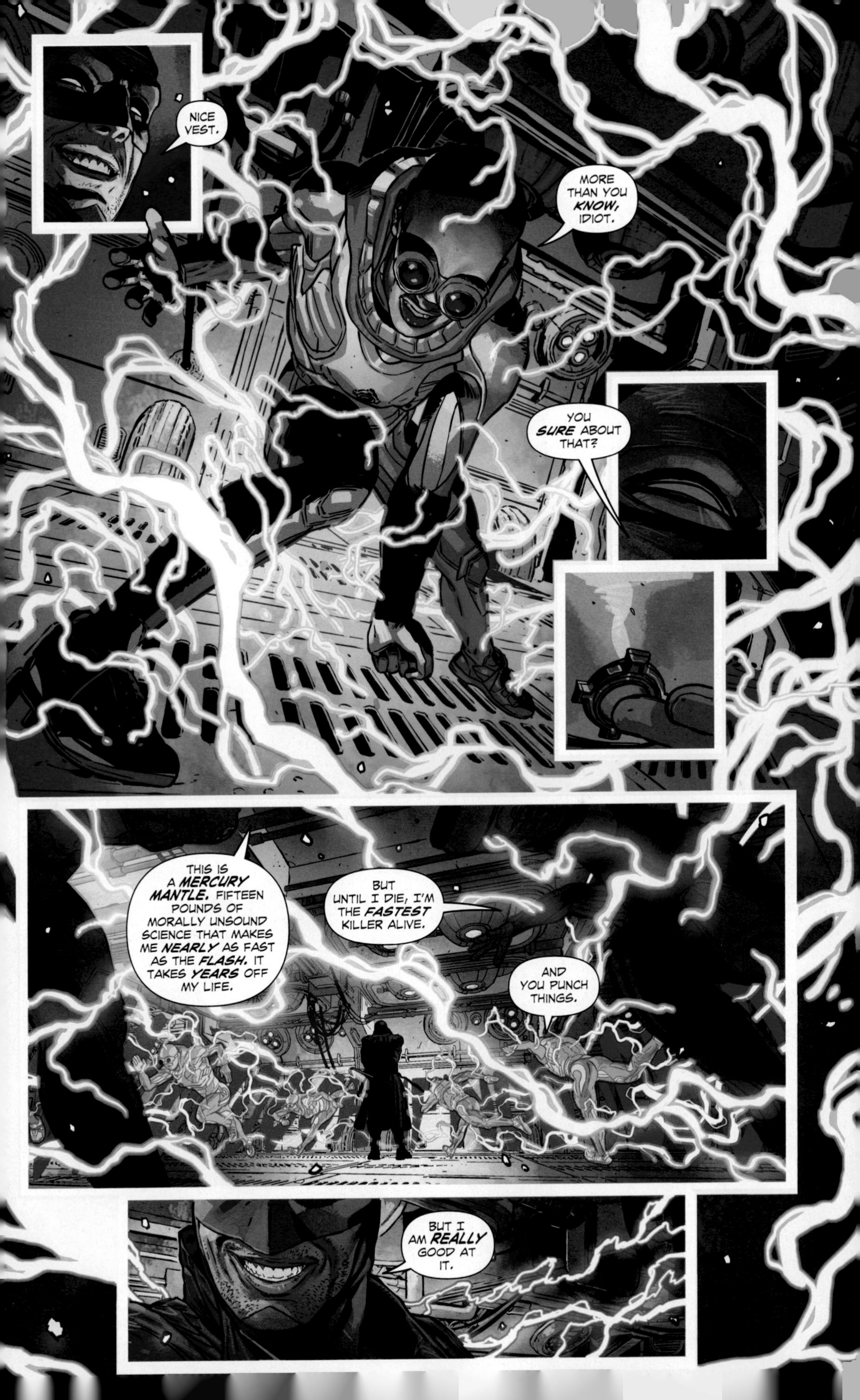
NICE VEST.
MORE THAN YOU KNOW, IDIOT.
YOU SURE ABOUT THAT?
THIS IS A MERCURY MANTLE. FIFTEEN POUNDS OF MORALLY UNSOUND SCIENCE THAT MAKES ME NEARLY AS FAST AS THE FLASH. IT TAKES YEARS OFF MY LIFE.
BUT UNTIL I DIE, I'M THE FASTEST KILLER ALIVE.
AND YOU PUNCH THINGS.
BUT I AM REALLY GOOD AT IT.

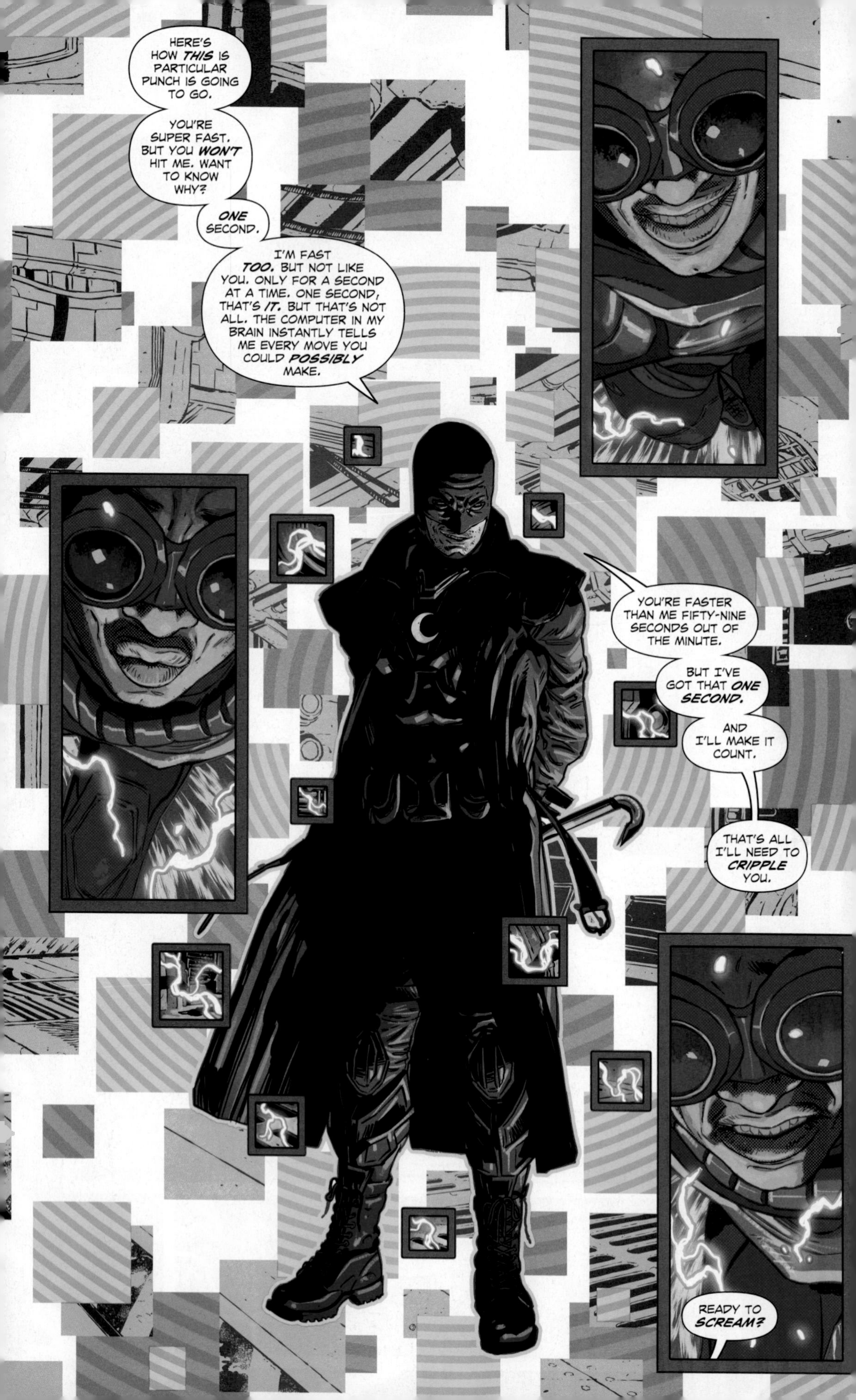

HERE'S HOW THIS IS PARTICULAR PUNCH IS GOING TO GO.
YOU'RE SUPER FAST. BUT YOU WON'T HIT ME. WANT TO KNOW WHY?
ONE SECOND.
I'M FAST TOO. BUT NOT LIKE YOU. ONLY FOR A SECOND AT A TIME. ONE SECOND, THAT'S IT. BUT THAT'S NOT ALL. THE COMPUTER IN MY BRAIN INSTANTLY TELLS ME EVERY MOVE YOU COULD POSSIBLY MAKE.
YOU'RE FASTER THAN ME FIFTY-NINE SECONDS OUT OF THE MINUTE.
BUT I'VE GOT THAT ONE SECOND.
AND I'LL MAKE IT COUNT.
THAT'S ALL I'LL NEED TO CRIPPLE YOU.
READY TO SCREAM?

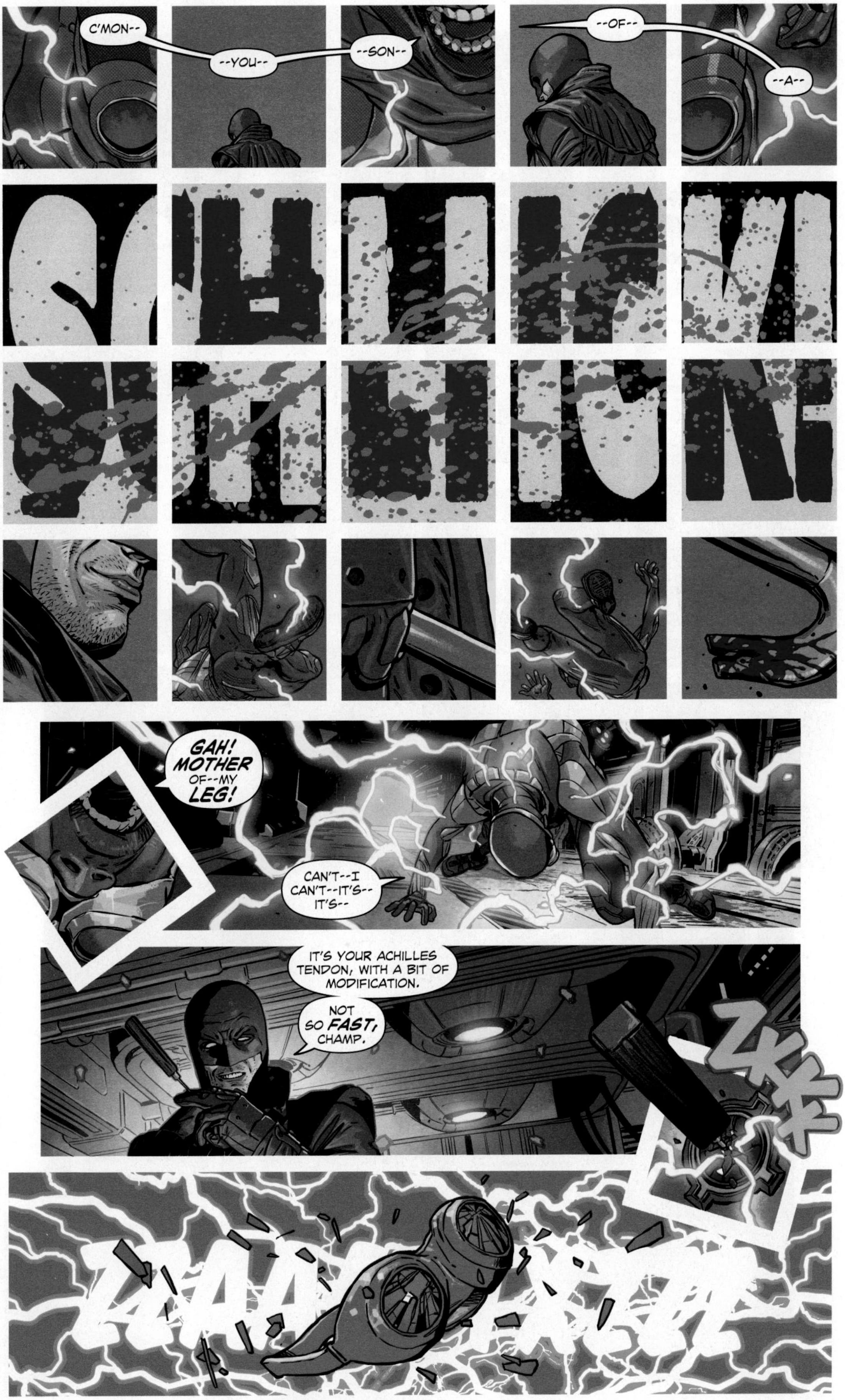

C'MON--
--YOU--
--SON--
--OF--
--A--
GAH! MOTHER OF--MY LEG!
CAN'T--I CAN'T--IT'S-- IT'S--
IT'S YOUR ACHILLES TENDON, WITH A BIT OF MODIFICATION.
NOT SO FAST, CHAMP.

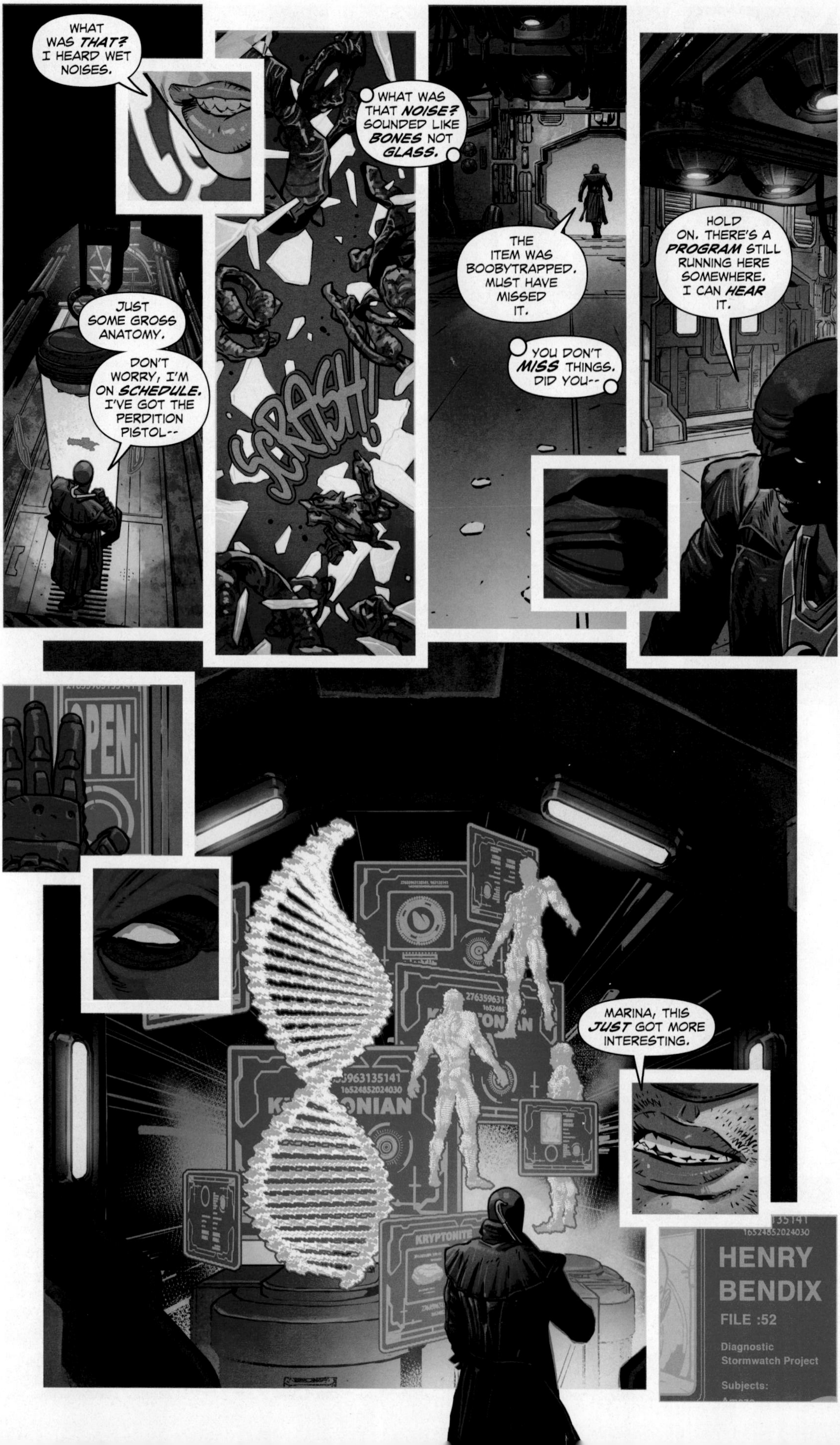

WHAT WAS THAT? I HEARD WET NOISES.
WHAT WAS THAT NOISE? SOUNDED LIKE BONES NOT GLASS.
JUST SOME GROSS ANATOMY.
DON'T WORRY, I'M ON SCHEDULE. I'VE GOT THE PERDITION PISTOL--
SCRASH!
THE ITEM WAS BOOBYTRAPPED. MUST HAVE MISSED IT.
YOU DON'T MISS THINGS. DID YOU--
HOLD ON. THERE'S A PROGRAM STILL RUNNING HERE SOMEWHERE. I CAN HEAR IT.
OPEN
KRYPTONITE
MARINA, THIS JUST GOT MORE INTERESTING.
16524852024030
HENRY BENDIX
FILE :52
Diagnostic
Stormwatch Project
Subjects:

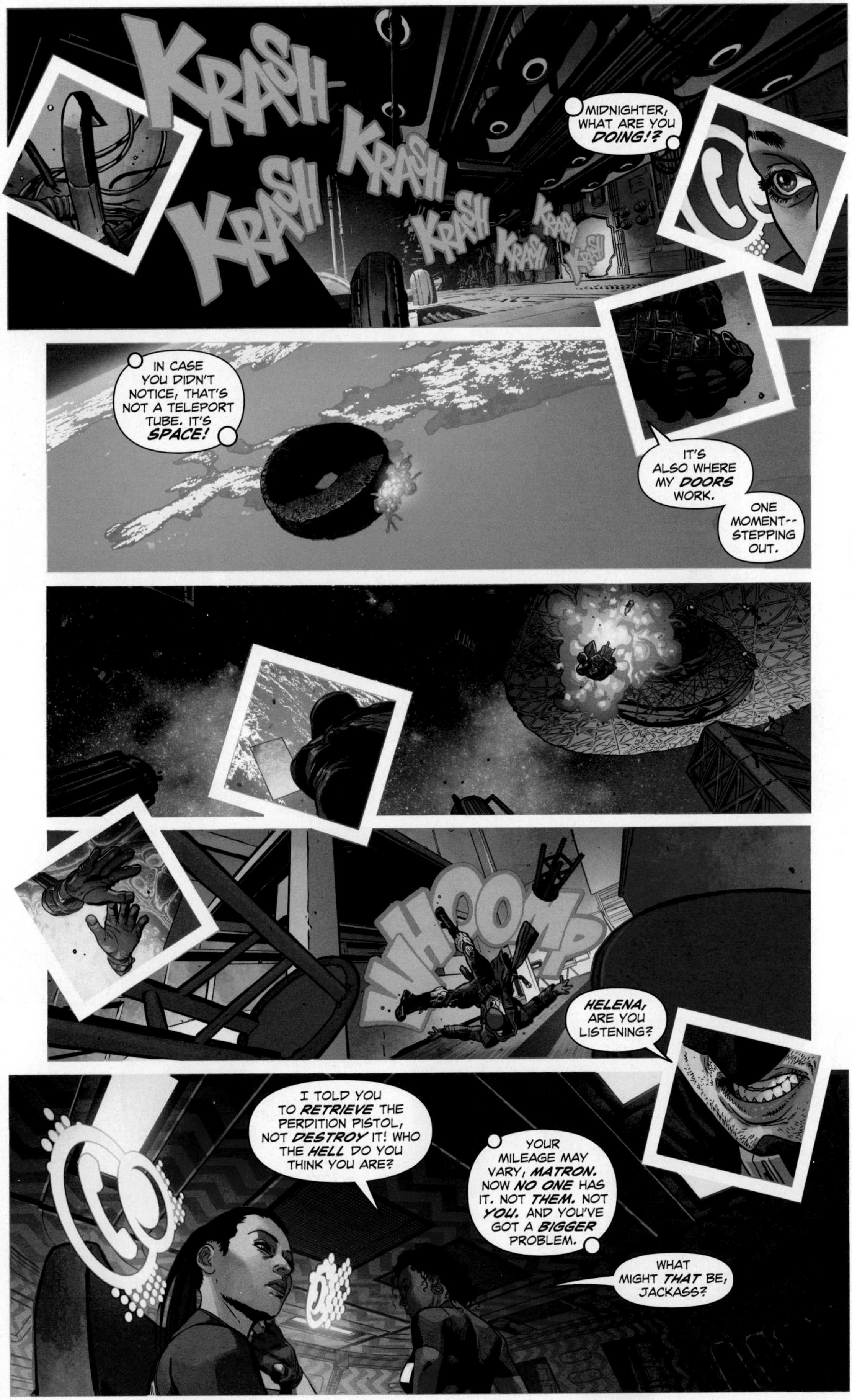
KRASH-KRASH
KRASH
KRASH
KRASH
KRASH
KRASH
MIDNIGHTER, WHAT ARE YOU DOING!?
IN CASE YOU DIDN'T NOTICE, THAT'S NOT A TELEPORT TUBE. IT'S SPACE!
IT'S ALSO WHERE MY DOORS WORK.
ONE MOMENT--STEPPING OUT.
WHOOMP
HELENA, ARE YOU LISTENING?
I TOLD YOU TO RETRIEVE THE PERDITION PISTOL, NOT DESTROY IT! WHO THE HELL DO YOU THINK YOU ARE?
YOUR MILEAGE MAY VARY, MATRON. NOW NO ONE HAS IT. NOT THEM. NOT YOU. AND YOU'VE GOT A BIGGER PROBLEM.
WHAT MIGHT THAT BE, JACKASS?

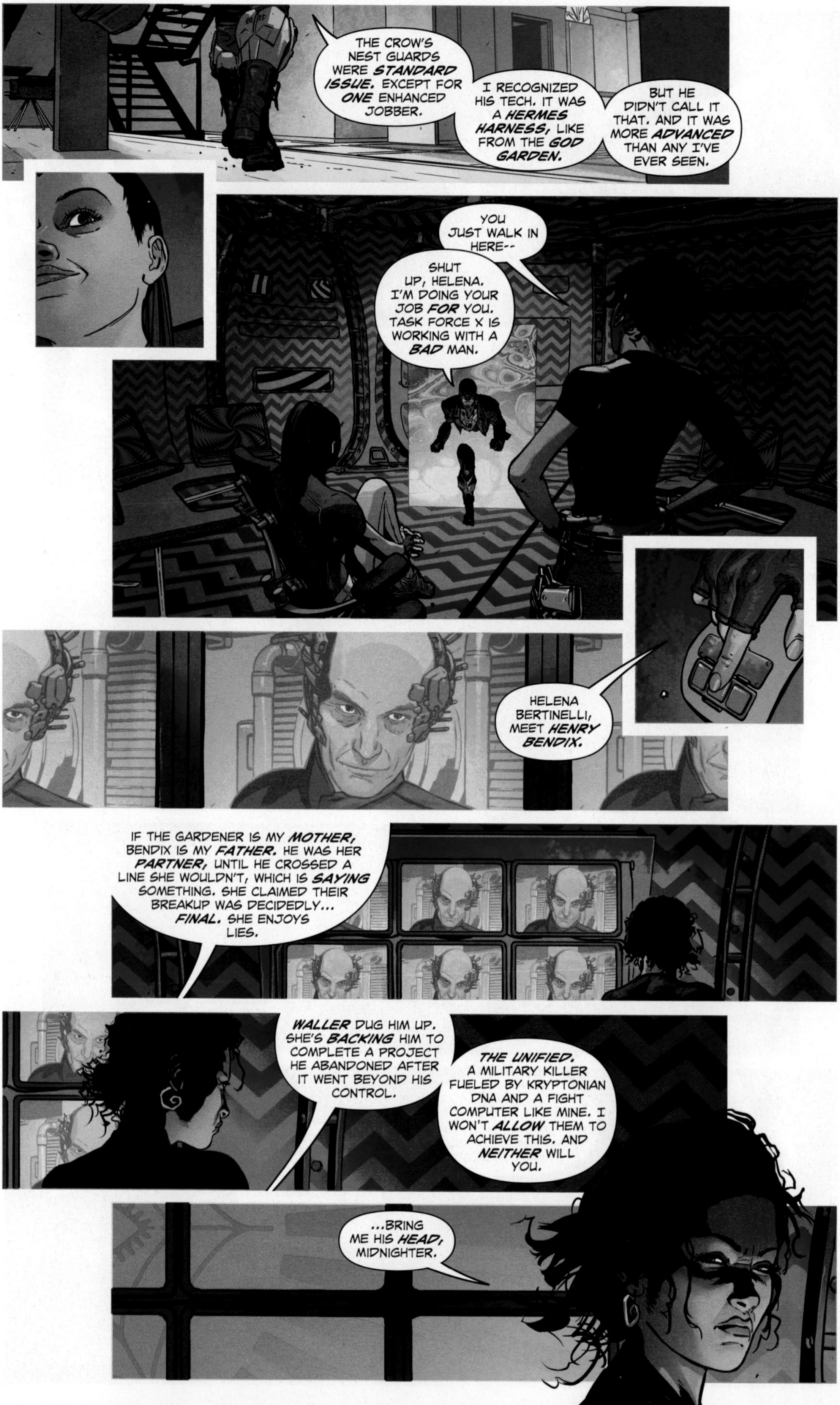
THE CROW'S NEST GUARDS WERE STANDARD ISSUE. EXCEPT FOR ONE ENHANCED JOBBER.
I RECOGNIZED HIS TECH. IT WAS A HERMES HARNESS, LIKE FROM THE GOD GARDEN.
BUT HE DIDN'T CALL IT THAT. AND IT WAS MORE ADVANCED THAN ANY I'VE EVER SEEN.
YOU JUST WALK IN HERE--
SHUT UP, HELENA. I'M DOING YOUR JOB FOR YOU. TASK FORCE X IS WORKING WITH A BAD MAN.
HELENA BERTINELLI, MEET HENRY BENDIX.
IF THE GARDENER IS MY MOTHER, BENDIX IS MY FATHER. HE WAS HER PARTNER, UNTIL HE CROSSED A LINE SHE WOULDN'T, WHICH IS SAYING SOMETHING. SHE CLAIMED THEIR BREAKUP WAS DECIDEDLY... FINAL. SHE ENJOYS LIES.
WALLER DUG HIM UP. SHE'S BACKING HIM TO COMPLETE A PROJECT HE ABANDONED AFTER IT WENT BEYOND HIS CONTROL.
THE UNIFIED. A MILITARY KILLER FUELED BY KRYPTONIAN DNA AND A FIGHT COMPUTER LIKE MINE. I WON'T ALLOW THEM TO ACHIEVE THIS. AND NEITHER WILL YOU.
...BRING ME HIS HEAD, MIDNIGHTER.

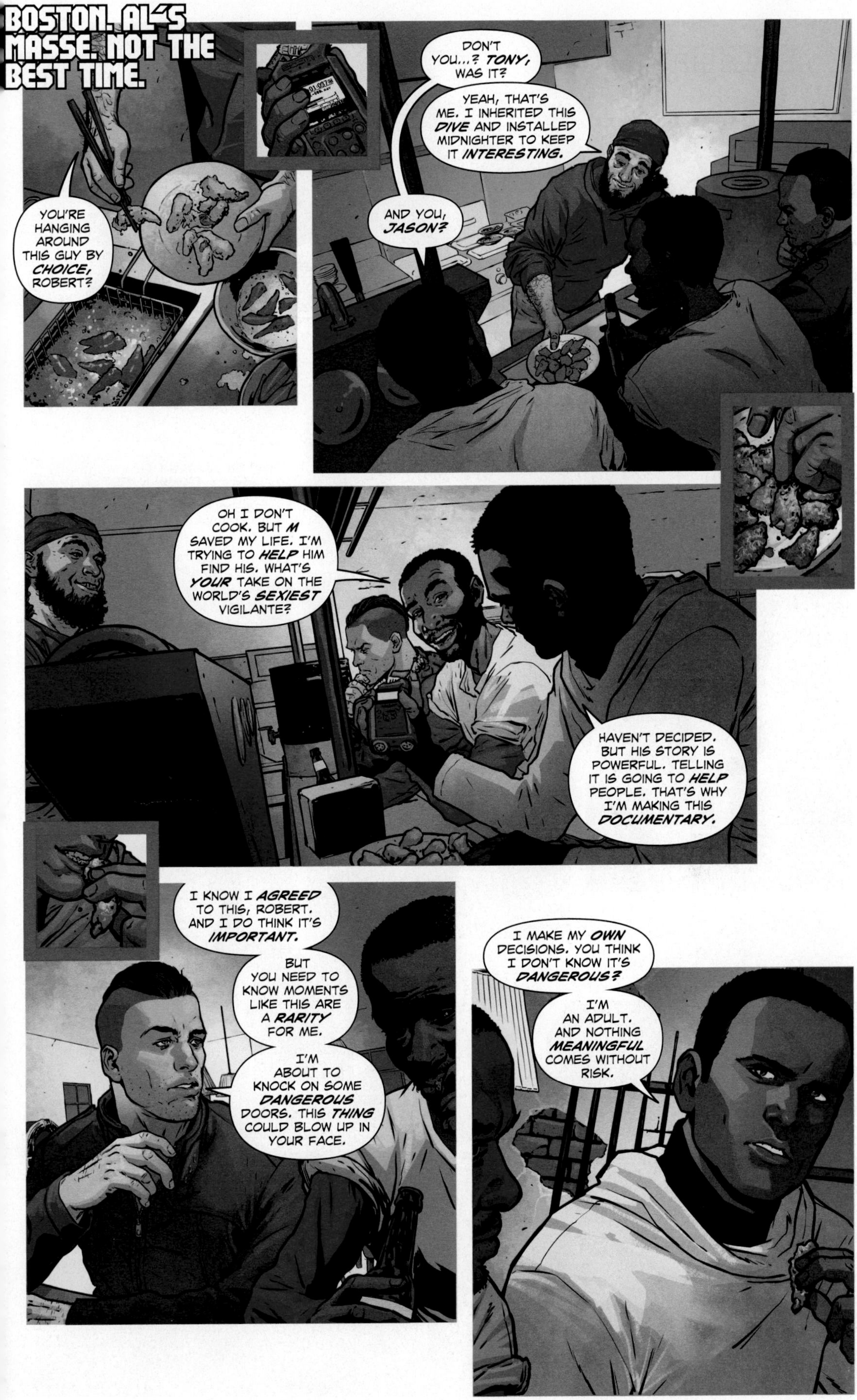
BOSTON. AL'S MASSE. NOT THE BEST TIME.
YOU'RE HANGING AROUND THIS GUY BY CHOICE, ROBERT?
DON'T YOU...? TONY, WAS IT?
YEAH, THAT'S ME. I INHERITED THIS DIVE AND INSTALLED MIDNIGHTER TO KEEP IT INTERESTING.
AND YOU, JASON?
OH I DON'T COOK. BUT M SAVED MY LIFE. I'M TRYING TO HELP HIM FIND HIS. WHAT'S YOUR TAKE ON THE WORLD'S SEXIEST VIGILANTE?
HAVEN'T DECIDED. BUT HIS STORY IS POWERFUL. TELLING IT IS GOING TO HELP PEOPLE. THAT'S WHY I'M MAKING THIS DOCUMENTARY.
I KNOW I AGREED TO THIS, ROBERT. AND I DO THINK IT'S IMPORTANT.
BUT YOU NEED TO KNOW MOMENTS LIKE THIS ARE A RARITY FOR ME.
I'M ABOUT TO KNOCK ON SOME DANGEROUS DOORS. THIS THING COULD BLOW UP IN YOUR FACE.
I MAKE MY OWN DECISIONS. YOU THINK I DON'T KNOW IT'S DANGEROUS?
I'M AN ADULT. AND NOTHING MEANINGFUL COMES WITHOUT RISK.

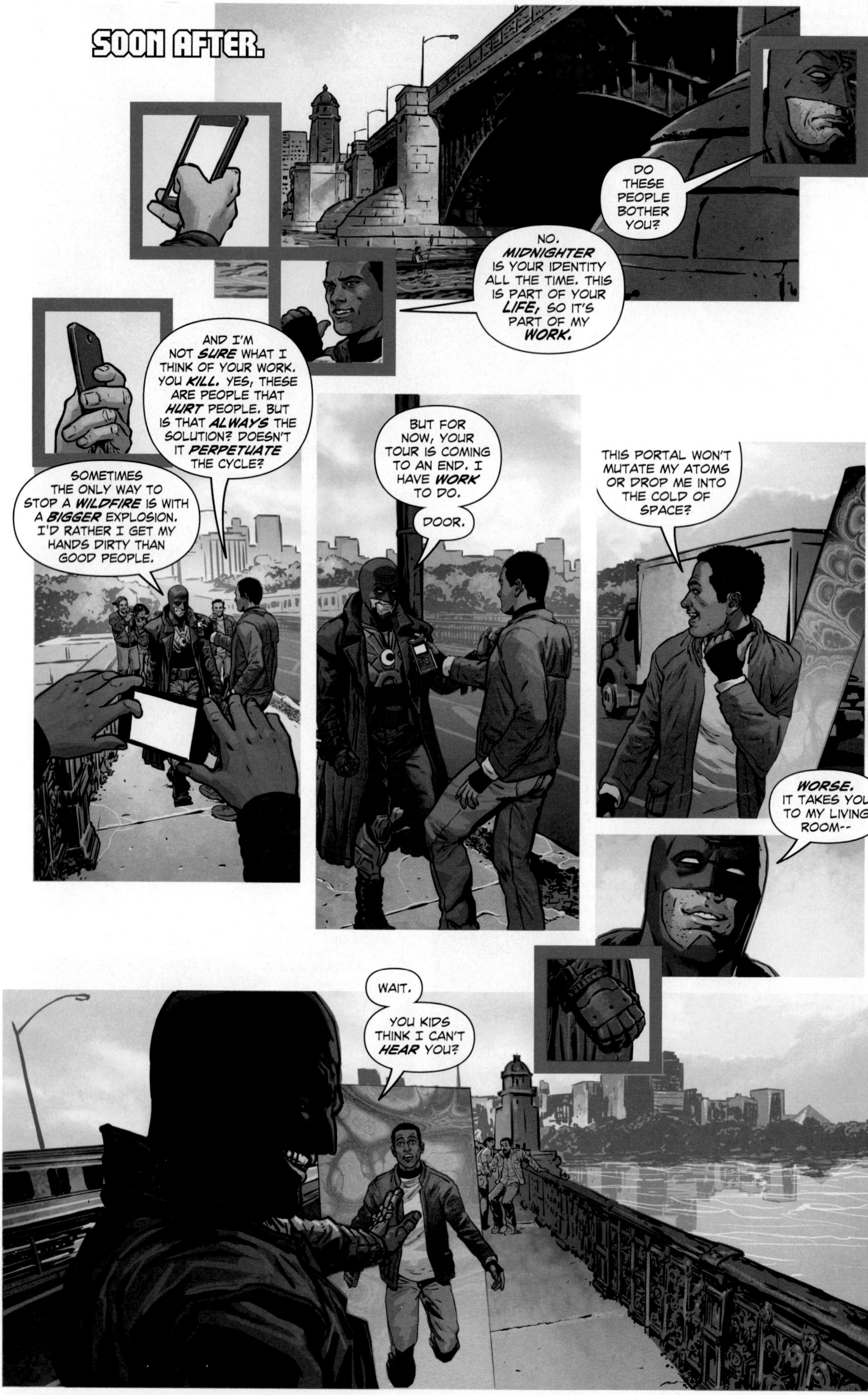
SOON AFTER.
DO THESE PEOPLE BOTHER YOU?
NO. MIDNIGHTER IS YOUR IDENTITY ALL THE TIME. THIS IS PART OF YOUR LIFE, SO IT'S PART OF MY WORK.
AND I'M NOT SURE WHAT I THINK OF YOUR WORK. YOU KILL. YES, THESE ARE PEOPLE THAT HURT PEOPLE. BUT IS THAT ALWAYS THE SOLUTION? DOESN'T IT PERPETUATE THE CYCLE?
SOMETIMES THE ONLY WAY TO STOP A WILDFIRE IS WITH A BIGGER EXPLOSION. I'D RATHER I GET MY HANDS DIRTY THAN GOOD PEOPLE.
BUT FOR NOW, YOUR TOUR IS COMING TO AN END. I HAVE WORK TO DO.
DOOR.
THIS PORTAL WON'T MUTATE MY ATOMS OR DROP ME INTO THE COLD OF SPACE?
WORSE. IT TAKES YOU TO MY LIVING ROOM--
WAIT.
YOU KIDS THINK I CAN'T HEAR YOU?

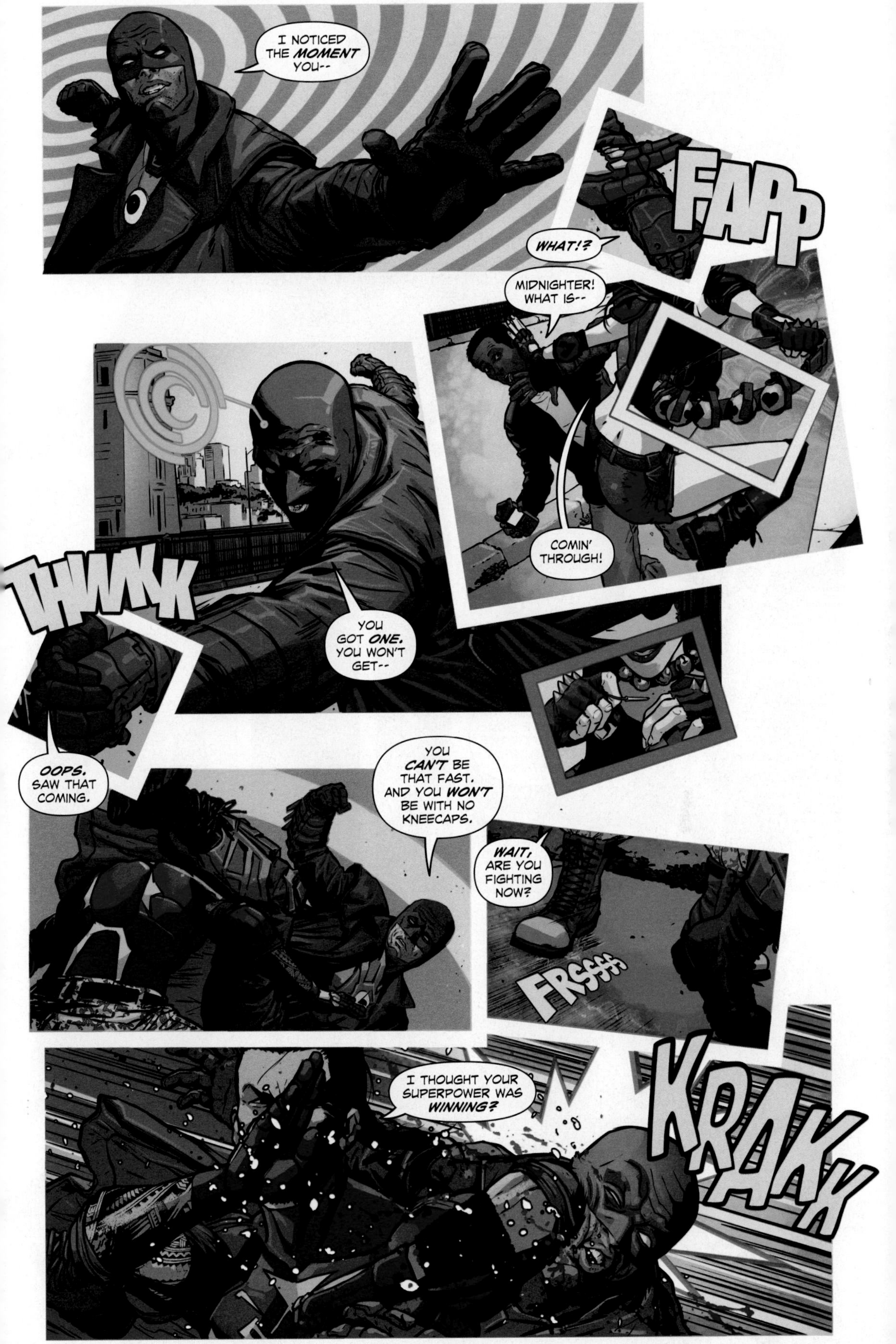
I NOTICED THE MOMENT YOU--
FAPP
WHAT!?
MIDNIGHTER! WHAT IS--
COMIN' THROUGH!
YOU GOT ONE. YOU WON'T GET--
THWAKK
OOPS. SAW THAT COMING.
YOU CAN'T BE THAT FAST. AND YOU WON'T BE WITH NO KNEECAPS.
WAIT, ARE YOU FIGHTING NOW?
FRSSSS
I THOUGHT YOUR SUPERPOWER WAS WINNING?
KRAKK

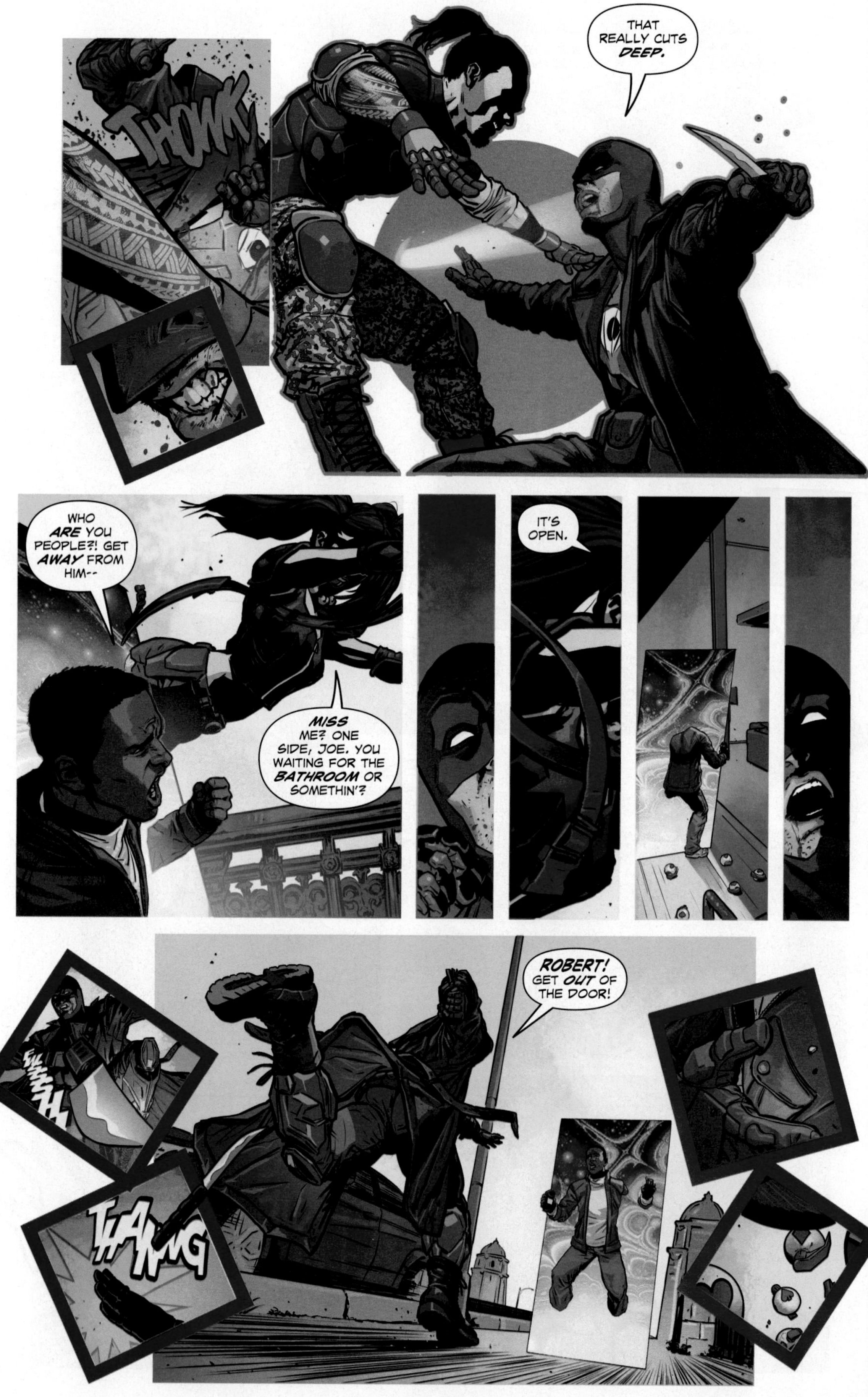
THONK
THAT REALLY CUTS DEEP.
WHO ARE YOU PEOPLE?! GET AWAY FROM HIM--
MISS ME? ONE SIDE, JOE. YOU WAITING FOR THE BATHROOM OR SOMETHIN'?
IT'S OPEN.
ROBERT! GET OUT OF THE DOOR!
THANG

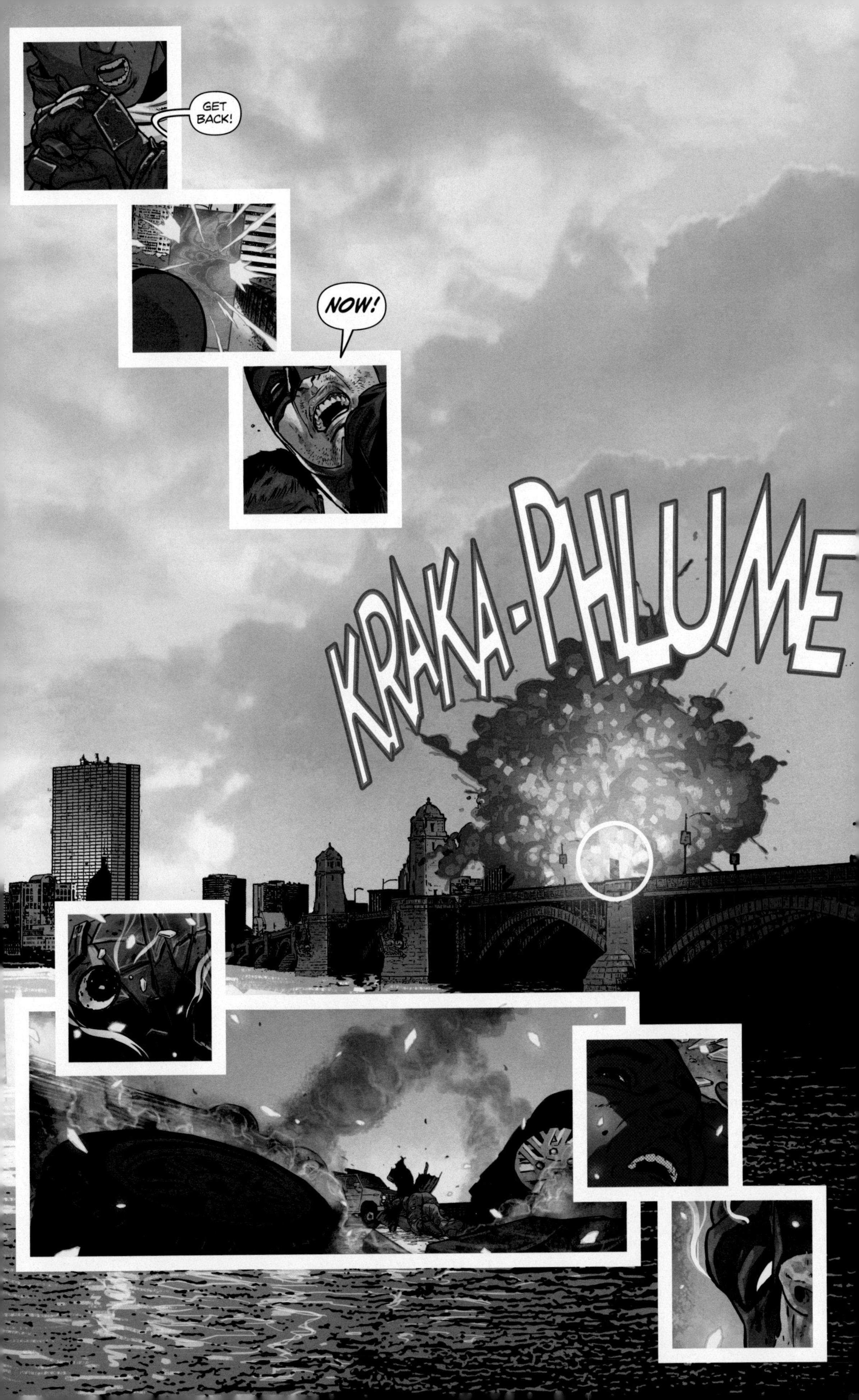
GET BACK!
NOW!
KRAKA-PHLUME

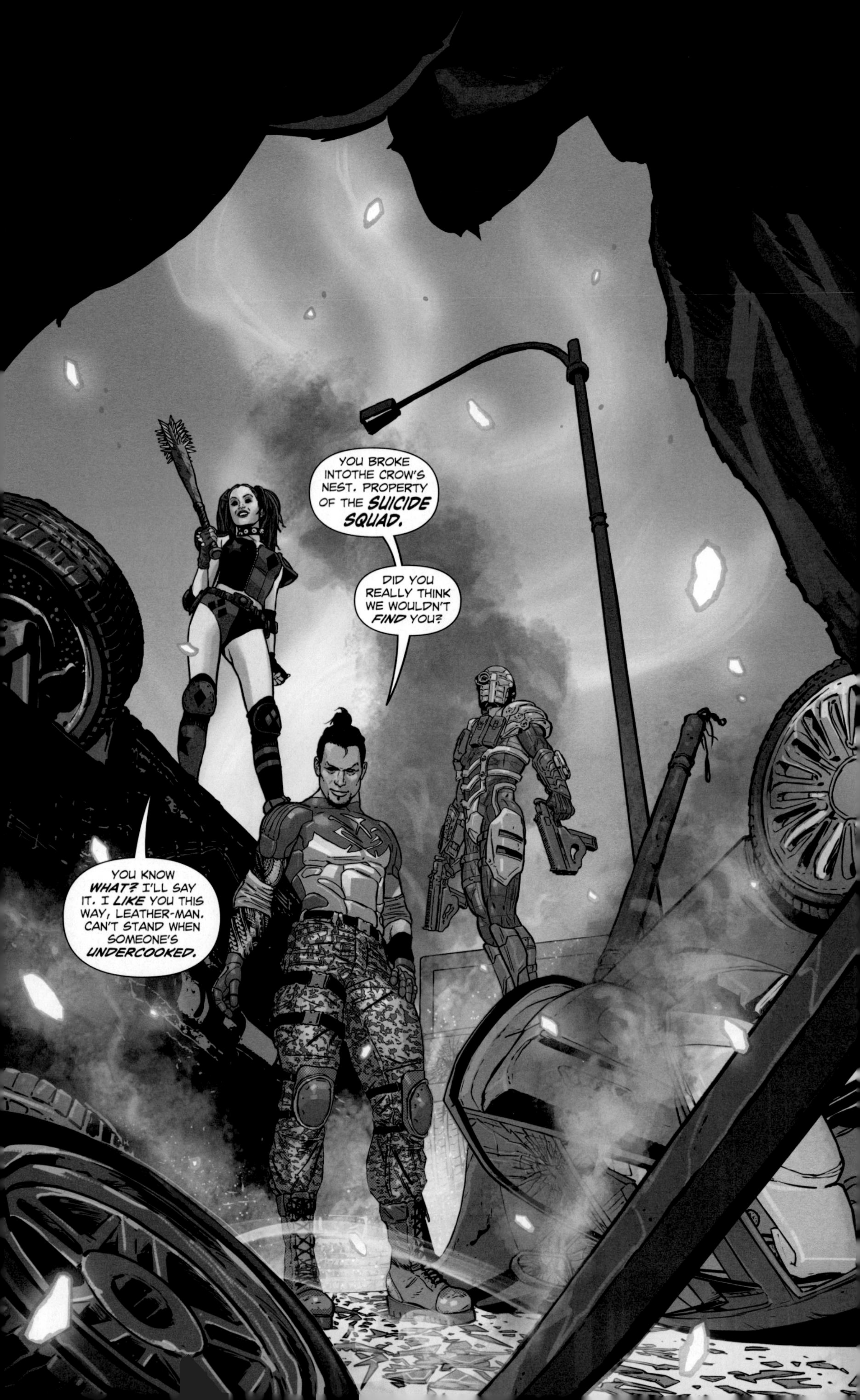
YOU BROKE INTOTHE CROW'S NEST. PROPERTY OF THE SUICIDE SQUAD.
DID YOU REALLY THINK WE WOULDN'T FIND YOU?
YOU KNOW WHAT? I'LL SAY IT. I LIKE YOU THIS WAY, LEATHER-MAN. CAN'T STAND WHEN SOMEONE'S UNDERCOOKED.

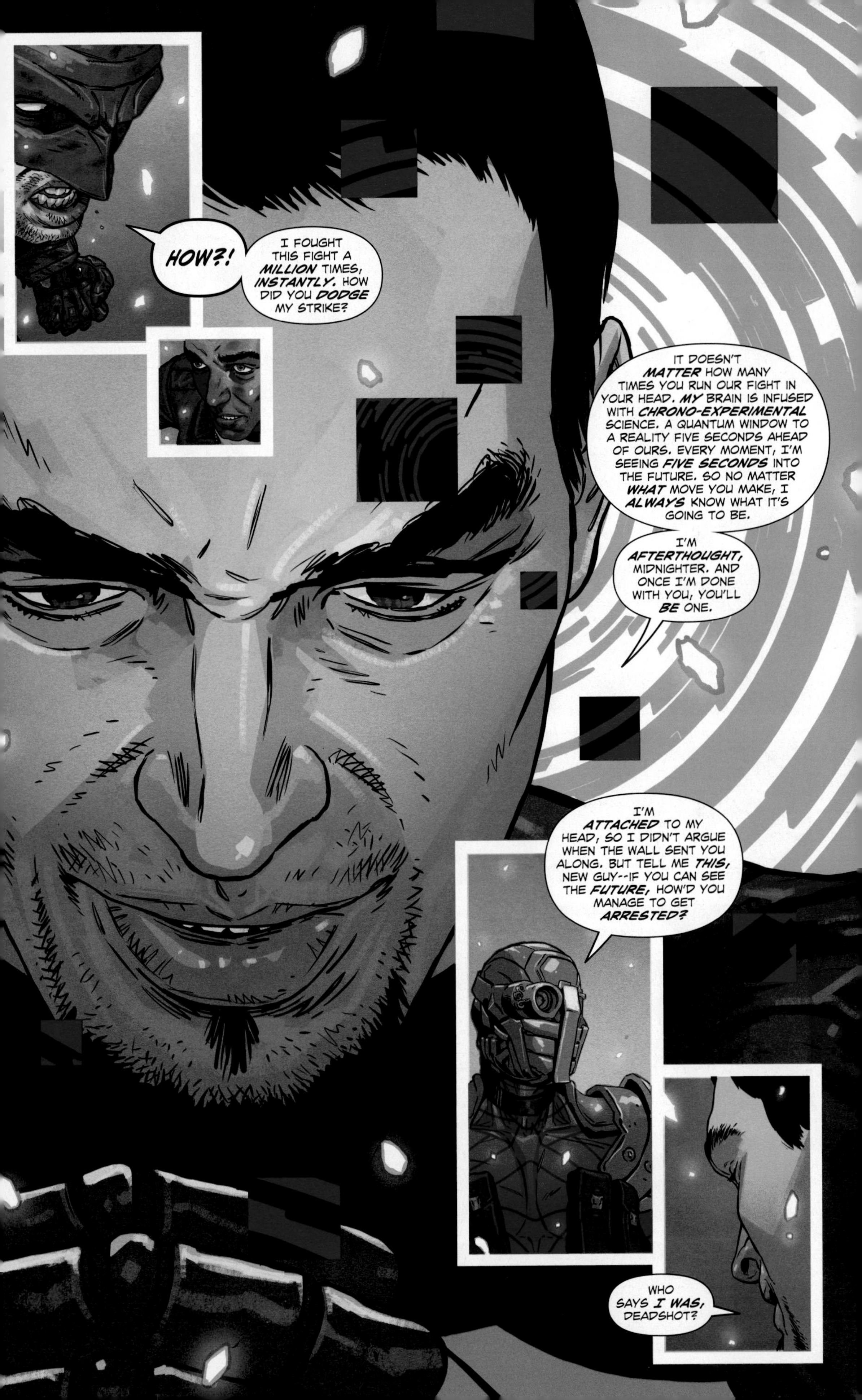
HOW?!
I FOUGHT THIS FIGHT A MILLION TIMES, INSTANTLY. HOW DID YOU DODGE MY STRIKE?
IT DOESN'T MATTER HOW MANY TIMES YOU RUN OUR FIGHT IN YOUR HEAD. MY BRAIN IS INFUSED WITH CHRONO-EXPERIMENTAL SCIENCE. A QUANTUM WINDOW TO A REALITY FIVE SECONDS AHEAD OF OURS. EVERY MOMENT, I'M SEEING FIVE SECONDS INTO THE FUTURE. SO NO MATTER WHAT MOVE YOU MAKE, I ALWAYS KNOW WHAT IT'S GOING TO BE.
I'M AFTERTHOUGHT, MIDNIGHTER. AND ONCE I'M DONE WITH YOU, YOU'LL BE ONE.
I'M ATTACHED TO MY HEAD, SO I DIDN'T ARGUE WHEN THE WALL SENT YOU ALONG. BUT TELL ME THIS, NEW GUY--IF YOU CAN SEE THE FUTURE, HOW'D YOU MANAGE TO GET ARRESTED?
WHO SAYS I WAS, DEADSHOT?

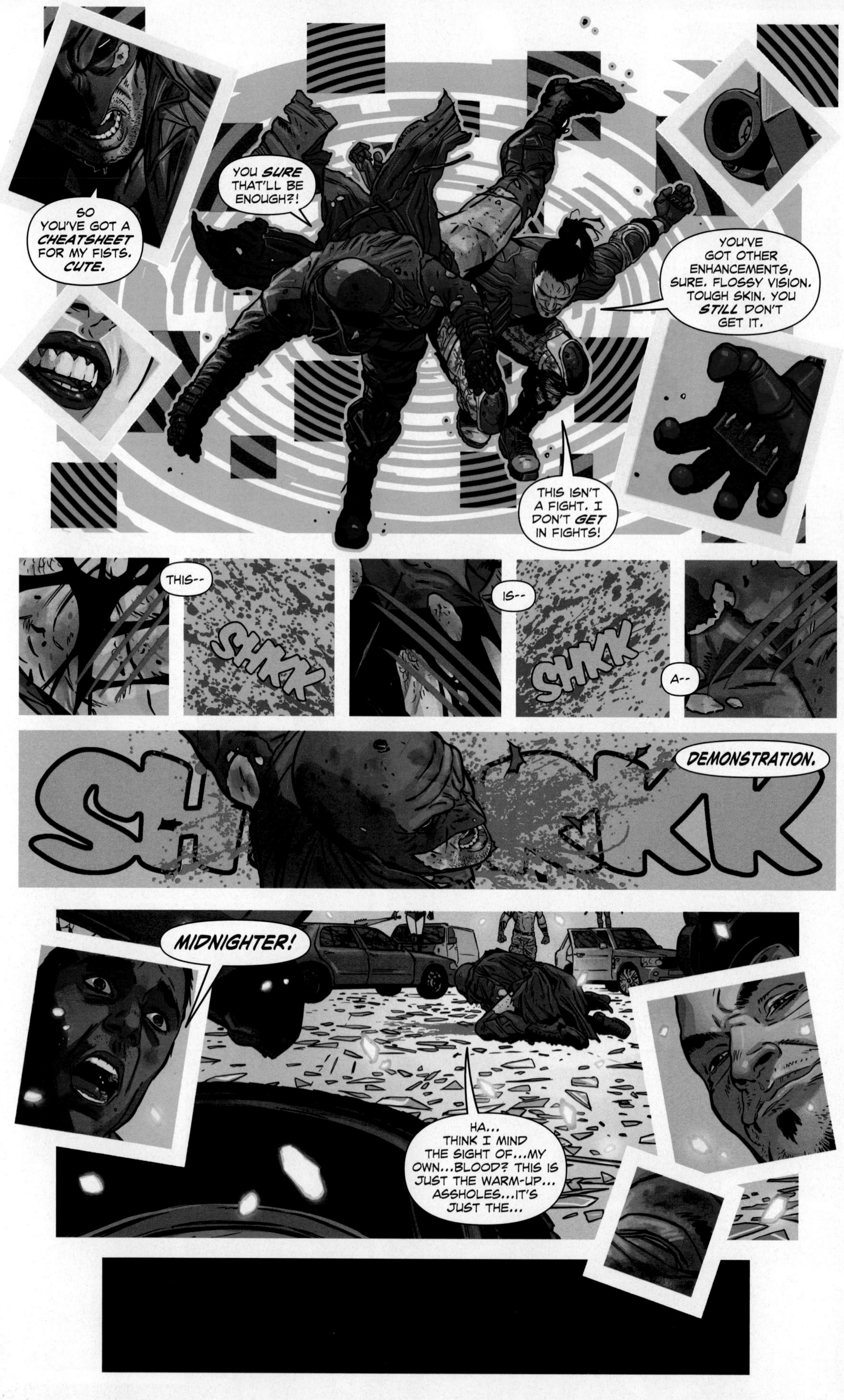
SO YOU'VE GOT A CHEATSHEET FOR MY FISTS. CUTE.
YOU SURE THAT'LL BE ENOUGH?!
YOU'VE GOT OTHER ENHANCEMENTS, SURE. FLOSSY VISION. TOUGH SKIN. YOU STILL DON'T GET IT.
THIS ISN'T A FIGHT. I DON'T GET IN FIGHTS!
THIS--
SHKK
IS--
SHKK
A--
SHKK
DEMONSTRATION.
MIDNIGHTER!
HA... THINK I MIND THE SIGHT OF...MY OWN...BLOOD? THIS IS JUST THE WARM-UP... ASSHOLES...IT'S JUST THE...

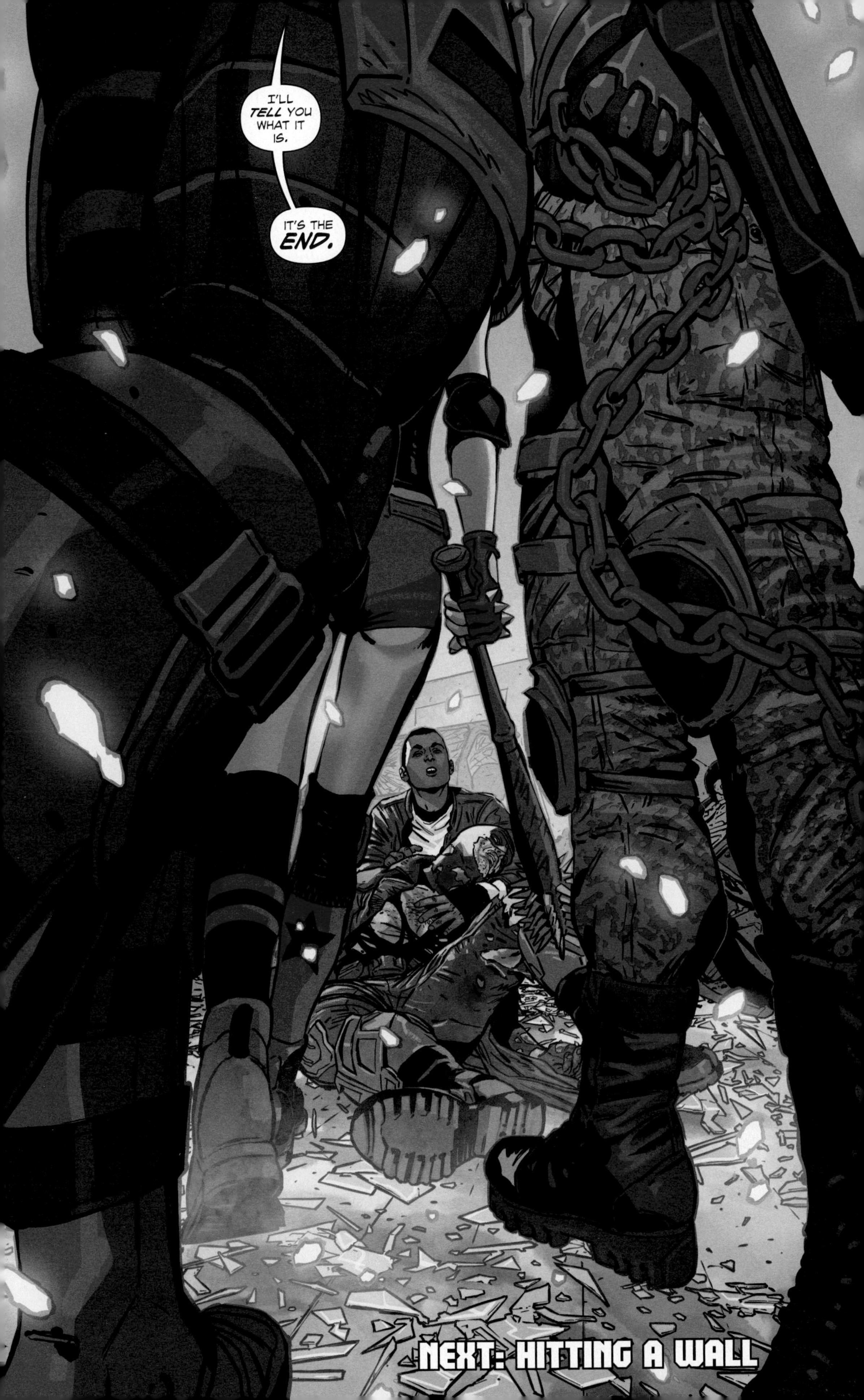
I'LL TELL YOU WHAT IT IS.
IT'S THE END.
NEXT: HITTING A WALL

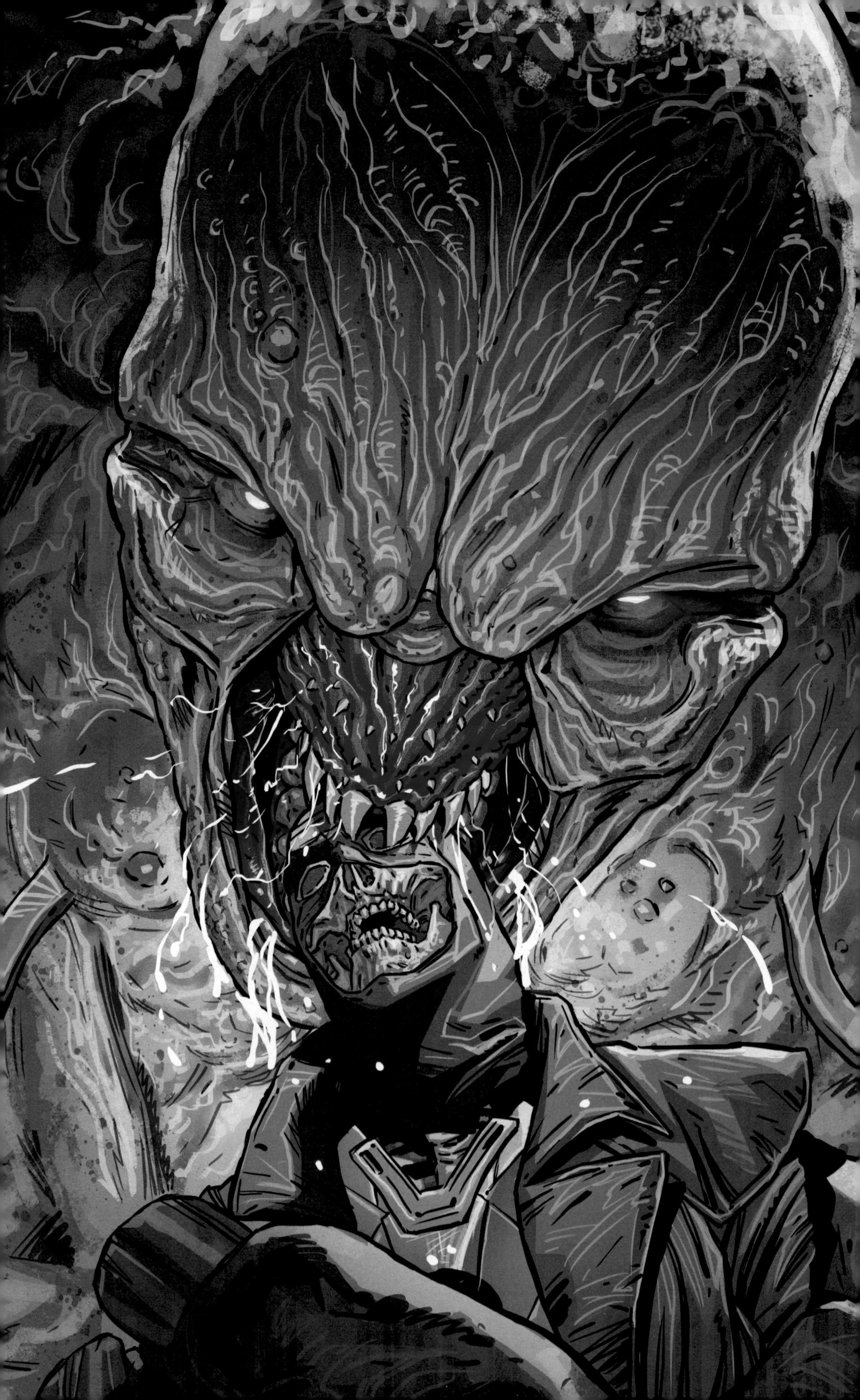

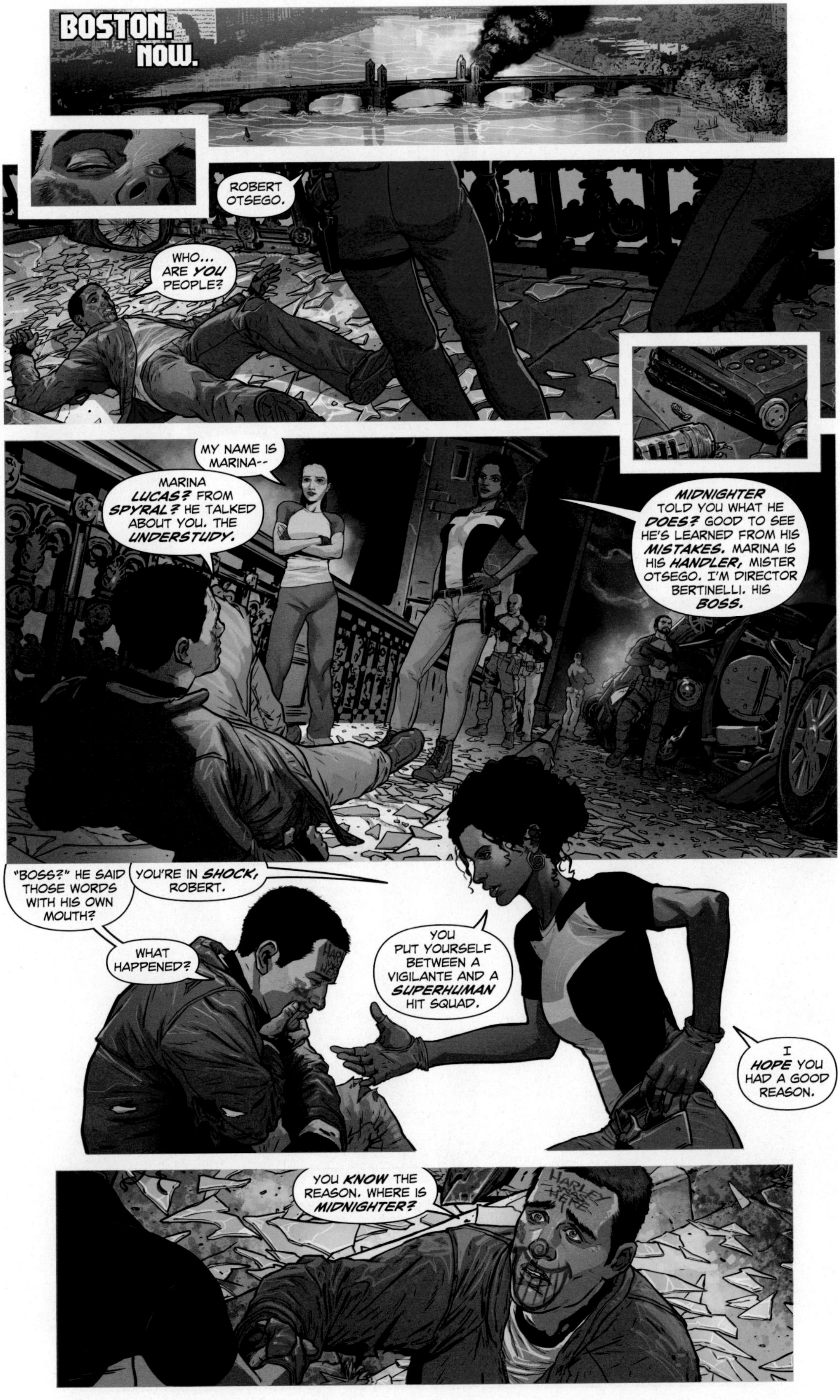
BOSTON. NOW.
ROBERT OTSEGO.
WHO... ARE YOU PEOPLE?
MY NAME IS MARINA--
MARINA LUCAS? FROM SPYRAL? HE TALKED ABOUT YOU. THE UNDERSTUDY.
MIDNIGHTER TOLD YOU WHAT HE DOES? GOOD TO SEE HE'S LEARNED FROM HIS MISTAKES. MARINA IS HIS HANDLER, MISTER OTSEGO. I'M DIRECTOR BERTINELLI. HIS BOSS.
"BOSS?" HE SAID THOSE WORDS WITH HIS OWN MOUTH?
YOU'RE IN SHOCK, ROBERT.
WHAT HAPPENED?
YOU PUT YOURSELF BETWEEN A VIGILANTE AND A SUPERHUMAN HIT SQUAD.
I HOPE YOU HAD A GOOD REASON.
YOU KNOW THE REASON. WHERE IS MIDNIGHTER?

MIDNIGHTER WAS M.I.A BEFORE WE WERE ON SITE. LOOKS LIKE YOU PUT UP A GOOD FIGHT, FOR AN ARTIST.

IS THAT SUPPOSED TO BE FUNNY? HE'S *GONE!*

HE'D BE WAY *LESS* GONE IF HE HAD WORKED *WITH* ME, INSTEAD OF IN *SPITE* OF ME.

MIDNIGHTER *REFUSED* THE NANOTECH VIRUS WE USE TO TRACK OTHER SPYRAL AGENTS. WE'RE *LOOKING* FOR HIM. BUT WE HAVE TO DO IT THE OLD FASHIONED WAY.

DON'T WORRY. HE'S A *BIG BOY.* HE'LL--

I'M GOING TO SAY SOMETHING HERE.

I DON'T AGREE WITH *EVERYTHING* MIDNIGHTER DOES. BUT HE WORKS HIMSELF TO THE BONE TO *HELP* PEOPLE. AND HE DOES IT *DESPITE* WHAT WAS DONE TO HIM-- EXPERIMENTS AND *MANIPULATION.*

YOU *KNOW* THAT, AND YOU HANG HIM OUT TO DRY TO PROVE A POINT? YOU'RE *STILL* MANIPULATING HIM.

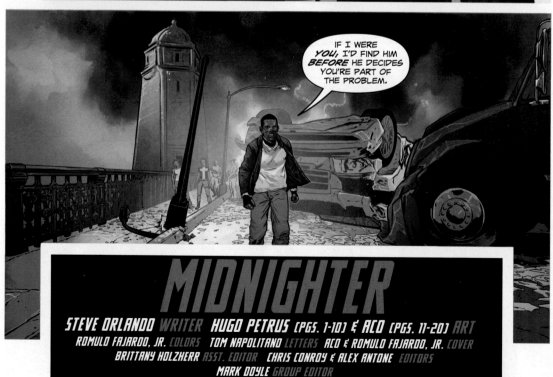

IF I WERE *YOU,* I'D FIND HIM *BEFORE* HE DECIDES YOU'RE PART OF THE PROBLEM.

MIDNIGHTER

STEVE ORLANDO WRITER **HUGO PETRUS** (PGS. 1-10) & **ACO** (PGS. 11-20) ART
ROMULO FAJARDO, JR. COLORS **TOM NAPOLITANO** LETTERS **ACO & ROMULO FAJARDO, JR.** COVER
BRITTANY HOLZHERR ASST. EDITOR **CHRIS CONROY & ALEX ANTONE** EDITORS
MARK DOYLE GROUP EDITOR

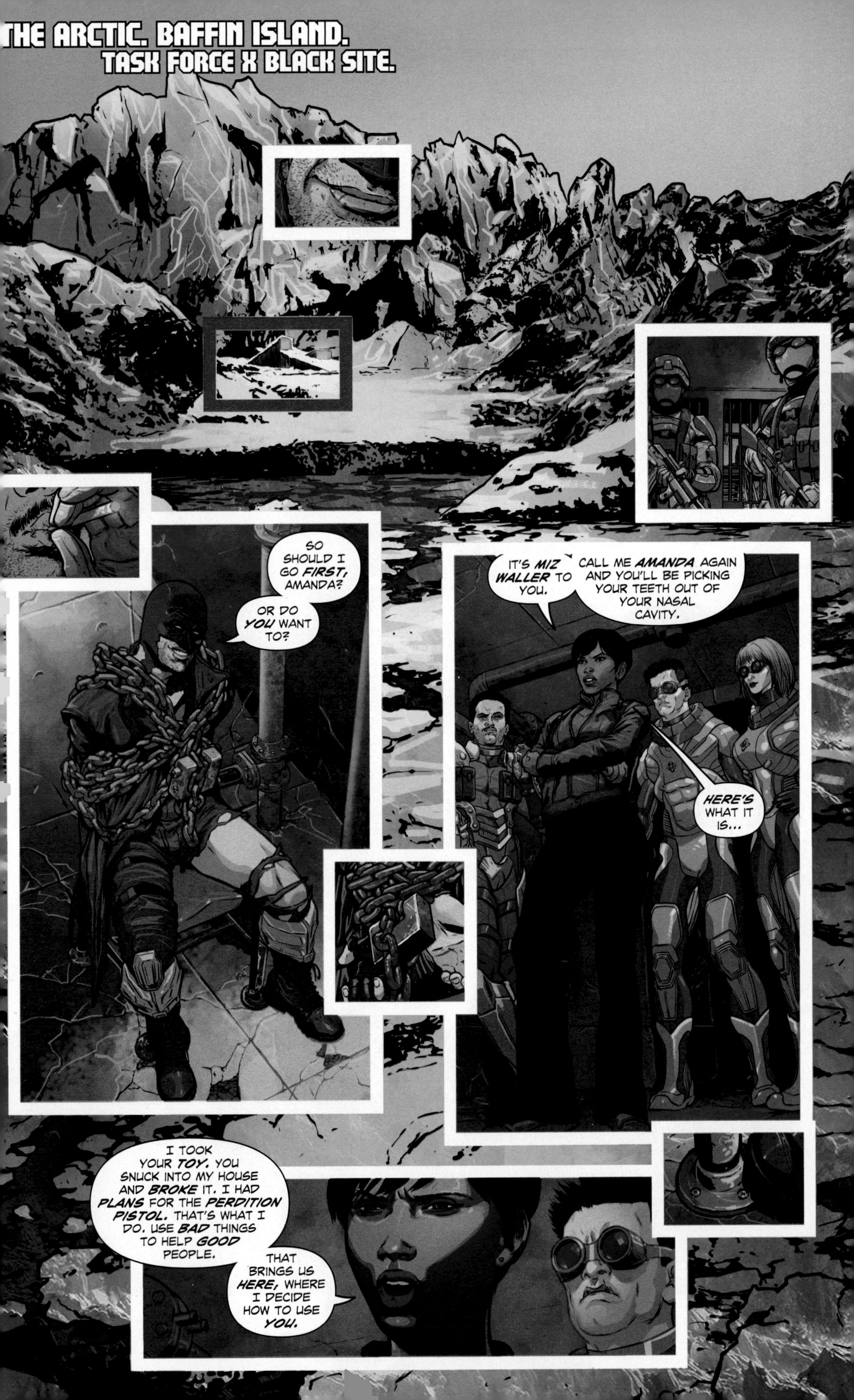
THE ARCTIC. BAFFIN ISLAND.
TASK FORCE X BLACK SITE.
SO SHOULD I GO FIRST, AMANDA?
OR DO YOU WANT TO?
IT'S MIZ WALLER TO YOU.
CALL ME AMANDA AGAIN AND YOU'LL BE PICKING YOUR TEETH OUT OF YOUR NASAL CAVITY.
HERE'S WHAT IT IS...
I TOOK YOUR TOY. YOU SNUCK INTO MY HOUSE AND BROKE IT. I HAD PLANS FOR THE PERDITION PISTOL. THAT'S WHAT I DO. USE BAD THINGS TO HELP GOOD PEOPLE.
THAT BRINGS US HERE, WHERE I DECIDE HOW TO USE YOU.

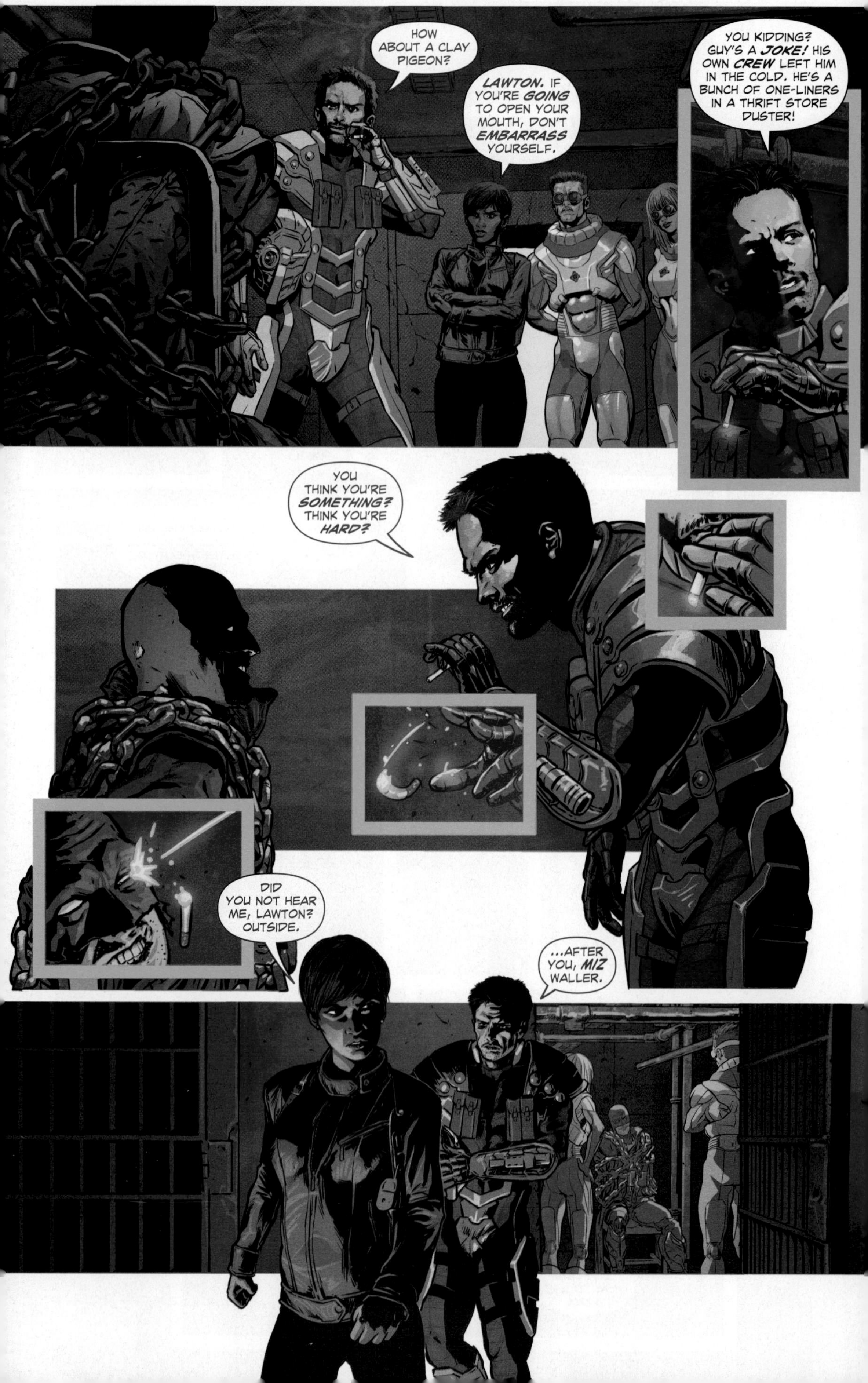

HOW ABOUT A CLAY PIGEON?
LAWTON. IF YOU'RE GOING TO OPEN YOUR MOUTH, DON'T EMBARRASS YOURSELF.
YOU KIDDING? GUY'S A JOKE! HIS OWN CREW LEFT HIM IN THE COLD. HE'S A BUNCH OF ONE-LINERS IN A THRIFT STORE DUSTER!
YOU THINK YOU'RE SOMETHING? THINK YOU'RE HARD?
DID YOU NOT HEAR ME, LAWTON? OUTSIDE.
...AFTER YOU, MIZ WALLER.

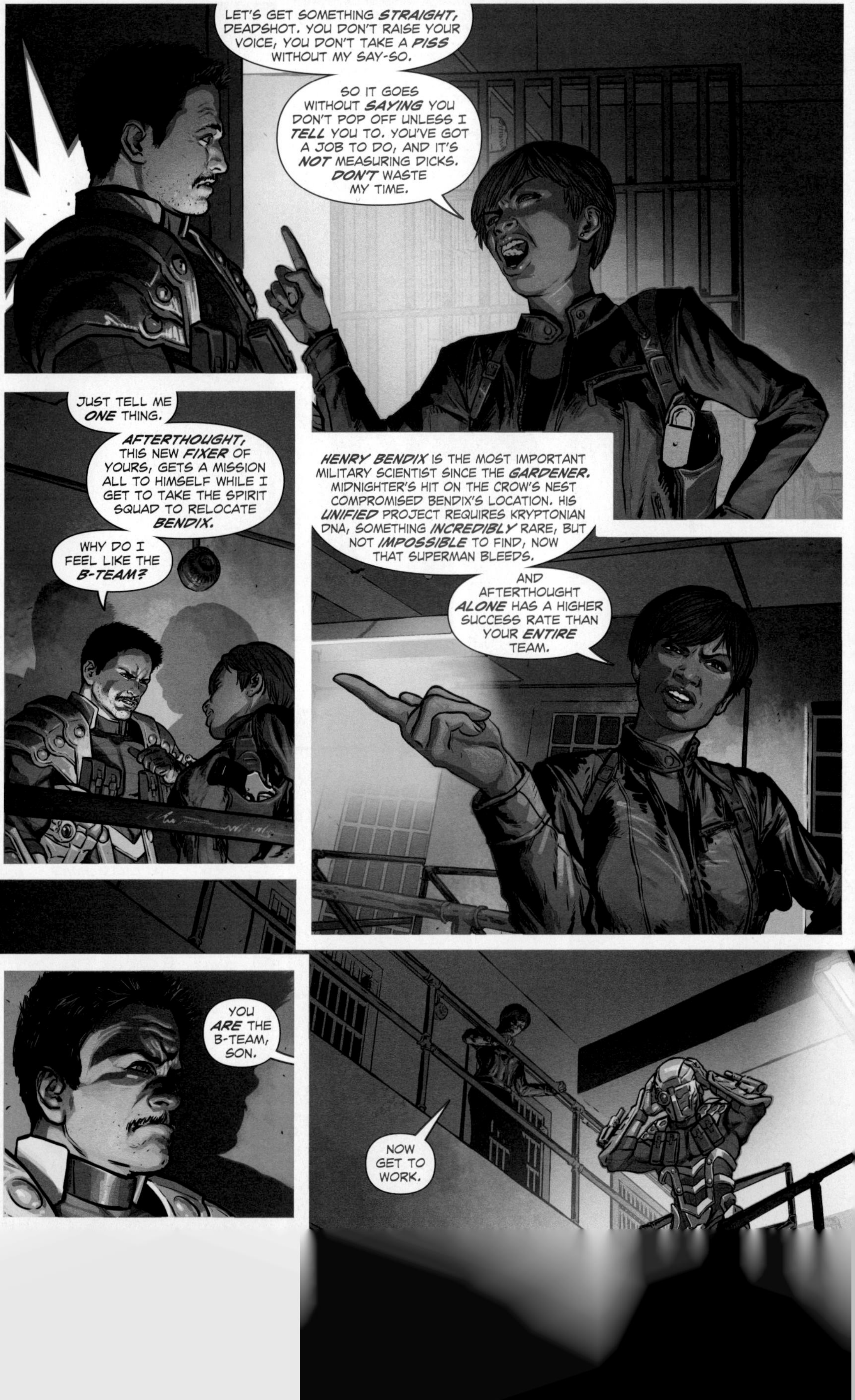
LET'S GET SOMETHING STRAIGHT, DEADSHOT. YOU DON'T RAISE YOUR VOICE, YOU DON'T TAKE A PISS WITHOUT MY SAY-SO.
SO IT GOES WITHOUT SAYING YOU DON'T POP OFF UNLESS I TELL YOU TO. YOU'VE GOT A JOB TO DO, AND IT'S NOT MEASURING DICKS. DON'T WASTE MY TIME.
JUST TELL ME ONE THING.
AFTERTHOUGHT, THIS NEW FIXER OF YOURS, GETS A MISSION ALL TO HIMSELF WHILE I GET TO TAKE THE SPIRIT SQUAD TO RELOCATE BENDIX.
WHY DO I FEEL LIKE THE B-TEAM?
HENRY BENDIX IS THE MOST IMPORTANT MILITARY SCIENTIST SINCE THE GARDENER. MIDNIGHTER'S HIT ON THE CROW'S NEST COMPROMISED BENDIX'S LOCATION. HIS UNIFIED PROJECT REQUIRES KRYPTONIAN DNA, SOMETHING INCREDIBLY RARE; BUT NOT IMPOSSIBLE TO FIND, NOW THAT SUPERMAN BLEEDS.
AND AFTERTHOUGHT ALONE HAS A HIGHER SUCCESS RATE THAN YOUR ENTIRE TEAM.
YOU ARE THE B-TEAM, SON.
NOW GET TO WORK.

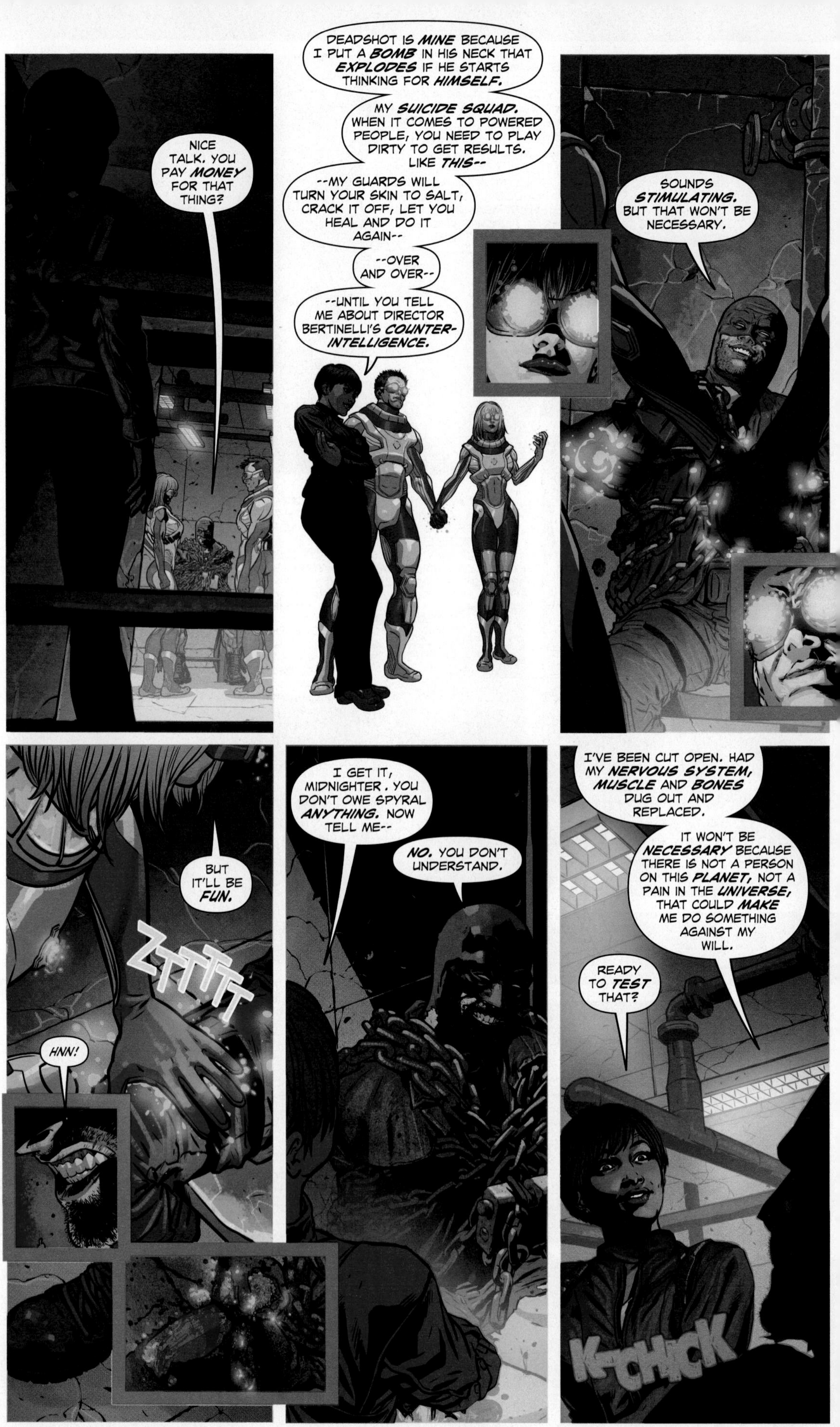

NICE TALK. YOU PAY MONEY FOR THAT THING?
DEADSHOT IS MINE BECAUSE I PUT A BOMB IN HIS NECK THAT EXPLODES IF HE STARTS THINKING FOR HIMSELF.
MY SUICIDE SQUAD. WHEN IT COMES TO POWERED PEOPLE, YOU NEED TO PLAY DIRTY TO GET RESULTS. LIKE THIS--
--MY GUARDS WILL TURN YOUR SKIN TO SALT, CRACK IT OFF, LET YOU HEAL AND DO IT AGAIN--
--OVER AND OVER--
--UNTIL YOU TELL ME ABOUT DIRECTOR BERTINELLI'S COUNTER-INTELLIGENCE.
SOUNDS STIMULATING. BUT THAT WON'T BE NECESSARY.
BUT IT'LL BE FUN.
ZTTTTT
HNN!
I GET IT, MIDNIGHTER. YOU DON'T OWE SPYRAL ANYTHING. NOW TELL ME--
NO. YOU DON'T UNDERSTAND.
I'VE BEEN CUT OPEN. HAD MY NERVOUS SYSTEM, MUSCLE AND BONES DUG OUT AND REPLACED.
IT WON'T BE NECESSARY BECAUSE THERE IS NOT A PERSON ON THIS PLANET, NOT A PAIN IN THE UNIVERSE, THAT COULD MAKE ME DO SOMETHING AGAINST MY WILL.
READY TO TEST THAT?
K-CHICK

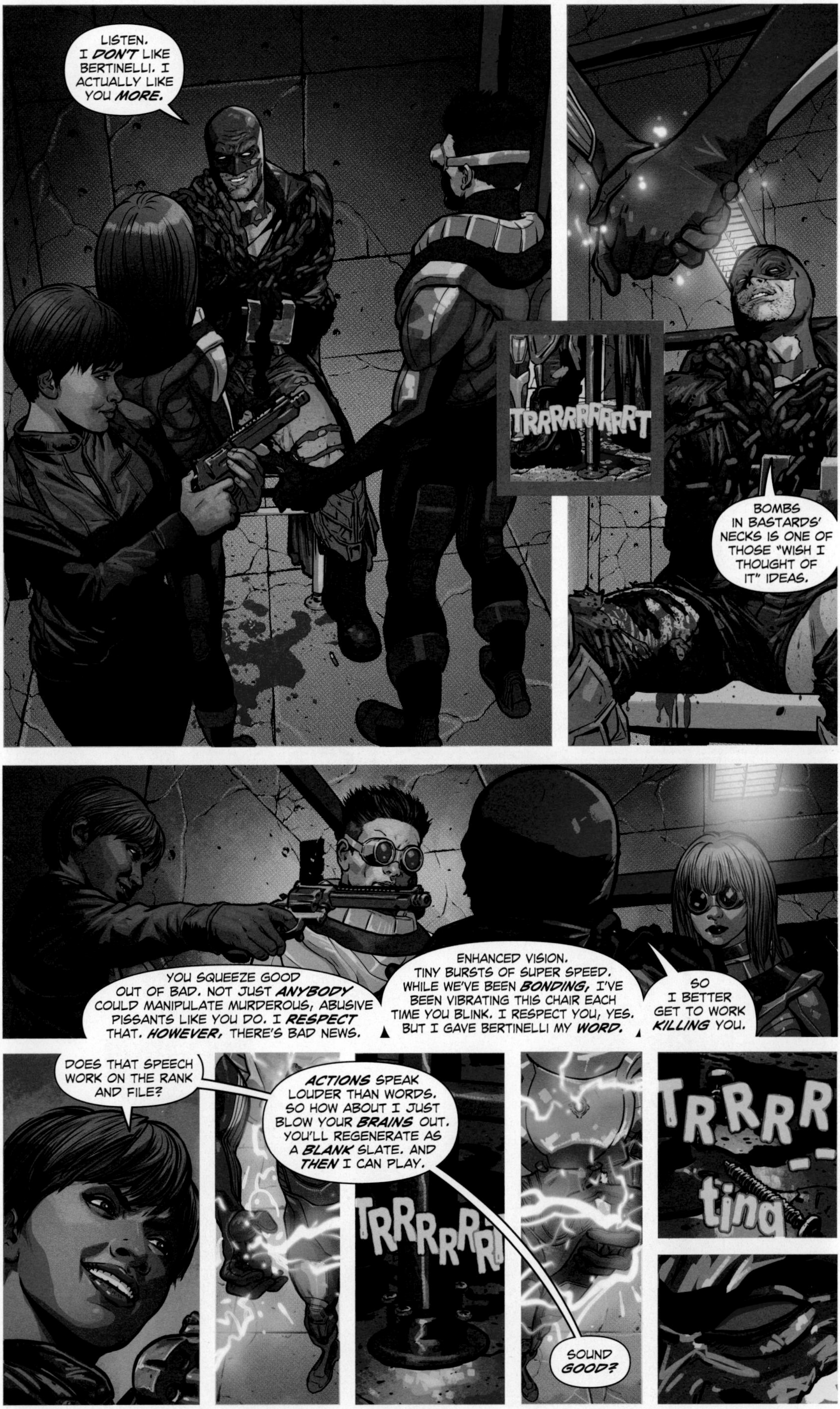

LISTEN. I DON'T LIKE BERTINELLI. I ACTUALLY LIKE YOU MORE.
TRRRRRRRRT
BOMBS IN BASTARDS' NECKS IS ONE OF THOSE "WISH I THOUGHT OF IT" IDEAS.
YOU SQUEEZE GOOD OUT OF BAD. NOT JUST ANYBODY COULD MANIPULATE MURDEROUS, ABUSIVE PISSANTS LIKE YOU DO. I RESPECT THAT. HOWEVER, THERE'S BAD NEWS.
ENHANCED VISION. TINY BURSTS OF SUPER SPEED. WHILE WE'VE BEEN BONDING, I'VE BEEN VIBRATING THIS CHAIR EACH TIME YOU BLINK. I RESPECT YOU, YES. BUT I GAVE BERTINELLI MY WORD.
SO I BETTER GET TO WORK KILLING YOU.
DOES THAT SPEECH WORK ON THE RANK AND FILE?
ACTIONS SPEAK LOUDER THAN WORDS. SO HOW ABOUT I JUST BLOW YOUR BRAINS OUT. YOU'LL REGENERATE AS A BLANK SLATE. AND THEN I CAN PLAY.
TRRRRRRI
SOUND GOOD?
TRRRR
ting

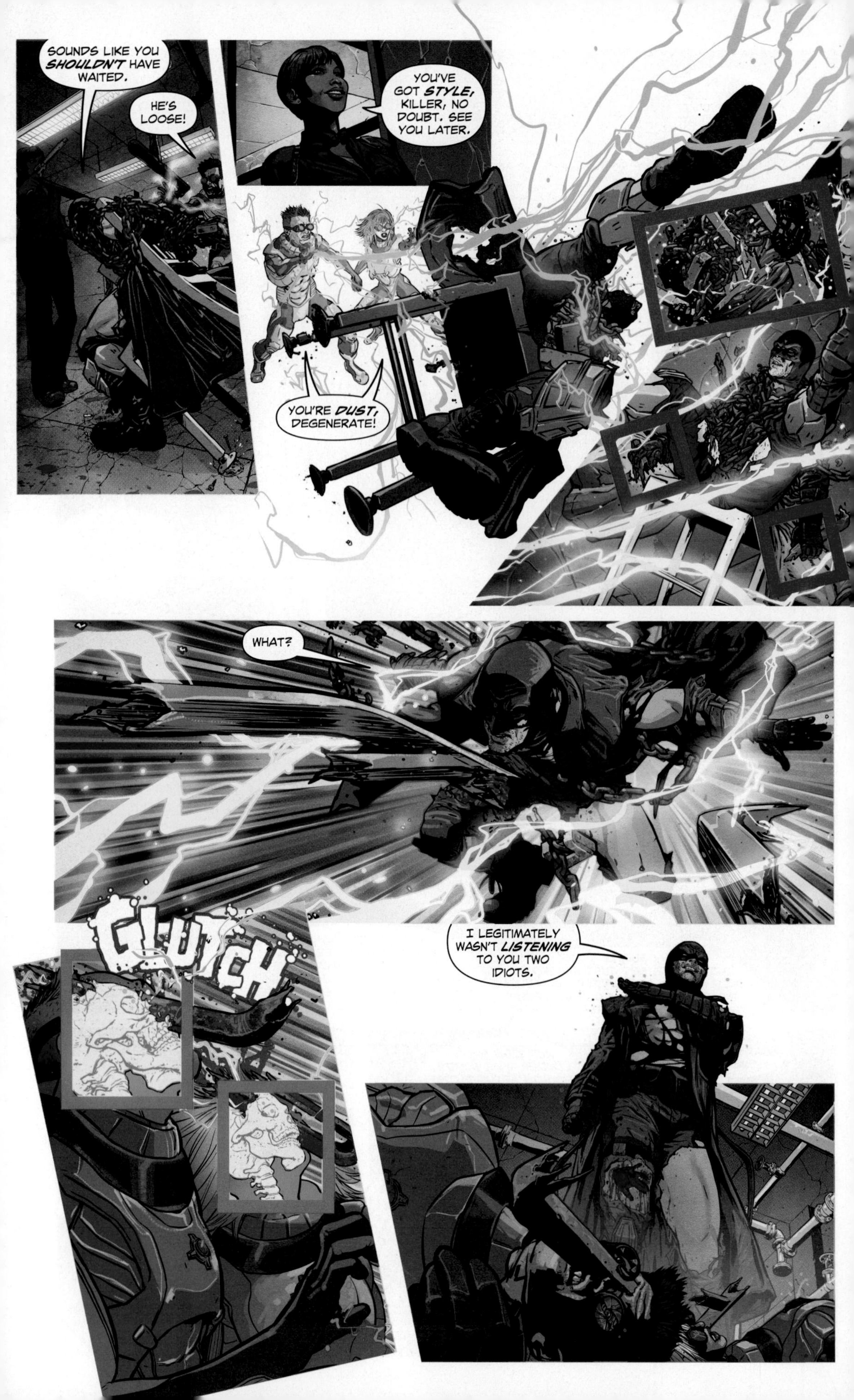
SOUNDS LIKE YOU *SHOULDN'T* HAVE WAITED.
HE'S LOOSE!
YOU'VE GOT *STYLE,* KILLER, NO DOUBT. SEE YOU LATER.
YOU'RE *DUST,* DEGENERATE!
WHAT?
GLUTCH
I LEGITIMATELY WASN'T *LISTENING* TO YOU TWO IDIOTS.

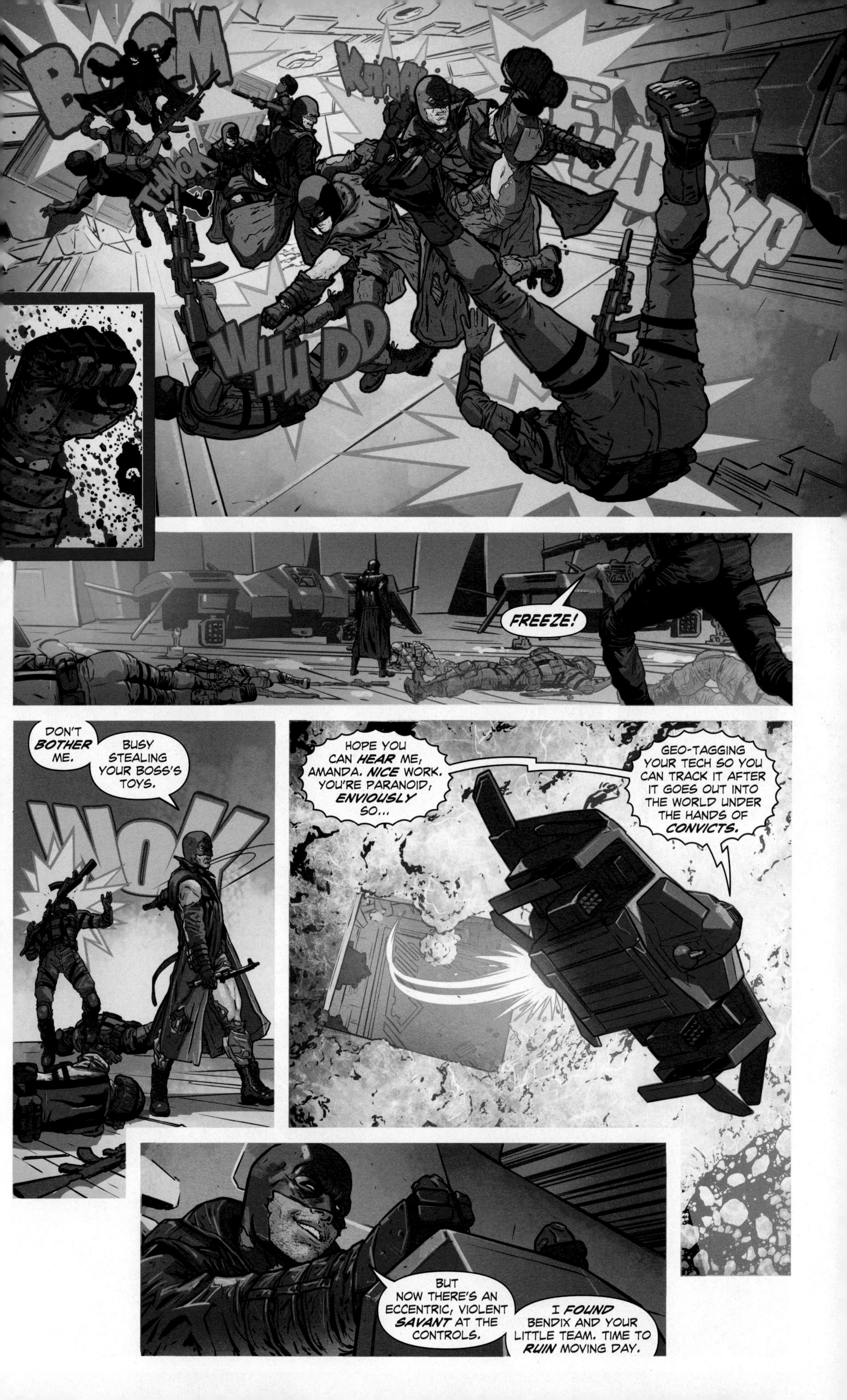
BOOM
THWOK
WHUDD
FREEZE!
DON'T BOTHER ME.
BUSY STEALING YOUR BOSS'S TOYS.
HOPE YOU CAN HEAR ME, AMANDA. NICE WORK. YOU'RE PARANOID, ENVIOUSLY SO...
GEO-TAGGING YOUR TECH SO YOU CAN TRACK IT AFTER IT GOES OUT INTO THE WORLD UNDER THE HANDS OF CONVICTS.
BUT NOW THERE'S AN ECCENTRIC, VIOLENT SAVANT AT THE CONTROLS.
I FOUND BENDIX AND YOUR LITTLE TEAM. TIME TO RUIN MOVING DAY.

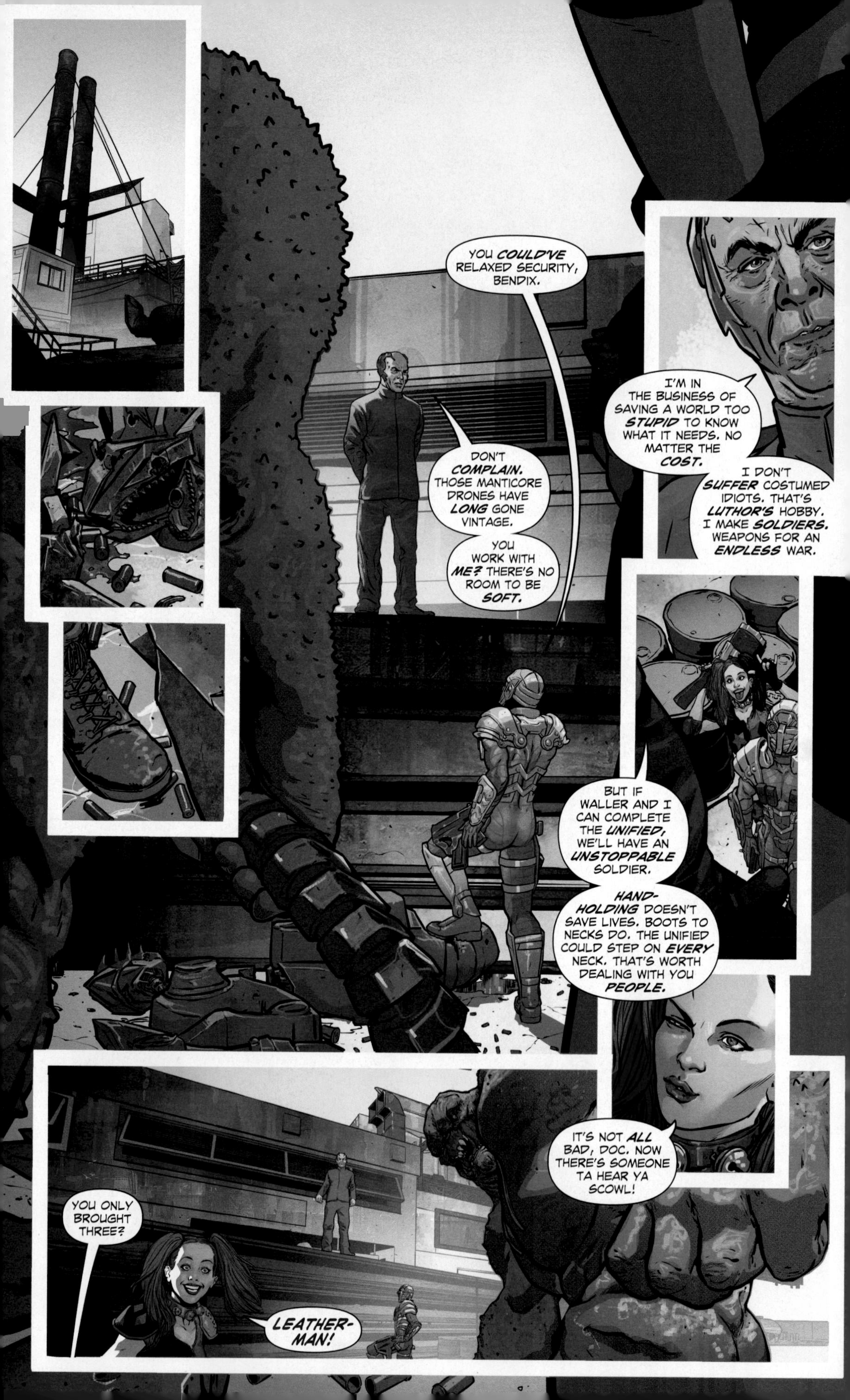
YOU COULD'VE RELAXED SECURITY, BENDIX.
DON'T COMPLAIN. THOSE MANTICORE DRONES HAVE LONG GONE VINTAGE.
YOU WORK WITH ME? THERE'S NO ROOM TO BE SOFT.
I'M IN THE BUSINESS OF SAVING A WORLD TOO STUPID TO KNOW WHAT IT NEEDS. NO MATTER THE COST.
I DON'T SUFFER COSTUMED IDIOTS. THAT'S LUTHOR'S HOBBY. I MAKE SOLDIERS. WEAPONS FOR AN ENDLESS WAR.
BUT IF WALLER AND I CAN COMPLETE THE UNIFIED, WE'LL HAVE AN UNSTOPPABLE SOLDIER.
HAND-HOLDING DOESN'T SAVE LIVES. BOOTS TO NECKS DO. THE UNIFIED COULD STEP ON EVERY NECK. THAT'S WORTH DEALING WITH YOU PEOPLE.
IT'S NOT ALL BAD, DOC. NOW THERE'S SOMEONE TA HEAR YA SCOWL!
YOU ONLY BROUGHT THREE?
LEATHER-MAN!

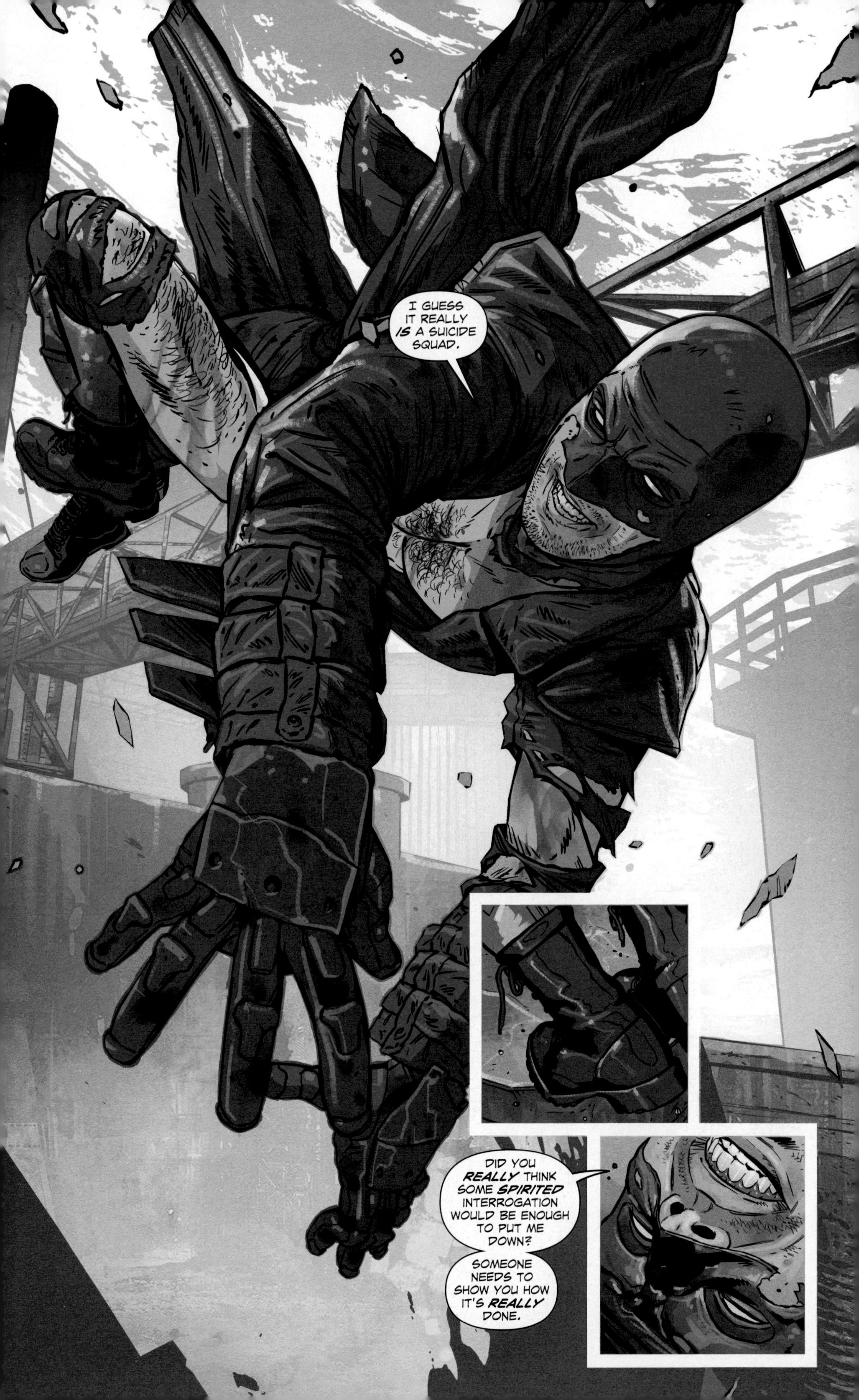
I GUESS IT REALLY IS A SUICIDE SQUAD.
DID YOU REALLY THINK SOME SPIRITED INTERROGATION WOULD BE ENOUGH TO PUT ME DOWN?
SOMEONE NEEDS TO SHOW YOU HOW IT'S REALLY DONE.

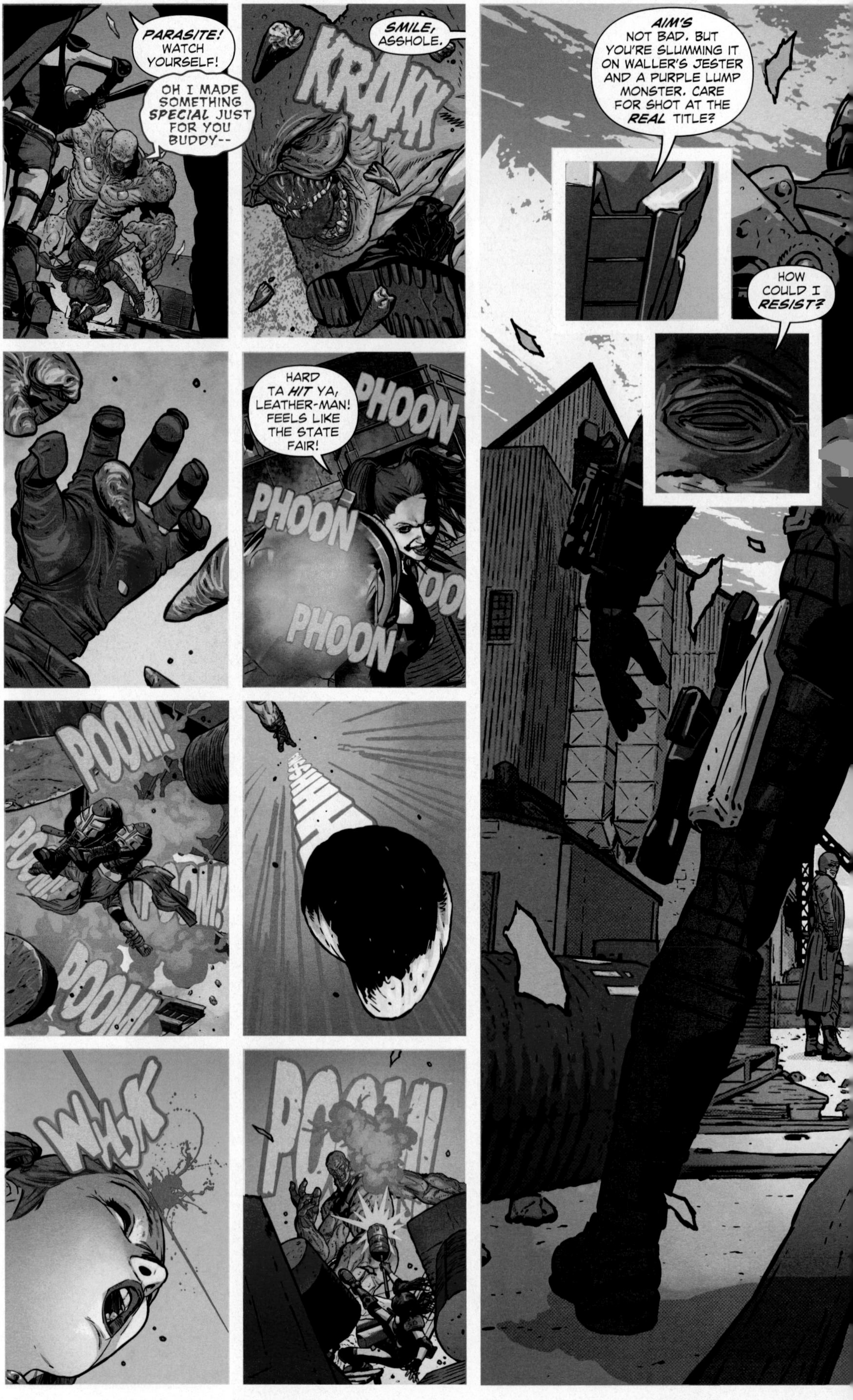
PARASITE! WATCH YOURSELF!
OH I MADE SOMETHING SPECIAL JUST FOR YOU BUDDY--
SMILE, ASSHOLE.
AIM'S NOT BAD. BUT YOU'RE SLUMMING IT ON WALLER'S JESTER AND A PURPLE LUMP MONSTER. CARE FOR SHOT AT THE REAL TITLE?
HOW COULD I RESIST?
HARD TA HIT YA, LEATHER-MAN! FEELS LIKE THE STATE FAIR!
PHOON
PHOON
PHOON
POOM!
POOM!

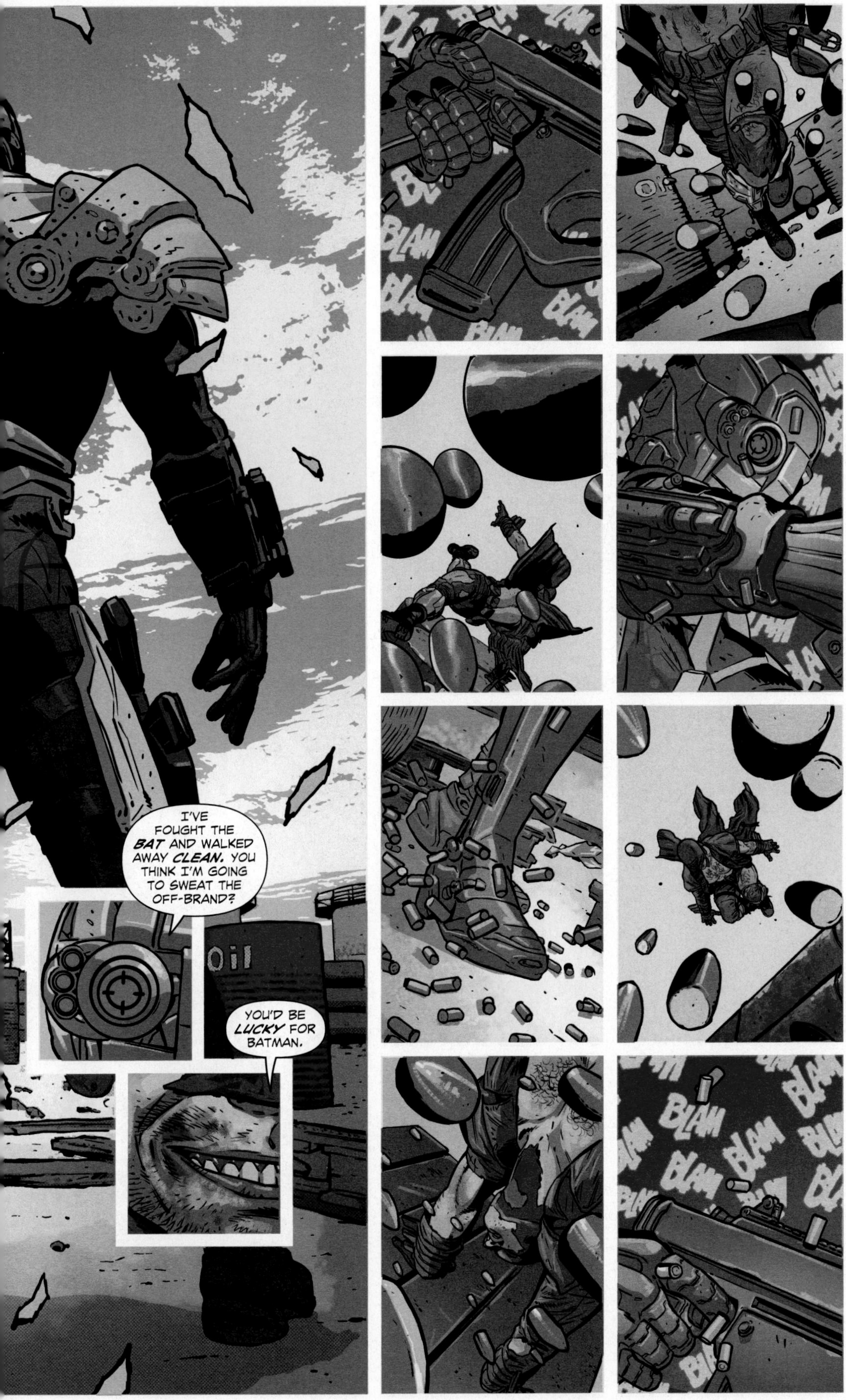
BLAM
BLAM
BLAM
I'VE FOUGHT THE BAT AND WALKED AWAY CLEAN. YOU THINK I'M GOING TO SWEAT THE OFF-BRAND?
Oil
YOU'D BE LUCKY FOR BATMAN.
BLAM
BLAM
BLAM
BLAM
BLAM

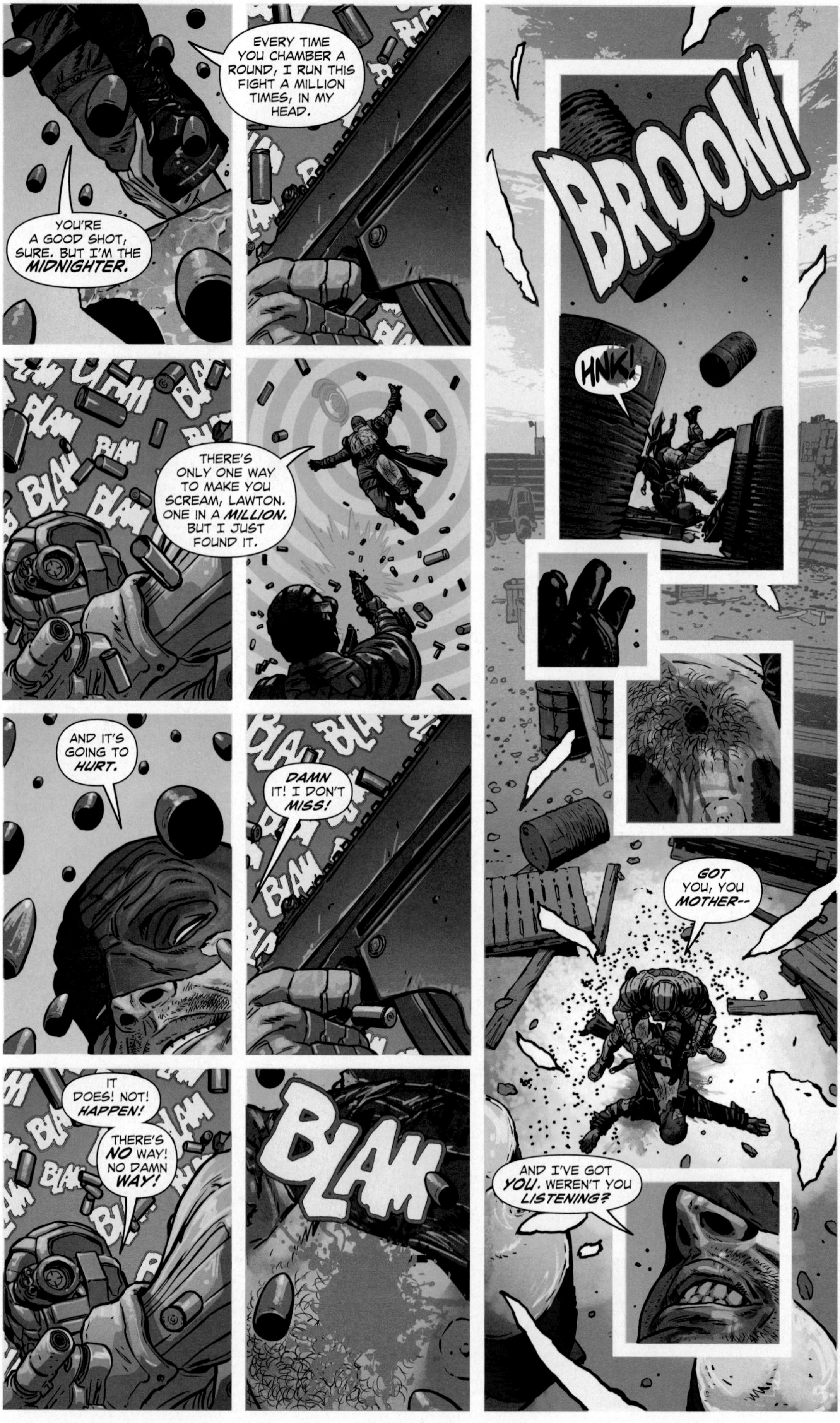
YOU'RE A GOOD SHOT, SURE. BUT I'M THE MIDNIGHTER.
EVERY TIME YOU CHAMBER A ROUND, I RUN THIS FIGHT A MILLION TIMES, IN MY HEAD.
THERE'S ONLY ONE WAY TO MAKE YOU SCREAM, LAWTON. ONE IN A MILLION. BUT I JUST FOUND IT.
AND IT'S GOING TO HURT.
DAMN IT! I DON'T MISS!
IT DOES! NOT! HAPPEN!
THERE'S NO WAY! NO DAMN WAY!
BLAM
BROOM
HNK!
GOT YOU, YOU MOTHER--
AND I'VE GOT YOU. WEREN'T YOU LISTENING?

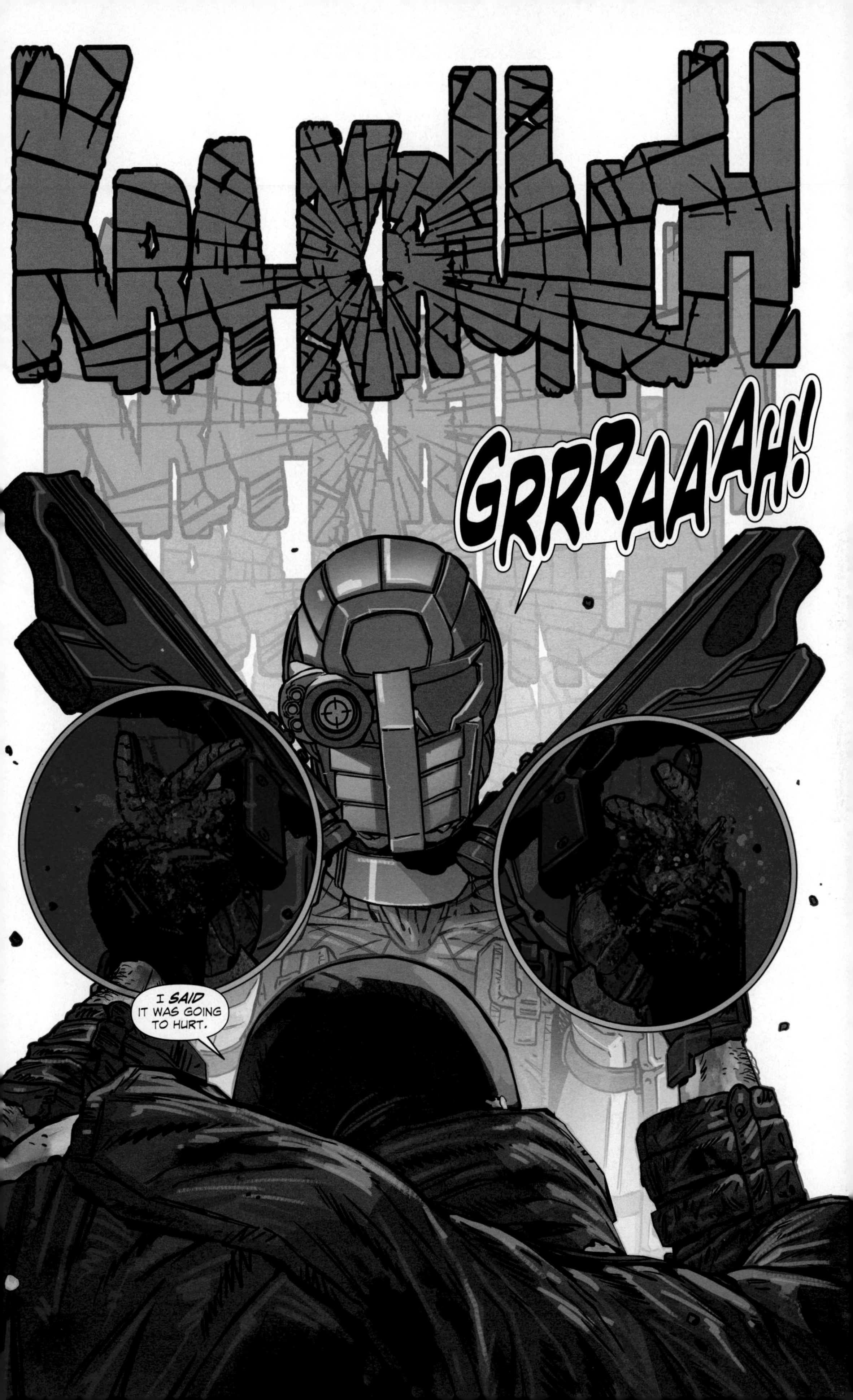
KRAKRUNCH!
GRRRAAAH!
I SAID IT WAS GOING TO HURT.

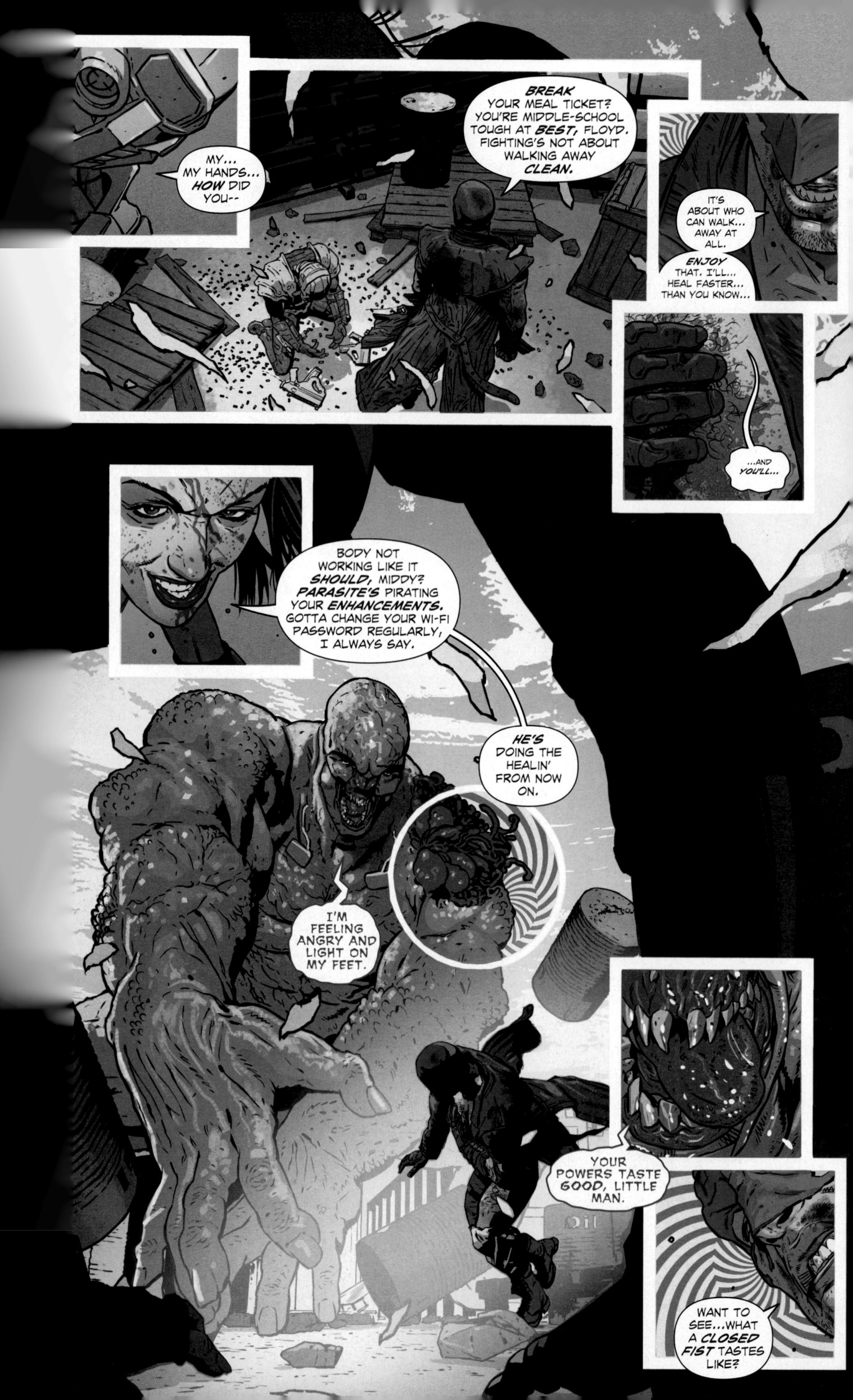
MY... MY HANDS... HOW DID YOU--
BREAK YOUR MEAL TICKET? YOU'RE MIDDLE-SCHOOL TOUGH AT BEST, FLOYD. FIGHTING'S NOT ABOUT WALKING AWAY CLEAN.
IT'S ABOUT WHO CAN WALK... AWAY AT ALL.
ENJOY THAT. I'LL... HEAL FASTER... THAN YOU KNOW...
...AND YOU'LL...
BODY NOT WORKING LIKE IT SHOULD, MIDDY? PARASITE'S PIRATING YOUR ENHANCEMENTS. GOTTA CHANGE YOUR WI-FI PASSWORD REGULARLY, I ALWAYS SAY.
HE'S DOING THE HEALIN' FROM NOW ON.
I'M FEELING ANGRY AND LIGHT ON MY FEET.
YOUR POWERS TASTE GOOD, LITTLE MAN.
WANT TO SEE...WHAT A CLOSED FIST TASTES LIKE?

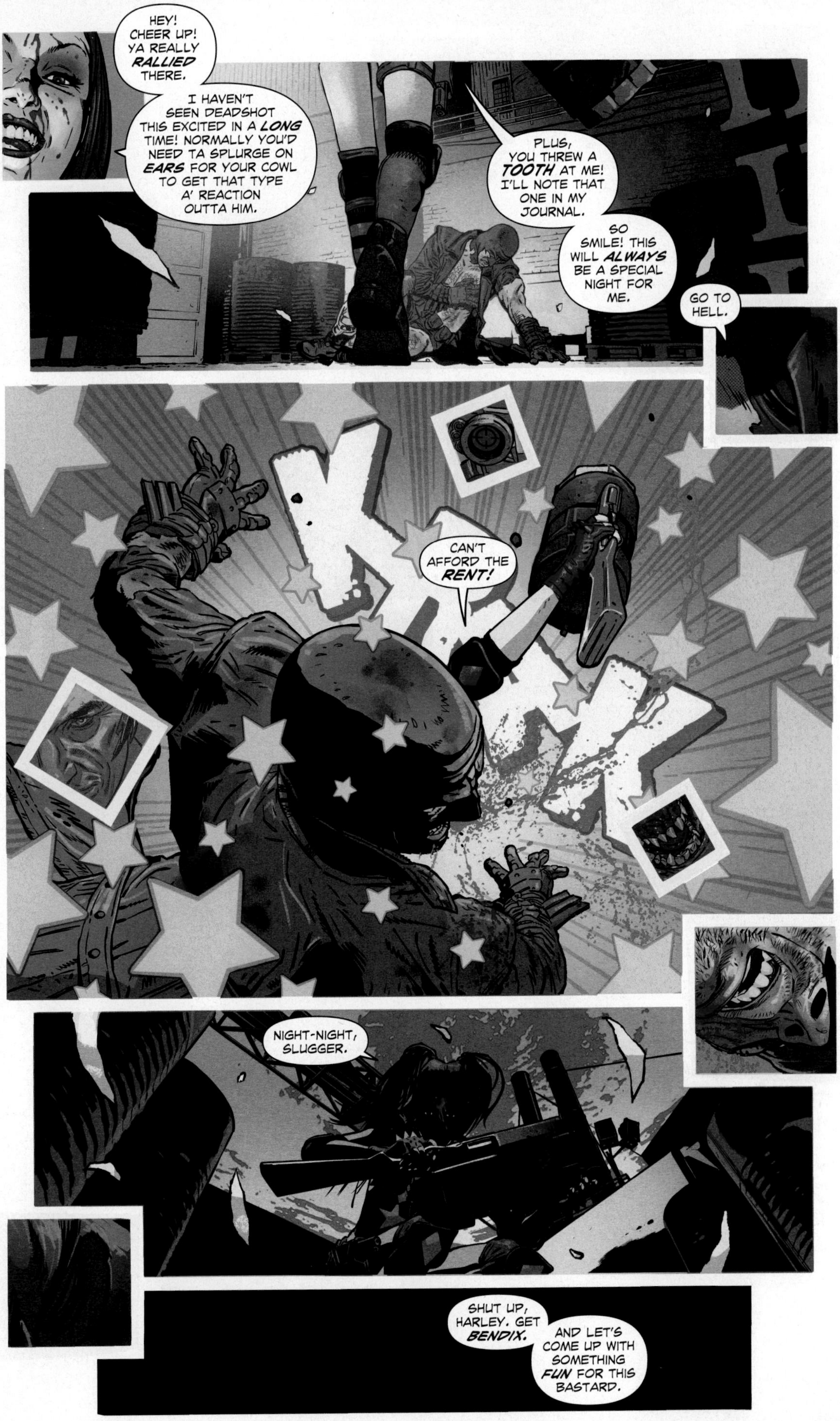
HEY! CHEER UP! YA REALLY RALLIED THERE.
I HAVEN'T SEEN DEADSHOT THIS EXCITED IN A LONG TIME! NORMALLY YOU'D NEED TA SPLURGE ON EARS FOR YOUR COWL TO GET THAT TYPE A' REACTION OUTTA HIM.
PLUS, YOU THREW A TOOTH AT ME! I'LL NOTE THAT ONE IN MY JOURNAL.
SO SMILE! THIS WILL ALWAYS BE A SPECIAL NIGHT FOR ME.
GO TO HELL.
CAN'T AFFORD THE RENT!
NIGHT-NIGHT, SLUGGER.
SHUT UP, HARLEY. GET BENDIX.
AND LET'S COME UP WITH SOMETHING FUN FOR THIS BASTARD.

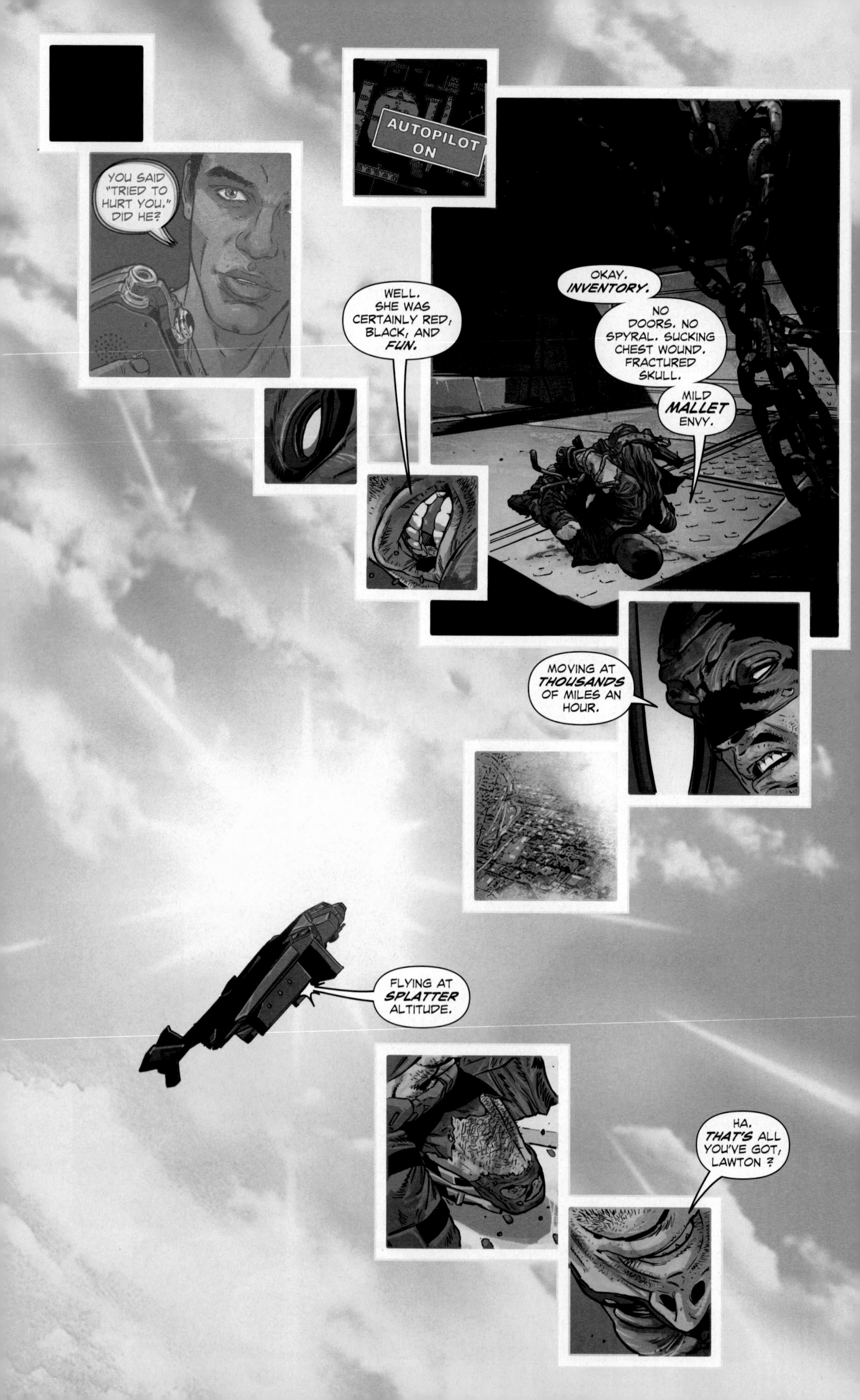

YOU SAID "TRIED TO HURT YOU." DID HE?
AUTOPILOT ON
WELL. SHE WAS CERTAINLY RED, BLACK, AND *FUN.*
OKAY. *INVENTORY.*
NO DOORS. NO SPYRAL. SUCKING CHEST WOUND. FRACTURED SKULL.
MILD *MALLET* ENVY.
MOVING AT *THOUSANDS* OF MILES AN HOUR.
FLYING AT *SPLATTER* ALTITUDE.
HA. *THAT'S* ALL YOU'VE GOT, LAWTON?

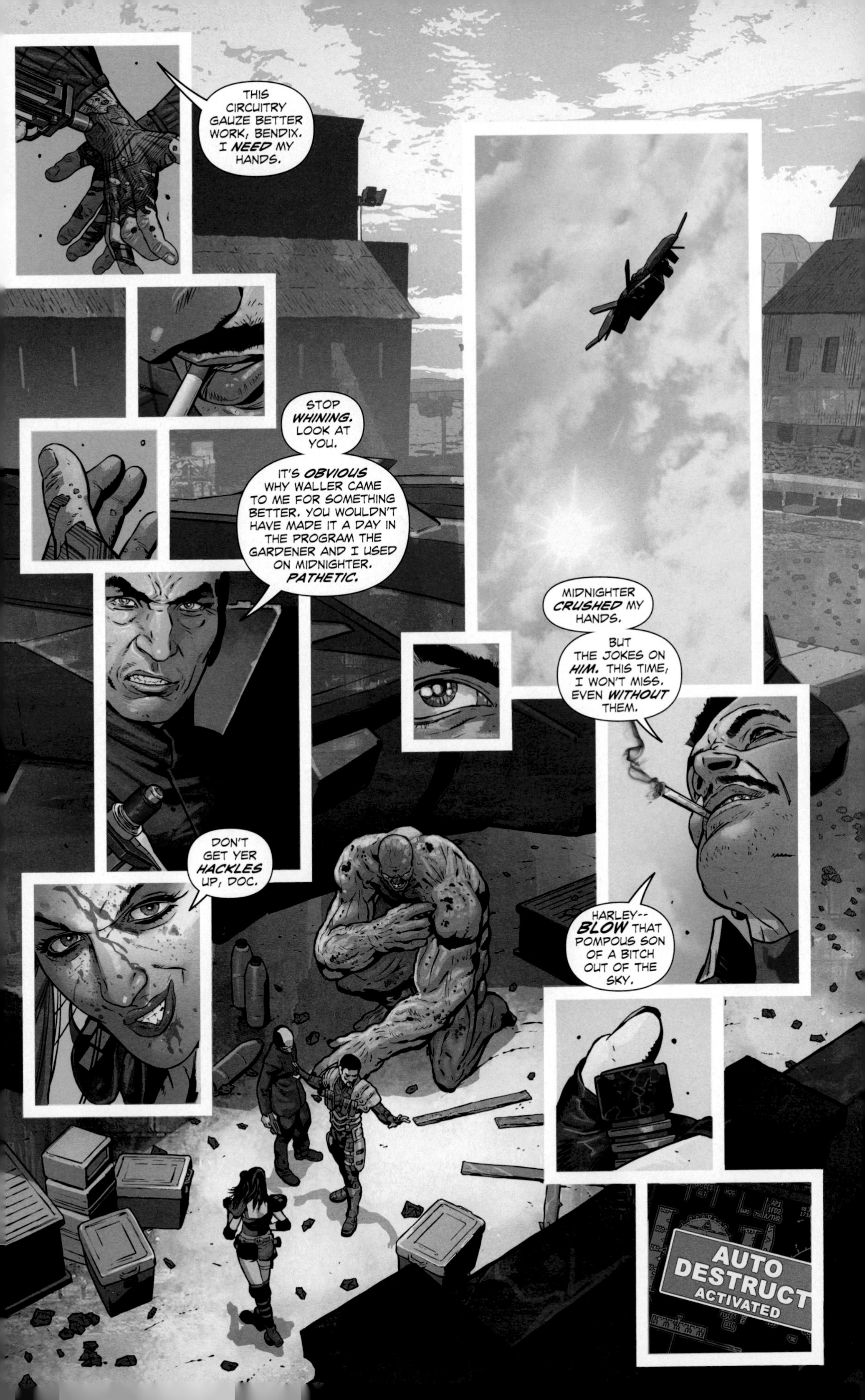
THIS CIRCUITRY GAUZE BETTER WORK, BENDIX. I NEED MY HANDS.
STOP WHINING. LOOK AT YOU.
IT'S OBVIOUS WHY WALLER CAME TO ME FOR SOMETHING BETTER. YOU WOULDN'T HAVE MADE IT A DAY IN THE PROGRAM THE GARDENER AND I USED ON MIDNIGHTER. PATHETIC.
DON'T GET YER HACKLES UP, DOC.
MIDNIGHTER CRUSHED MY HANDS.
BUT THE JOKES ON HIM. THIS TIME, I WON'T MISS. EVEN WITHOUT THEM.
HARLEY-- BLOW THAT POMPOUS SON OF A BITCH OUT OF THE SKY.
AUTO DESTRUCT ACTIVATED

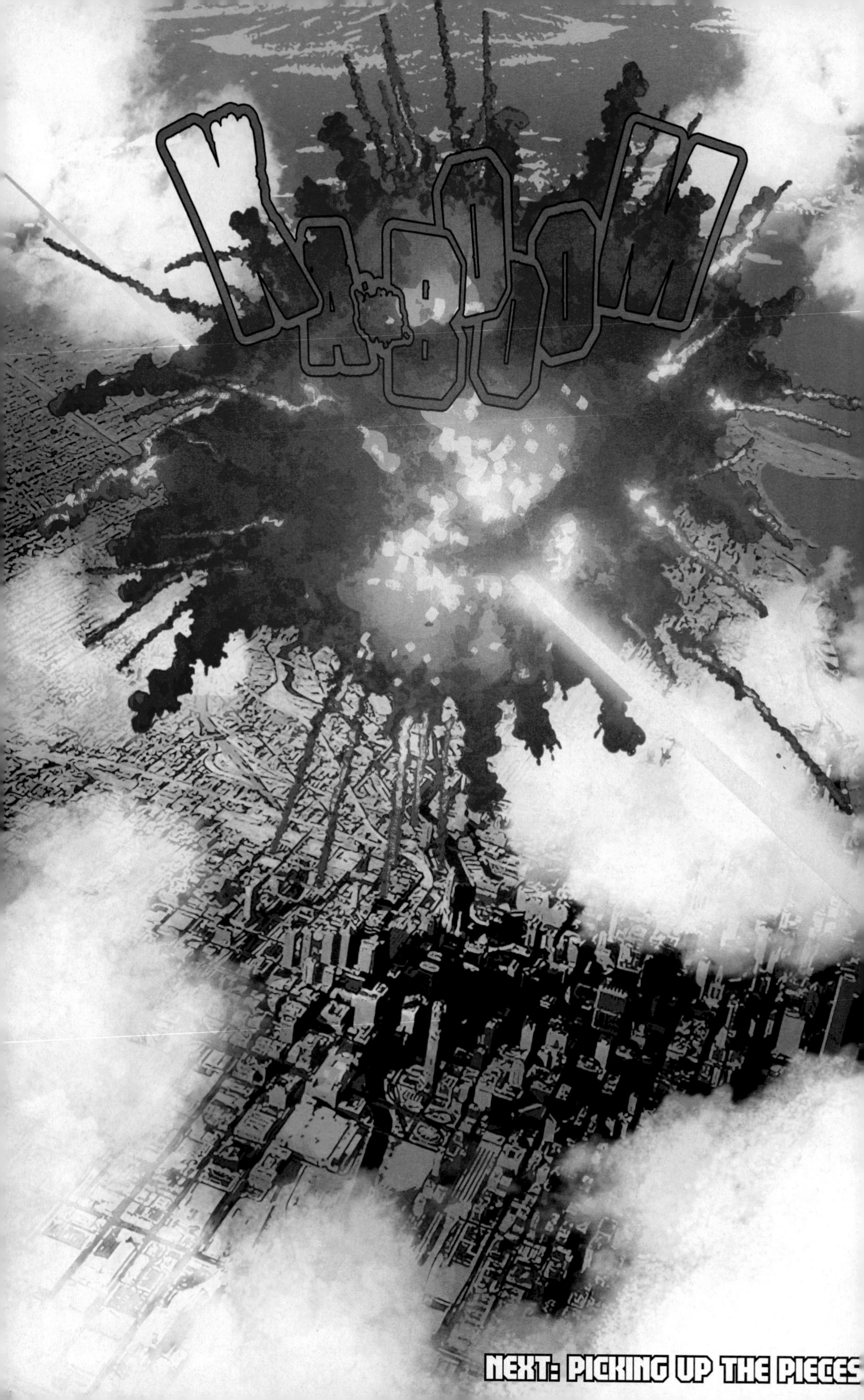
KABOOM
NEXT: PICKING UP THE PIECES

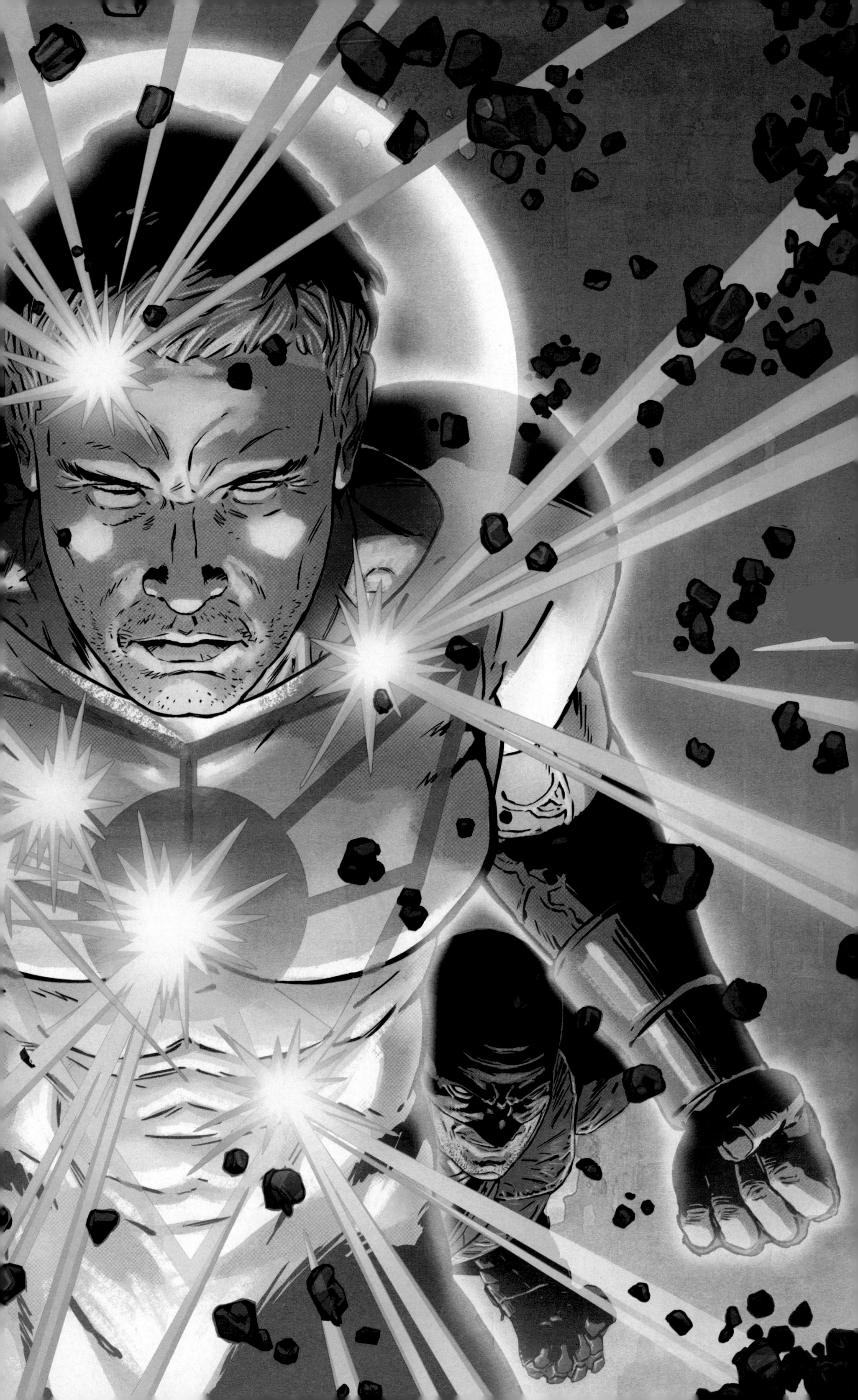

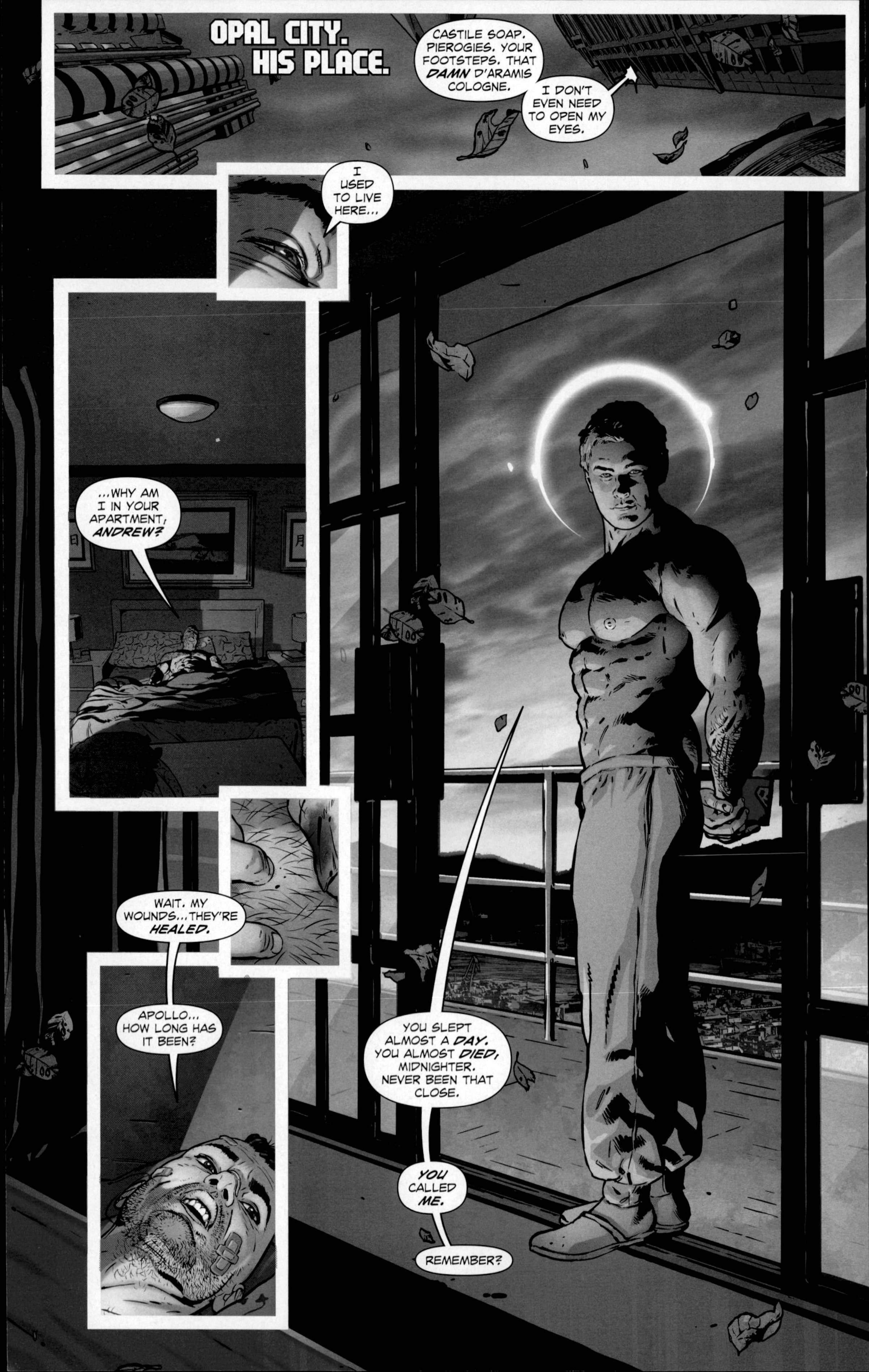

OPAL CITY.
HIS PLACE.
CASTILE SOAP. PIEROGIES. YOUR FOOTSTEPS. THAT DAMN D'ARAMIS COLOGNE.
I DON'T EVEN NEED TO OPEN MY EYES.
I USED TO LIVE HERE...
...WHY AM I IN YOUR APARTMENT, ANDREW?
WAIT. MY WOUNDS...THEY'RE HEALED.
APOLLO... HOW LONG HAS IT BEEN?
YOU SLEPT ALMOST A DAY. YOU ALMOST DIED, MIDNIGHTER. NEVER BEEN THAT CLOSE.
YOU CALLED ME.
REMEMBER?

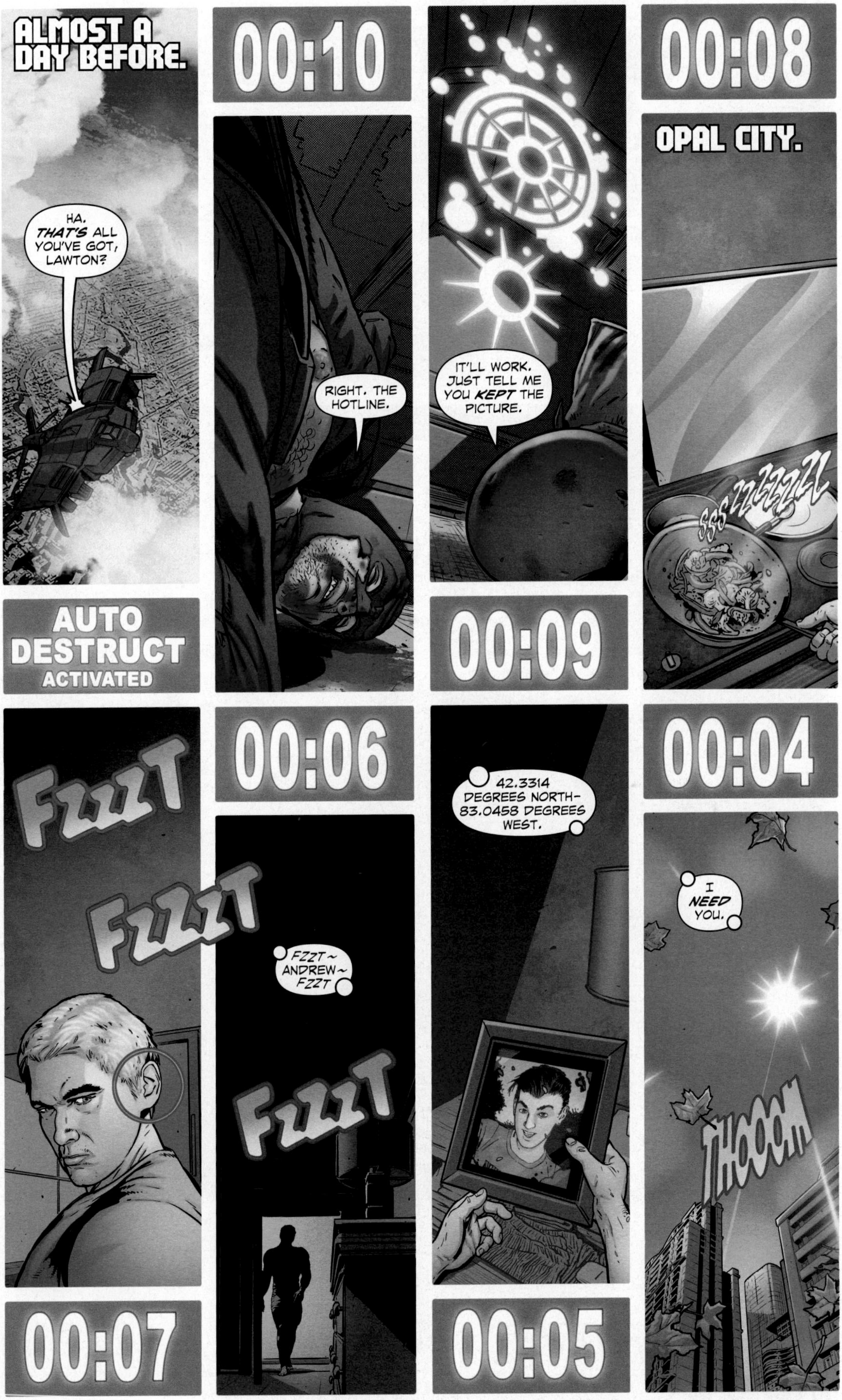
ALMOST A DAY BEFORE.
HA. *THAT'S* ALL YOU'VE GOT, LAWTON?
AUTO DESTRUCT ACTIVATED
00:10
RIGHT. THE HOTLINE.
IT'LL WORK. JUST TELL ME YOU *KEPT* THE PICTURE.
00:09
00:08
OPAL CITY.
SSSZZZZZZZ
FZZZT
FZZZT
00:07
00:06
FZZT~ ANDREW~ FZZT
FZZZT
42.3314 DEGREES NORTH- 83.0458 DEGREES WEST.
00:05
00:04
I *NEED* YOU.
THOOOM

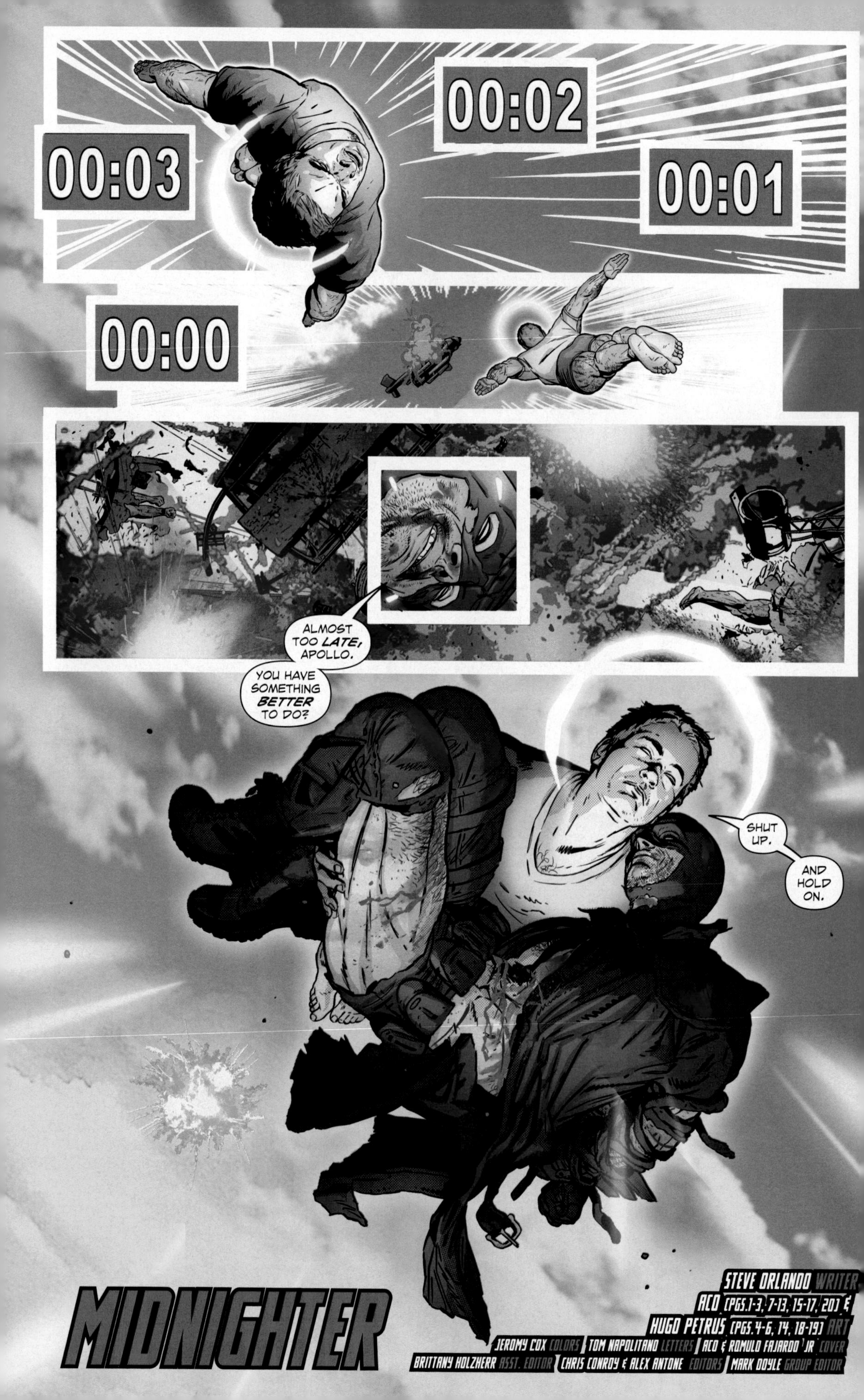
00:03
00:02
00:01
00:00
ALMOST TOO *LATE,* APOLLO.
YOU HAVE SOMETHING *BETTER* TO DO?
SHUT UP.
AND HOLD ON.
MIDNIGHTER
STEVE ORLANDO WRITER
ACO (PGS.1-3, 7-13, 15-17, 20) &
HUGO PETRUS (PGS.4-6, 14, 18-19) ART
JEROMY COX COLORS | TOM NAPOLITANO LETTERS | ACO & ROMULO FAJARDO JR COVER
BRITTANY HOLZHERR ASST. EDITOR | CHRIS CONROY & ALEX ANTONE EDITORS | MARK DOYLE GROUP EDITOR

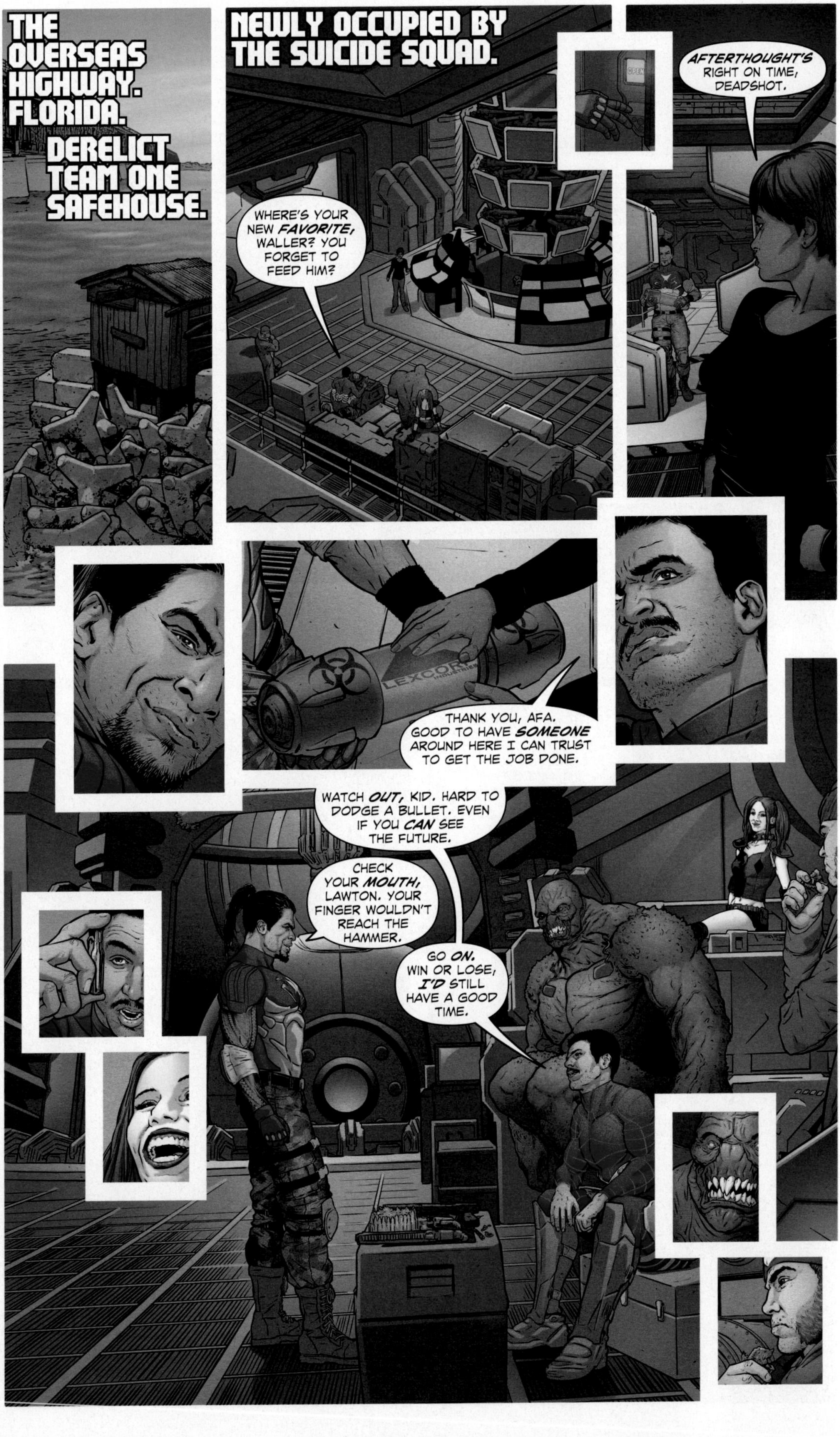
THE OVERSEAS HIGHWAY. FLORIDA.
DERELICT TEAM ONE SAFEHOUSE.
NEWLY OCCUPIED BY THE SUICIDE SQUAD.
WHERE'S YOUR NEW FAVORITE, WALLER? YOU FORGET TO FEED HIM?
AFTERTHOUGHT'S RIGHT ON TIME, DEADSHOT.
THANK YOU, AFA. GOOD TO HAVE SOMEONE AROUND HERE I CAN TRUST TO GET THE JOB DONE.
WATCH OUT, KID. HARD TO DODGE A BULLET. EVEN IF YOU CAN SEE THE FUTURE.
CHECK YOUR MOUTH, LAWTON. YOUR FINGER WOULDN'T REACH THE HAMMER.
GO ON. WIN OR LOSE, I'D STILL HAVE A GOOD TIME.

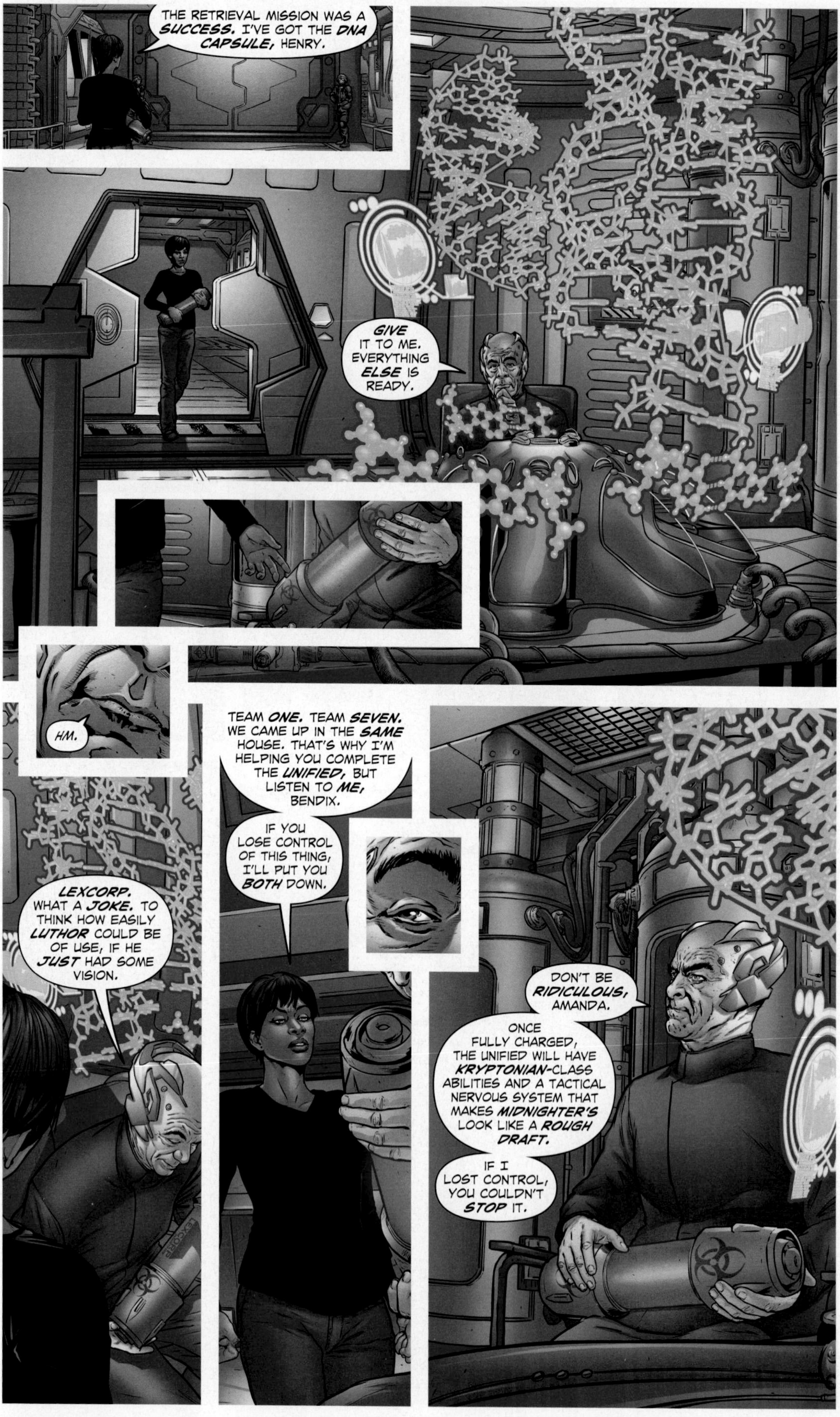
THE RETRIEVAL MISSION WAS A SUCCESS. I'VE GOT THE DNA CAPSULE, HENRY.
GIVE IT TO ME. EVERYTHING ELSE IS READY.
HM.
TEAM ONE. TEAM SEVEN. WE CAME UP IN THE SAME HOUSE. THAT'S WHY I'M HELPING YOU COMPLETE THE UNIFIED, BUT LISTEN TO ME, BENDIX.
IF YOU LOSE CONTROL OF THIS THING, I'LL PUT YOU BOTH DOWN.
LEXCORP. WHAT A JOKE. TO THINK HOW EASILY LUTHOR COULD BE OF USE, IF HE JUST HAD SOME VISION.
DON'T BE RIDICULOUS, AMANDA.
ONCE FULLY CHARGED, THE UNIFIED WILL HAVE KRYPTONIAN-CLASS ABILITIES AND A TACTICAL NERVOUS SYSTEM THAT MAKES MIDNIGHTER'S LOOK LIKE A ROUGH DRAFT.
IF I LOST CONTROL, YOU COULDN'T STOP IT.

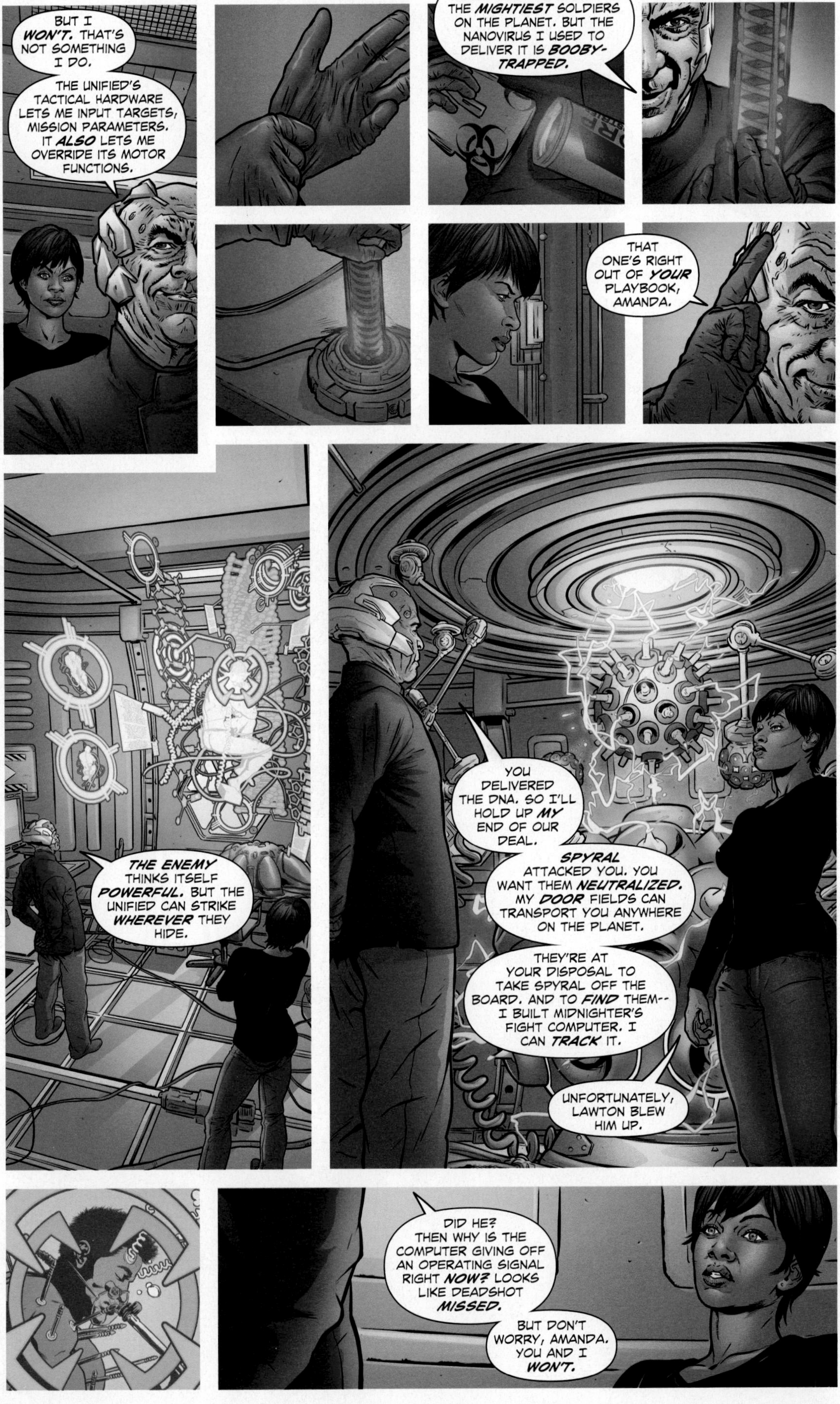

BUT I WON'T. THAT'S NOT SOMETHING I DO.
THE UNIFIED'S TACTICAL HARDWARE LETS ME INPUT TARGETS, MISSION PARAMETERS. IT ALSO LETS ME OVERRIDE ITS MOTOR FUNCTIONS.
KRYPTONIAN GENE THERAPY MAKES IT ONE OF THE MIGHTIEST SOLDIERS ON THE PLANET. BUT THE NANOVIRUS I USED TO DELIVER IT IS BOOBY-TRAPPED.
THAT ONE'S RIGHT OUT OF YOUR PLAYBOOK, AMANDA.
THE ENEMY THINKS ITSELF POWERFUL. BUT THE UNIFIED CAN STRIKE WHEREVER THEY HIDE.
YOU DELIVERED THE DNA. SO I'LL HOLD UP MY END OF OUR DEAL.
SPYRAL ATTACKED YOU. YOU WANT THEM NEUTRALIZED. MY DOOR FIELDS CAN TRANSPORT YOU ANYWHERE ON THE PLANET.
THEY'RE AT YOUR DISPOSAL TO TAKE SPYRAL OFF THE BOARD. AND TO FIND THEM-- I BUILT MIDNIGHTER'S FIGHT COMPUTER. I CAN TRACK IT.
UNFORTUNATELY, LAWTON BLEW HIM UP.
DID HE? THEN WHY IS THE COMPUTER GIVING OFF AN OPERATING SIGNAL RIGHT NOW? LOOKS LIKE DEADSHOT MISSED.
BUT DON'T WORRY, AMANDA. YOU AND I WON'T.

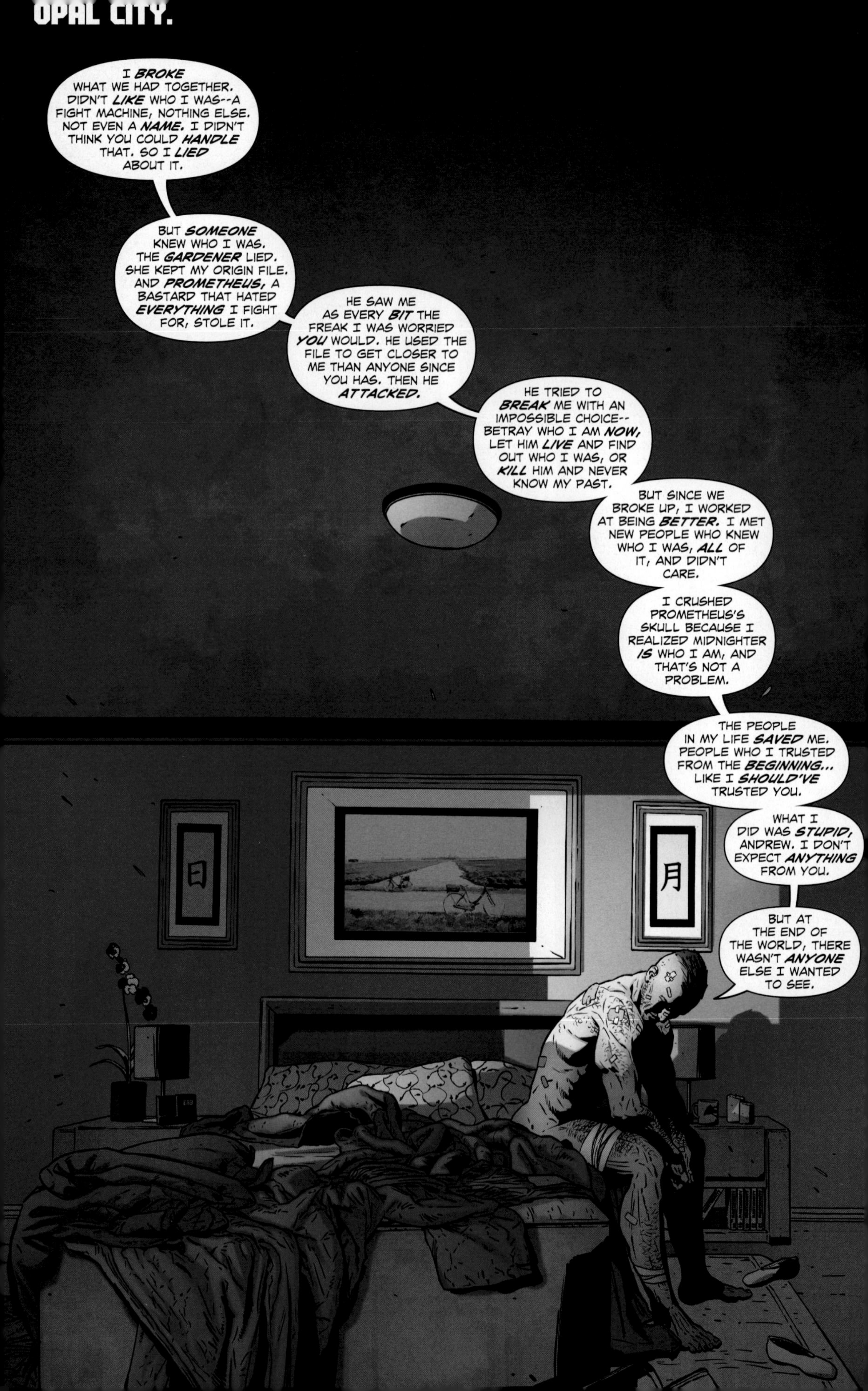
OPAL CITY.
I BROKE WHAT WE HAD TOGETHER. DIDN'T LIKE WHO I WAS--A FIGHT MACHINE, NOTHING ELSE. NOT EVEN A NAME. I DIDN'T THINK YOU COULD HANDLE THAT. SO I LIED ABOUT IT.
BUT SOMEONE KNEW WHO I WAS. THE GARDENER LIED. SHE KEPT MY ORIGIN FILE. AND PROMETHEUS, A BASTARD THAT HATED EVERYTHING I FIGHT FOR, STOLE IT.
HE SAW ME AS EVERY BIT THE FREAK I WAS WORRIED YOU WOULD. HE USED THE FILE TO GET CLOSER TO ME THAN ANYONE SINCE YOU HAS. THEN HE ATTACKED.
HE TRIED TO BREAK ME WITH AN IMPOSSIBLE CHOICE--BETRAY WHO I AM NOW, LET HIM LIVE AND FIND OUT WHO I WAS, OR KILL HIM AND NEVER KNOW MY PAST.
BUT SINCE WE BROKE UP, I WORKED AT BEING BETTER. I MET NEW PEOPLE WHO KNEW WHO I WAS, ALL OF IT, AND DIDN'T CARE.
I CRUSHED PROMETHEUS'S SKULL BECAUSE I REALIZED MIDNIGHTER IS WHO I AM, AND THAT'S NOT A PROBLEM.
THE PEOPLE IN MY LIFE SAVED ME. PEOPLE WHO I TRUSTED FROM THE BEGINNING... LIKE I SHOULD'VE TRUSTED YOU.
WHAT I DID WAS STUPID, ANDREW. I DON'T EXPECT ANYTHING FROM YOU.
BUT AT THE END OF THE WORLD, THERE WASN'T ANYONE ELSE I WANTED TO SEE.

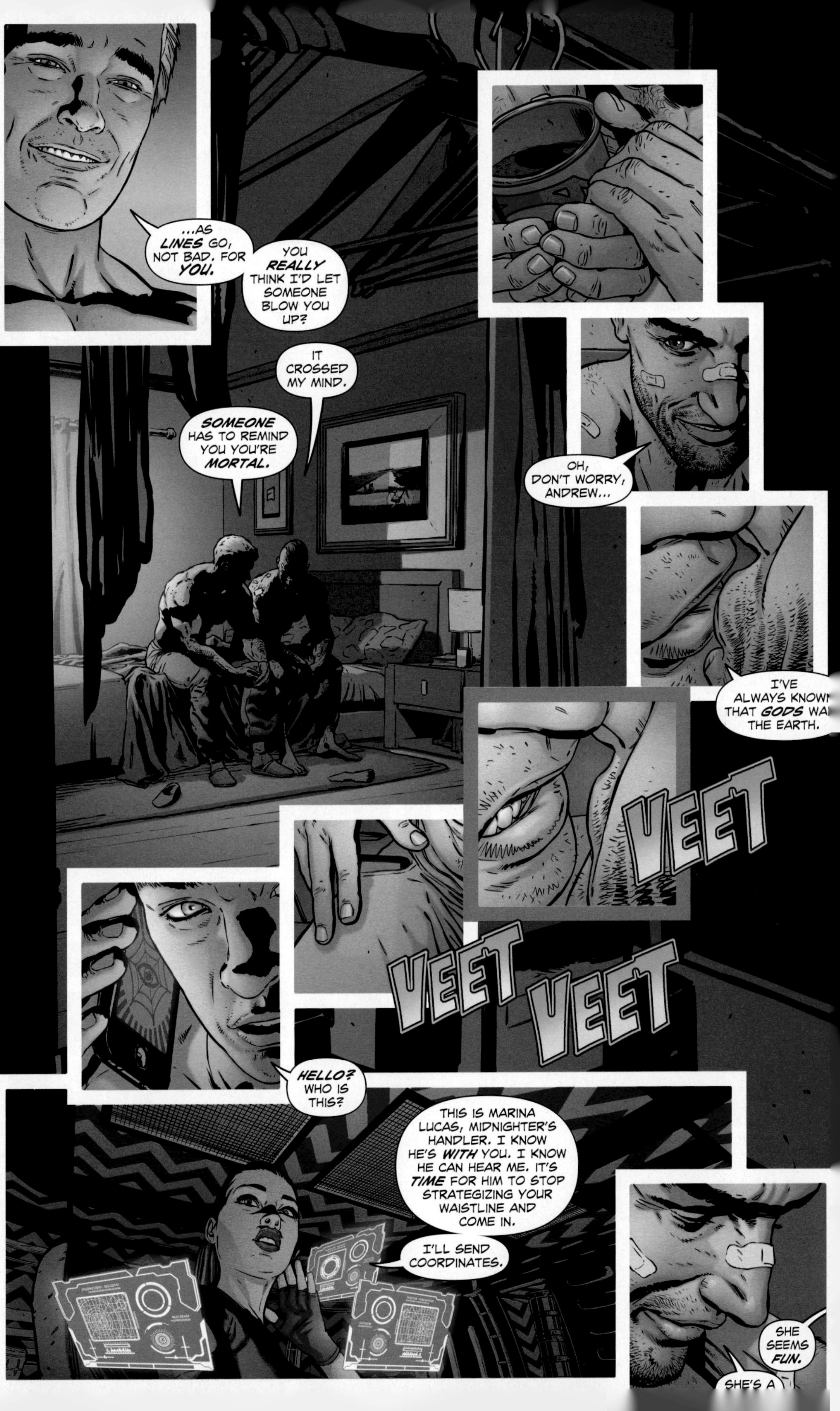
...AS LINES GO, NOT BAD. FOR YOU.
YOU REALLY THINK I'D LET SOMEONE BLOW YOU UP?
IT CROSSED MY MIND.
SOMEONE HAS TO REMIND YOU YOU'RE MORTAL.
OH, DON'T WORRY, ANDREW...
I'VE ALWAYS KNOWN THAT GODS WA THE EARTH.
VEET
VEET
VEET
HELLO? WHO IS THIS?
THIS IS MARINA LUCAS, MIDNIGHTER'S HANDLER. I KNOW HE'S WITH YOU. I KNOW HE CAN HEAR ME. IT'S TIME FOR HIM TO STOP STRATEGIZING YOUR WAISTLINE AND COME IN.
I'LL SEND COORDINATES.
SHE SEEMS FUN.
SHE'S A

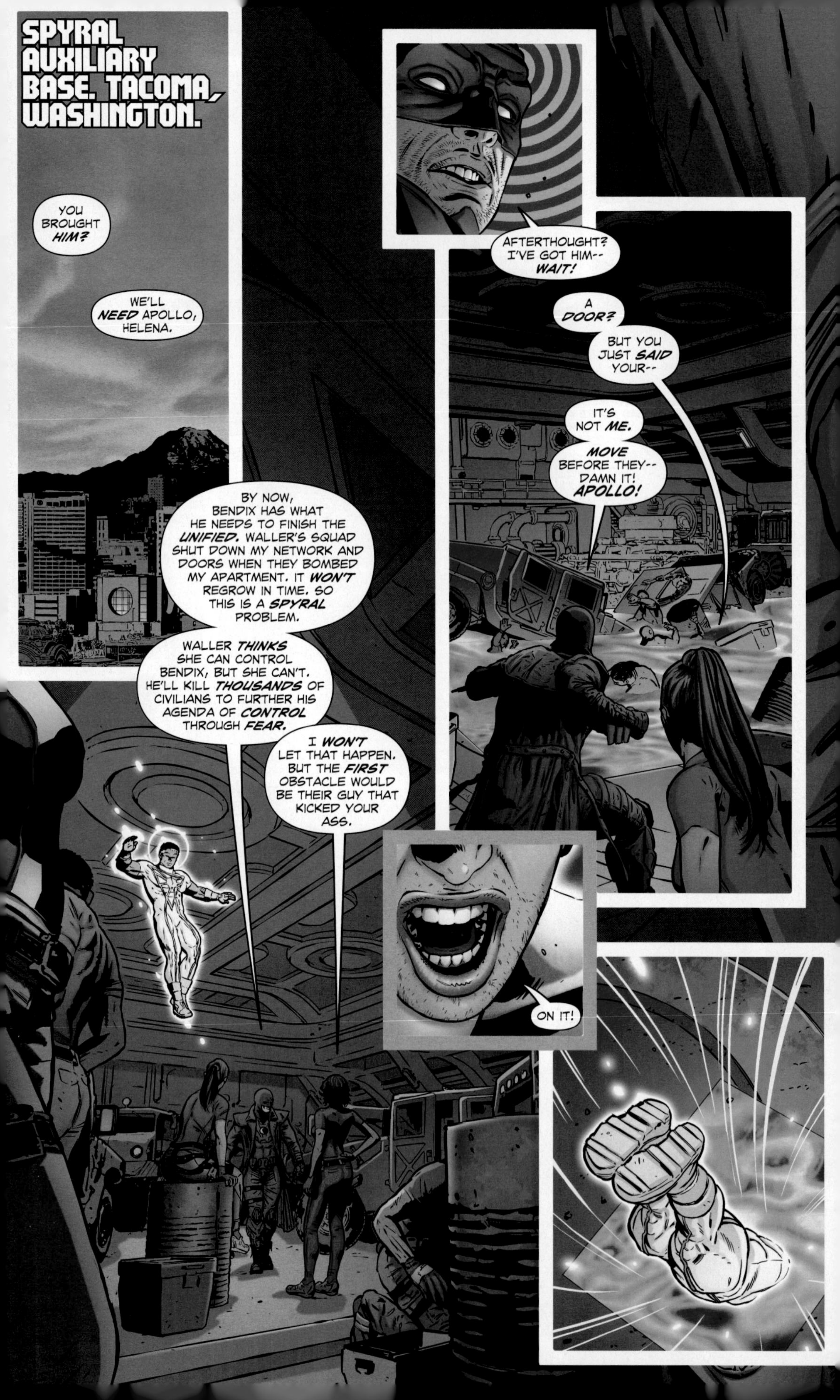
SPYRAL AUXILIARY BASE. TACOMA, WASHINGTON.
YOU BROUGHT HIM?
WE'LL NEED APOLLO, HELENA.
BY NOW, BENDIX HAS WHAT HE NEEDS TO FINISH THE UNIFIED. WALLER'S SQUAD SHUT DOWN MY NETWORK AND DOORS WHEN THEY BOMBED MY APARTMENT. IT WON'T REGROW IN TIME. SO THIS IS A SPYRAL PROBLEM.
WALLER THINKS SHE CAN CONTROL BENDIX, BUT SHE CAN'T. HE'LL KILL THOUSANDS OF CIVILIANS TO FURTHER HIS AGENDA OF CONTROL THROUGH FEAR.
I WON'T LET THAT HAPPEN. BUT THE FIRST OBSTACLE WOULD BE THEIR GUY THAT KICKED YOUR ASS.
AFTERTHOUGHT? I'VE GOT HIM-- WAIT!
A DOOR?
BUT YOU JUST SAID YOUR--
IT'S NOT ME.
MOVE BEFORE THEY-- DAMN IT! APOLLO!
ON IT!

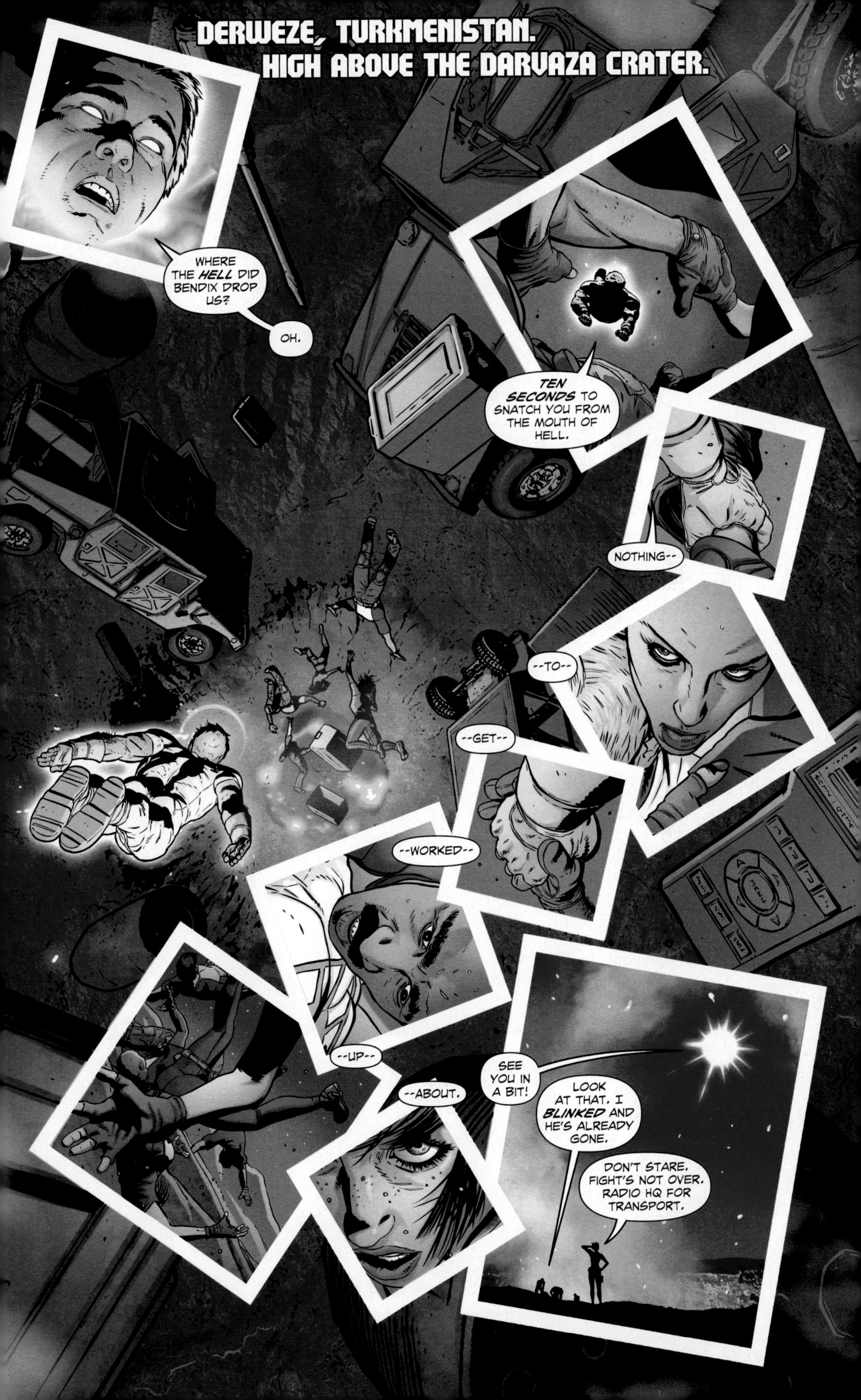

DERWEZE, TURKMENISTAN.
HIGH ABOVE THE DARVAZA CRATER.
WHERE THE HELL DID BENDIX DROP US?
OH.
TEN SECONDS TO SNATCH YOU FROM THE MOUTH OF HELL.
NOTHING--
--TO--
--GET--
--WORKED--
--UP--
--ABOUT.
SEE YOU IN A BIT!
LOOK AT THAT. I BLINKED AND HE'S ALREADY GONE.
DON'T STARE. FIGHT'S NOT OVER. RADIO HQ FOR TRANSPORT.

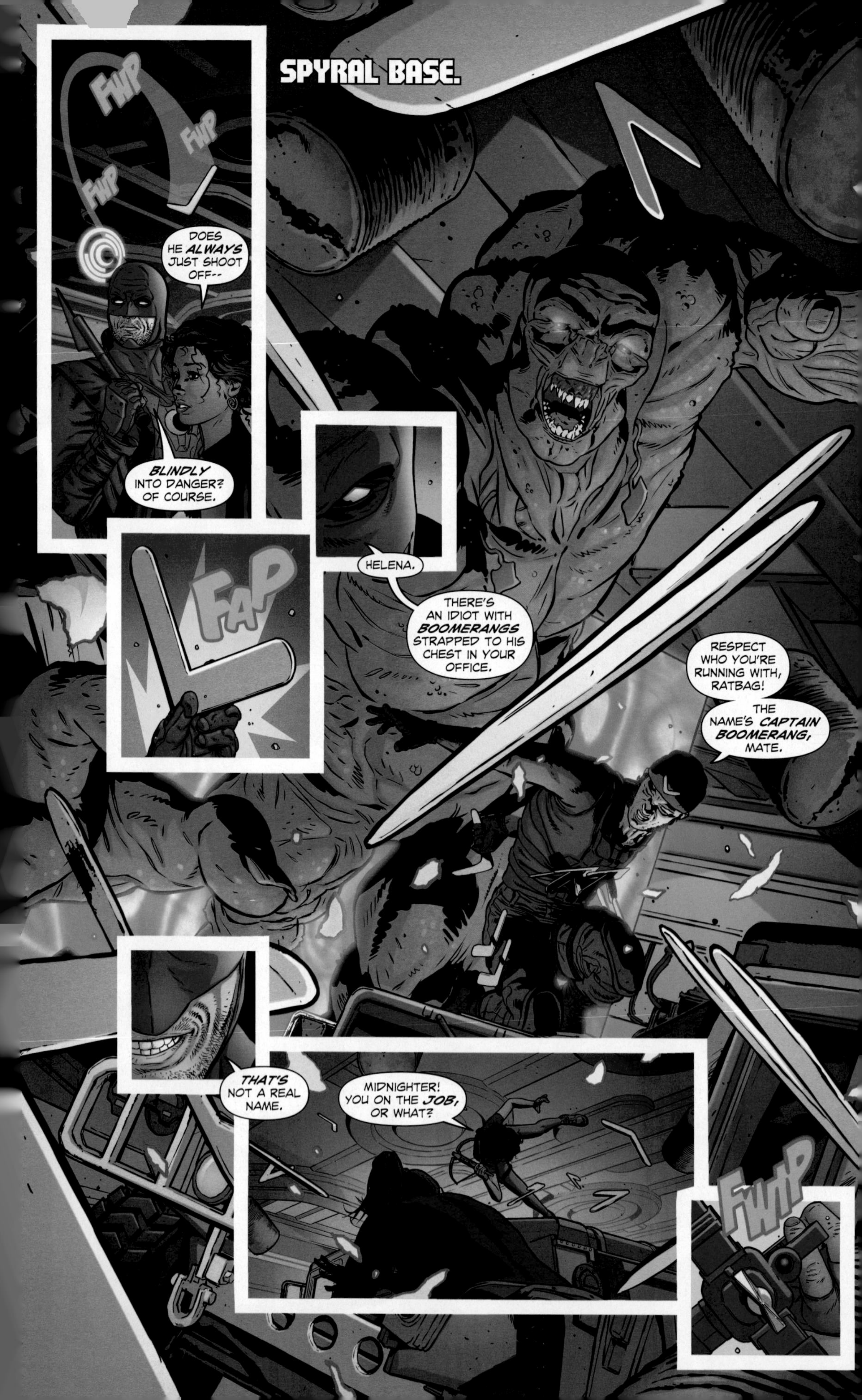
SPYRAL BASE.
FWP
FWP
FWP
DOES HE ALWAYS JUST SHOOT OFF--
BLINDLY INTO DANGER? OF COURSE.
FAP
HELENA.
THERE'S AN IDIOT WITH BOOMERANGS STRAPPED TO HIS CHEST IN YOUR OFFICE.
RESPECT WHO YOU'RE RUNNING WITH, RATBAG!
THE NAME'S CAPTAIN BOOMERANG, MATE.
THAT'S NOT A REAL NAME.
MIDNIGHTER! YOU ON THE JOB, OR WHAT?
FWIP

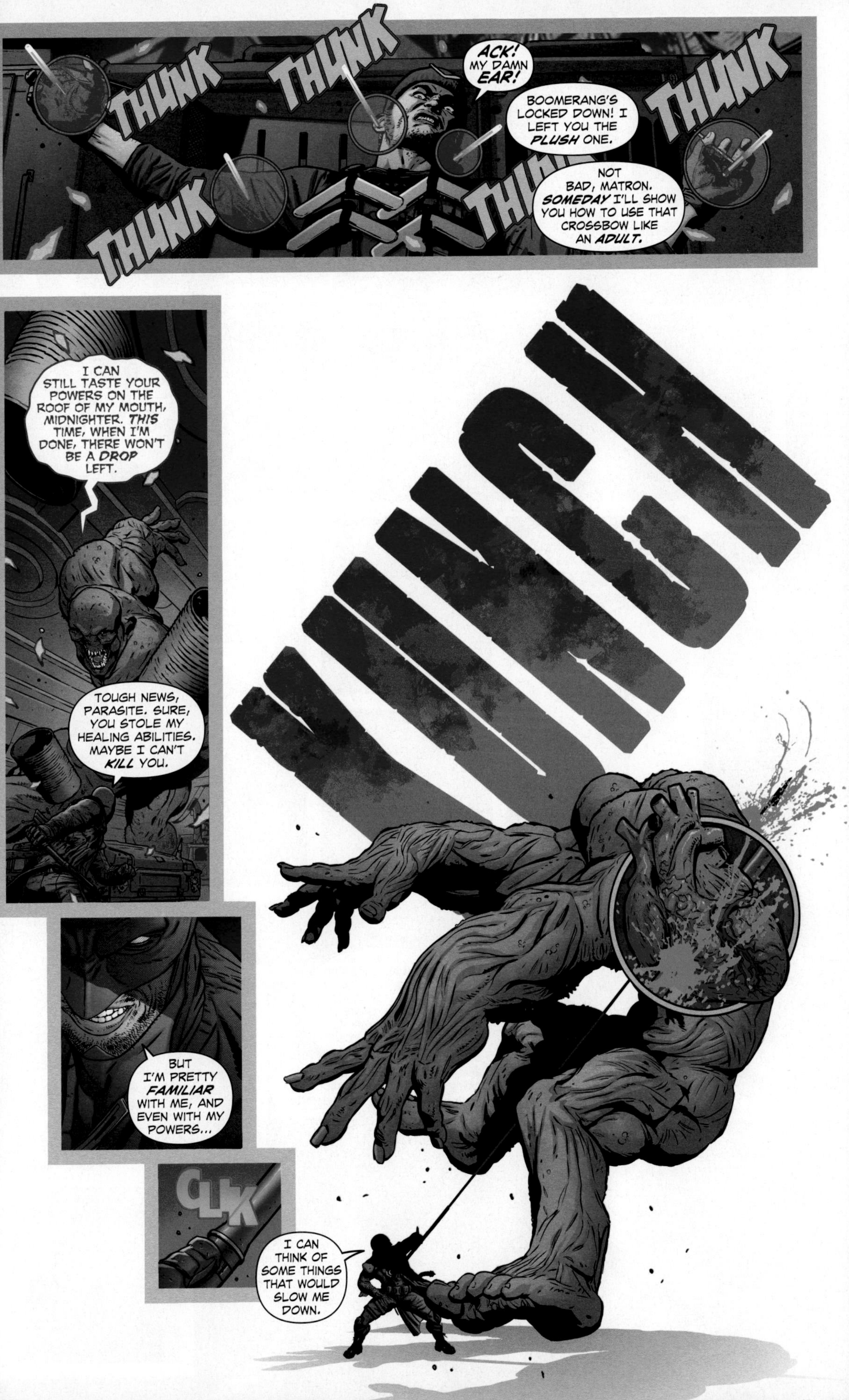
THUNK
THUNK
THUNK
ACK! MY DAMN EAR!
BOOMERANG'S LOCKED DOWN! I LEFT YOU THE PLUSH ONE.
THUNK
NOT BAD, MATRON. SOMEDAY I'LL SHOW YOU HOW TO USE THAT CROSSBOW LIKE AN ADULT.
I CAN STILL TASTE YOUR POWERS ON THE ROOF OF MY MOUTH, MIDNIGHTER. THIS TIME, WHEN I'M DONE, THERE WON'T BE A DROP LEFT.
TOUGH NEWS, PARASITE. SURE, YOU STOLE MY HEALING ABILITIES. MAYBE I CAN'T KILL YOU.
BUT I'M PRETTY FAMILIAR WITH ME, AND EVEN WITH MY POWERS...
CLIK
YUNCH
I CAN THINK OF SOME THINGS THAT WOULD SLOW ME DOWN.

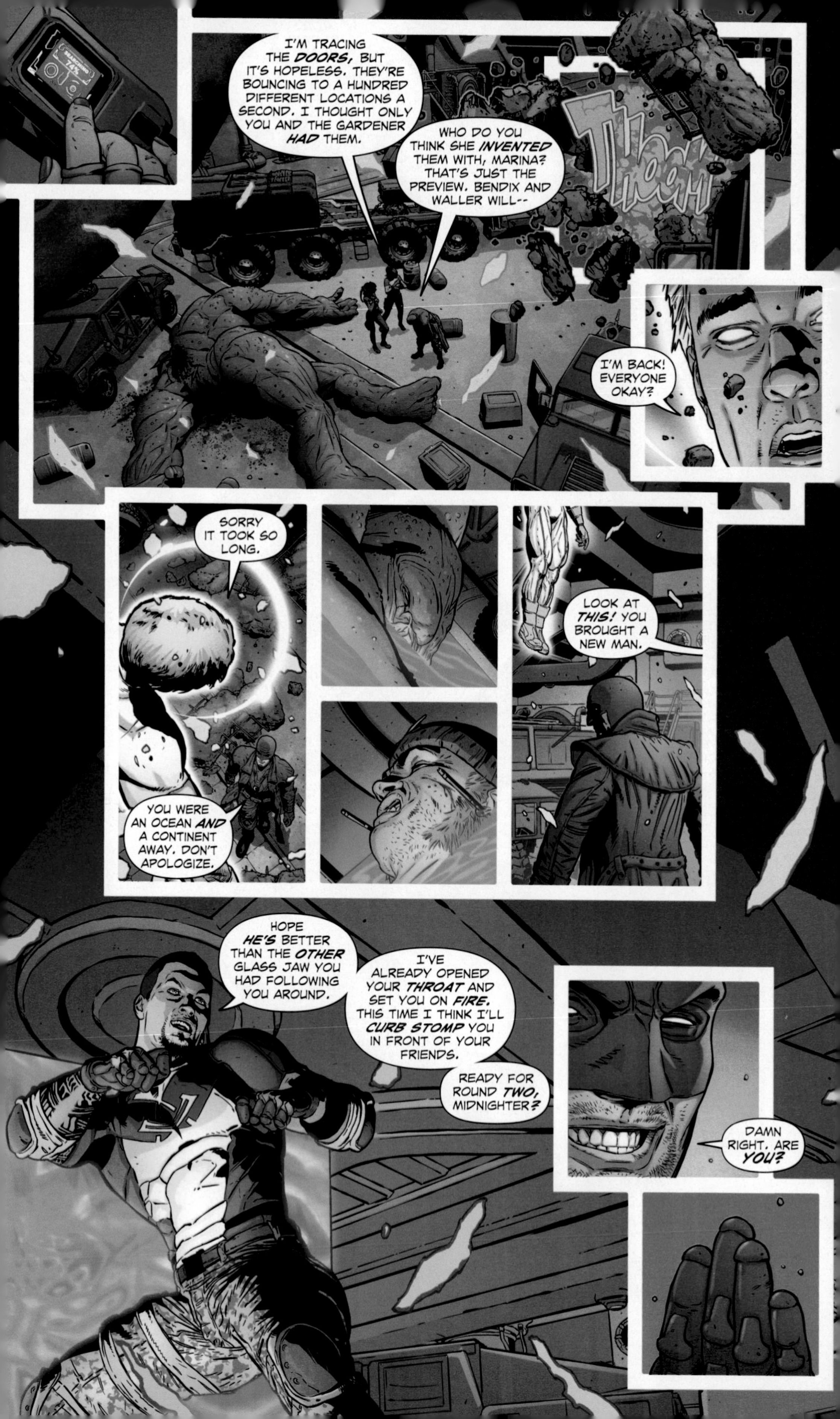
SEARCHING 74%
I'M TRACING THE DOORS, BUT IT'S HOPELESS. THEY'RE BOUNCING TO A HUNDRED DIFFERENT LOCATIONS A SECOND. I THOUGHT ONLY YOU AND THE GARDENER HAD THEM.
WHO DO YOU THINK SHE INVENTED THEM WITH, MARINA? THAT'S JUST THE PREVIEW. BENDIX AND WALLER WILL--
THOOM
I'M BACK! EVERYONE OKAY?
SORRY IT TOOK SO LONG.
YOU WERE AN OCEAN AND A CONTINENT AWAY. DON'T APOLOGIZE.
LOOK AT THIS! YOU BROUGHT A NEW MAN.
HOPE HE'S BETTER THAN THE OTHER GLASS JAW YOU HAD FOLLOWING YOU AROUND.
I'VE ALREADY OPENED YOUR THROAT AND SET YOU ON FIRE. THIS TIME I THINK I'LL CURB STOMP YOU IN FRONT OF YOUR FRIENDS.
READY FOR ROUND TWO, MIDNIGHTER?
DAMN RIGHT. ARE YOU?

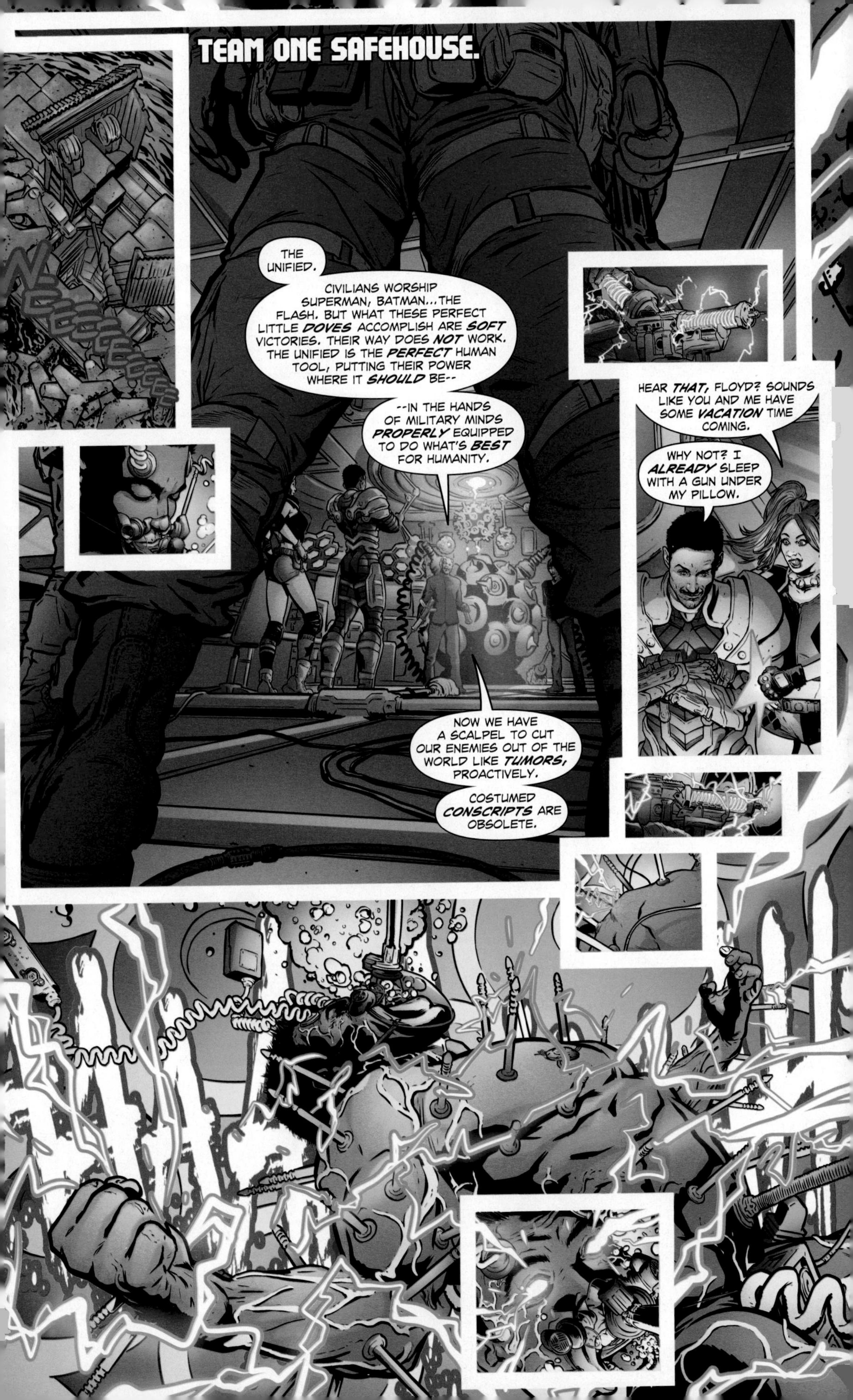
TEAM ONE SAFEHOUSE.
NGEEEEEEEE
THE UNIFIED.
CIVILIANS WORSHIP SUPERMAN, BATMAN...THE FLASH. BUT WHAT THESE PERFECT LITTLE DOVES ACCOMPLISH ARE SOFT VICTORIES. THEIR WAY DOES NOT WORK. THE UNIFIED IS THE PERFECT HUMAN TOOL, PUTTING THEIR POWER WHERE IT SHOULD BE--
--IN THE HANDS OF MILITARY MINDS PROPERLY EQUIPPED TO DO WHAT'S BEST FOR HUMANITY.
NOW WE HAVE A SCALPEL TO CUT OUR ENEMIES OUT OF THE WORLD LIKE TUMORS, PROACTIVELY.
COSTUMED CONSCRIPTS ARE OBSOLETE.
HEAR THAT, FLOYD? SOUNDS LIKE YOU AND ME HAVE SOME VACATION TIME COMING.
WHY NOT? I ALREADY SLEEP WITH A GUN UNDER MY PILLOW.

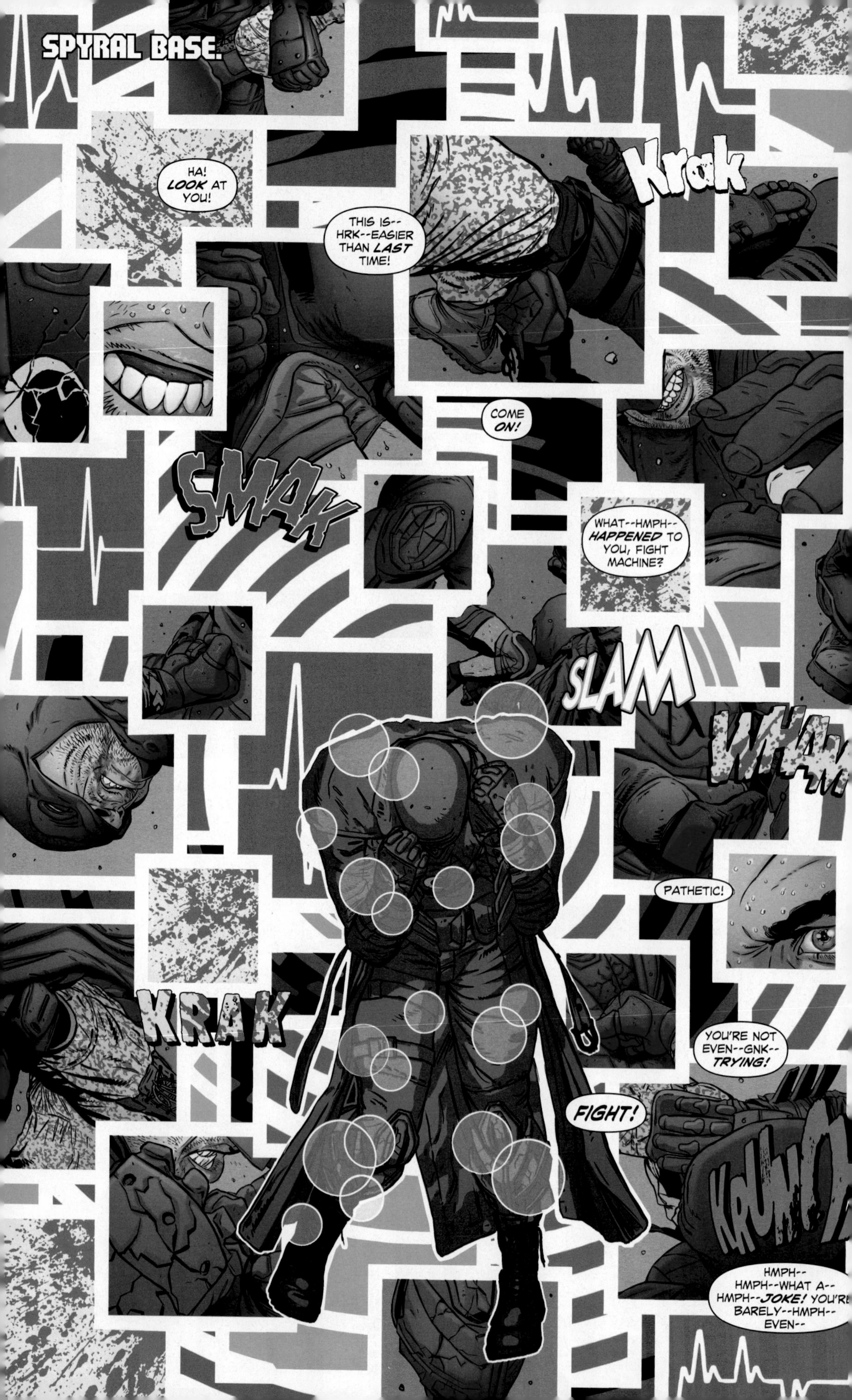
SPYRAL BASE.
HA! LOOK AT YOU!
THIS IS--HRK--EASIER THAN LAST TIME!
Krak
COME ON!
SMAK
WHAT--HMPH--HAPPENED TO YOU, FIGHT MACHINE?
SLAM
PATHETIC!
KRAK
YOU'RE NOT EVEN--GNK--TRYING!
FIGHT!
HMPH--HMPH--WHAT A--HMPH--JOKE! YOU'RE BARELY--HMPH--EVEN--

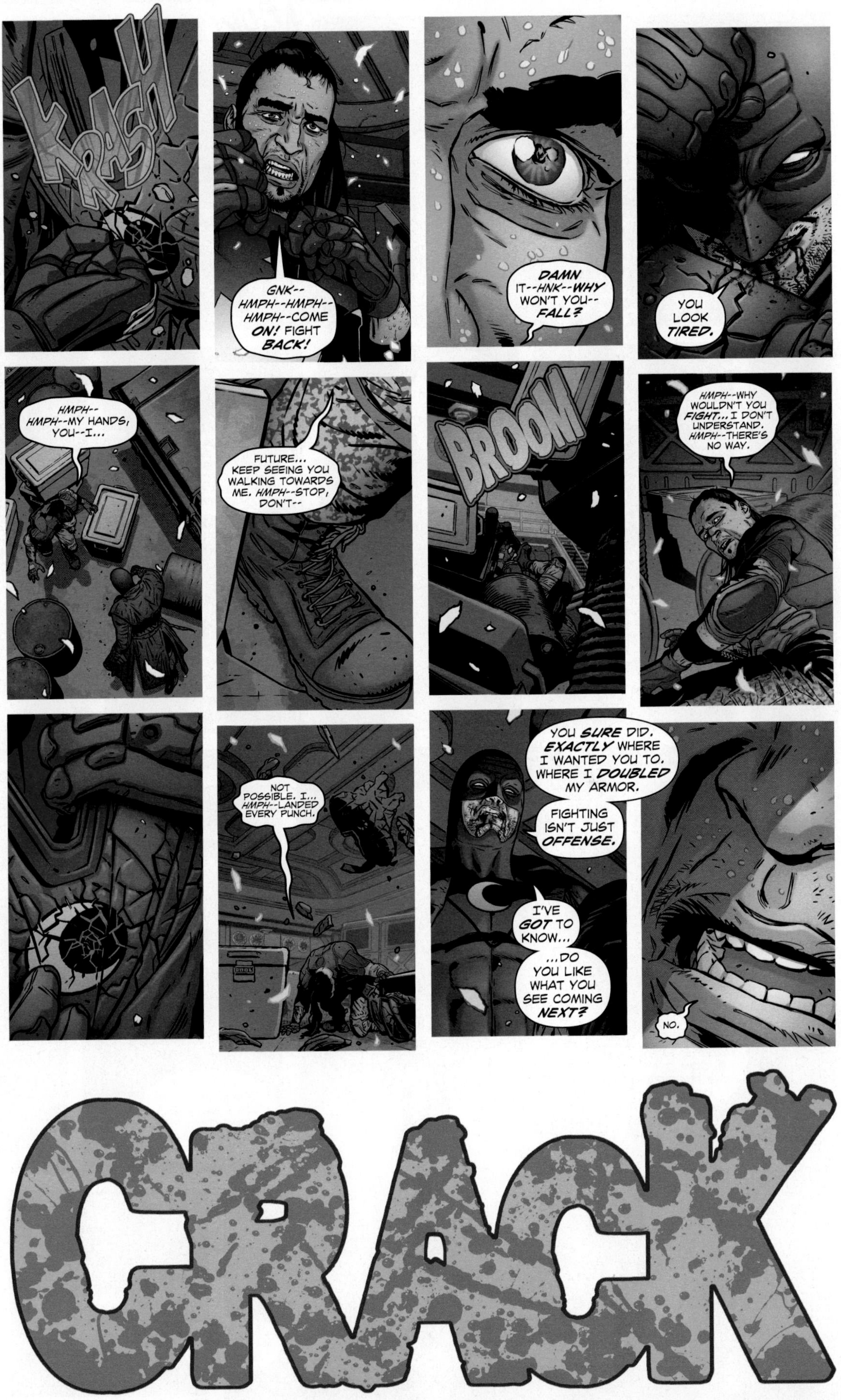
KRASH
GNK--HMPH--HMPH--HMPH--COME ON! FIGHT BACK!
DAMN IT--HNK--WHY WON'T YOU--FALL?
YOU LOOK TIRED.
HMPH--HMPH--MY HANDS, YOU--I...
FUTURE... KEEP SEEING YOU WALKING TOWARDS ME. HMPH--STOP, DON'T--
BROOM
HMPH--WHY WOULDN'T YOU FIGHT... I DON'T UNDERSTAND. HMPH--THERE'S NO WAY.
NOT POSSIBLE. I... HMPH--LANDED EVERY PUNCH.
YOU SURE DID. EXACTLY WHERE I WANTED YOU TO. WHERE I DOUBLED MY ARMOR.
FIGHTING ISN'T JUST OFFENSE.
I'VE GOT TO KNOW...
...DO YOU LIKE WHAT YOU SEE COMING NEXT?
NO.
CRACK

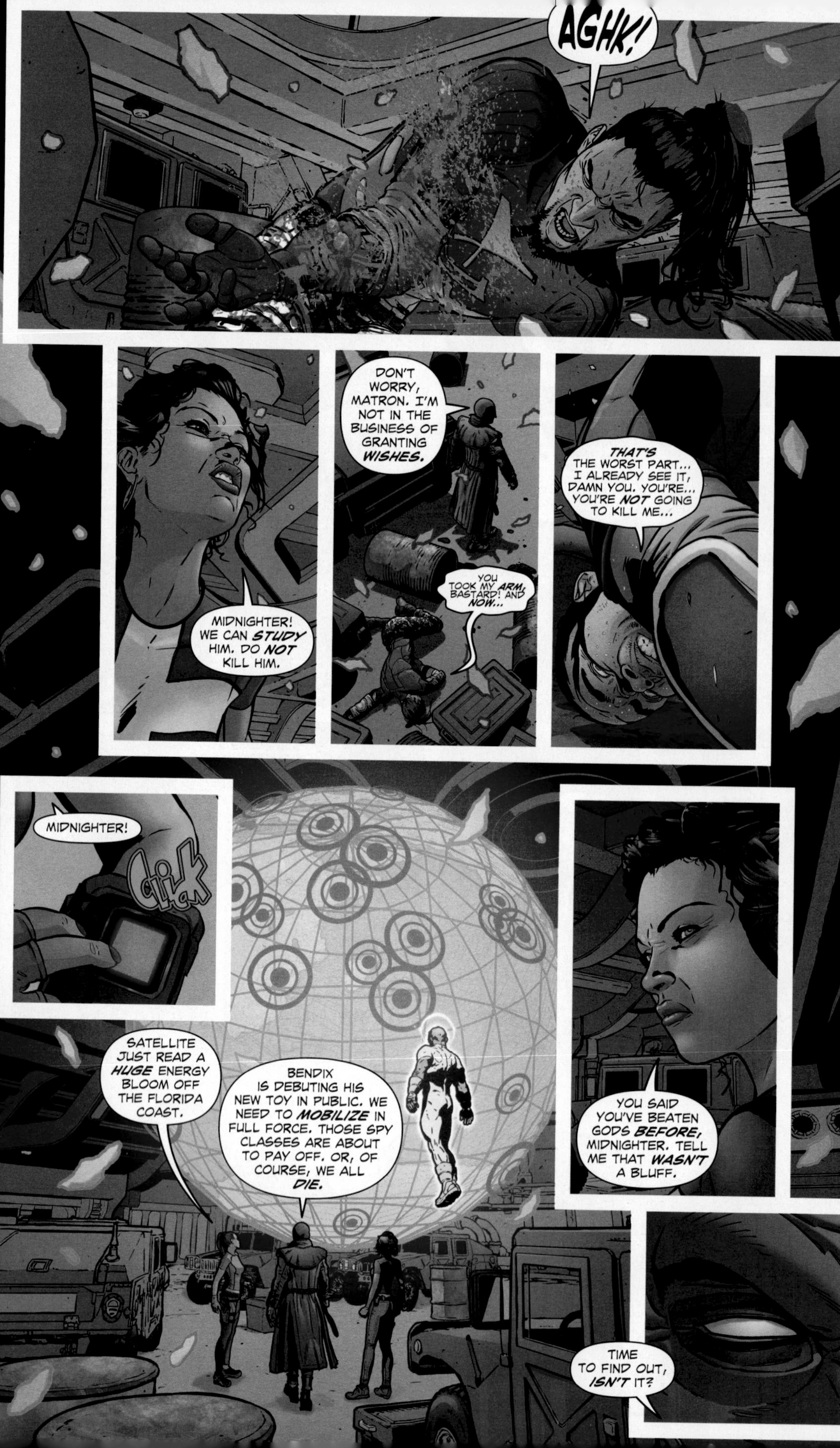
AGHK!
MIDNIGHTER! WE CAN STUDY HIM. DO NOT KILL HIM.
DON'T WORRY, MATRON. I'M NOT IN THE BUSINESS OF GRANTING WISHES.
YOU TOOK MY ARM, BASTARD! AND NOW...
THAT'S THE WORST PART... I ALREADY SEE IT, DAMN YOU. YOU'RE... YOU'RE NOT GOING TO KILL ME...
MIDNIGHTER!
CLICK
SATELLITE JUST READ A HUGE ENERGY BLOOM OFF THE FLORIDA COAST.
BENDIX IS DEBUTING HIS NEW TOY IN PUBLIC. WE NEED TO MOBILIZE IN FULL FORCE. THOSE SPY CLASSES ARE ABOUT TO PAY OFF. OR, OF COURSE, WE ALL DIE.
YOU SAID YOU'VE BEATEN GODS BEFORE, MIDNIGHTER. TELL ME THAT WASN'T A BLUFF.
TIME TO FIND OUT, ISN'T IT?

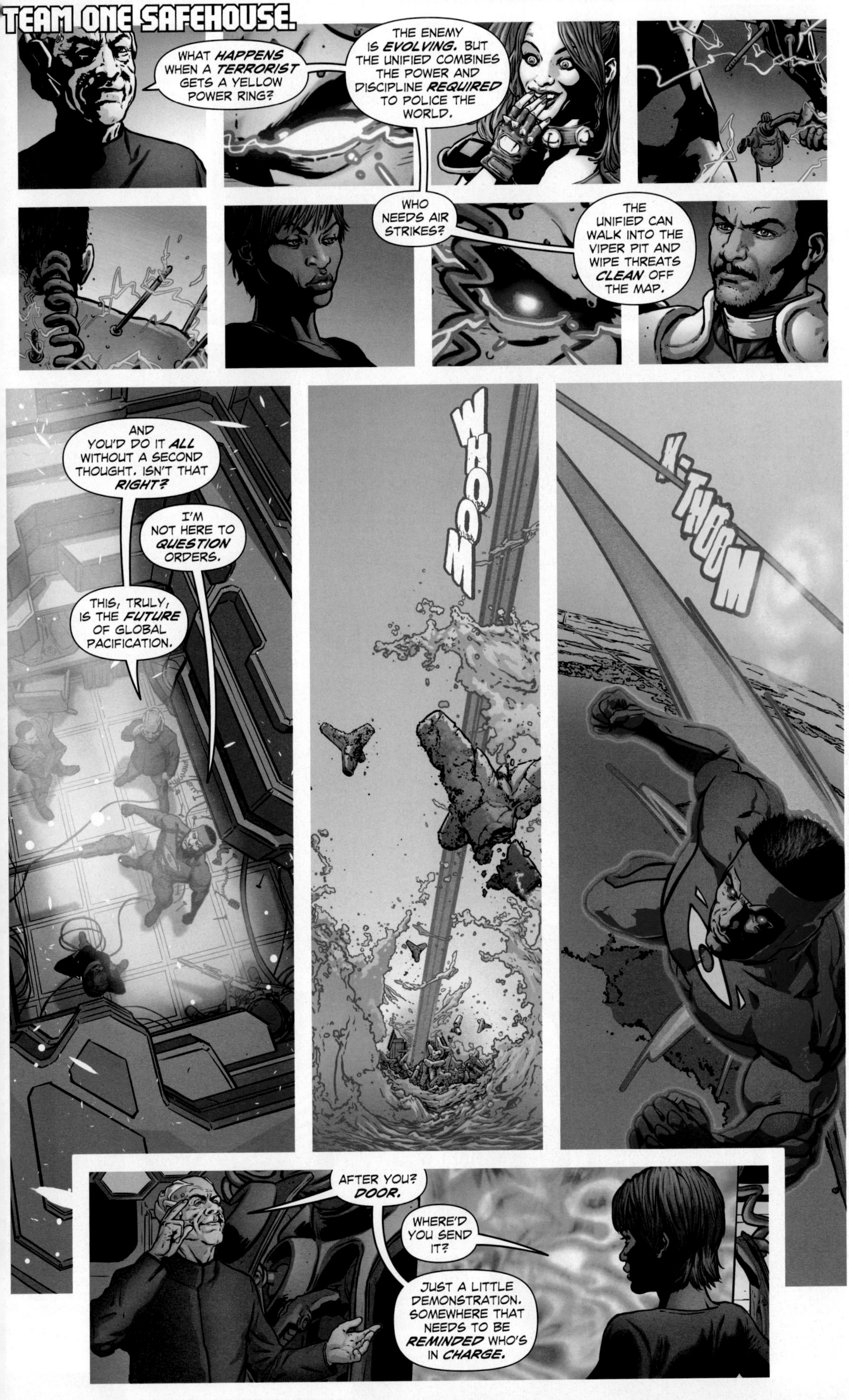
TEAM ONE SAFEHOUSE.
WHAT HAPPENS WHEN A TERRORIST GETS A YELLOW POWER RING?
THE ENEMY IS EVOLVING. BUT THE UNIFIED COMBINES THE POWER AND DISCIPLINE REQUIRED TO POLICE THE WORLD.
WHO NEEDS AIR STRIKES?
THE UNIFIED CAN WALK INTO THE VIPER PIT AND WIPE THREATS CLEAN OFF THE MAP.
AND YOU'D DO IT ALL WITHOUT A SECOND THOUGHT. ISN'T THAT RIGHT?
I'M NOT HERE TO QUESTION ORDERS.
THIS, TRULY, IS THE FUTURE OF GLOBAL PACIFICATION.
WHOOOM
K-THOOM
AFTER YOU? DOOR.
WHERE'D YOU SEND IT?
JUST A LITTLE DEMONSTRATION. SOMEWHERE THAT NEEDS TO BE REMINDED WHO'S IN CHARGE.

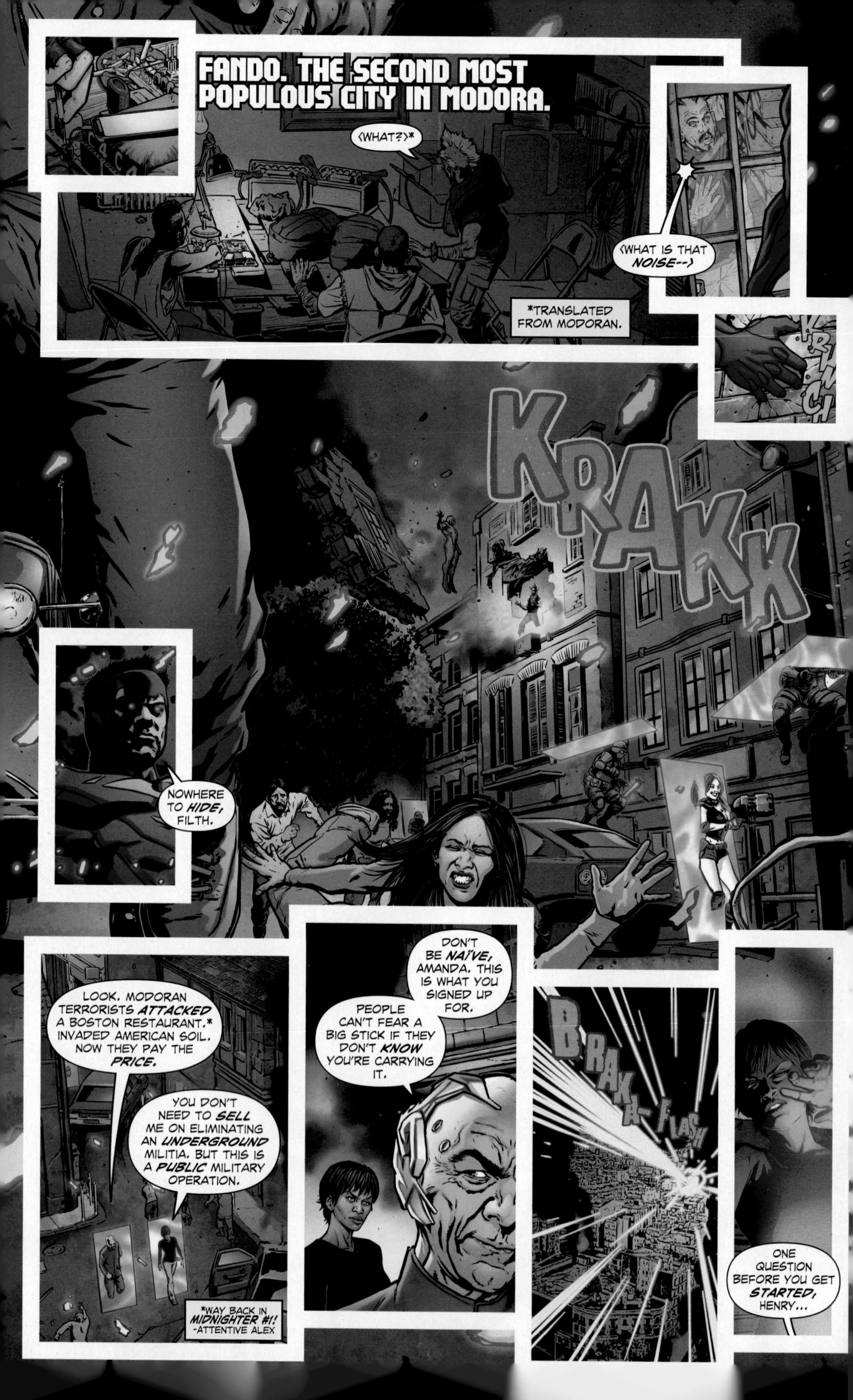
FANDO. THE SECOND MOST POPULOUS CITY IN MODORA.
‹WHAT?›*
*TRANSLATED FROM MODORAN.
‹WHAT IS THAT NOISE--›
KRAKK
NOWHERE TO HIDE, FILTH.
LOOK. MODORAN TERRORISTS ATTACKED A BOSTON RESTAURANT.* INVADED AMERICAN SOIL. NOW THEY PAY THE PRICE.
YOU DON'T NEED TO SELL ME ON ELIMINATING AN UNDERGROUND MILITIA. BUT THIS IS A PUBLIC MILITARY OPERATION.
*WAY BACK IN MIDNIGHTER #1! -ATTENTIVE ALEX
DON'T BE NAÏVE, AMANDA. THIS IS WHAT YOU SIGNED UP FOR.
PEOPLE CAN'T FEAR A BIG STICK IF THEY DON'T KNOW YOU'RE CARRYING IT.
BRAKKA-FLASH
ONE QUESTION BEFORE YOU GET STARTED, HENRY...

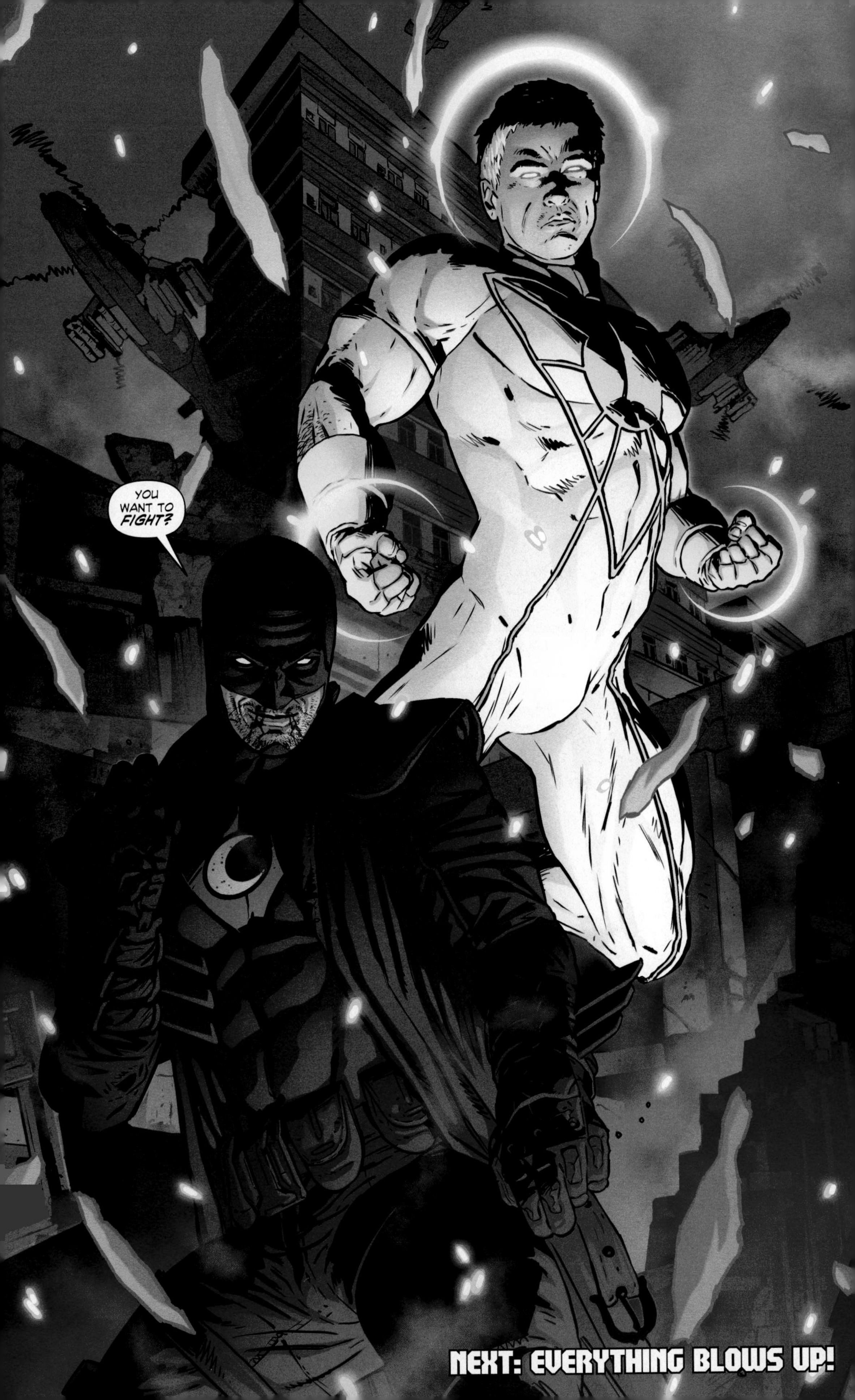
YOU WANT TO FIGHT?
NEXT: EVERYTHING BLOWS UP!

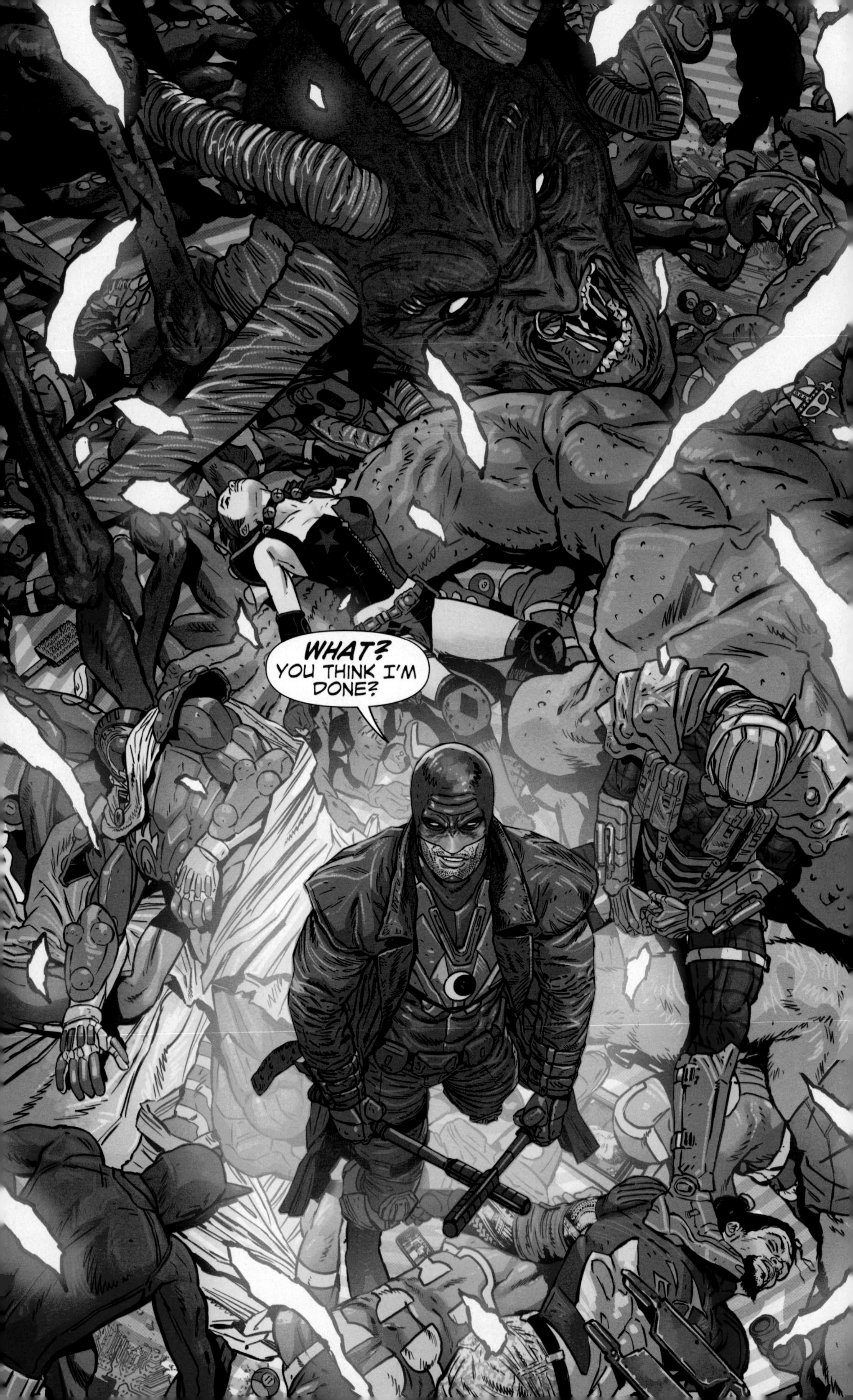
WHAT? YOU THINK I'M DONE?

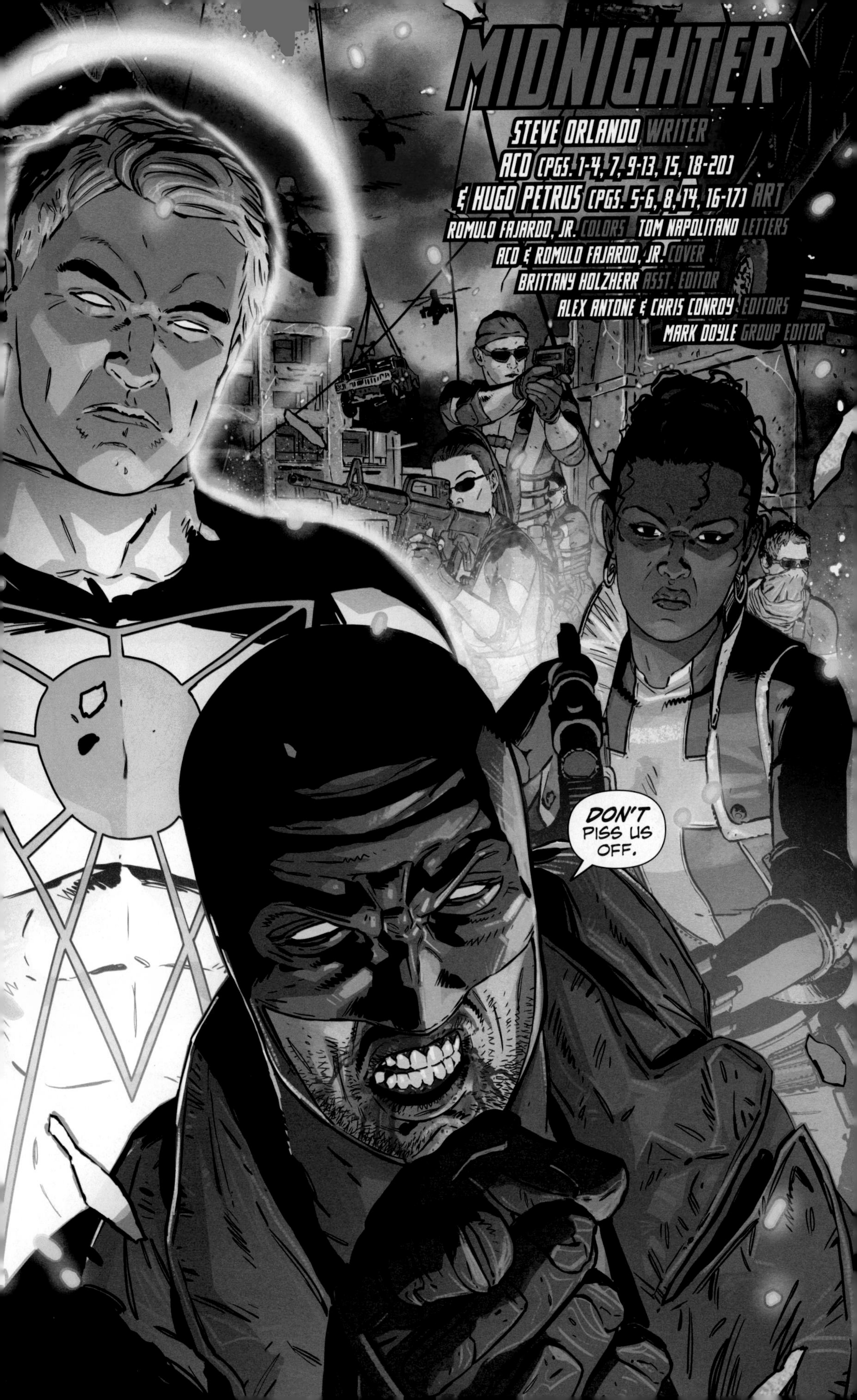
MIDNIGHTER
STEVE ORLANDO WRITER
ACO (PGS. 1-4, 7, 9-13, 15, 18-20)
& HUGO PETRUS (PGS. 5-6, 8, 14, 16-17) ART
ROMULO FAJARDO, JR. COLORS TOM NAPOLITANO LETTERS
ACO & ROMULO FAJARDO, JR. COVER
BRITTANY HOLZHERR ASST. EDITOR
ALEX ANTONE & CHRIS CONROY EDITORS
MARK DOYLE GROUP EDITOR
DON'T PISS US OFF.

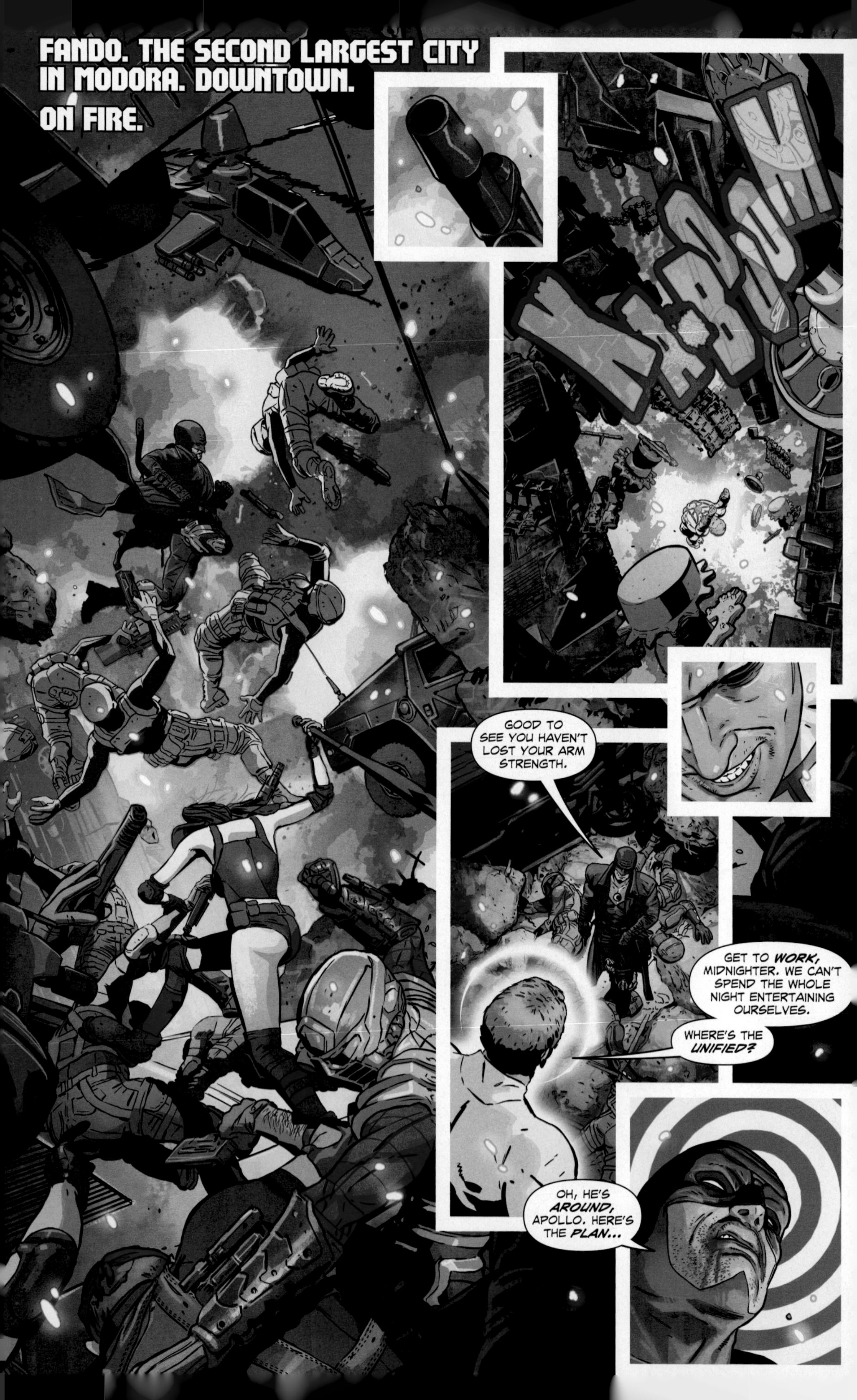

FANDO. THE SECOND LARGEST CITY IN MODORA. DOWNTOWN.
ON FIRE.
GOOD TO SEE YOU HAVEN'T LOST YOUR ARM STRENGTH.
GET TO WORK, MIDNIGHTER. WE CAN'T SPEND THE WHOLE NIGHT ENTERTAINING OURSELVES.
WHERE'S THE UNIFIED?
OH, HE'S AROUND, APOLLO. HERE'S THE PLAN...

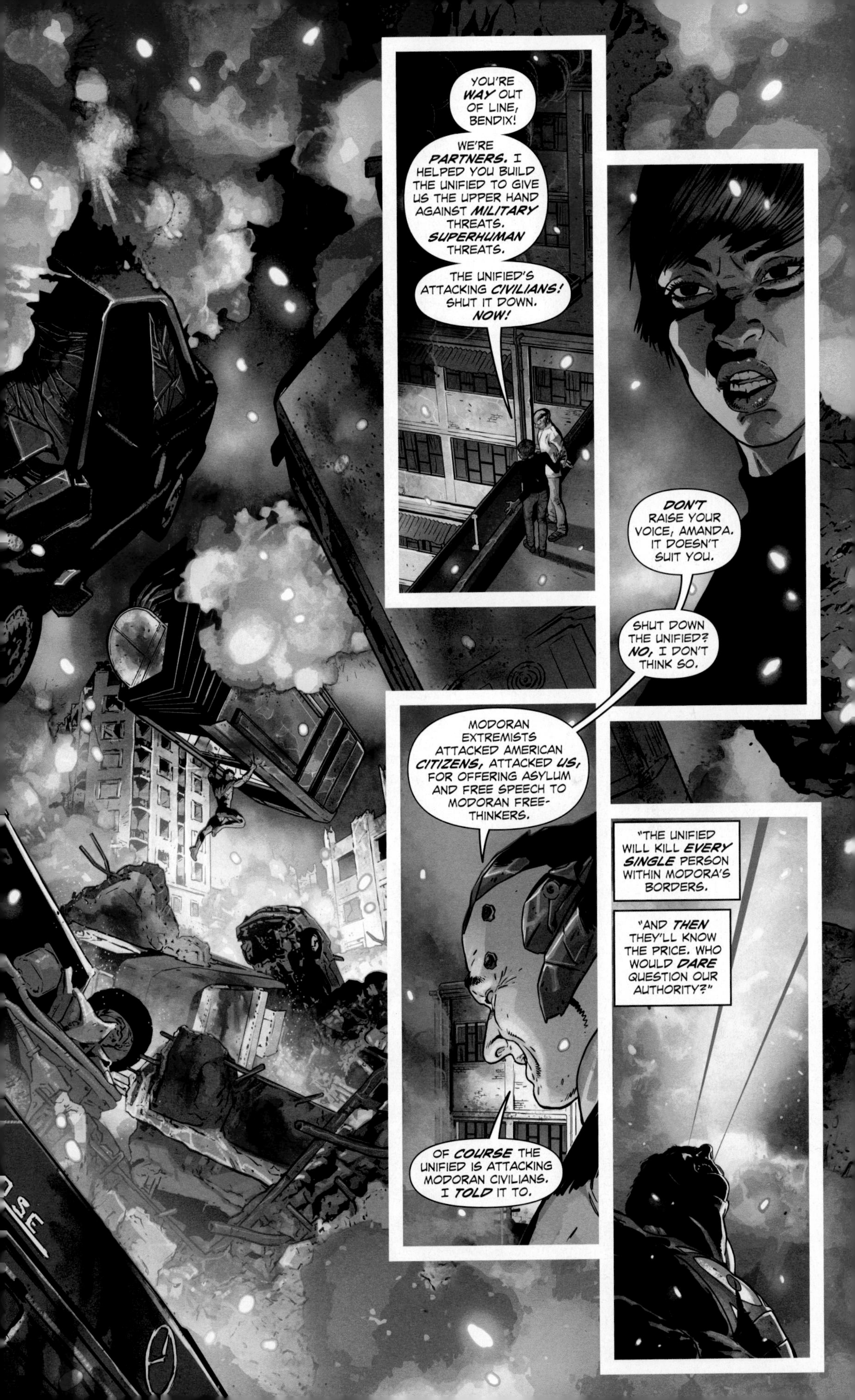

YOU'RE WAY OUT OF LINE, BENDIX!
WE'RE PARTNERS. I HELPED YOU BUILD THE UNIFIED TO GIVE US THE UPPER HAND AGAINST MILITARY THREATS. SUPERHUMAN THREATS.
THE UNIFIED'S ATTACKING CIVILIANS! SHUT IT DOWN. NOW!
DON'T RAISE YOUR VOICE, AMANDA. IT DOESN'T SUIT YOU.
SHUT DOWN THE UNIFIED? NO, I DON'T THINK SO.
MODORAN EXTREMISTS ATTACKED AMERICAN CITIZENS, ATTACKED US, FOR OFFERING ASYLUM AND FREE SPEECH TO MODORAN FREE-THINKERS.
OF COURSE THE UNIFIED IS ATTACKING MODORAN CIVILIANS. I TOLD IT TO.
"THE UNIFIED WILL KILL EVERY SINGLE PERSON WITHIN MODORA'S BORDERS.
"AND THEN THEY'LL KNOW THE PRICE. WHO WOULD DARE QUESTION OUR AUTHORITY?"

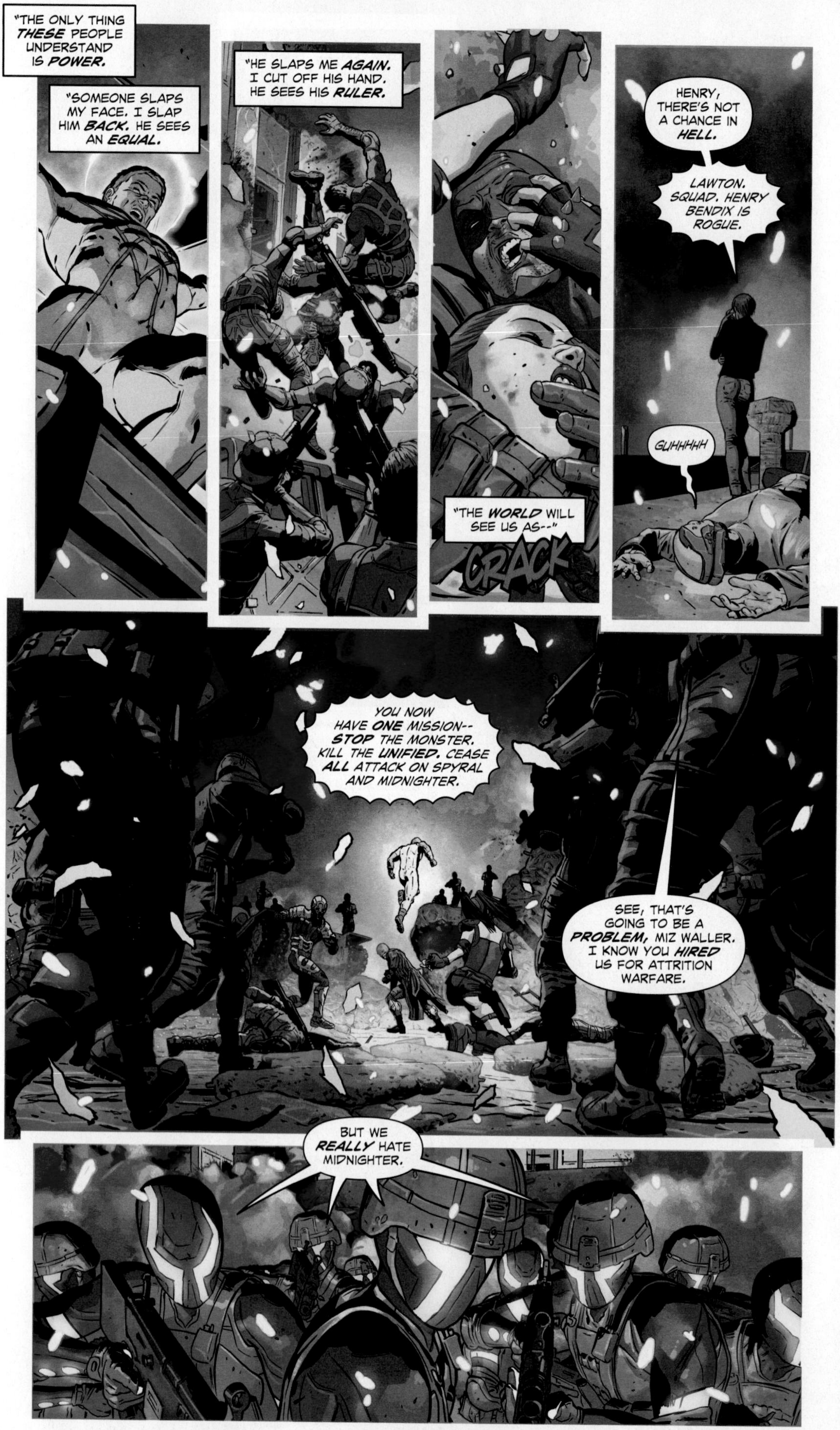
"THE ONLY THING *THESE* PEOPLE UNDERSTAND IS *POWER.*
"SOMEONE SLAPS MY FACE. I SLAP HIM *BACK.* HE SEES AN *EQUAL.*
"HE SLAPS ME *AGAIN.* I CUT OFF HIS HAND. HE SEES HIS *RULER.*
"THE *WORLD* WILL SEE US AS--"
CRACK
HENRY, THERE'S NOT A CHANCE IN *HELL.*
LAWTON. SQUAD. HENRY BENDIX IS ROGUE.
GUHHHHH
YOU NOW HAVE *ONE* MISSION-- *STOP* THE MONSTER. KILL THE *UNIFIED.* CEASE *ALL* ATTACK ON SPYRAL AND MIDNIGHTER.
SEE, THAT'S GOING TO BE A *PROBLEM,* MIZ WALLER. I KNOW YOU *HIRED* US FOR ATTRITION WARFARE.
BUT WE *REALLY* HATE MIDNIGHTER.

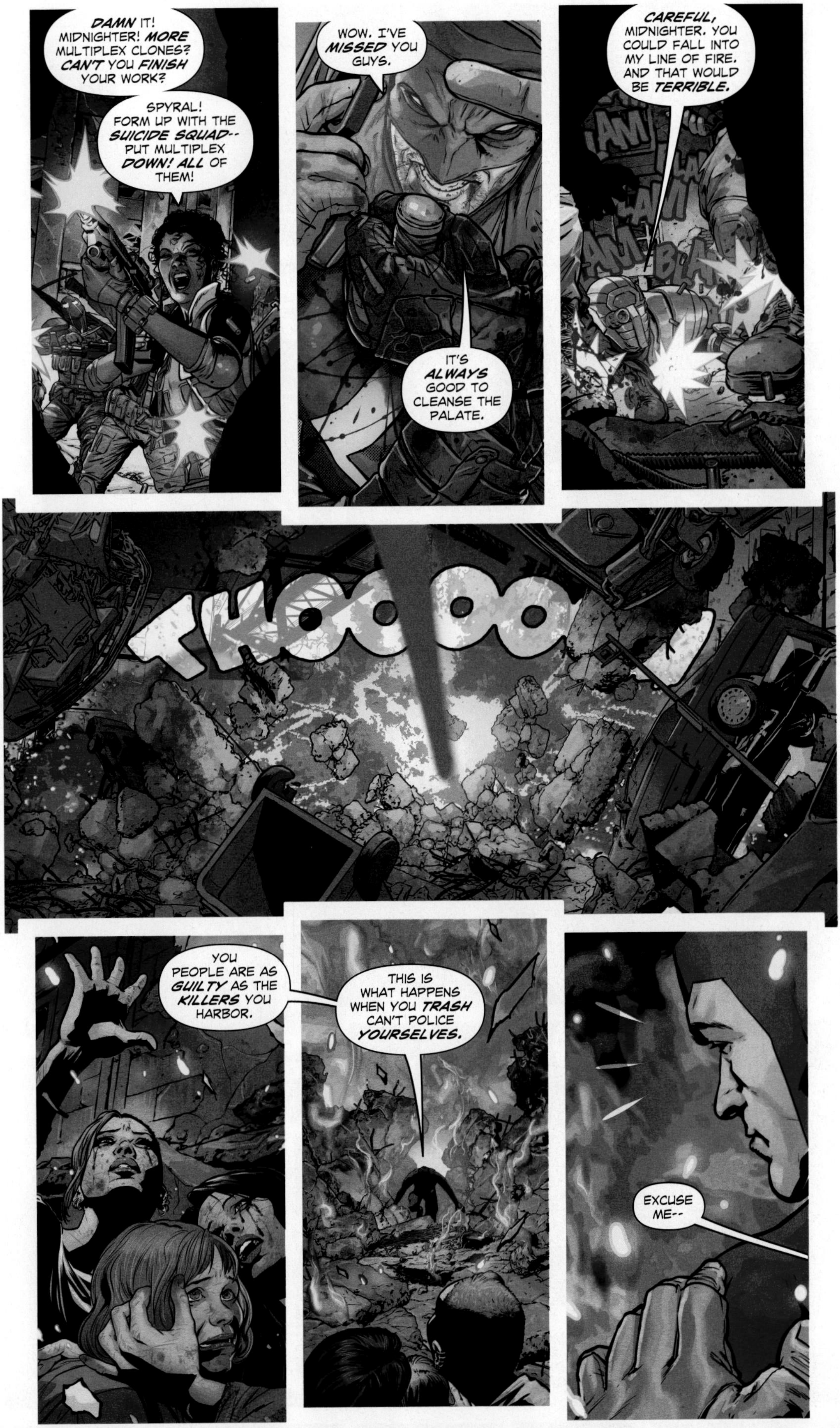

DAMN IT! MIDNIGHTER! MORE MULTIPLEX CLONES? CAN'T YOU FINISH YOUR WORK?
SPYRAL! FORM UP WITH THE SUICIDE SQUAD-- PUT MULTIPLEX DOWN! ALL OF THEM!
WOW. I'VE MISSED YOU GUYS.
IT'S ALWAYS GOOD TO CLEANSE THE PALATE.
CAREFUL, MIDNIGHTER. YOU COULD FALL INTO MY LINE OF FIRE. AND THAT WOULD BE TERRIBLE.
YOU PEOPLE ARE AS GUILTY AS THE KILLERS YOU HARBOR.
THIS IS WHAT HAPPENS WHEN YOU TRASH CAN'T POLICE YOURSELVES.
EXCUSE ME--

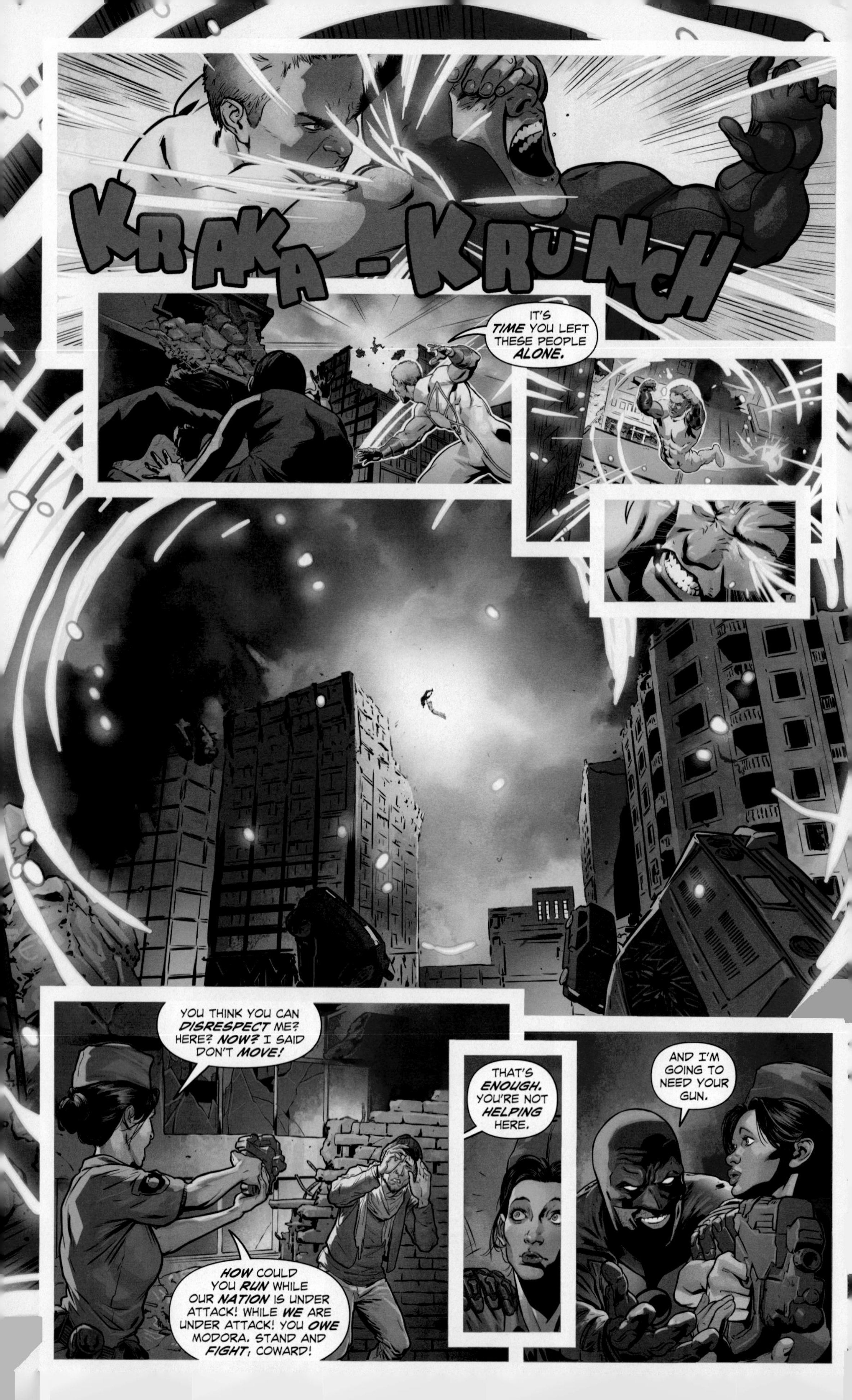
KRAKA - KRUNCH
IT'S TIME YOU LEFT THESE PEOPLE ALONE.
YOU THINK YOU CAN DISRESPECT ME? HERE? NOW? I SAID DON'T MOVE!
HOW COULD YOU RUN WHILE OUR NATION IS UNDER ATTACK! WHILE WE ARE UNDER ATTACK! YOU OWE MODORA. STAND AND FIGHT, COWARD!
THAT'S ENOUGH. YOU'RE NOT HELPING HERE.
AND I'M GOING TO NEED YOUR GUN.

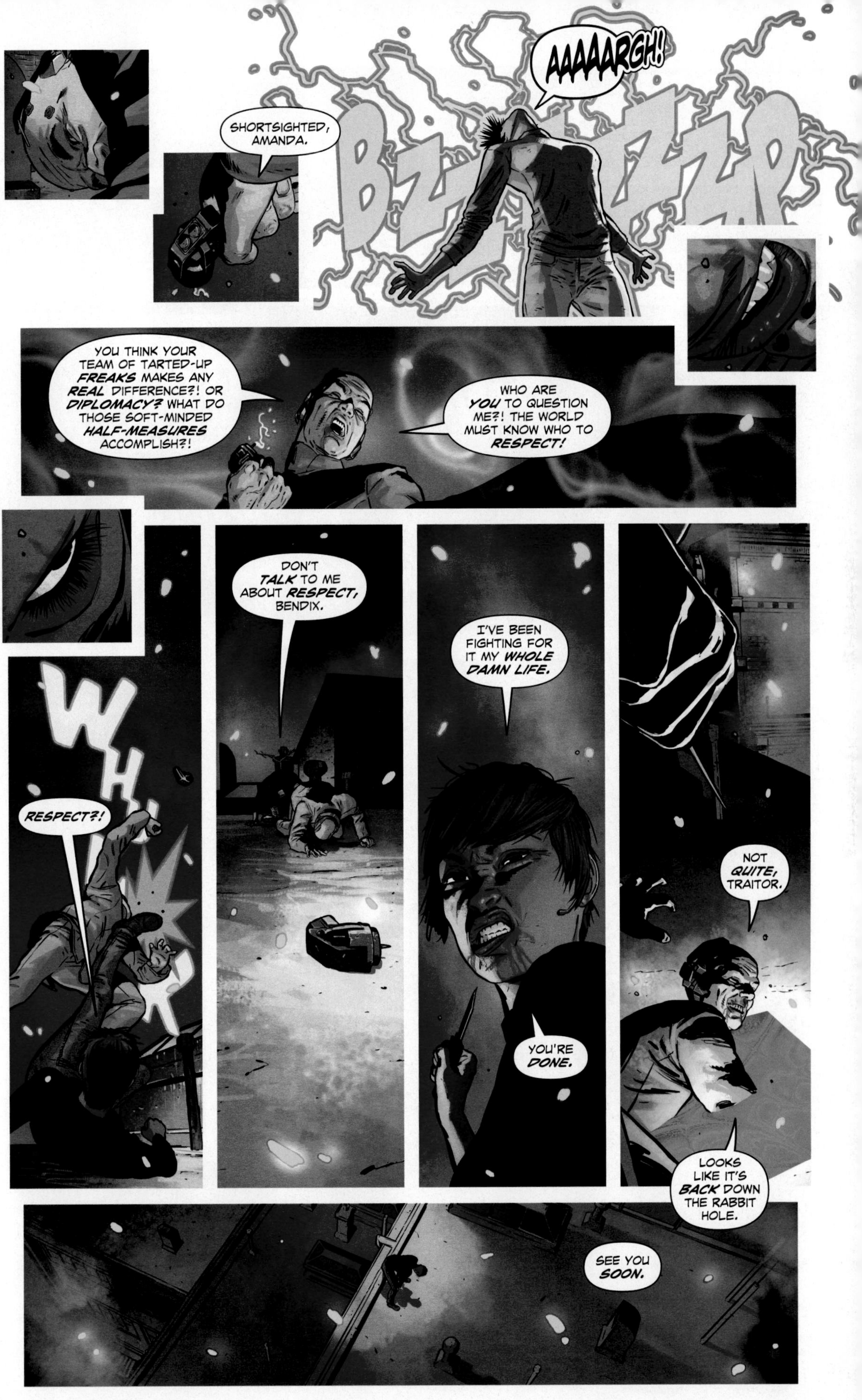

SHORTSIGHTED, AMANDA.
AAAAARGH!
BZZZZZT
YOU THINK YOUR TEAM OF TARTED-UP FREAKS MAKES ANY REAL DIFFERENCE?! OR DIPLOMACY? WHAT DO THOSE SOFT-MINDED HALF-MEASURES ACCOMPLISH?!
WHO ARE YOU TO QUESTION ME?! THE WORLD MUST KNOW WHO TO RESPECT!
RESPECT?!
DON'T TALK TO ME ABOUT RESPECT, BENDIX.
I'VE BEEN FIGHTING FOR IT MY WHOLE DAMN LIFE.
YOU'RE DONE.
NOT QUITE, TRAITOR.
LOOKS LIKE IT'S BACK DOWN THE RABBIT HOLE.
SEE YOU SOON.

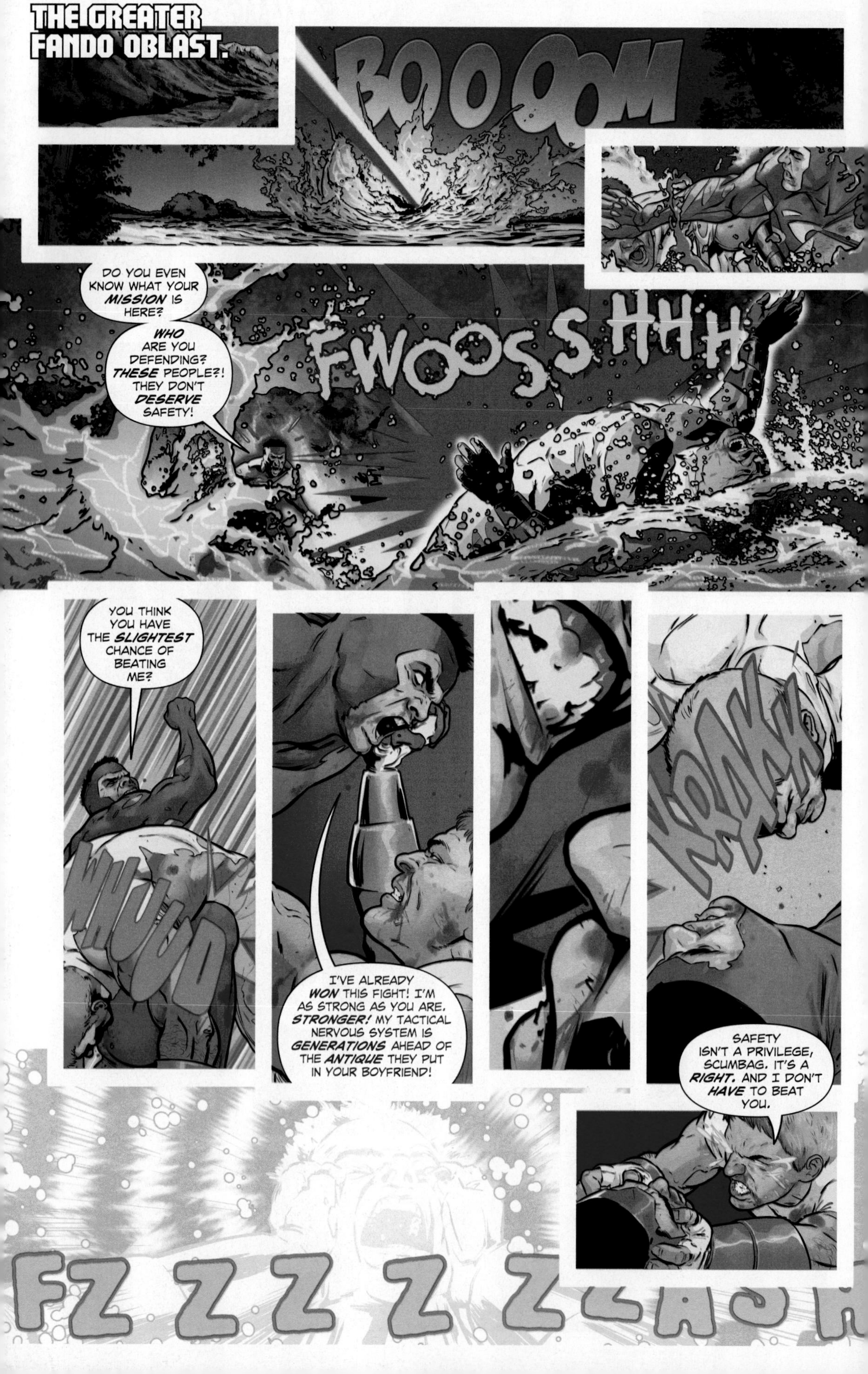
THE GREATER FANDO OBLAST.
BOOOOM
DO YOU EVEN KNOW WHAT YOUR MISSION IS HERE?
WHO ARE YOU DEFENDING? THESE PEOPLE?! THEY DON'T DESERVE SAFETY!
FWOOSSHHH
YOU THINK YOU HAVE THE SLIGHTEST CHANCE OF BEATING ME?
WHUUD
I'VE ALREADY WON THIS FIGHT! I'M AS STRONG AS YOU ARE. STRONGER! MY TACTICAL NERVOUS SYSTEM IS GENERATIONS AHEAD OF THE ANTIQUE THEY PUT IN YOUR BOYFRIEND!
SAFETY ISN'T A PRIVILEGE, SCUMBAG. IT'S A RIGHT. AND I DON'T HAVE TO BEAT YOU.
FZZZZZ

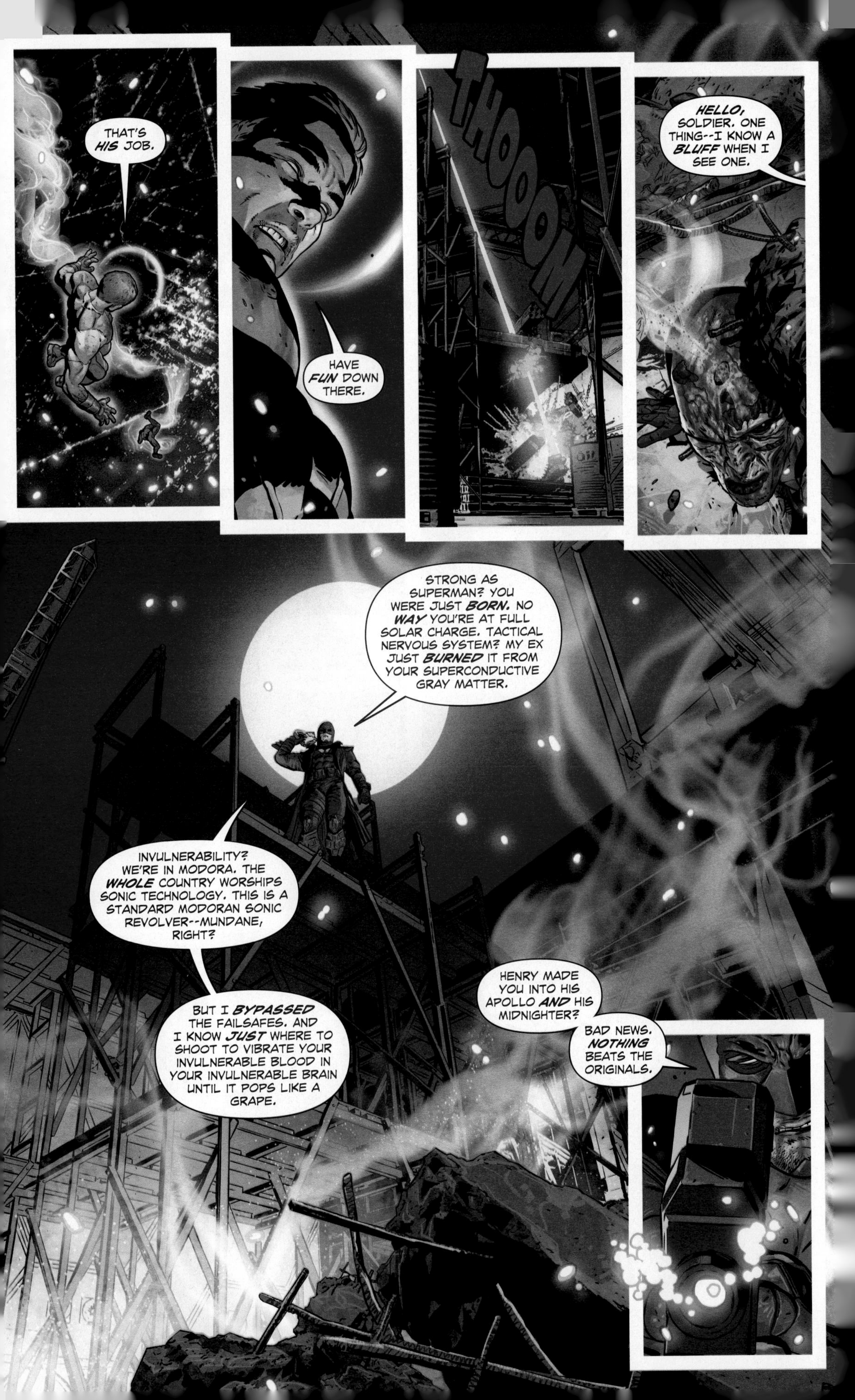
THAT'S HIS JOB.
HAVE FUN DOWN THERE.
THOOOM
HELLO, SOLDIER. ONE THING--I KNOW A BLUFF WHEN I SEE ONE.
STRONG AS SUPERMAN? YOU WERE JUST BORN. NO WAY YOU'RE AT FULL SOLAR CHARGE. TACTICAL NERVOUS SYSTEM? MY EX JUST BURNED IT FROM YOUR SUPERCONDUCTIVE GRAY MATTER.
INVULNERABILITY? WE'RE IN MODORA. THE WHOLE COUNTRY WORSHIPS SONIC TECHNOLOGY. THIS IS A STANDARD MODORAN SONIC REVOLVER--MUNDANE, RIGHT?
BUT I BYPASSED THE FAILSAFES. AND I KNOW JUST WHERE TO SHOOT TO VIBRATE YOUR INVULNERABLE BLOOD IN YOUR INVULNERABLE BRAIN UNTIL IT POPS LIKE A GRAPE.
HENRY MADE YOU INTO HIS APOLLO AND HIS MIDNIGHTER?
BAD NEWS. NOTHING BEATS THE ORIGINALS.

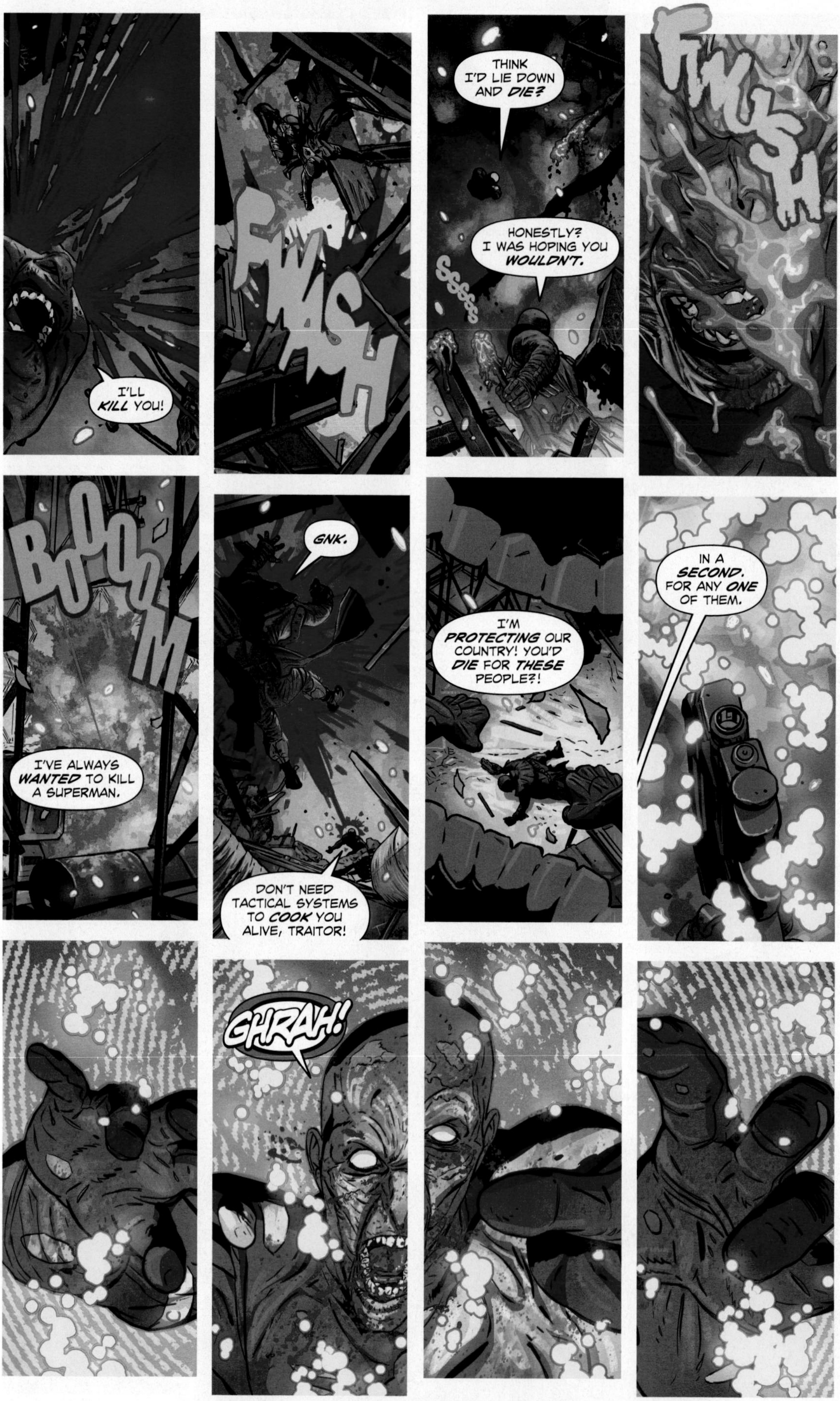
I'LL KILL YOU!
FWASH
THINK I'D LIE DOWN AND DIE?
HONESTLY? I WAS HOPING YOU WOULDN'T.
SSSSS
FWUSH
BOOOOOM
I'VE ALWAYS WANTED TO KILL A SUPERMAN.
GNK.
DON'T NEED TACTICAL SYSTEMS TO COOK YOU ALIVE, TRAITOR!
I'M PROTECTING OUR COUNTRY! YOU'D DIE FOR THESE PEOPLE?!
IN A SECOND. FOR ANY ONE OF THEM.
GHRAH!

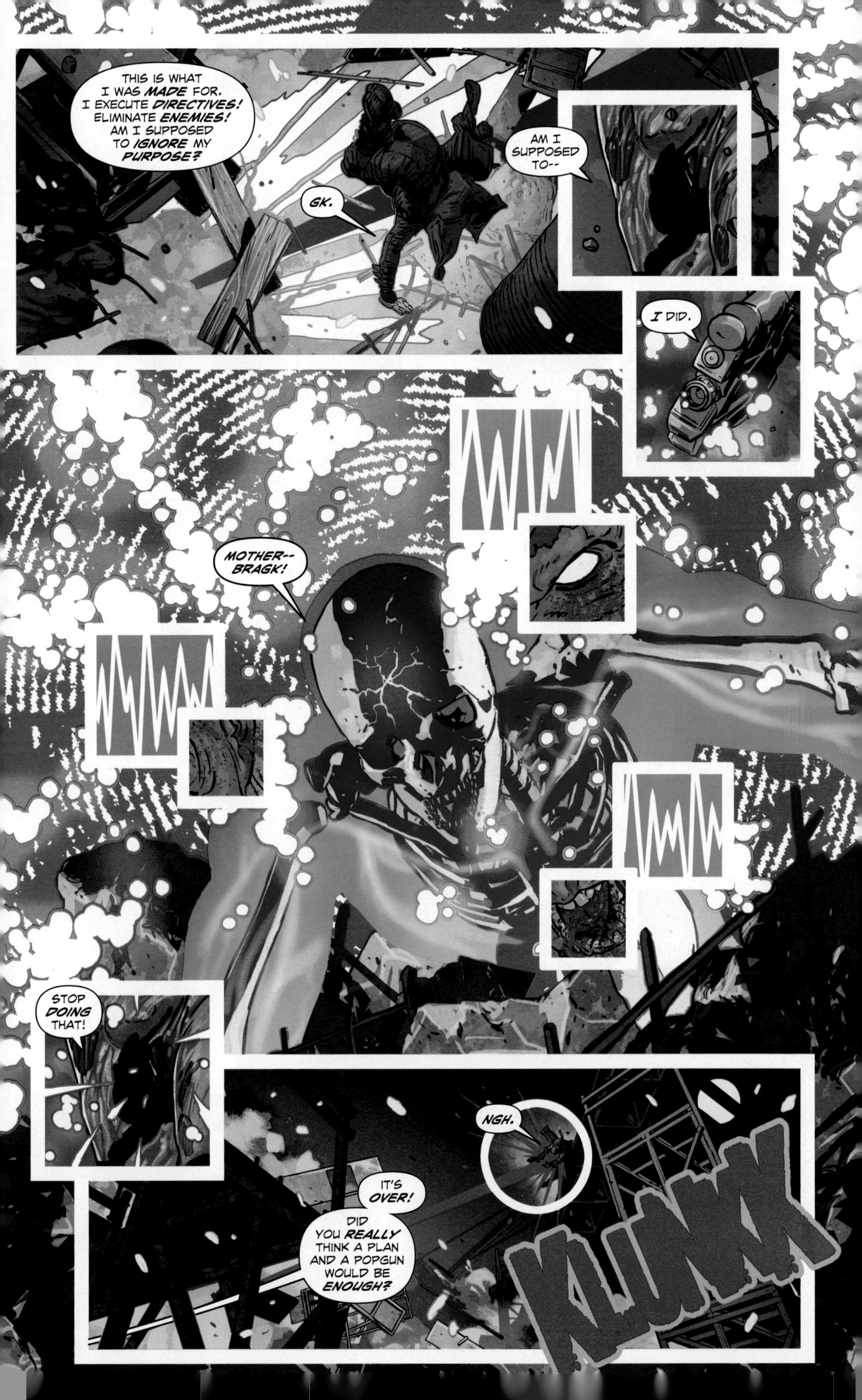
THIS IS WHAT I WAS MADE FOR. I EXECUTE DIRECTIVES! ELIMINATE ENEMIES! AM I SUPPOSED TO IGNORE MY PURPOSE?
GK.
AM I SUPPOSED TO--
I DID.
MOTHER-- BRAGK!
STOP DOING THAT!
NGH.
IT'S OVER!
DID YOU REALLY THINK A PLAN AND A POPGUN WOULD BE ENOUGH?
KLUNKK

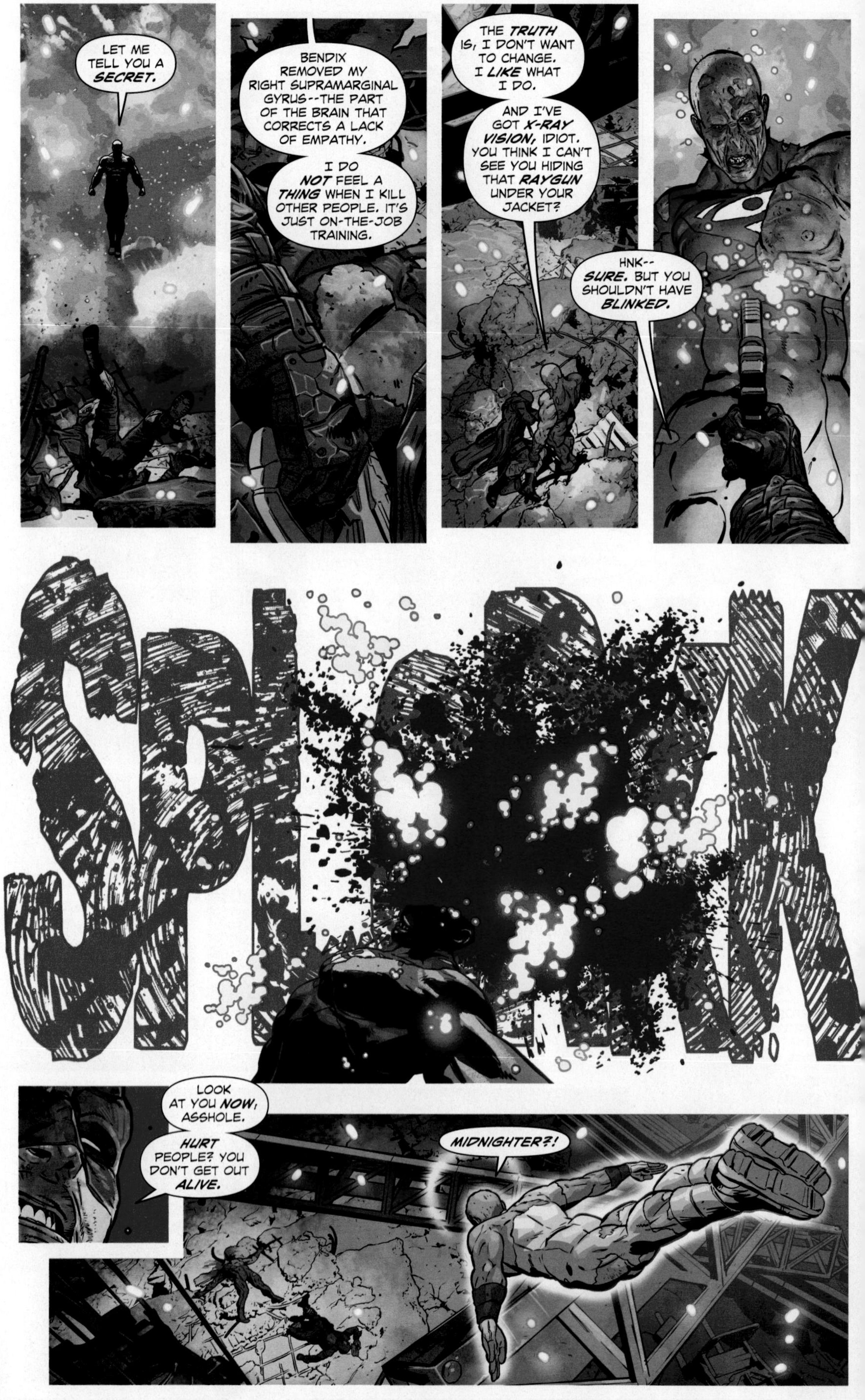
LET ME TELL YOU A SECRET.
BENDIX REMOVED MY RIGHT SUPRAMARGINAL GYRUS--THE PART OF THE BRAIN THAT CORRECTS A LACK OF EMPATHY.
I DO NOT FEEL A THING WHEN I KILL OTHER PEOPLE. IT'S JUST ON-THE-JOB TRAINING.
THE TRUTH IS, I DON'T WANT TO CHANGE. I LIKE WHAT I DO.
AND I'VE GOT X-RAY VISION, IDIOT. YOU THINK I CAN'T SEE YOU HIDING THAT RAYGUN UNDER YOUR JACKET?
HNK-- SURE. BUT YOU SHOULDN'T HAVE BLINKED.
LOOK AT YOU NOW, ASSHOLE.
HURT PEOPLE? YOU DON'T GET OUT ALIVE.
MIDNIGHTER?!

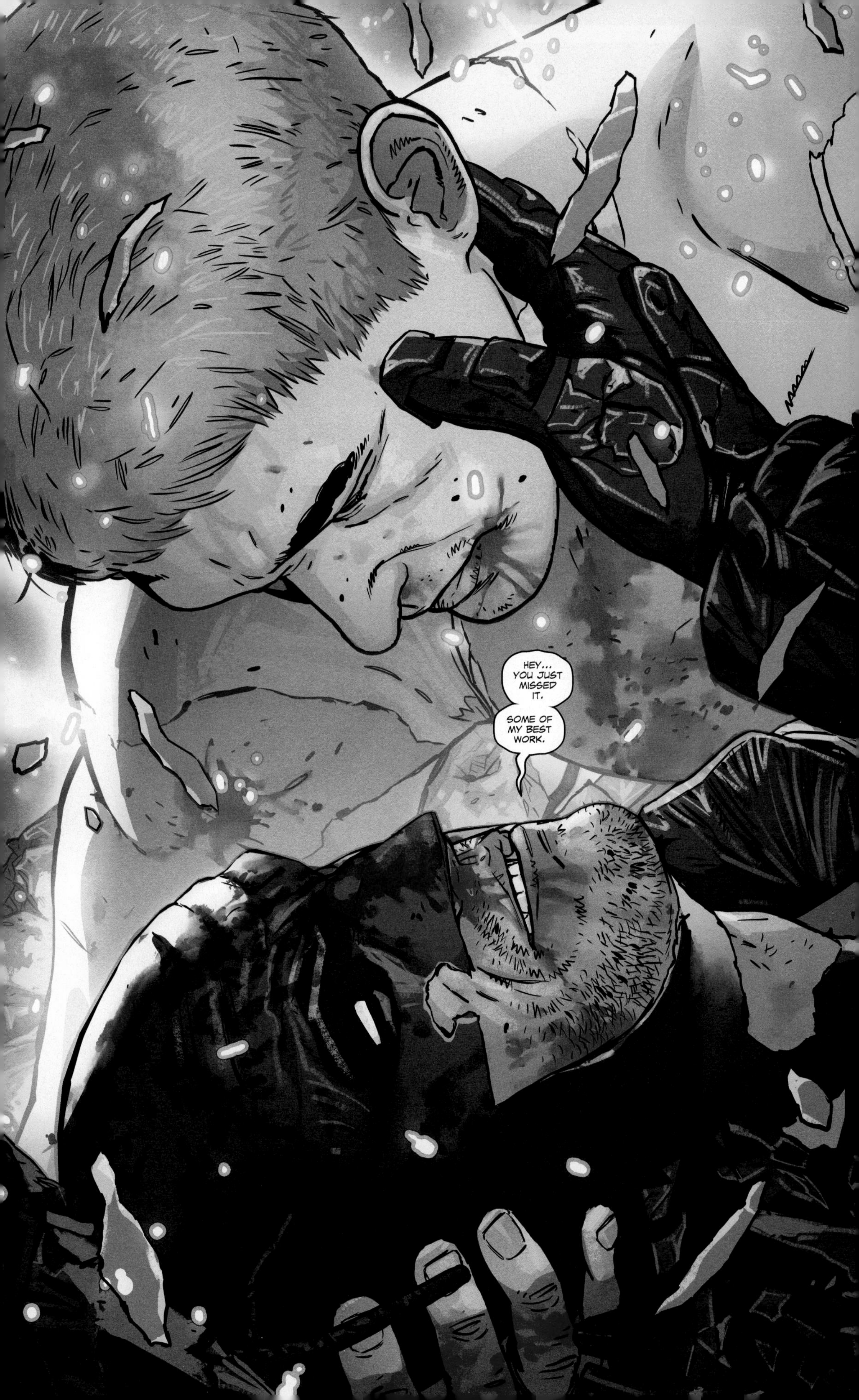
HEY... YOU JUST MISSED IT.
SOME OF MY BEST WORK.

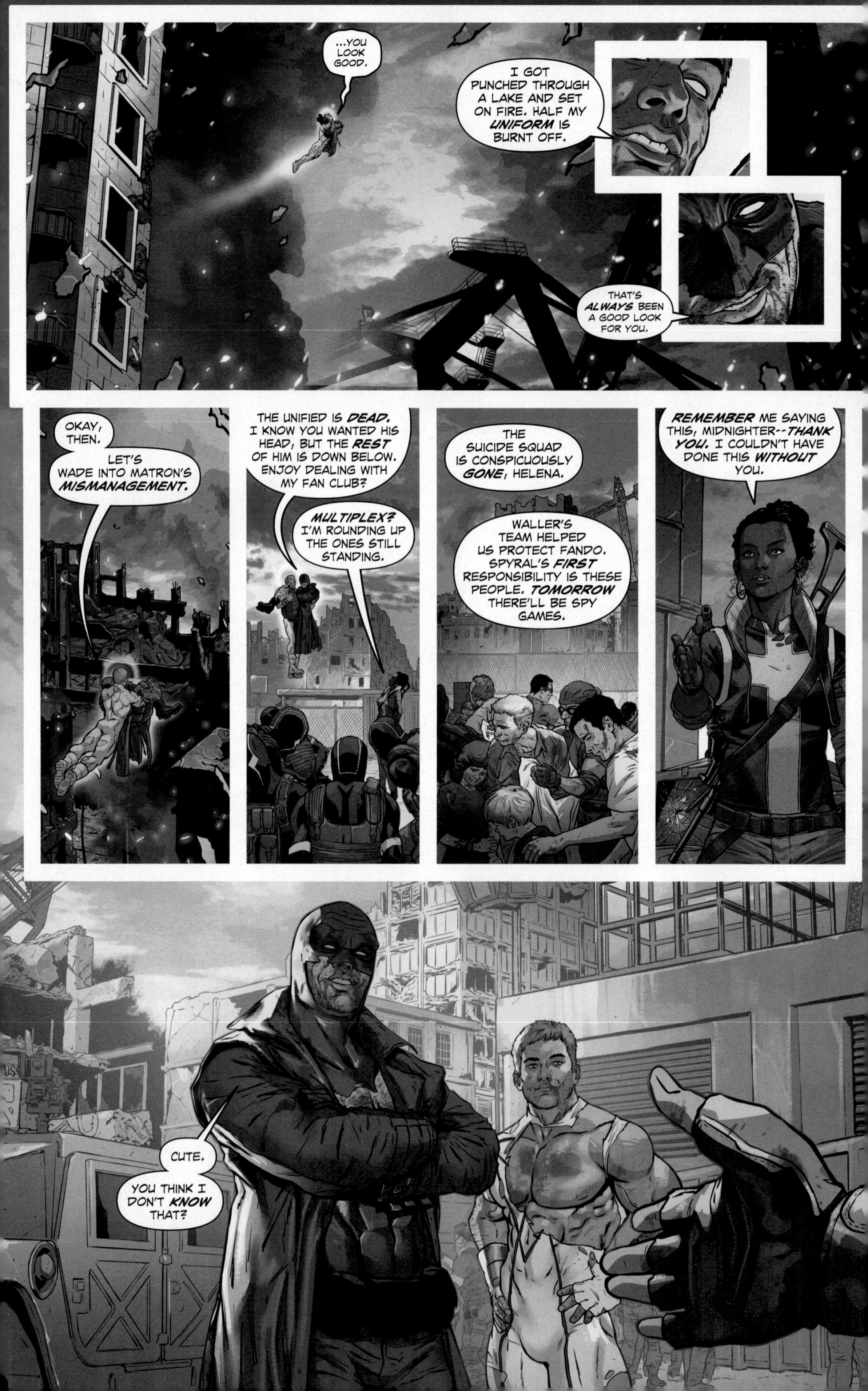
...YOU LOOK GOOD.
I GOT PUNCHED THROUGH A LAKE AND SET ON FIRE. HALF MY UNIFORM IS BURNT OFF.
THAT'S ALWAYS BEEN A GOOD LOOK FOR YOU.
OKAY, THEN.
LET'S WADE INTO MATRON'S MISMANAGEMENT.
THE UNIFIED IS DEAD. I KNOW YOU WANTED HIS HEAD, BUT THE REST OF HIM IS DOWN BELOW. ENJOY DEALING WITH MY FAN CLUB?
MULTIPLEX? I'M ROUNDING UP THE ONES STILL STANDING.
THE SUICIDE SQUAD IS CONSPICUOUSLY GONE, HELENA.
WALLER'S TEAM HELPED US PROTECT FANDO. SPYRAL'S FIRST RESPONSIBILITY IS THESE PEOPLE. TOMORROW THERE'LL BE SPY GAMES.
REMEMBER ME SAYING THIS, MIDNIGHTER--THANK YOU. I COULDN'T HAVE DONE THIS WITHOUT YOU.
CUTE.
YOU THINK I DON'T KNOW THAT?

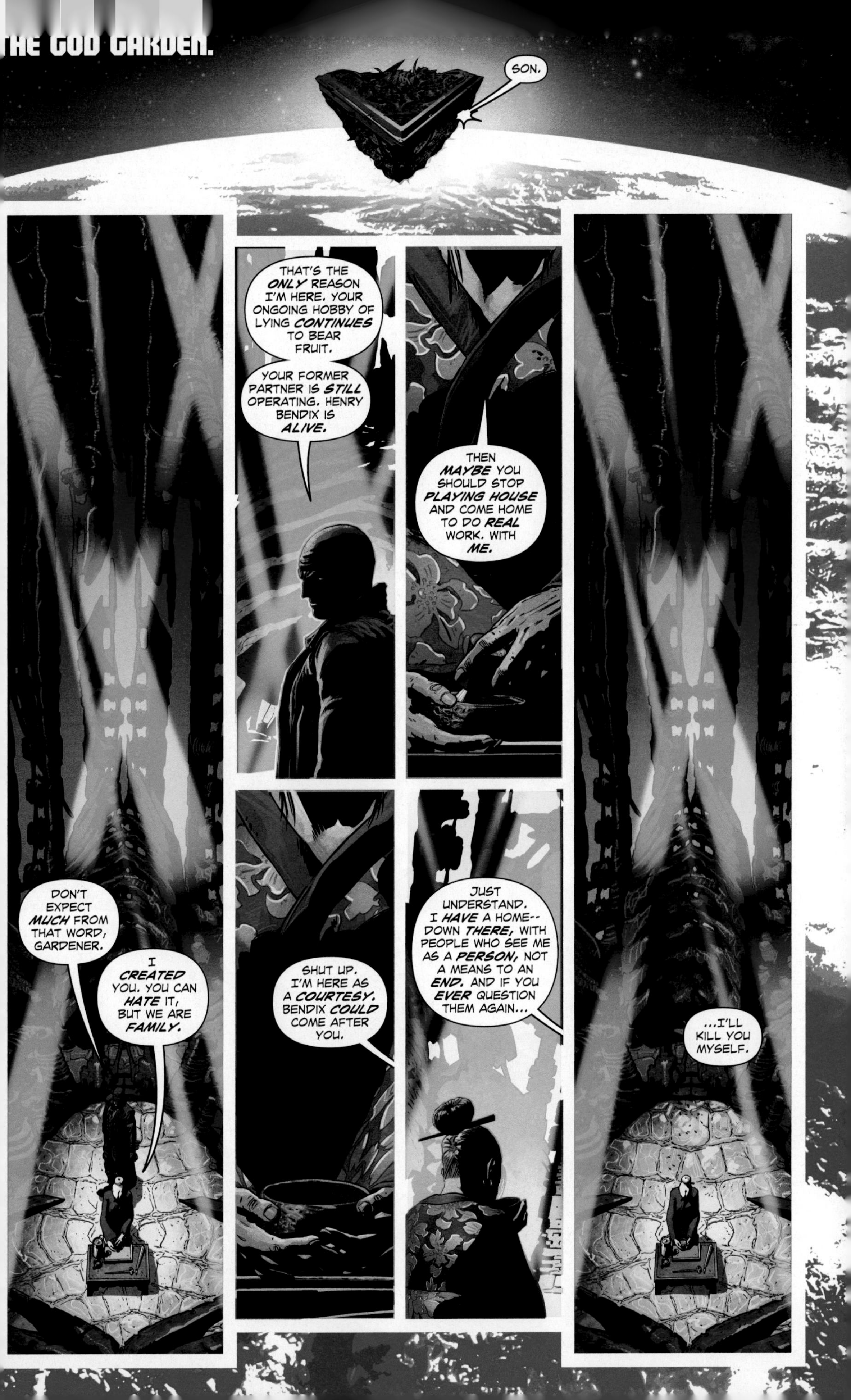
THE GOD GARDEN.
SON.
THAT'S THE ONLY REASON I'M HERE. YOUR ONGOING HOBBY OF LYING CONTINUES TO BEAR FRUIT.
YOUR FORMER PARTNER IS STILL OPERATING. HENRY BENDIX IS ALIVE.
THEN MAYBE YOU SHOULD STOP PLAYING HOUSE AND COME HOME TO DO REAL WORK. WITH ME.
DON'T EXPECT MUCH FROM THAT WORD, GARDENER.
I CREATED YOU. YOU CAN HATE IT, BUT WE ARE FAMILY.
SHUT UP. I'M HERE AS A COURTESY. BENDIX COULD COME AFTER YOU.
JUST UNDERSTAND. I HAVE A HOME-- DOWN THERE, WITH PEOPLE WHO SEE ME AS A PERSON, NOT A MEANS TO AN END. AND IF YOU EVER QUESTION THEM AGAIN...
...I'LL KILL YOU MYSELF.

BOSTON.

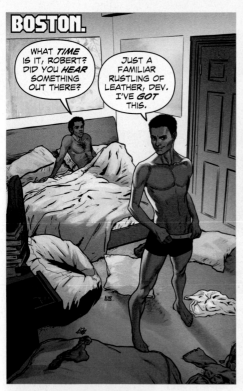

WHAT *TIME* IS IT, ROBERT? DID YOU *HEAR* SOMETHING OUT THERE?

JUST A FAMILIAR RUSTLING OF LEATHER, DEV. I'VE *GOT* THIS.

WE *ALMOST* STARTED WITHOUT YOU.

THANKS FOR *WARMING* HIM UP, WILL. SO, MIDNIGHTER, YOU GET *BLOWN UP.* YOU *DISAPPEAR.* YOUR BOSS DROPS ME HERE WITH AN N.D.A. AND A WAGGED FINGER. THEN I SEE YOU PUNCHING YOUR WAY AROUND THE *BALKANS* ON THE NEWS.

ANYTHING YOU WANT TO *TELL* ME?

I GOT HELD UP.

BUT, UNLESS I'M WRONG, YOU'VE GOT A *DOCUMENTARY* TO FINISH. WANT TO TELL PEOPLE MY *STORY.* GOOD *AND* BAD.

OKAY. YOUR *KIDNAPPING* AS A CHILD. YOUR *MANIPULATION.* THE *ATTACK* BY PROMETHEUS. YOUR *SURVIVOR* STORY. *READY* TO CONTINUE?

I'M *PERPETUALLY* READY.

GREAT. THEN TELL ME--WHAT'S *NEXT* FOR MIDNIGHTER?

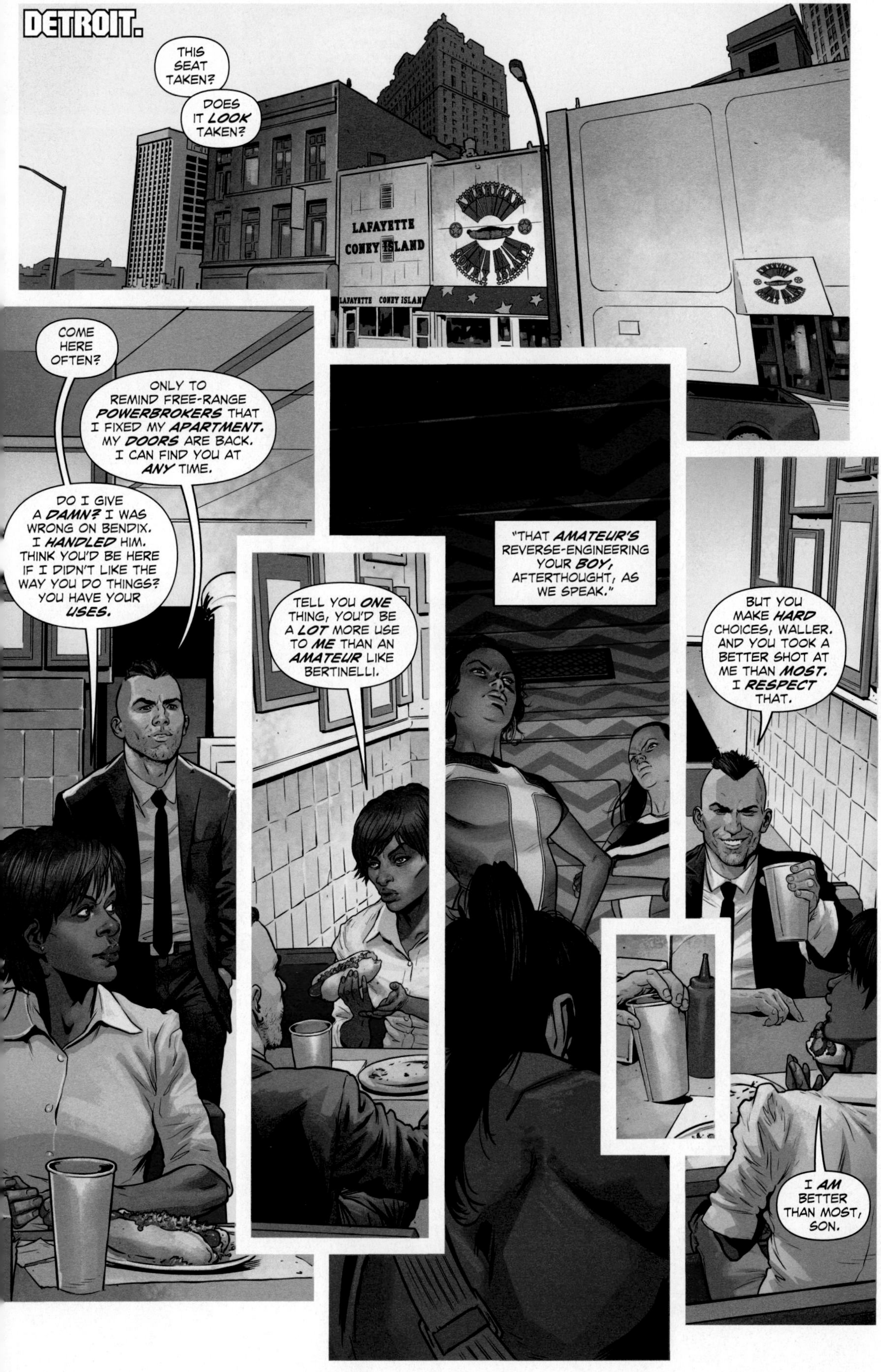
DETROIT.
THIS SEAT TAKEN?
DOES IT LOOK TAKEN?
LAFAYETTE CONEY ISLAND
AMERICAN CONEY ISLAND
LAFAYETTE CONEY ISLAND
COME HERE OFTEN?
ONLY TO REMIND FREE-RANGE POWERBROKERS THAT I FIXED MY APARTMENT. MY DOORS ARE BACK. I CAN FIND YOU AT ANY TIME.
DO I GIVE A DAMN? I WAS WRONG ON BENDIX. I HANDLED HIM. THINK YOU'D BE HERE IF I DIDN'T LIKE THE WAY YOU DO THINGS? YOU HAVE YOUR USES.
TELL YOU ONE THING, YOU'D BE A LOT MORE USE TO ME THAN AN AMATEUR LIKE BERTINELLI.
"THAT AMATEUR'S REVERSE-ENGINEERING YOUR BOY, AFTERTHOUGHT, AS WE SPEAK."
BUT YOU MAKE HARD CHOICES, WALLER. AND YOU TOOK A BETTER SHOT AT ME THAN MOST. I RESPECT THAT.
I AM BETTER THAN MOST, SON.

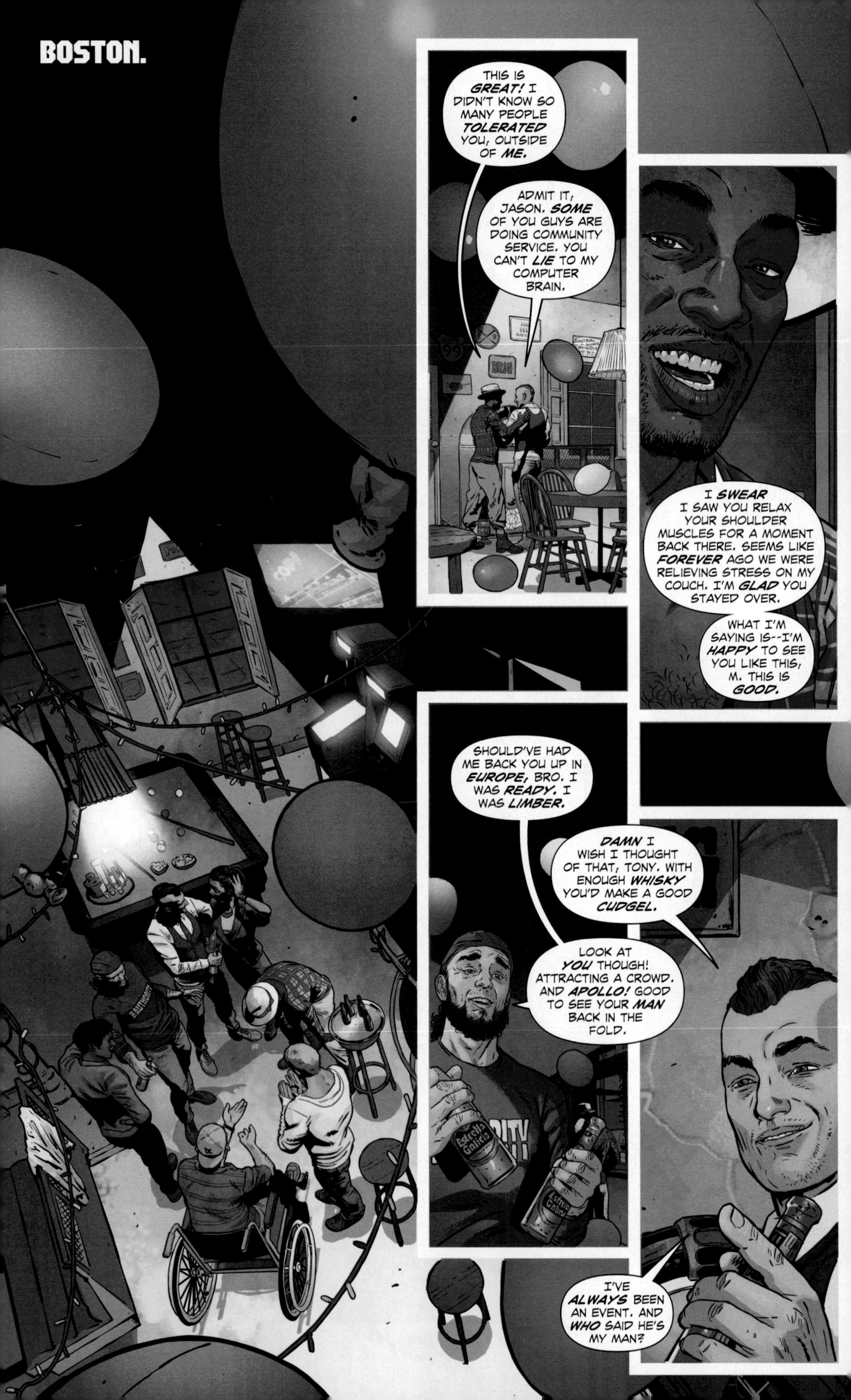
BOSTON.
THIS IS GREAT! I DIDN'T KNOW SO MANY PEOPLE TOLERATED YOU, OUTSIDE OF ME.
ADMIT IT, JASON. SOME OF YOU GUYS ARE DOING COMMUNITY SERVICE. YOU CAN'T LIE TO MY COMPUTER BRAIN.
BRIG
I SWEAR I SAW YOU RELAX YOUR SHOULDER MUSCLES FOR A MOMENT BACK THERE. SEEMS LIKE FOREVER AGO WE WERE RELIEVING STRESS ON MY COUCH. I'M GLAD YOU STAYED OVER.
WHAT I'M SAYING IS--I'M HAPPY TO SEE YOU LIKE THIS, M. THIS IS GOOD.
SHOULD'VE HAD ME BACK YOU UP IN EUROPE, BRO. I WAS READY. I WAS LIMBER.
DAMN I WISH I THOUGHT OF THAT, TONY. WITH ENOUGH WHISKY YOU'D MAKE A GOOD CUDGEL.
LOOK AT YOU THOUGH! ATTRACTING A CROWD. AND APOLLO! GOOD TO SEE YOUR MAN BACK IN THE FOLD.
I'VE ALWAYS BEEN AN EVENT. AND WHO SAID HE'S MY MAN?

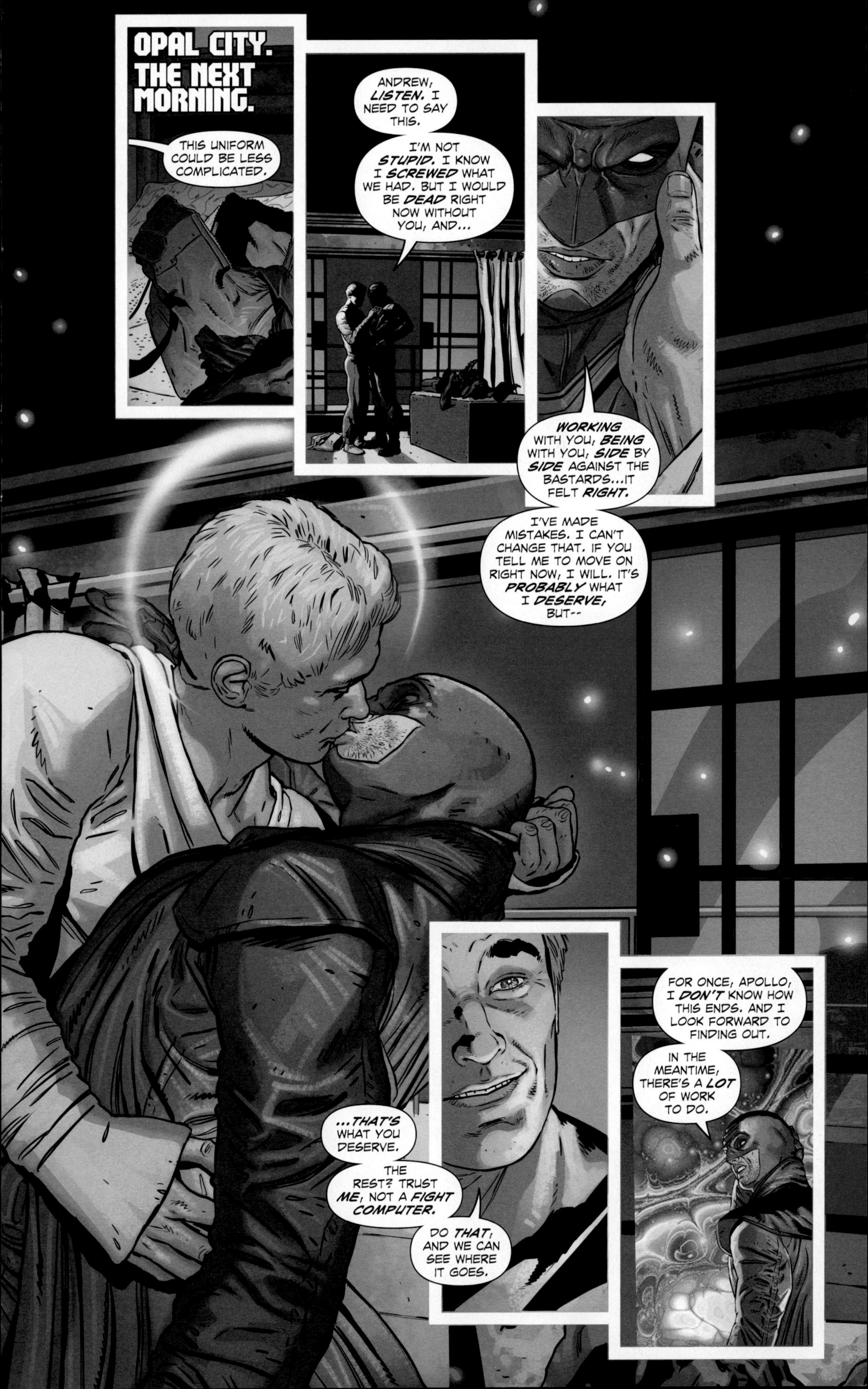
OPAL CITY. THE NEXT MORNING.
THIS UNIFORM COULD BE LESS COMPLICATED.
ANDREW, LISTEN. I NEED TO SAY THIS.
I'M NOT STUPID. I KNOW I SCREWED WHAT WE HAD. BUT I WOULD BE DEAD RIGHT NOW WITHOUT YOU, AND...
WORKING WITH YOU, BEING WITH YOU, SIDE BY SIDE AGAINST THE BASTARDS...IT FELT RIGHT.
I'VE MADE MISTAKES. I CAN'T CHANGE THAT. IF YOU TELL ME TO MOVE ON RIGHT NOW, I WILL. IT'S PROBABLY WHAT I DESERVE, BUT--
...THAT'S WHAT YOU DESERVE.
THE REST? TRUST ME, NOT A FIGHT COMPUTER.
DO THAT, AND WE CAN SEE WHERE IT GOES.
FOR ONCE, APOLLO, I DON'T KNOW HOW THIS ENDS. AND I LOOK FORWARD TO FINDING OUT.
IN THE MEANTIME, THERE'S A LOT OF WORK TO DO.

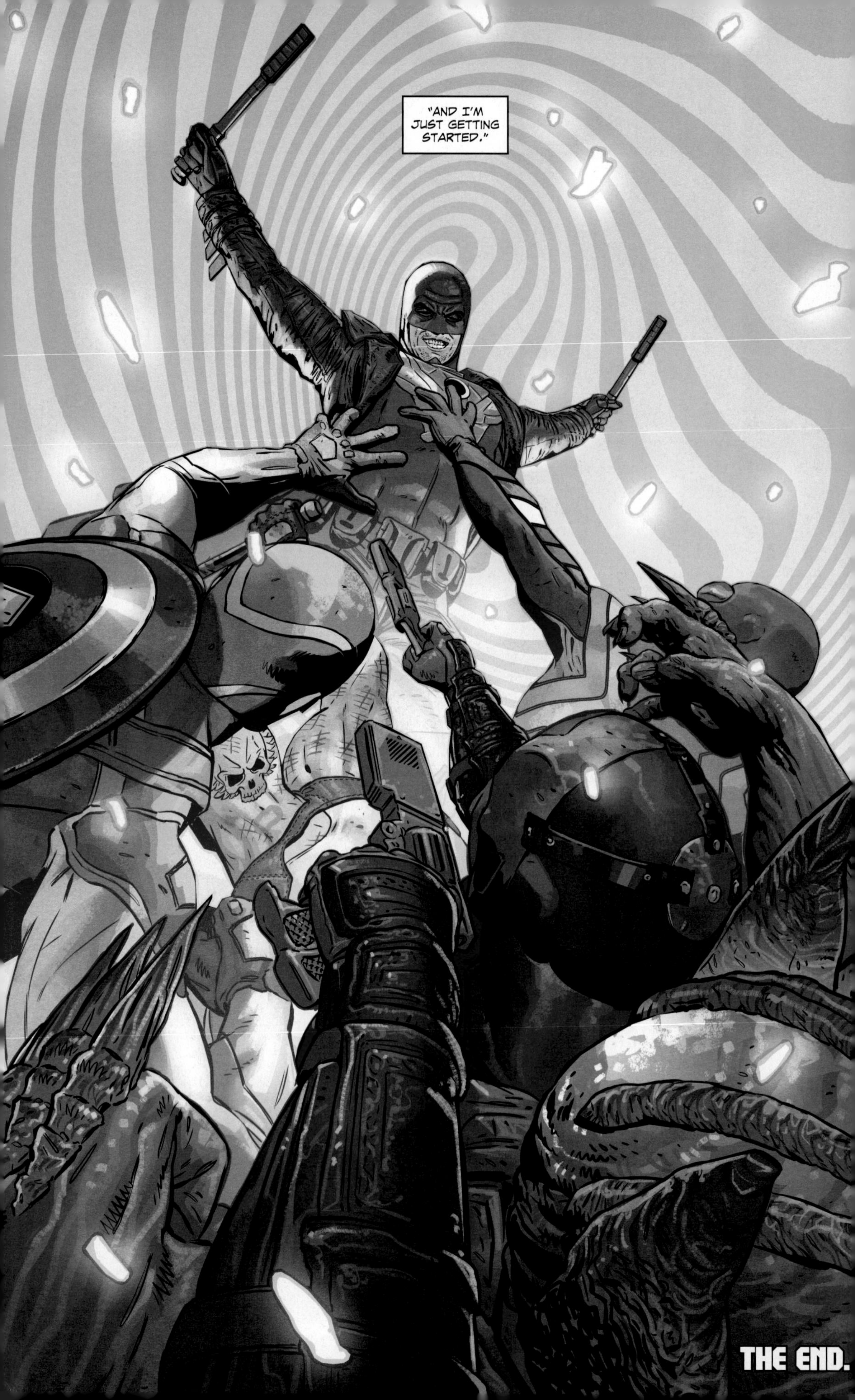
"AND I'M JUST GETTING STARTED."
THE END.

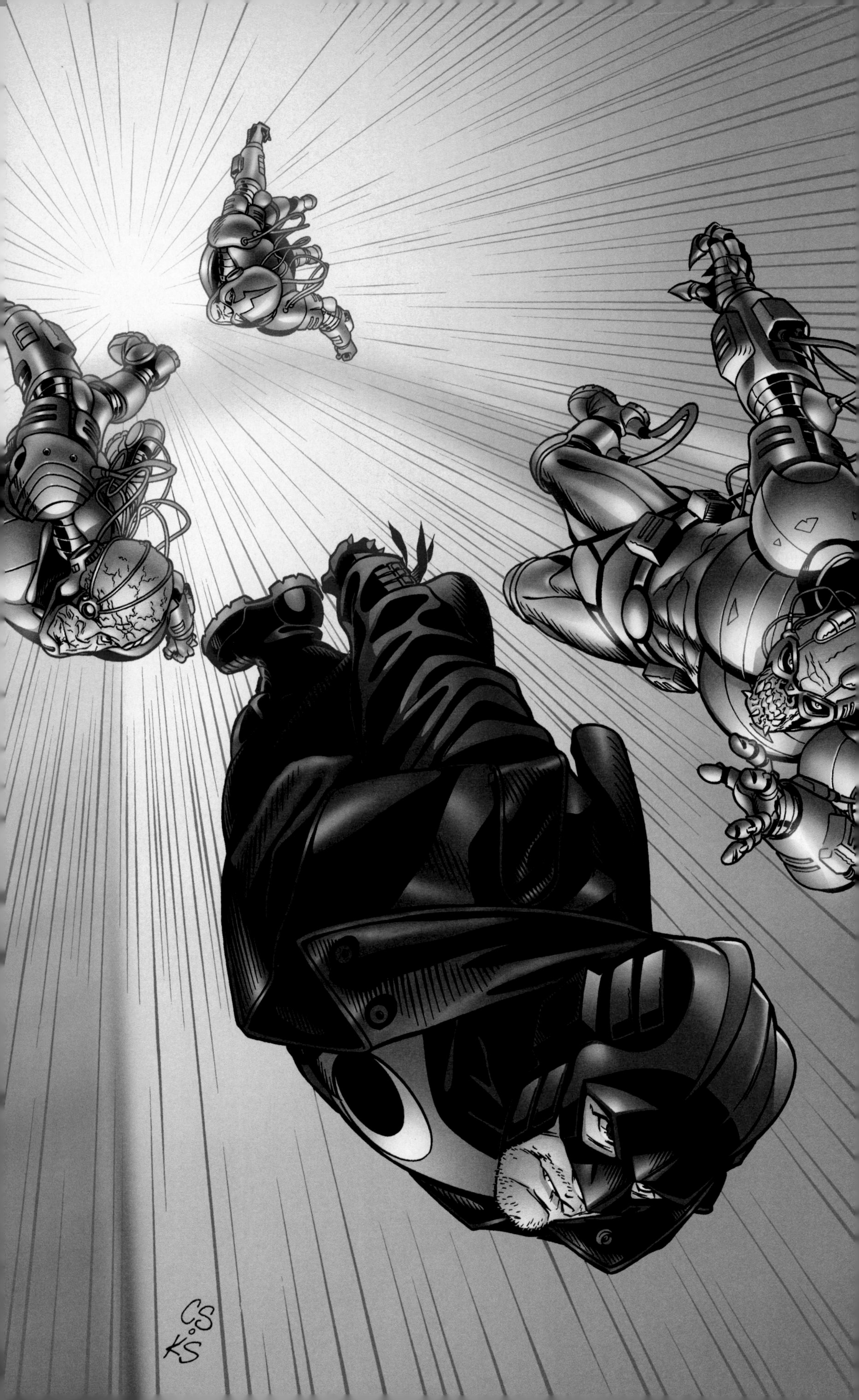
CS
KS

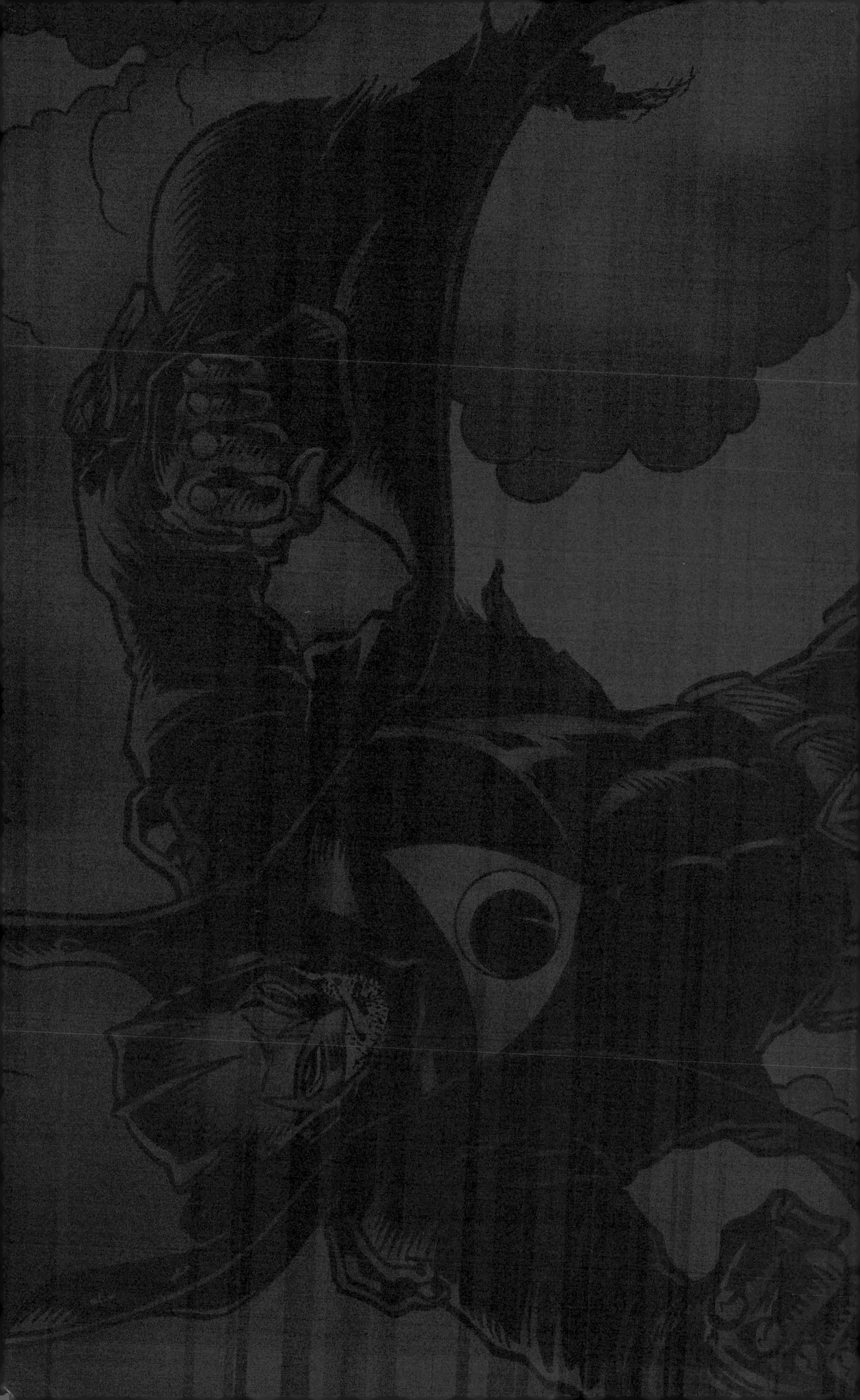

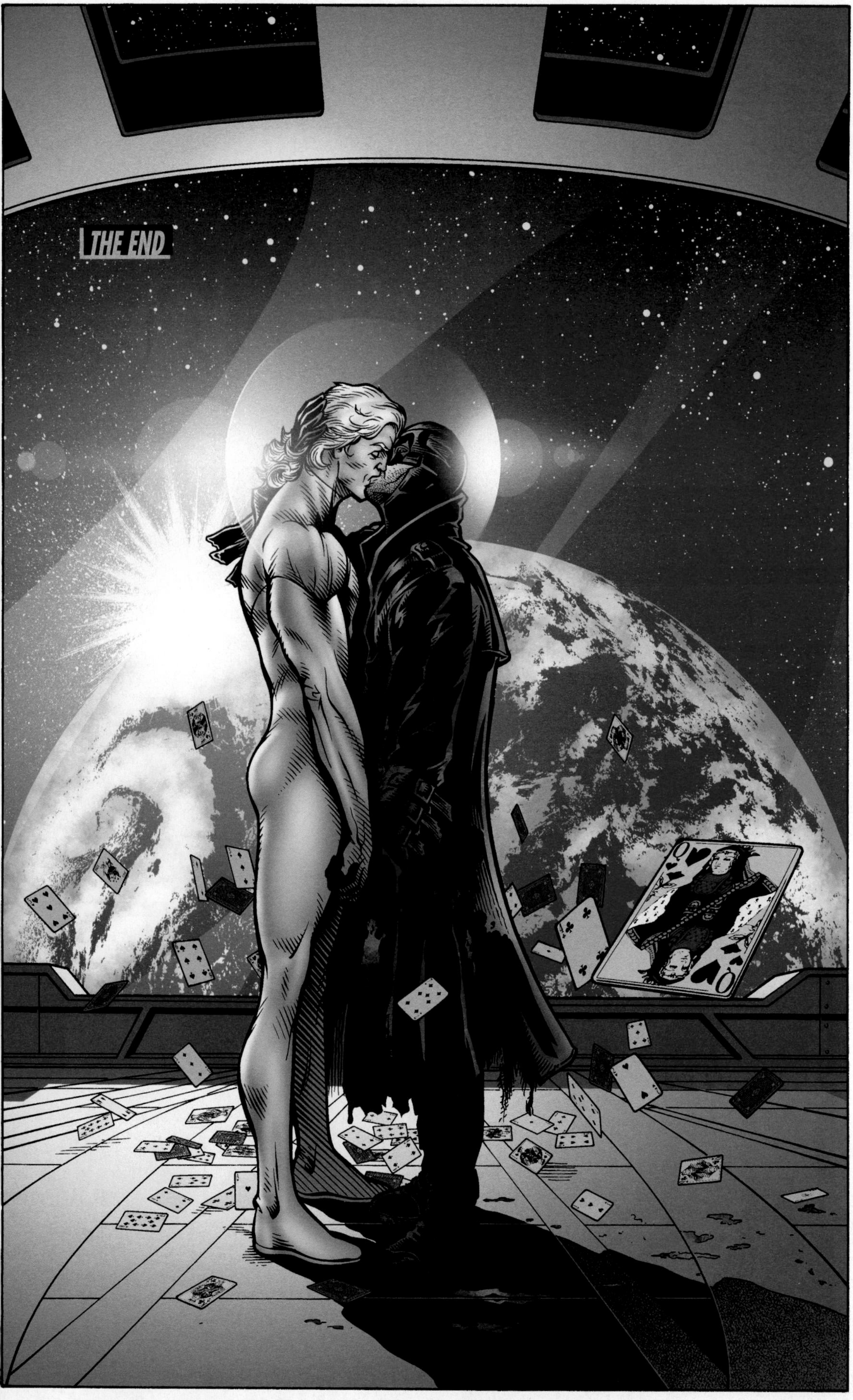
THE END

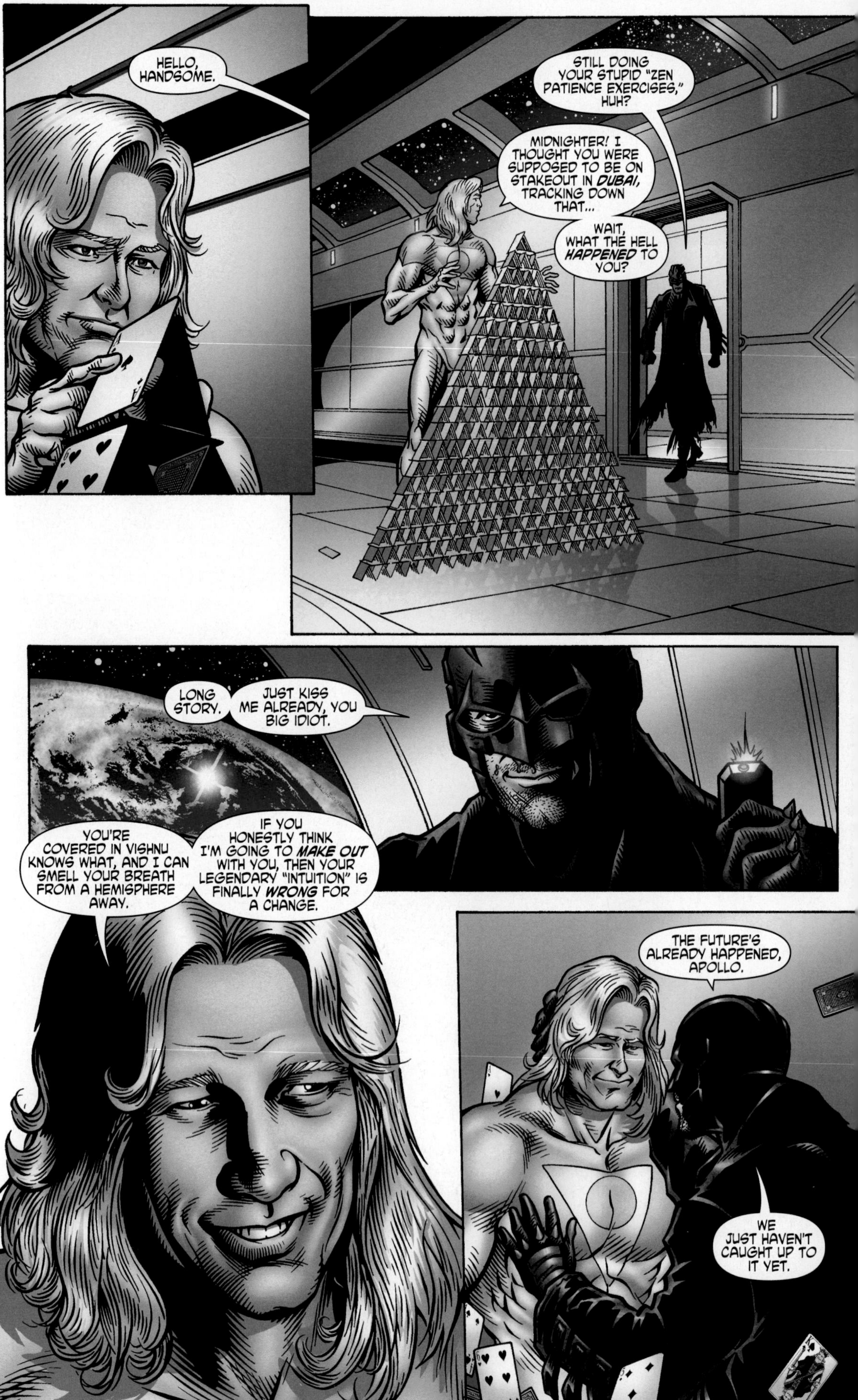
HELLO, HANDSOME.
STILL DOING YOUR STUPID "ZEN PATIENCE EXERCISES," HUH?
MIDNIGHTER! I THOUGHT YOU WERE SUPPOSED TO BE ON STAKEOUT IN DUBAI, TRACKING DOWN THAT...
WAIT, WHAT THE HELL HAPPENED TO YOU?
LONG STORY.
JUST KISS ME ALREADY, YOU BIG IDIOT.
YOU'RE COVERED IN VISHNU KNOWS WHAT, AND I CAN SMELL YOUR BREATH FROM A HEMISPHERE AWAY.
IF YOU HONESTLY THINK I'M GOING TO MAKE OUT WITH YOU, THEN YOUR LEGENDARY "INTUITION" IS FINALLY WRONG FOR A CHANGE.
THE FUTURE'S ALREADY HAPPENED, APOLLO.
WE JUST HAVEN'T CAUGHT UP TO IT YET.

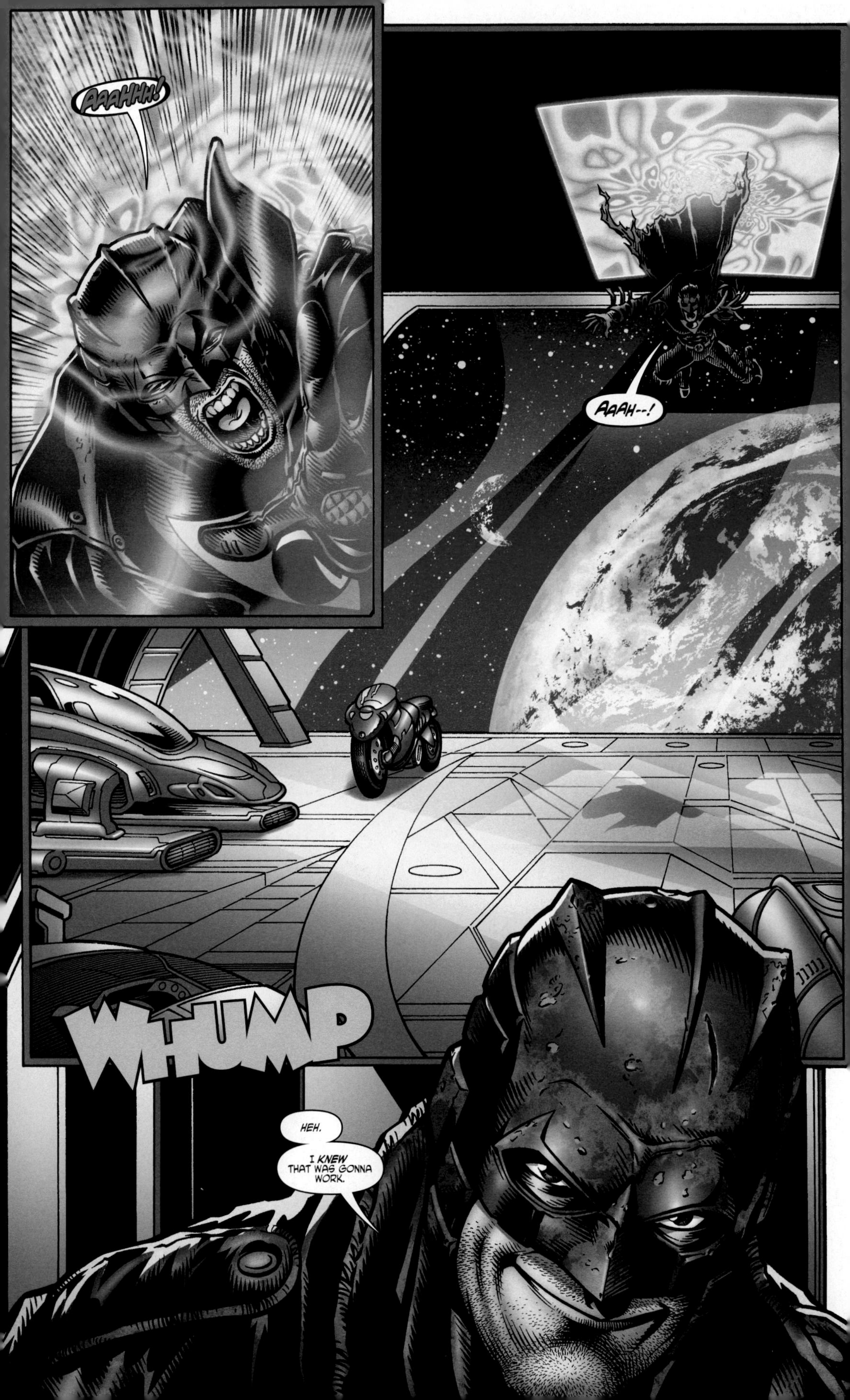
AAAHHH!
AAAH--!
WHUMP
HEH.
I KNEW THAT WAS GONNA WORK.

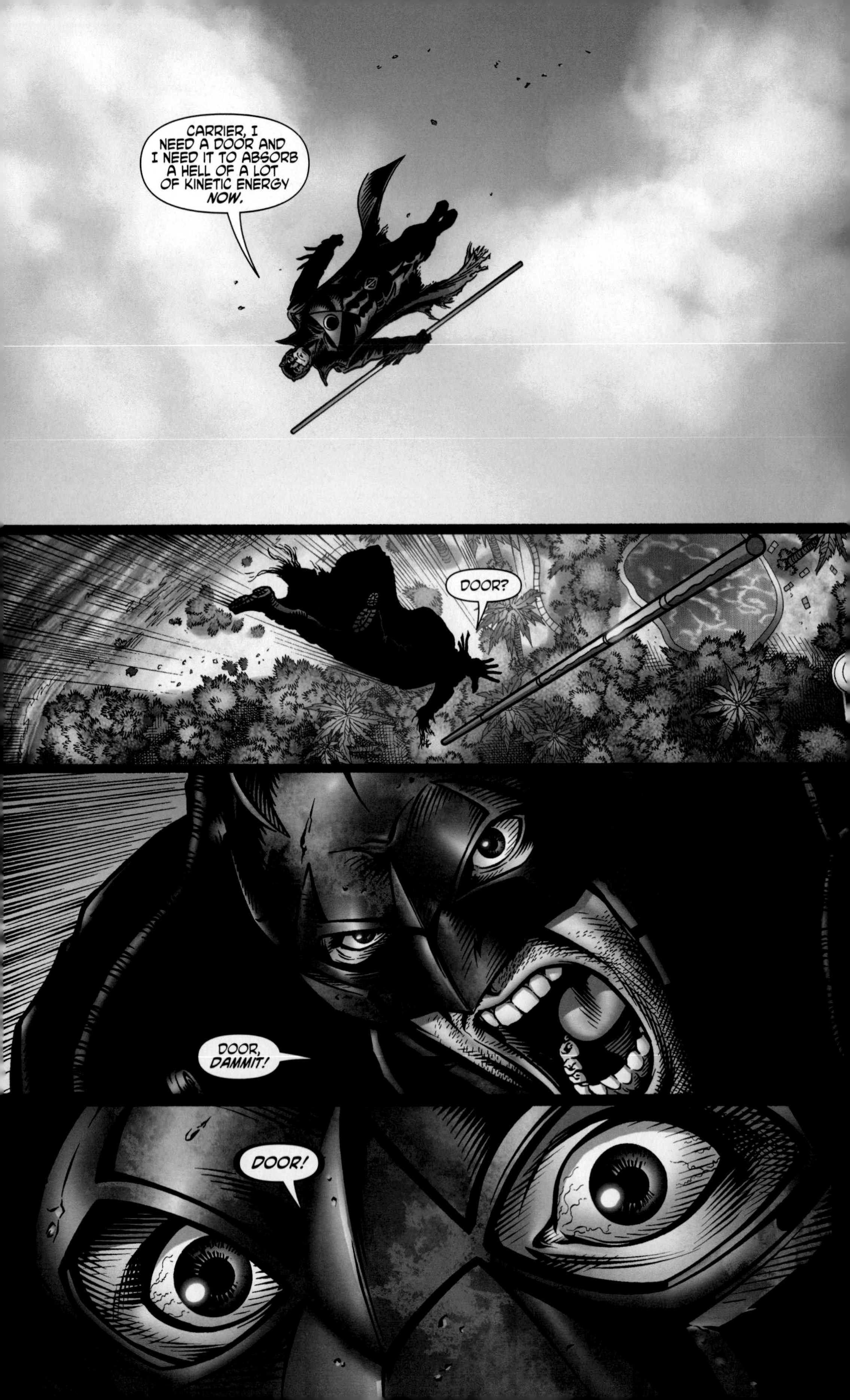
CARRIER, I NEED A DOOR AND I NEED IT TO ABSORB A HELL OF A LOT OF KINETIC ENERGY *NOW.*
DOOR?
DOOR, *DAMMIT!*
DOOR!

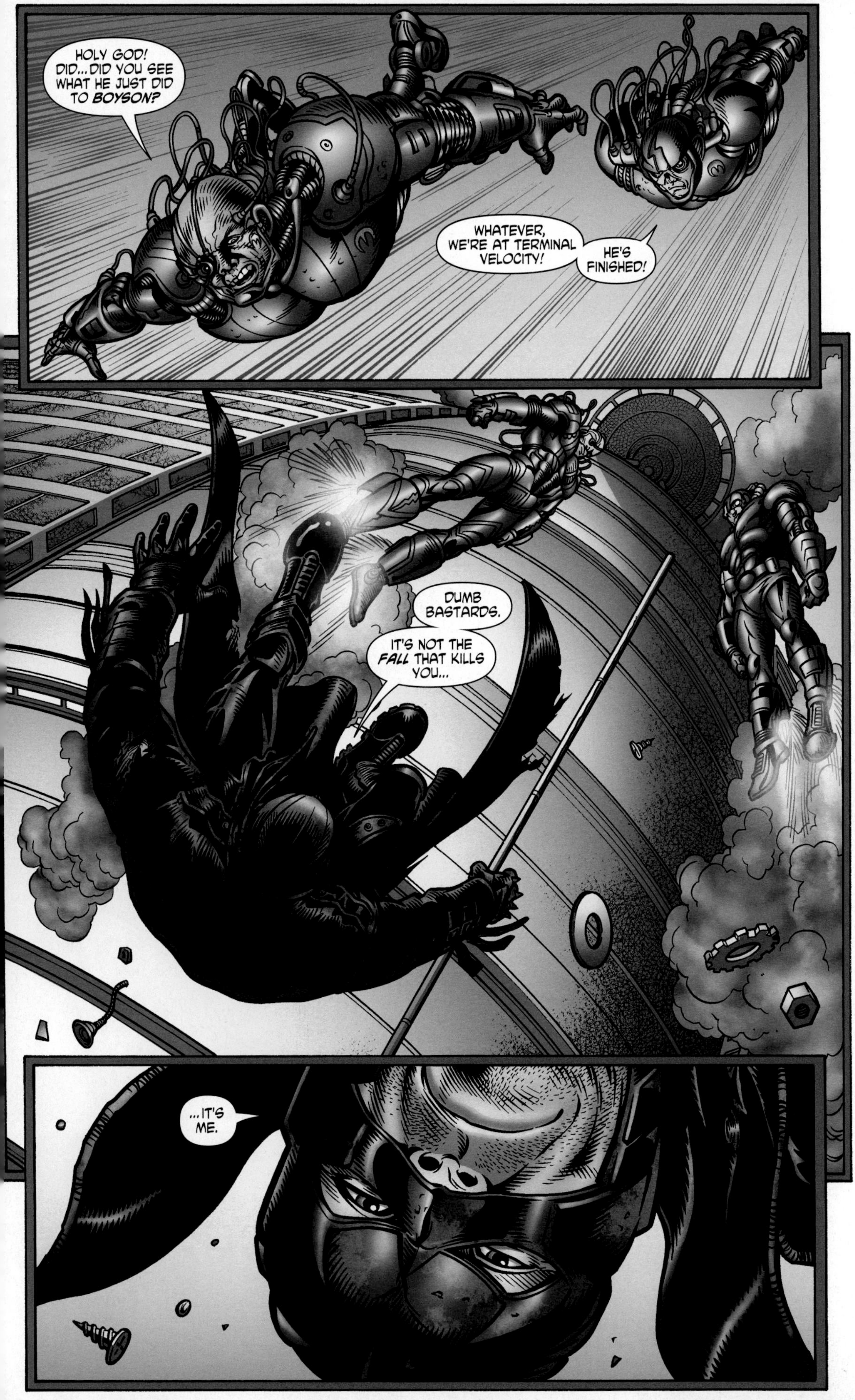
HOLY GOD! DID...DID YOU SEE WHAT HE JUST DID TO *BOYSON?*
WHATEVER, WE'RE AT TERMINAL VELOCITY!
HE'S FINISHED!
DUMB BASTARDS.
IT'S NOT THE *FALL* THAT KILLS YOU...
...IT'S ME.

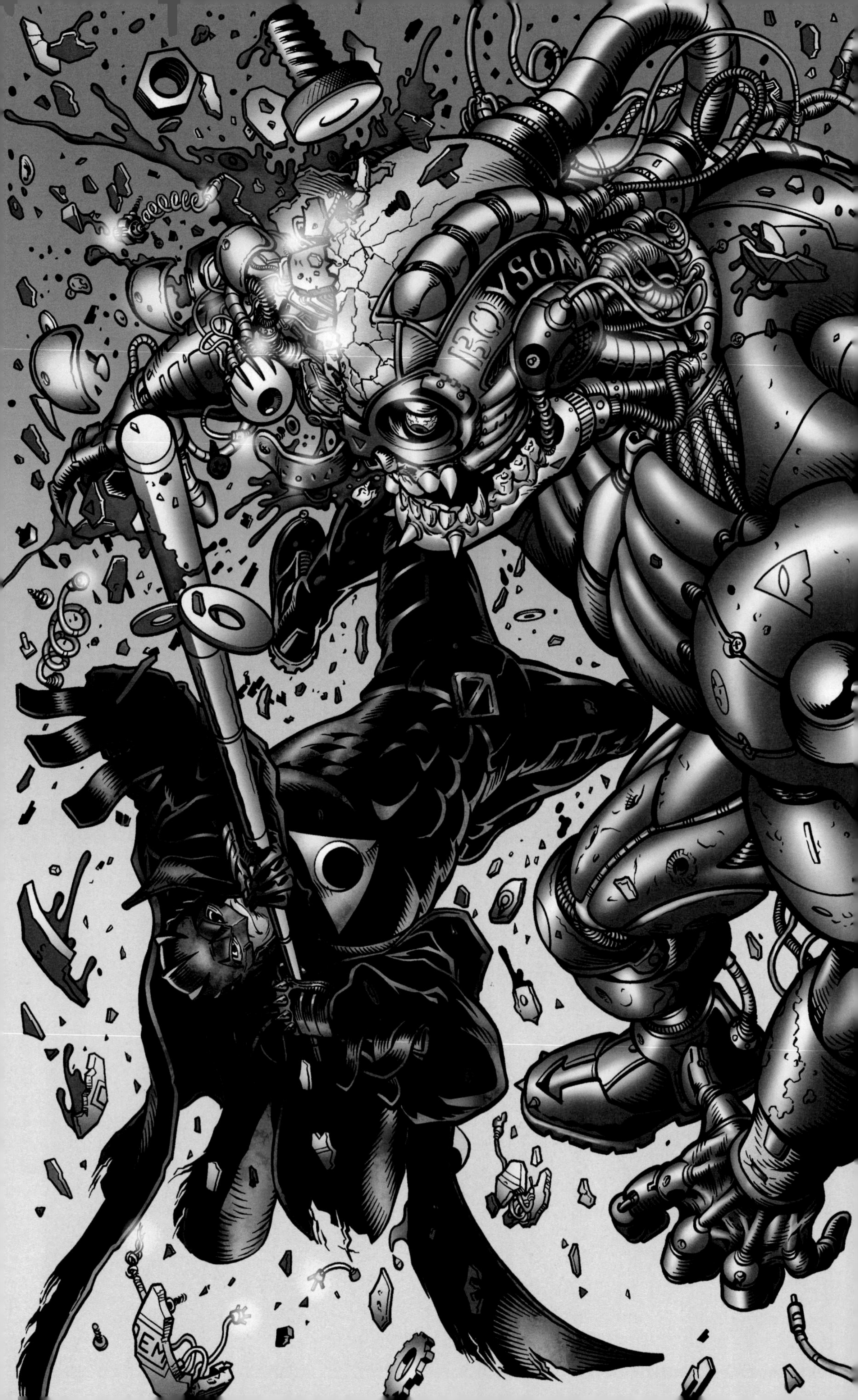

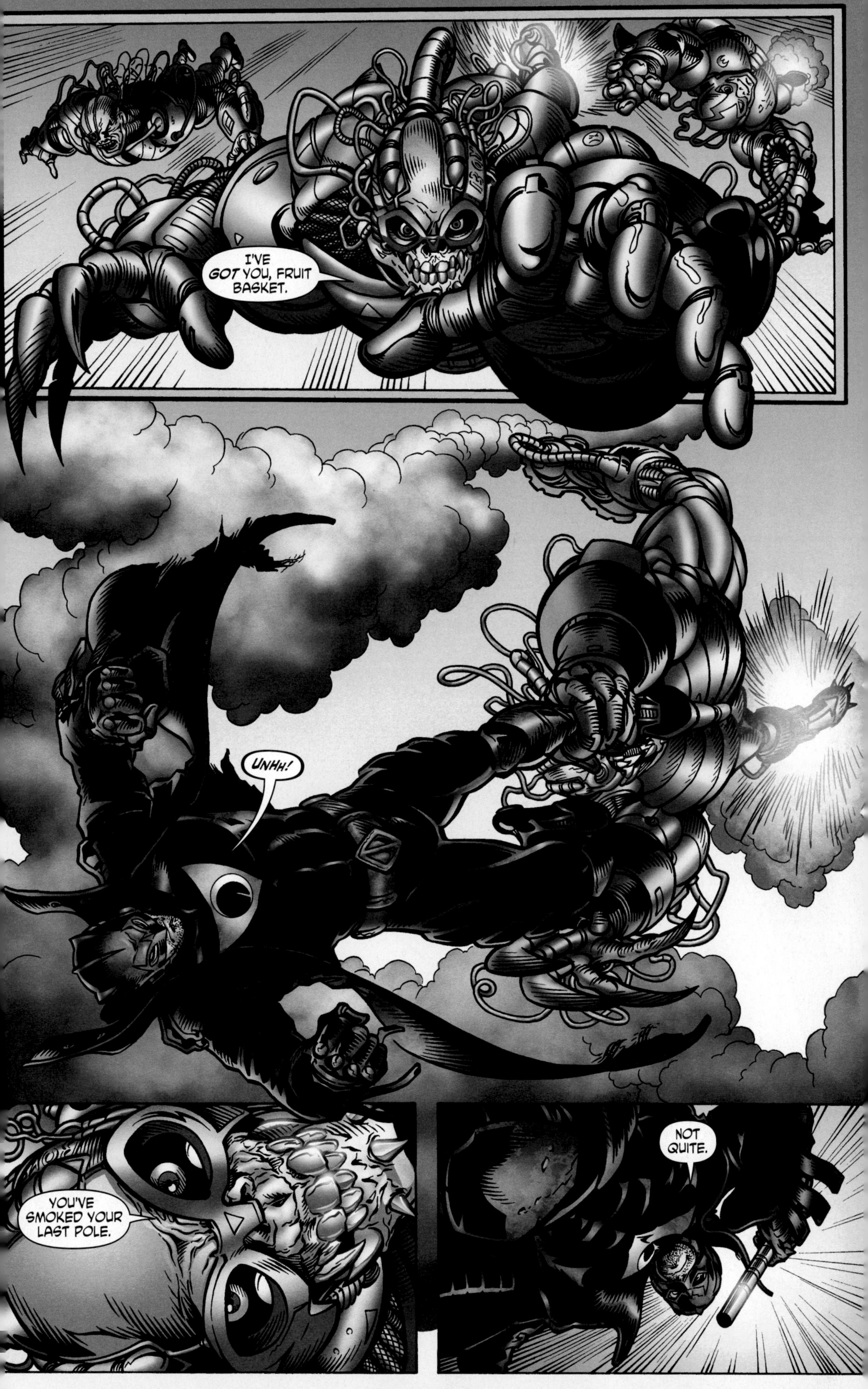
I'VE *GOT* YOU, FRUIT BASKET.
UNHH!
YOU'VE SMOKED YOUR LAST POLE.
NOT QUITE.

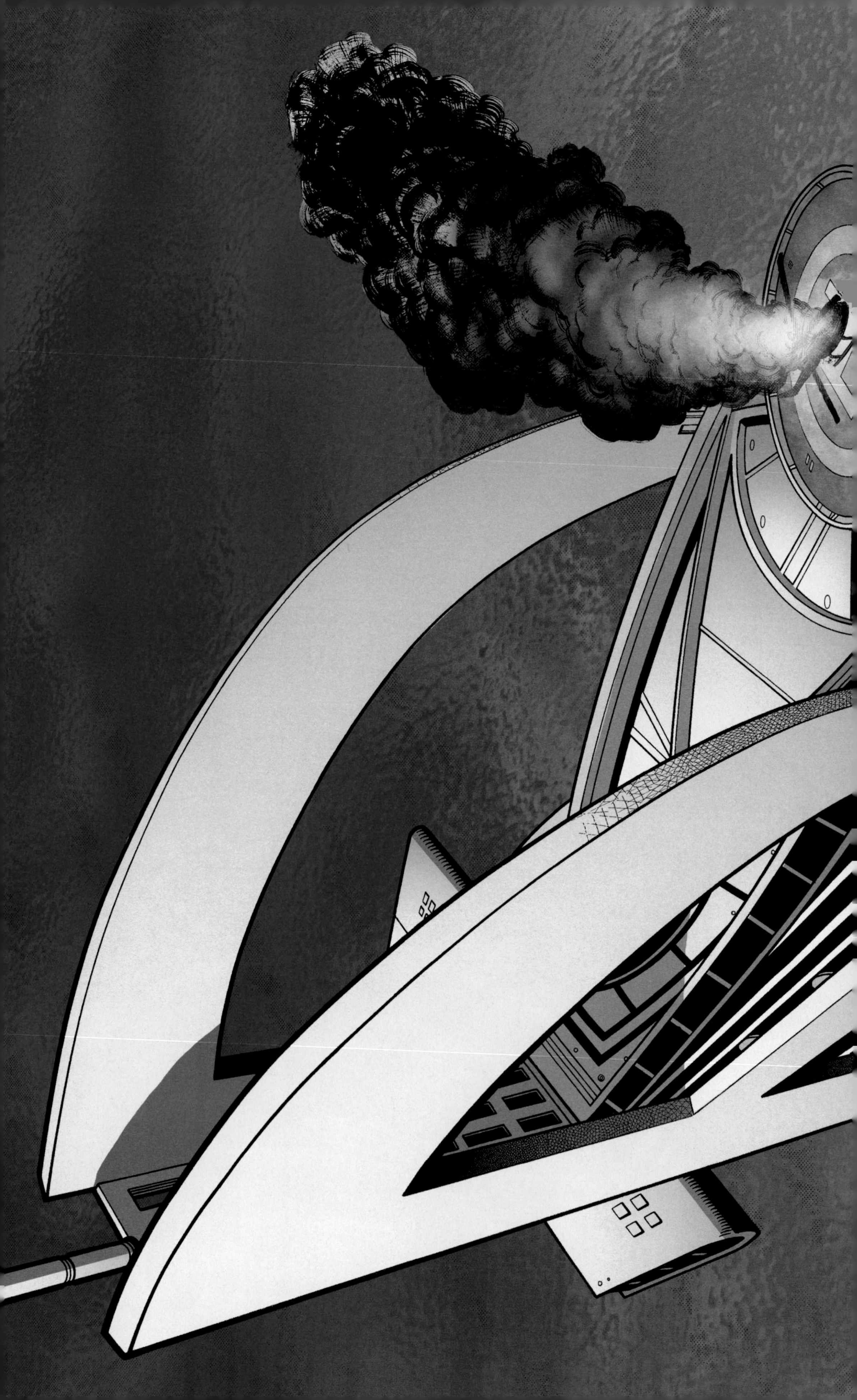

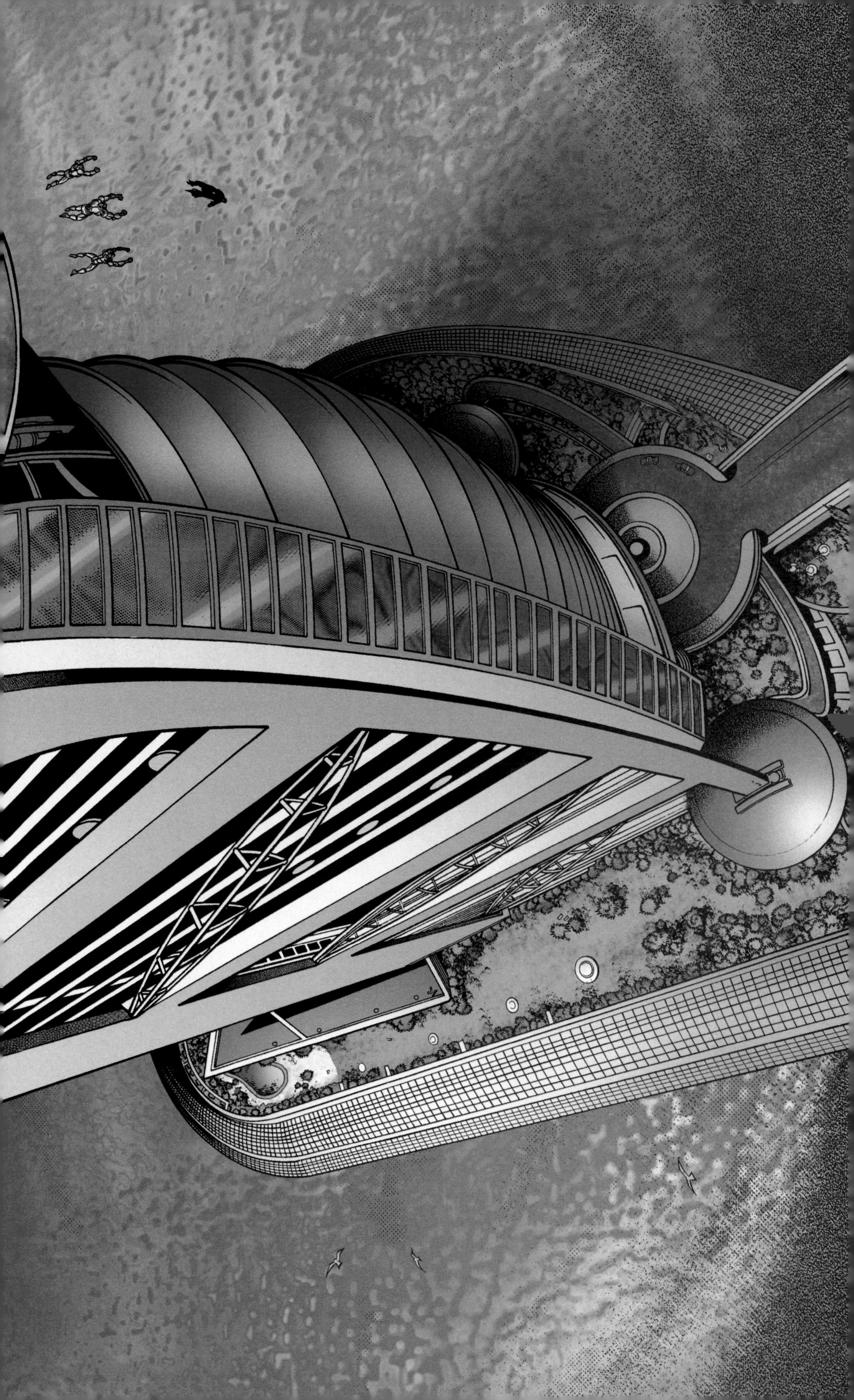

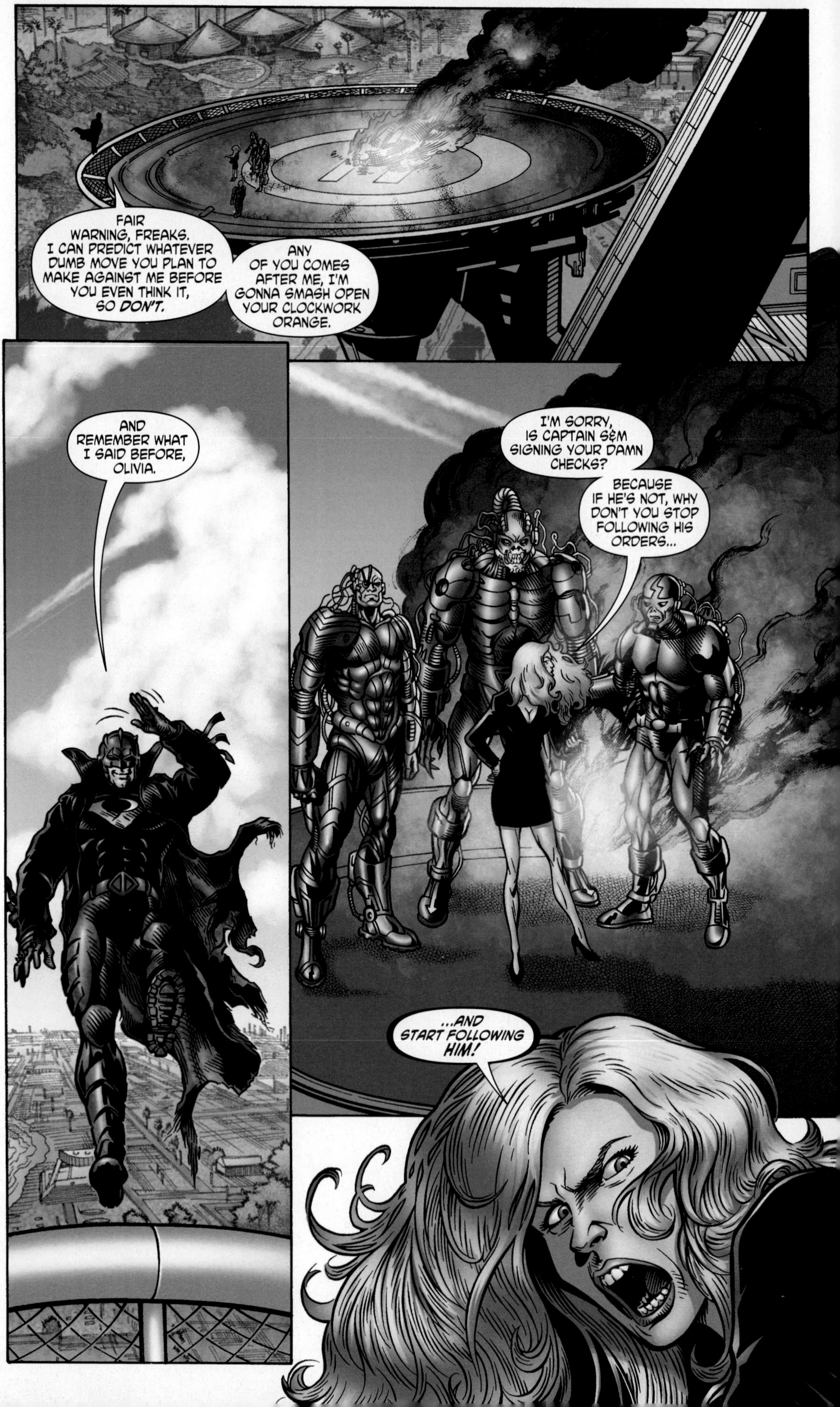
FAIR WARNING, FREAKS. I CAN PREDICT WHATEVER DUMB MOVE YOU PLAN TO MAKE AGAINST ME BEFORE YOU EVEN THINK IT, SO *DON'T.*
ANY OF YOU COMES AFTER ME, I'M GONNA SMASH OPEN YOUR CLOCKWORK ORANGE.
AND REMEMBER WHAT I SAID BEFORE, OLIVIA.
I'M SORRY, IS CAPTAIN S&M SIGNING YOUR DAMN CHECKS?
BECAUSE IF HE'S NOT, WHY DON'T YOU STOP FOLLOWING HIS ORDERS...
...AND START FOLLOWING *HIM!*

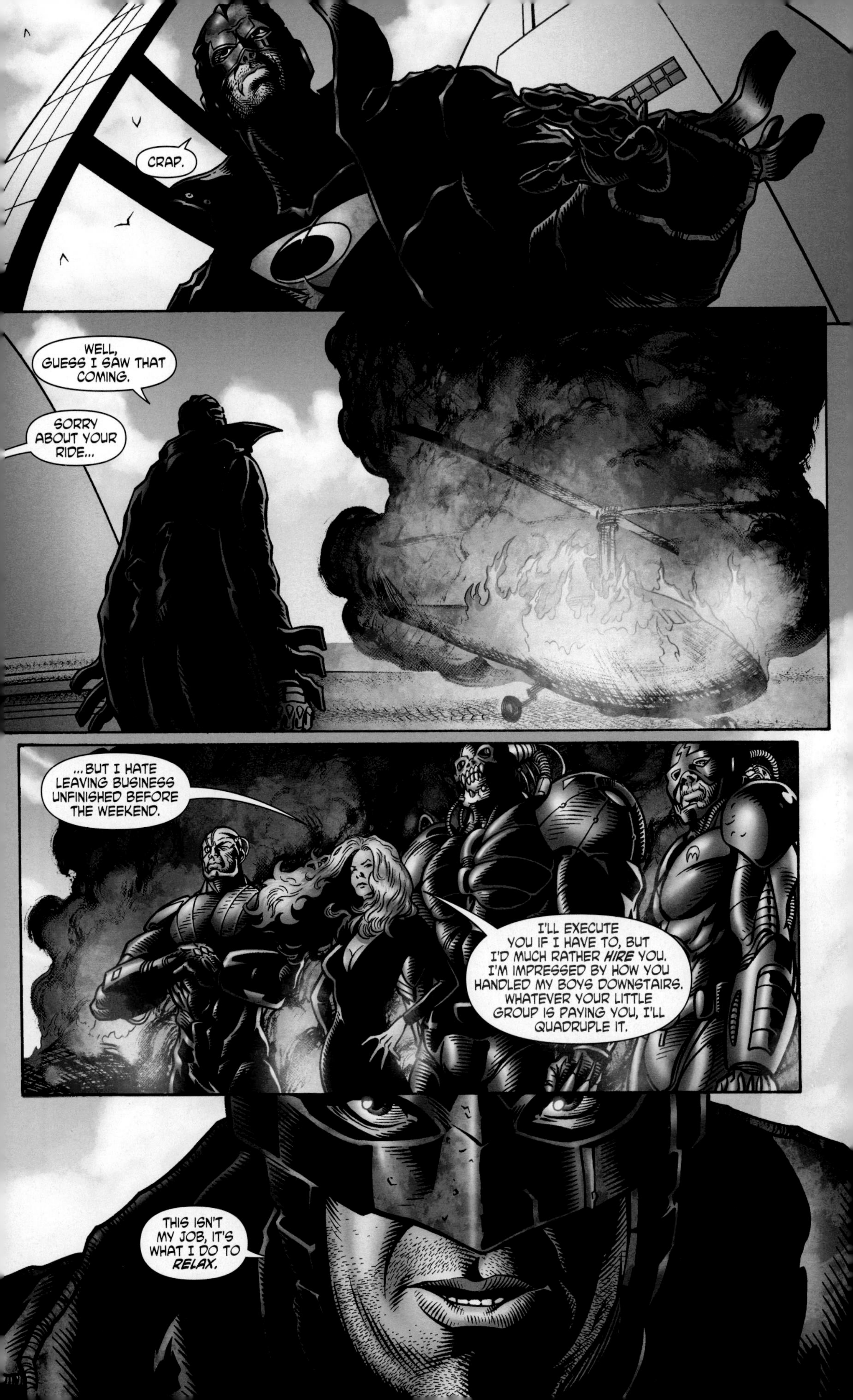
CRAP.
WELL, GUESS I SAW THAT COMING.
SORRY ABOUT YOUR RIDE...
...BUT I HATE LEAVING BUSINESS UNFINISHED BEFORE THE WEEKEND.
I'LL EXECUTE YOU IF I HAVE TO, BUT I'D MUCH RATHER HIRE YOU. I'M IMPRESSED BY HOW YOU HANDLED MY BOYS DOWNSTAIRS. WHATEVER YOUR LITTLE GROUP IS PAYING YOU, I'LL QUADRUPLE IT.
THIS ISN'T MY JOB, IT'S WHAT I DO TO RELAX.

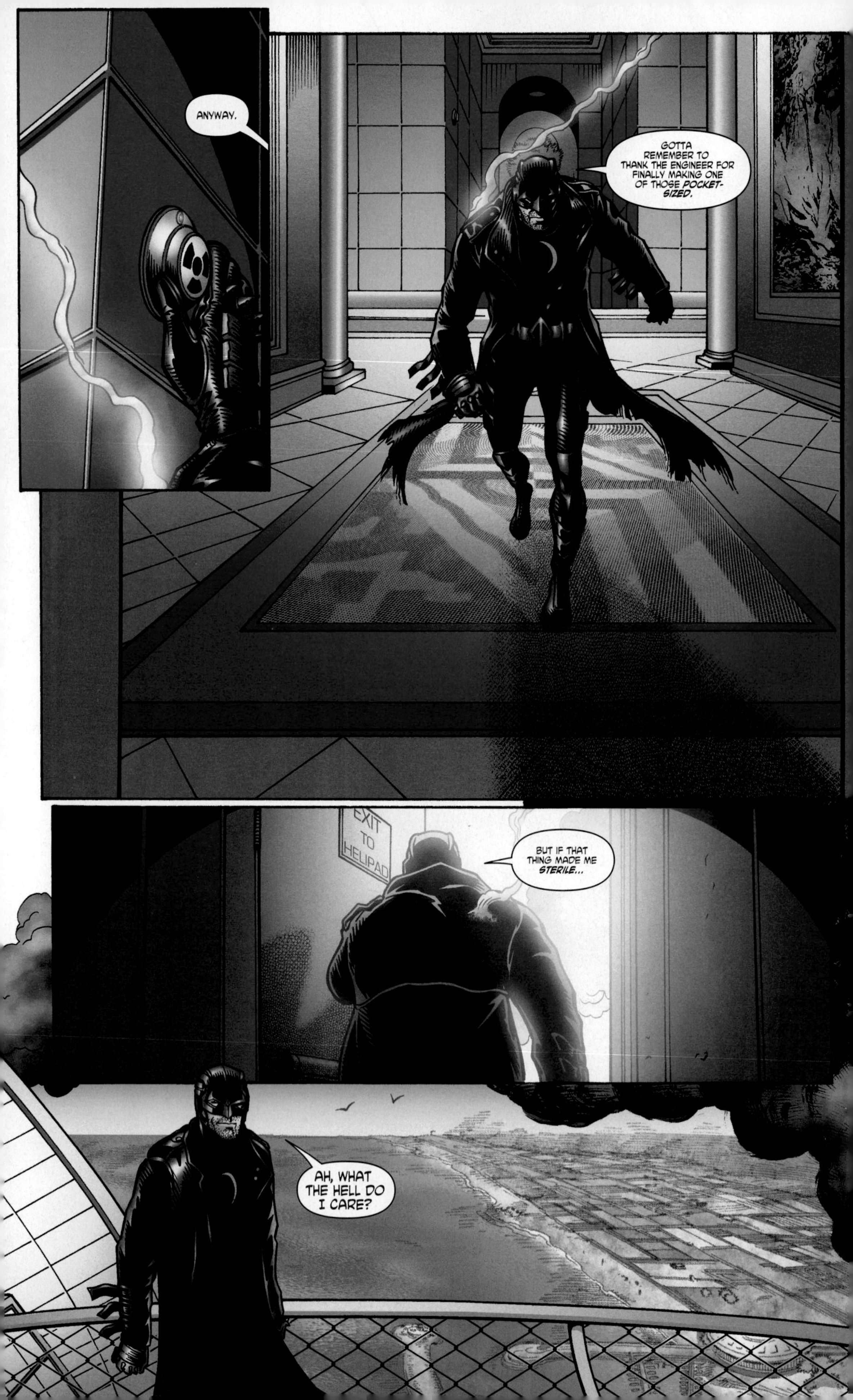
ANYWAY.
GOTTA REMEMBER TO THANK THE ENGINEER FOR FINALLY MAKING ONE OF THOSE POCKET-SIZED.
EXIT TO HELIPAD
BUT IF THAT THING MADE ME STERILE...
AH, WHAT THE HELL DO I CARE?

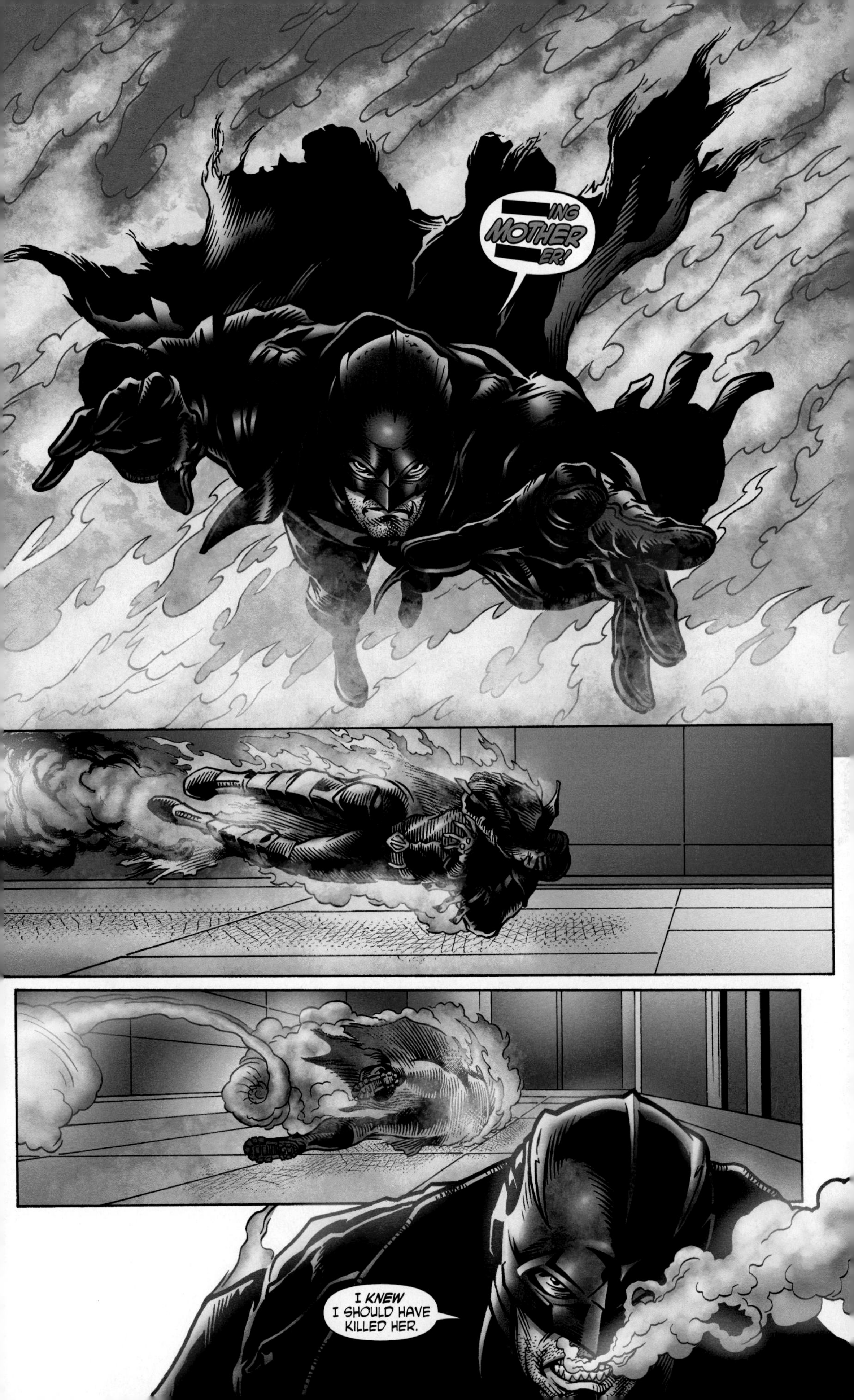
[redacted]ING MOTHER[redacted]ER!
I KNEW I SHOULD HAVE KILLED HER.

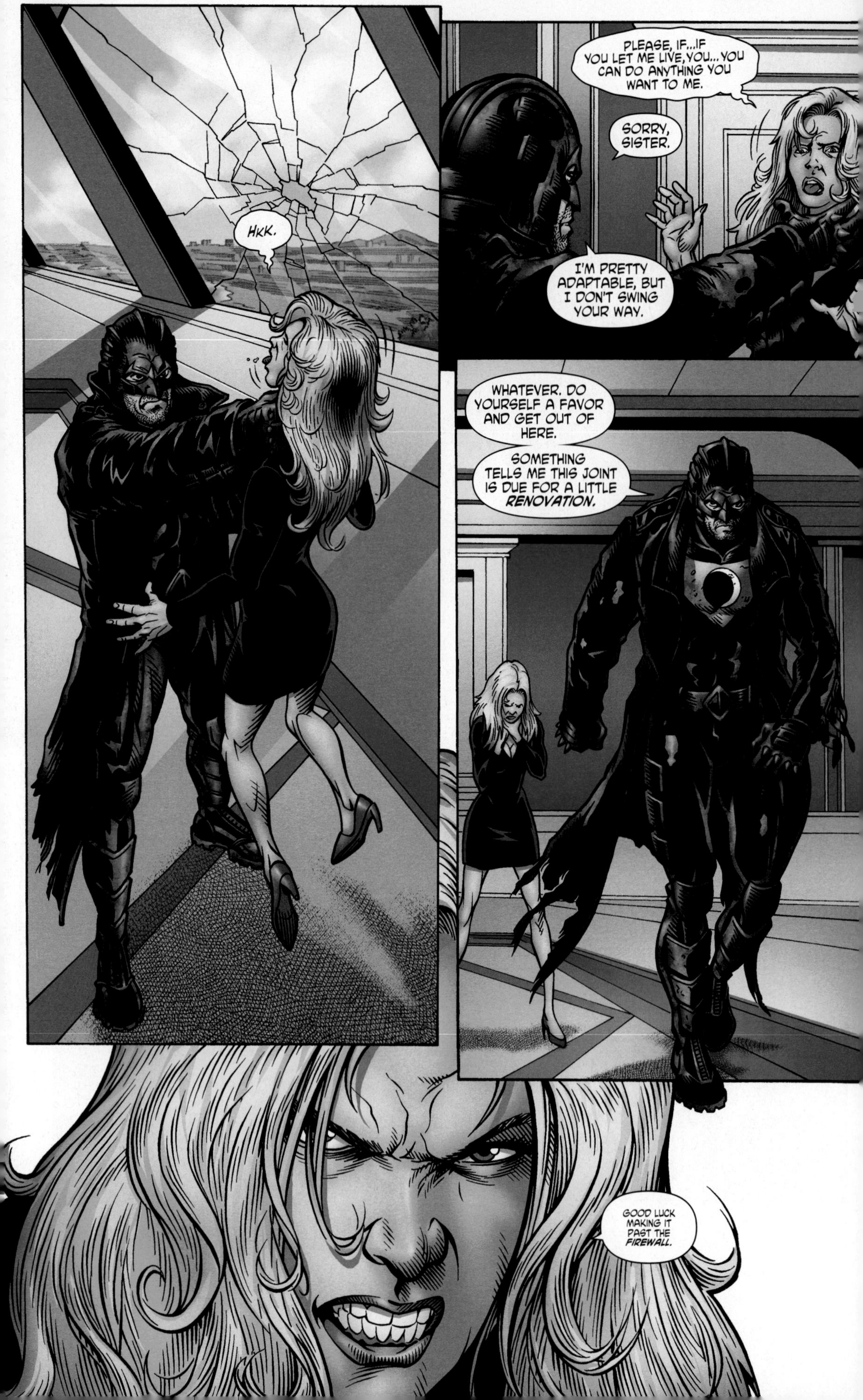
HKK.
PLEASE, IF...IF YOU LET ME LIVE, YOU...YOU CAN DO ANYTHING YOU WANT TO ME.
SORRY, SISTER.
I'M PRETTY ADAPTABLE, BUT I DON'T SWING YOUR WAY.
WHATEVER. DO YOURSELF A FAVOR AND GET OUT OF HERE.
SOMETHING TELLS ME THIS JOINT IS DUE FOR A LITTLE *RENOVATION.*
GOOD LUCK MAKING IT PAST THE *FIREWALL.*

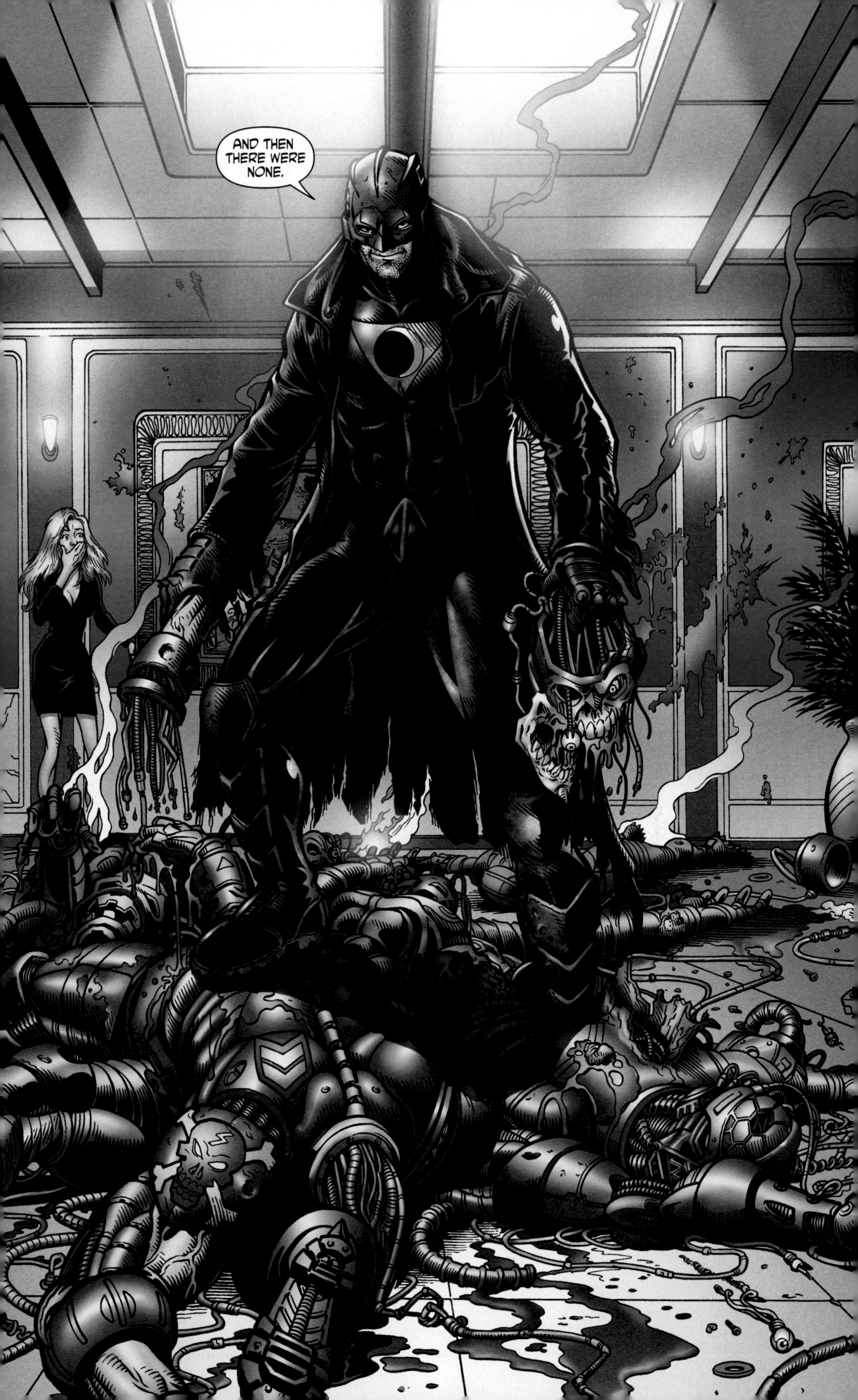
AND THEN THERE WERE NONE.

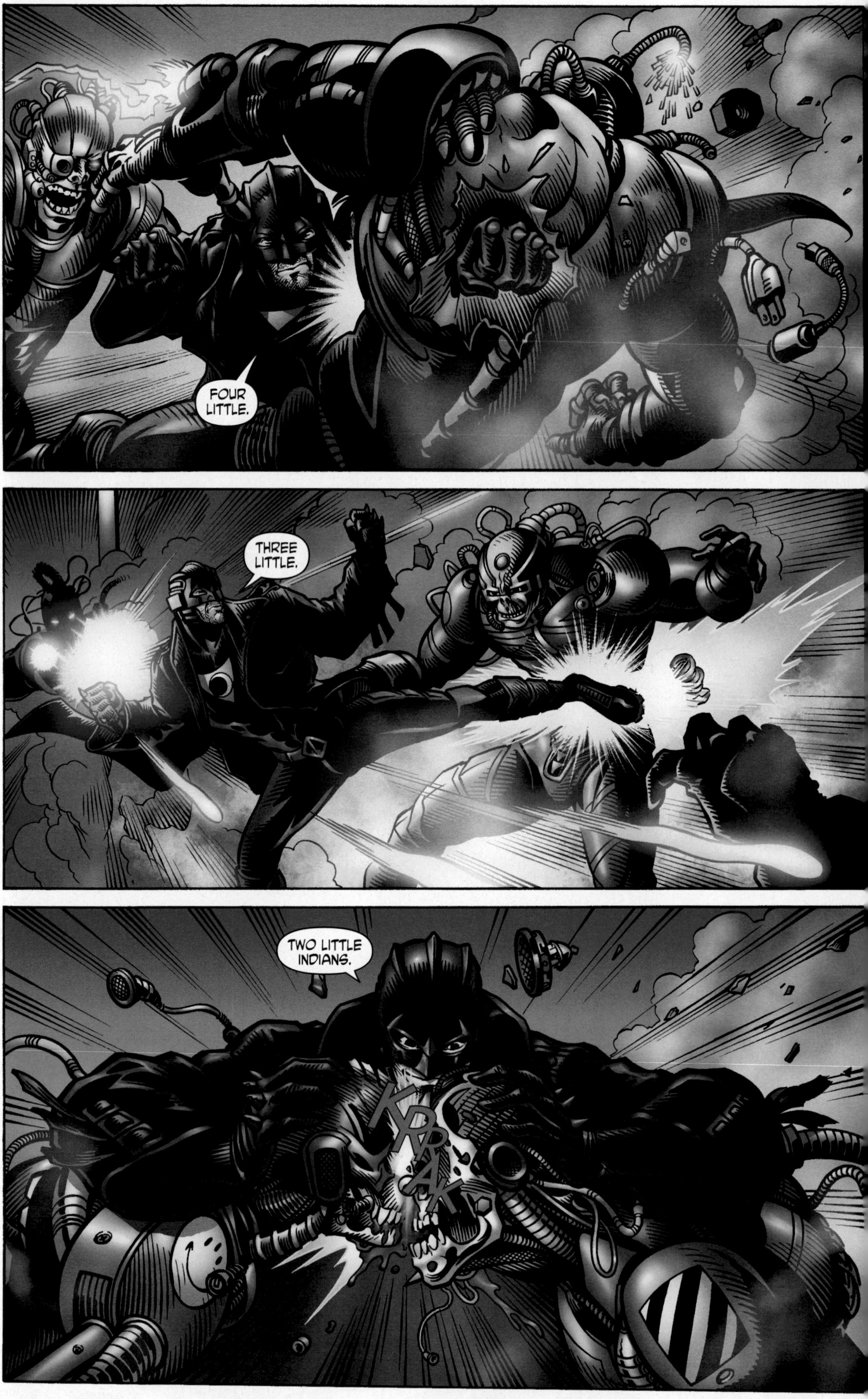
FOUR LITTLE.
THREE LITTLE.
TWO LITTLE INDIANS.
KRRAK

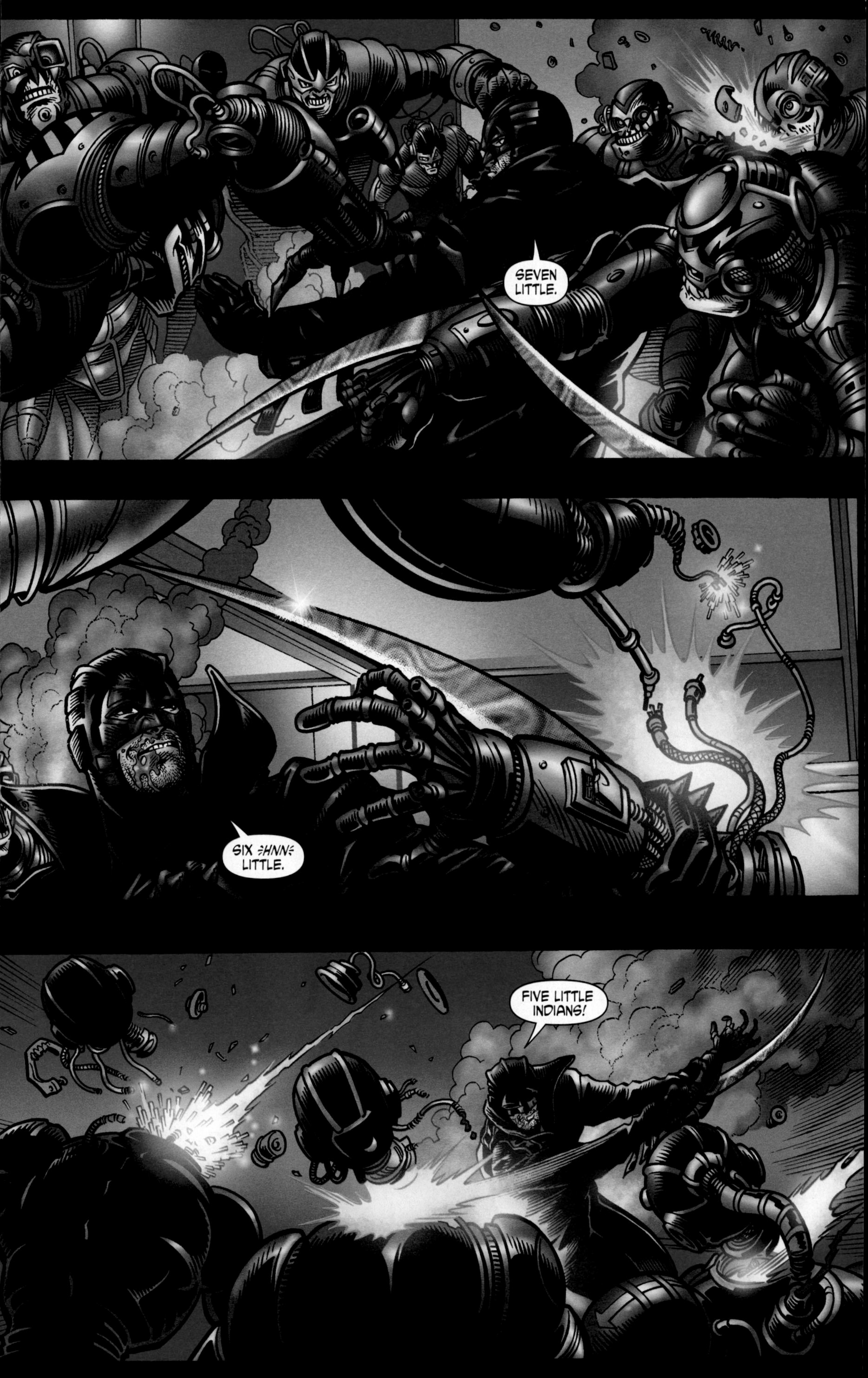
SEVEN LITTLE.
SIX =HNN= LITTLE.
FIVE LITTLE INDIANS!

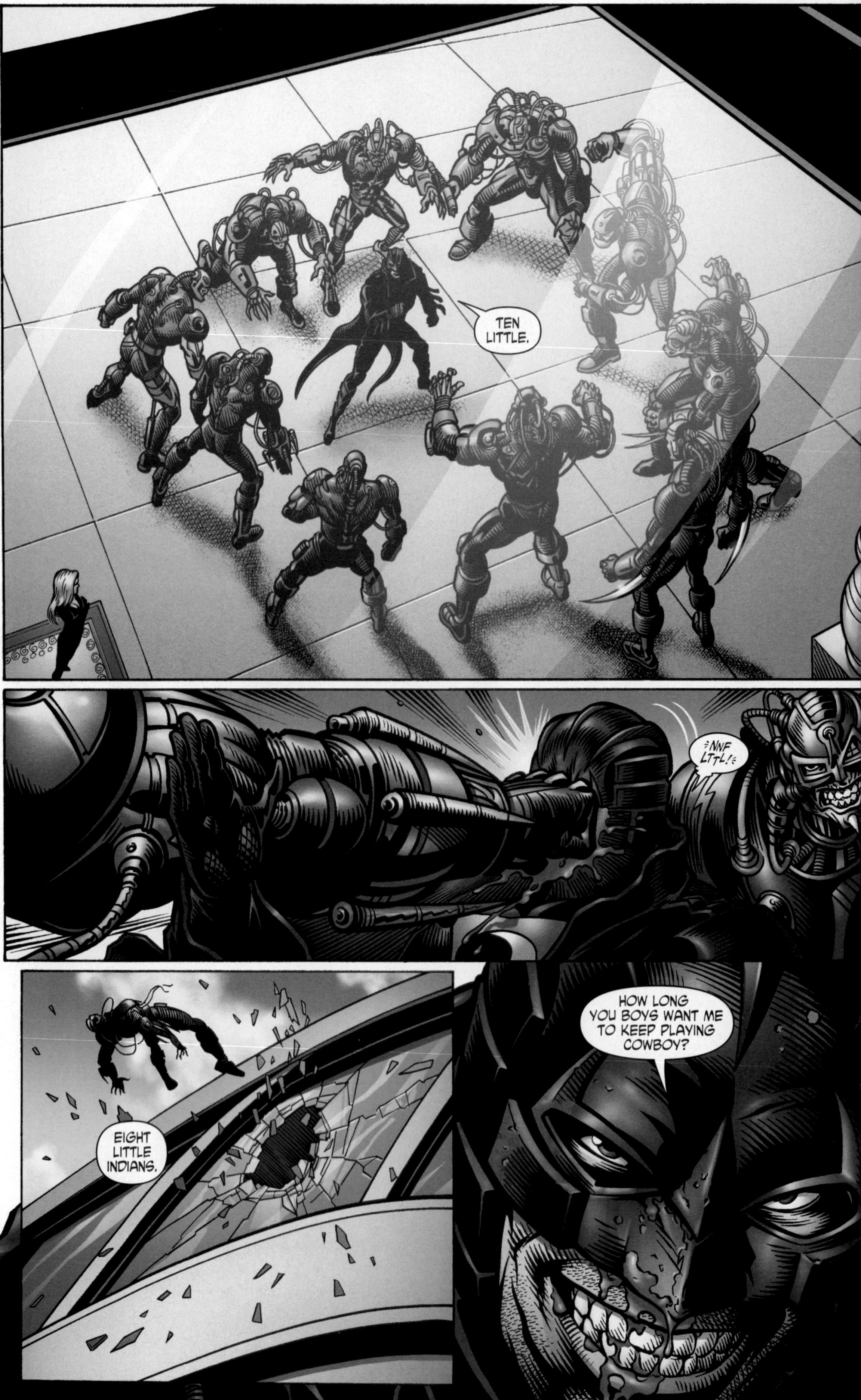
TEN LITTLE.
NNF LTTL!
EIGHT LITTLE INDIANS.
HOW LONG YOU BOYS WANT ME TO KEEP PLAYING COWBOY?

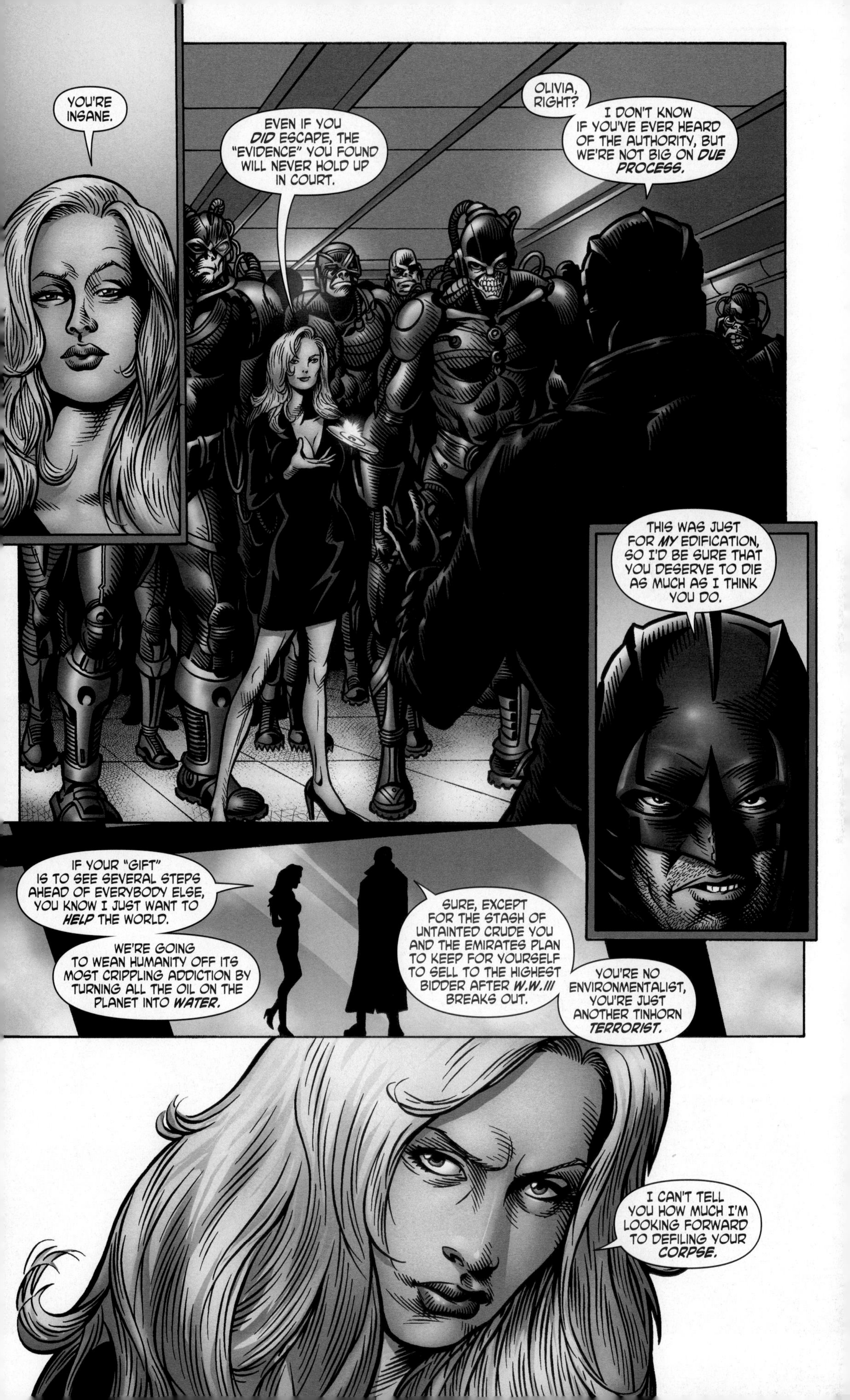
YOU'RE INSANE.
EVEN IF YOU DID ESCAPE, THE "EVIDENCE" YOU FOUND WILL NEVER HOLD UP IN COURT.
OLIVIA, RIGHT?
I DON'T KNOW IF YOU'VE EVER HEARD OF THE AUTHORITY, BUT WE'RE NOT BIG ON DUE PROCESS.
THIS WAS JUST FOR MY EDIFICATION, SO I'D BE SURE THAT YOU DESERVE TO DIE AS MUCH AS I THINK YOU DO.
IF YOUR "GIFT" IS TO SEE SEVERAL STEPS AHEAD OF EVERYBODY ELSE, YOU KNOW I JUST WANT TO HELP THE WORLD.
WE'RE GOING TO WEAN HUMANITY OFF ITS MOST CRIPPLING ADDICTION BY TURNING ALL THE OIL ON THE PLANET INTO WATER.
SURE, EXCEPT FOR THE STASH OF UNTAINTED CRUDE YOU AND THE EMIRATES PLAN TO KEEP FOR YOURSELF TO SELL TO THE HIGHEST BIDDER AFTER W.W.III BREAKS OUT.
YOU'RE NO ENVIRONMENTALIST, YOU'RE JUST ANOTHER TINHORN TERRORIST.
I CAN'T TELL YOU HOW MUCH I'M LOOKING FORWARD TO DEFILING YOUR CORPSE.

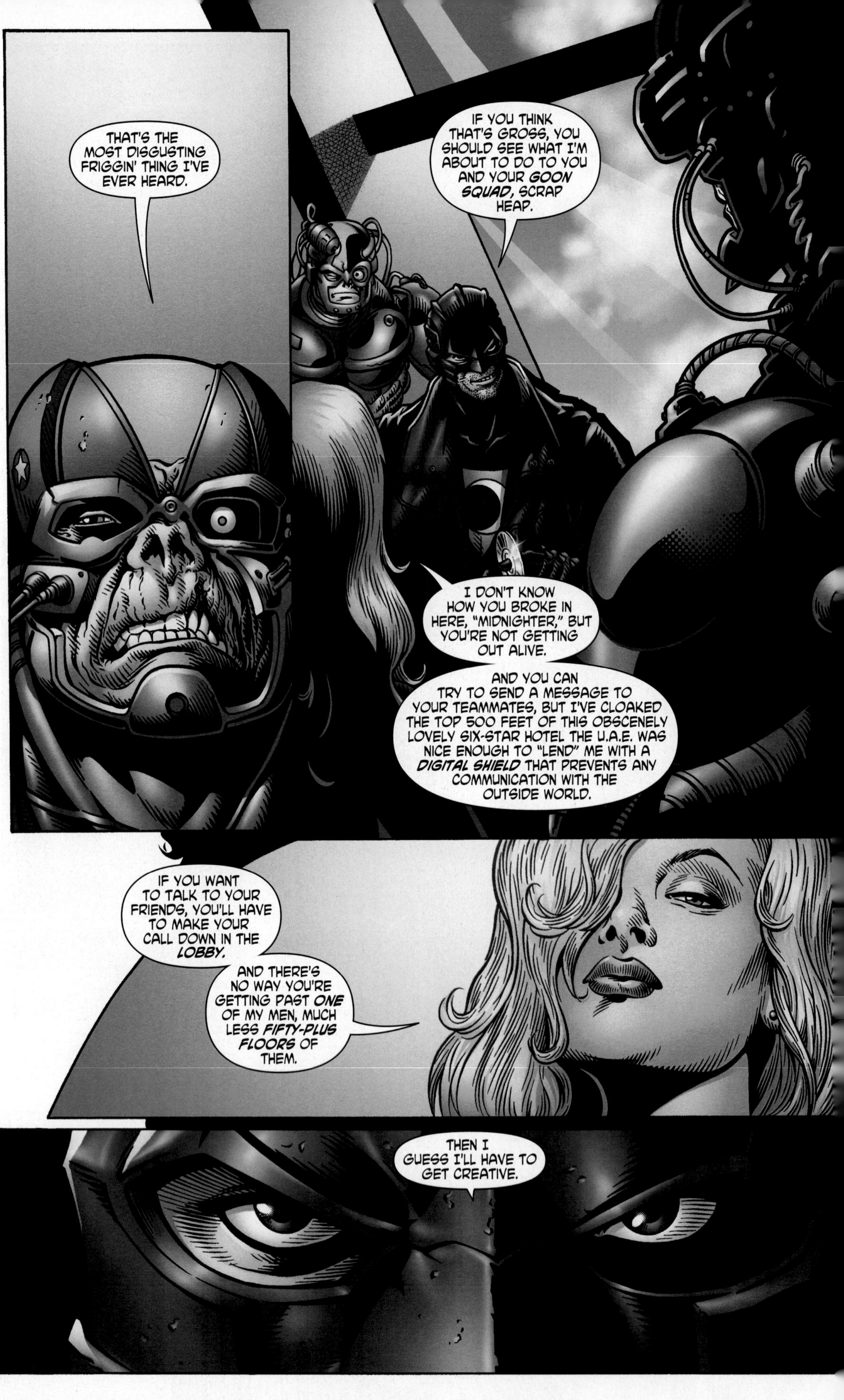

THAT'S THE MOST DISGUSTING FRIGGIN' THING I'VE EVER HEARD.
IF YOU THINK THAT'S GROSS, YOU SHOULD SEE WHAT I'M ABOUT TO DO TO YOU AND YOUR GOON SQUAD, SCRAP HEAP.
I DON'T KNOW HOW YOU BROKE IN HERE, "MIDNIGHTER," BUT YOU'RE NOT GETTING OUT ALIVE.
AND YOU CAN TRY TO SEND A MESSAGE TO YOUR TEAMMATES, BUT I'VE CLOAKED THE TOP 500 FEET OF THIS OBSCENELY LOVELY SIX-STAR HOTEL THE U.A.E. WAS NICE ENOUGH TO "LEND" ME WITH A DIGITAL SHIELD THAT PREVENTS ANY COMMUNICATION WITH THE OUTSIDE WORLD.
IF YOU WANT TO TALK TO YOUR FRIENDS, YOU'LL HAVE TO MAKE YOUR CALL DOWN IN THE LOBBY.
AND THERE'S NO WAY YOU'RE GETTING PAST ONE OF MY MEN, MUCH LESS FIFTY-PLUS FLOORS OF THEM.
THEN I GUESS I'LL HAVE TO GET CREATIVE.

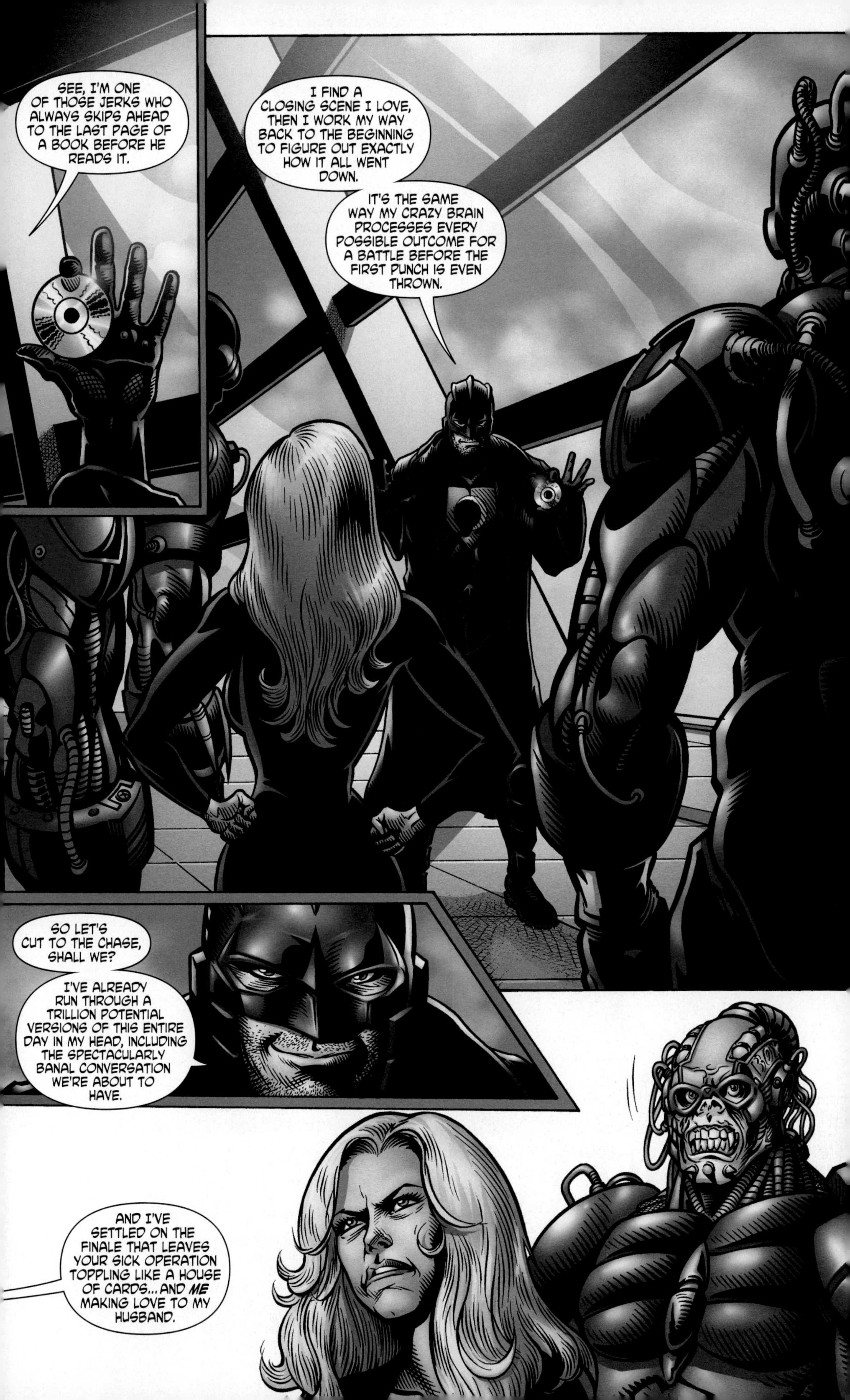
SEE, I'M ONE OF THOSE JERKS WHO ALWAYS SKIPS AHEAD TO THE LAST PAGE OF A BOOK BEFORE HE READS IT.
I FIND A CLOSING SCENE I LOVE, THEN I WORK MY WAY BACK TO THE BEGINNING TO FIGURE OUT EXACTLY HOW IT ALL WENT DOWN.
IT'S THE SAME WAY MY CRAZY BRAIN PROCESSES EVERY POSSIBLE OUTCOME FOR A BATTLE BEFORE THE FIRST PUNCH IS EVEN THROWN.
SO LET'S CUT TO THE CHASE, SHALL WE?
I'VE ALREADY RUN THROUGH A TRILLION POTENTIAL VERSIONS OF THIS ENTIRE DAY IN MY HEAD, INCLUDING THE SPECTACULARLY BANAL CONVERSATION WE'RE ABOUT TO HAVE.
AND I'VE SETTLED ON THE FINALE THAT LEAVES YOUR SICK OPERATION TOPPLING LIKE A HOUSE OF CARDS...AND *ME* MAKING LOVE TO MY HUSBAND.

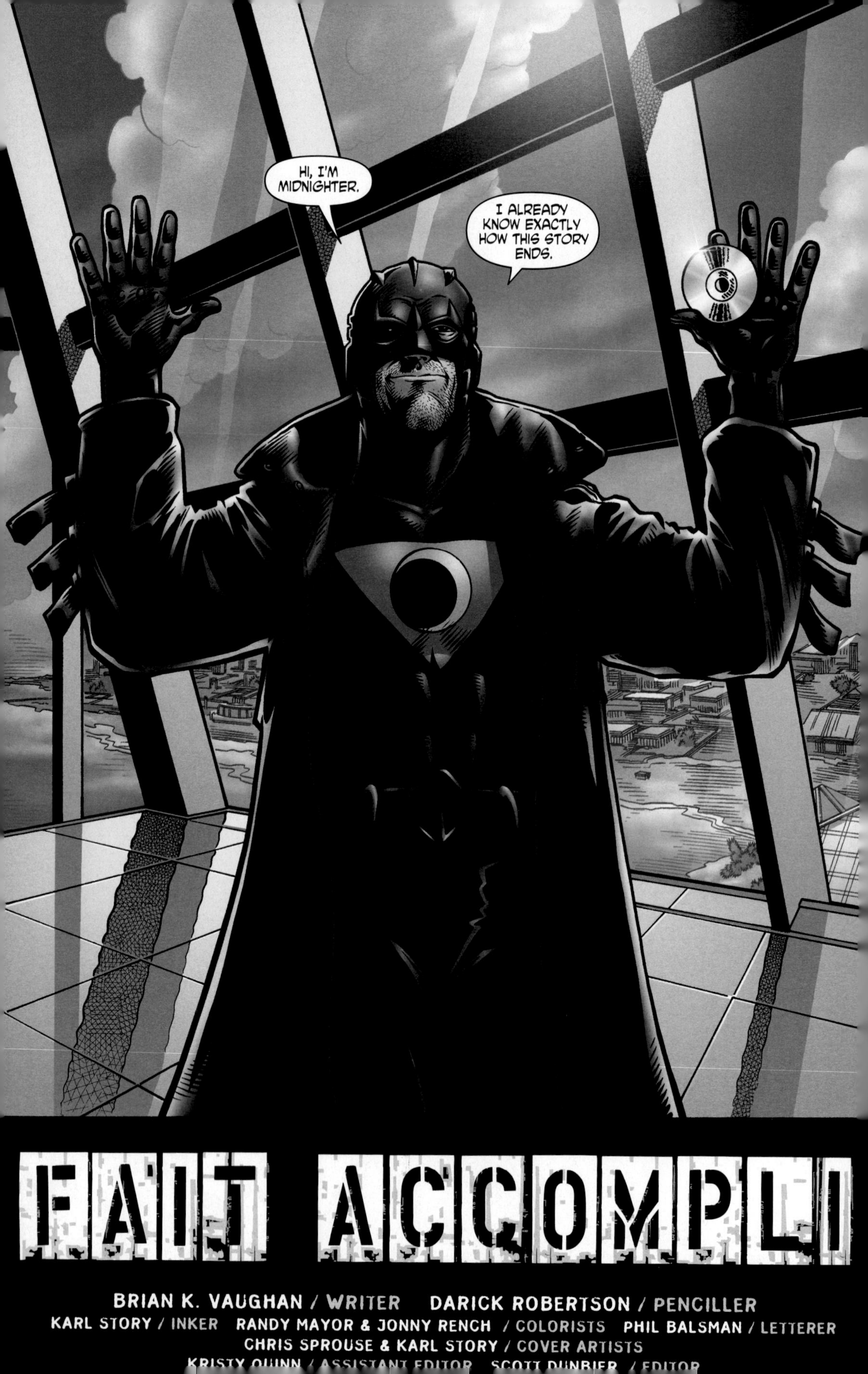
HI, I'M MIDNIGHTER.
I ALREADY KNOW EXACTLY HOW THIS STORY ENDS.

FAIT ACCOMPLI

BRIAN K. VAUGHAN / WRITER DARICK ROBERTSON / PENCILLER
KARL STORY / INKER RANDY MAYOR & JONNY RENCH / COLORISTS PHIL BALSMAN / LETTERER
CHRIS SPROUSE & KARL STORY / COVER ARTISTS
KRISTY QUINN / ASSISTANT EDITOR SCOTT DUNBIER / EDITOR

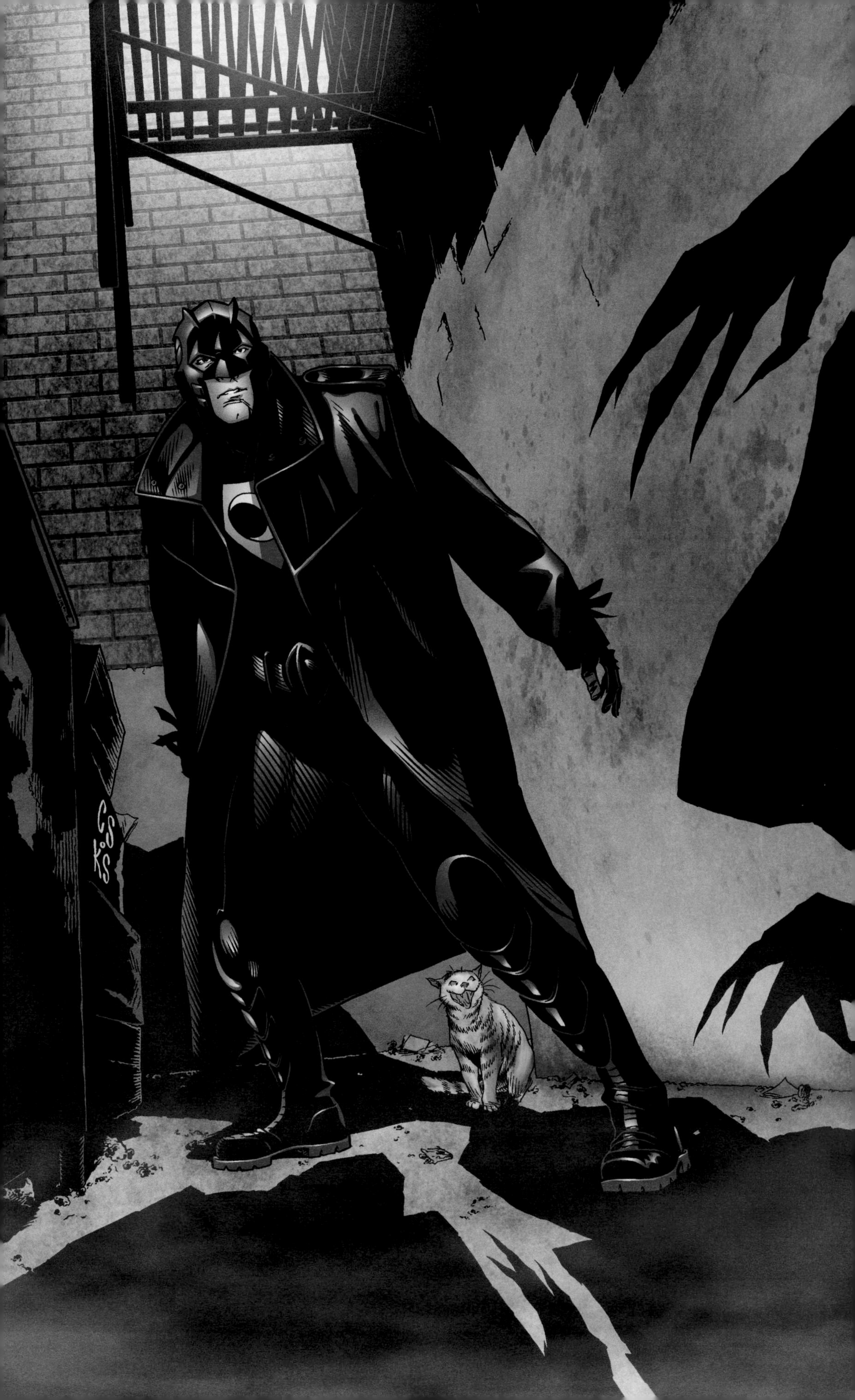
CS KoS

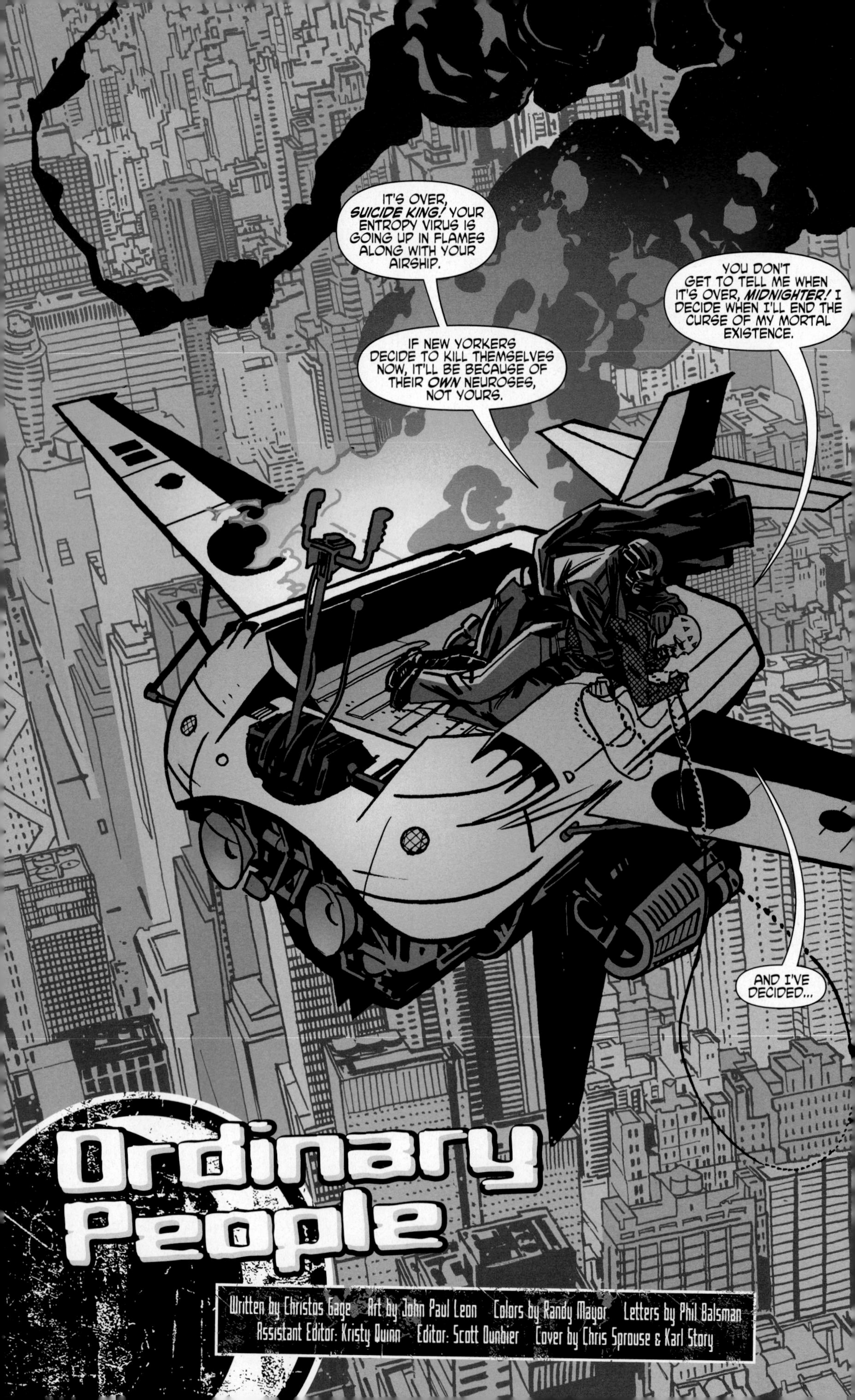

IT'S OVER, SUICIDE KING! YOUR ENTROPY VIRUS IS GOING UP IN FLAMES ALONG WITH YOUR AIRSHIP.
IF NEW YORKERS DECIDE TO KILL THEMSELVES NOW, IT'LL BE BECAUSE OF THEIR OWN NEUROSES, NOT YOURS.
YOU DON'T GET TO TELL ME WHEN IT'S OVER, MIDNIGHTER! I DECIDE WHEN I'LL END THE CURSE OF MY MORTAL EXISTENCE.
AND I'VE DECIDED...
Ordinary People
Written by Christos Gage Art by John Paul Leon Colors by Randy Mayor Letters by Phil Balsman
Assistant Editor: Kristy Quinn Editor: Scott Dunbier Cover by Chris Sprouse & Karl Story

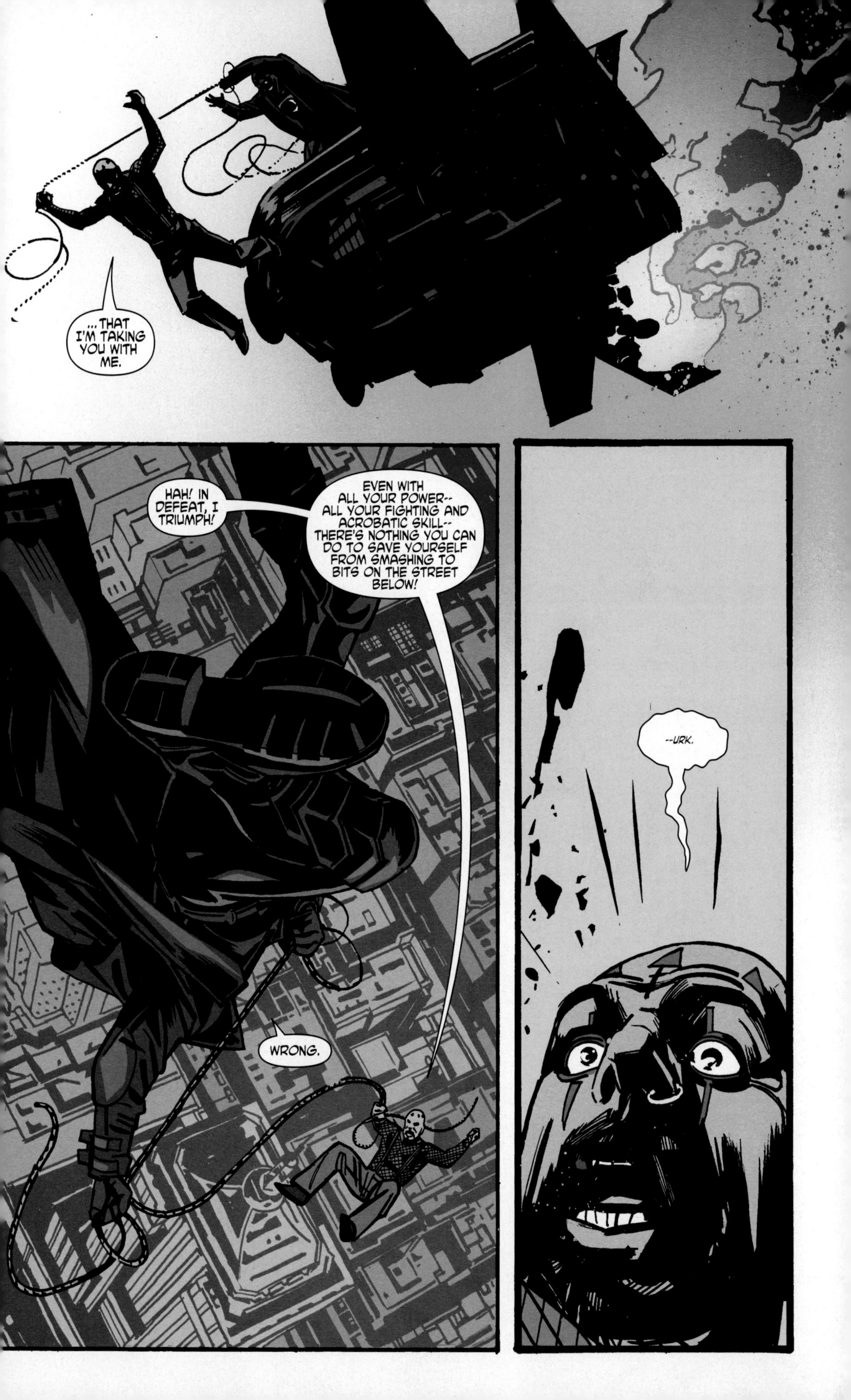
...THAT I'M TAKING YOU WITH ME.
HAH! IN DEFEAT, I TRIUMPH!
EVEN WITH ALL YOUR POWER-- ALL YOUR FIGHTING AND ACROBATIC SKILL-- THERE'S NOTHING YOU CAN DO TO SAVE YOURSELF FROM SMASHING TO BITS ON THE STREET BELOW!
WRONG.
--URK.

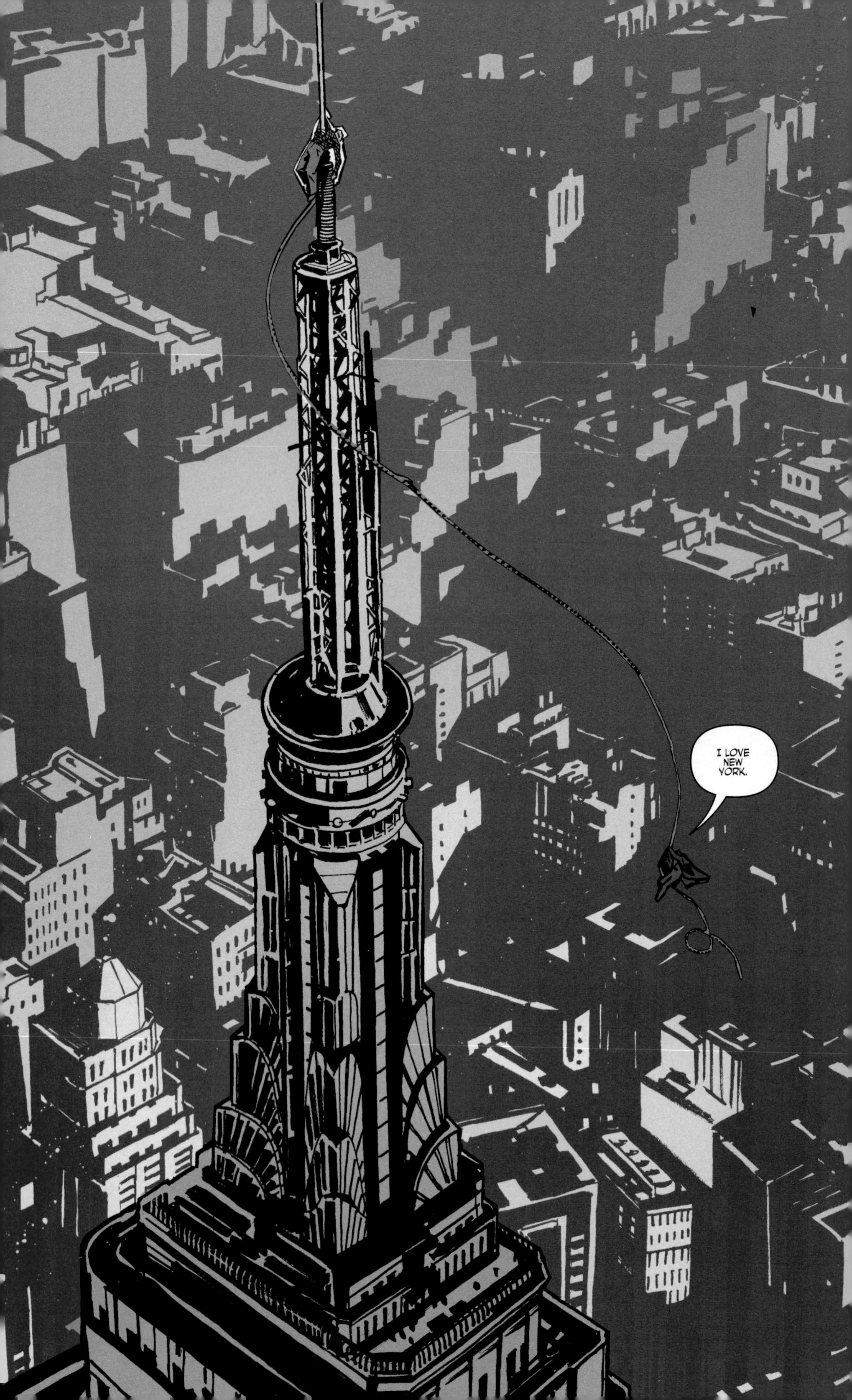
I LOVE NEW YORK.

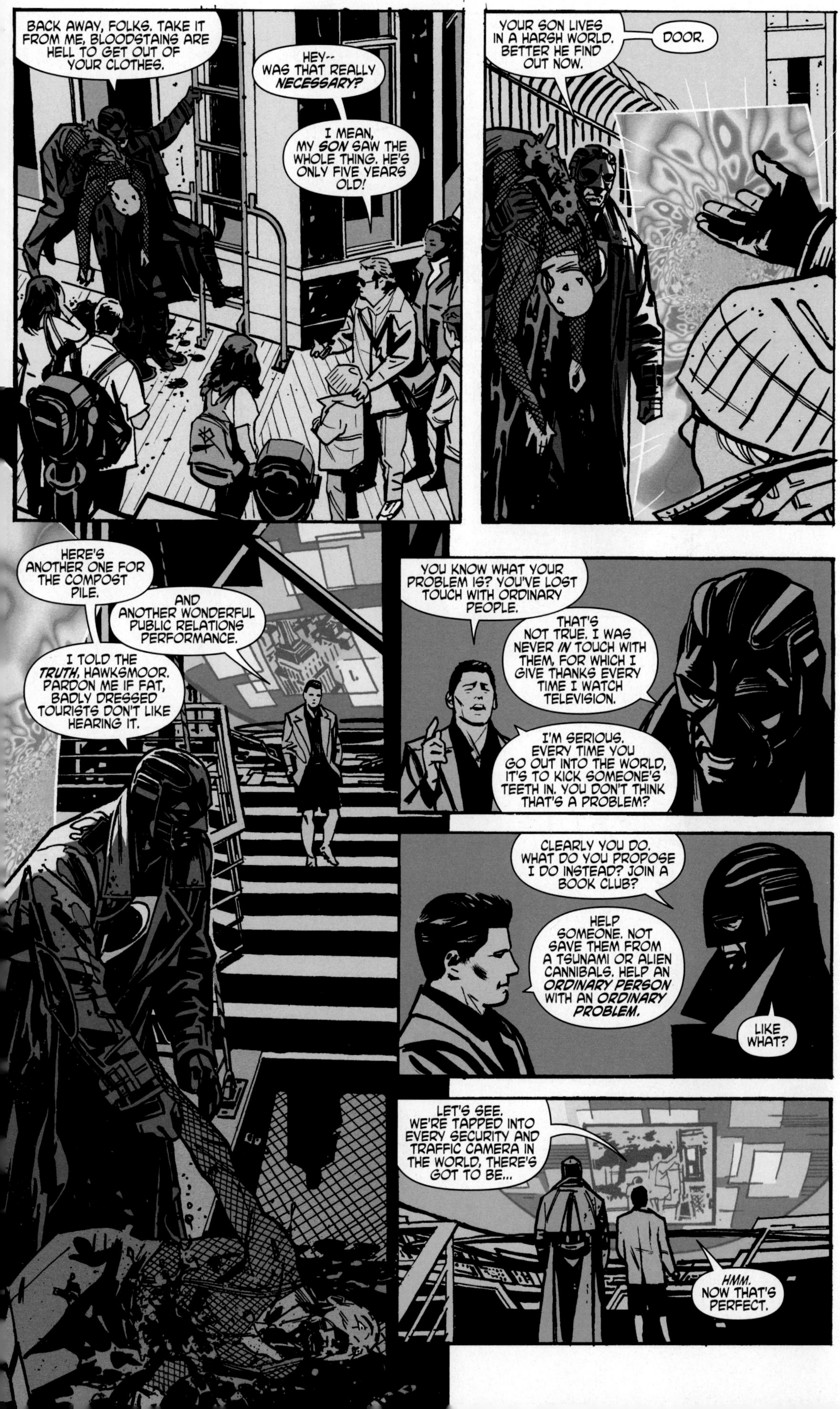
BACK AWAY, FOLKS. TAKE IT FROM ME, BLOODSTAINS ARE HELL TO GET OUT OF YOUR CLOTHES.
HEY-- WAS THAT REALLY NECESSARY?
I MEAN, MY SON SAW THE WHOLE THING. HE'S ONLY FIVE YEARS OLD!
YOUR SON LIVES IN A HARSH WORLD. BETTER HE FIND OUT NOW.
DOOR.
HERE'S ANOTHER ONE FOR THE COMPOST PILE.
AND ANOTHER WONDERFUL PUBLIC RELATIONS PERFORMANCE.
I TOLD THE TRUTH, HAWKSMOOR. PARDON ME IF FAT, BADLY DRESSED TOURISTS DON'T LIKE HEARING IT.
YOU KNOW WHAT YOUR PROBLEM IS? YOU'VE LOST TOUCH WITH ORDINARY PEOPLE.
THAT'S NOT TRUE. I WAS NEVER IN TOUCH WITH THEM, FOR WHICH I GIVE THANKS EVERY TIME I WATCH TELEVISION.
I'M SERIOUS. EVERY TIME YOU GO OUT INTO THE WORLD, IT'S TO KICK SOMEONE'S TEETH IN. YOU DON'T THINK THAT'S A PROBLEM?
CLEARLY YOU DO. WHAT DO YOU PROPOSE I DO INSTEAD? JOIN A BOOK CLUB?
HELP SOMEONE. NOT SAVE THEM FROM A TSUNAMI OR ALIEN CANNIBALS. HELP AN ORDINARY PERSON WITH AN ORDINARY PROBLEM.
LIKE WHAT?
LET'S SEE. WE'RE TAPPED INTO EVERY SECURITY AND TRAFFIC CAMERA IN THE WORLD, THERE'S GOT TO BE...
HMM. NOW THAT'S PERFECT.

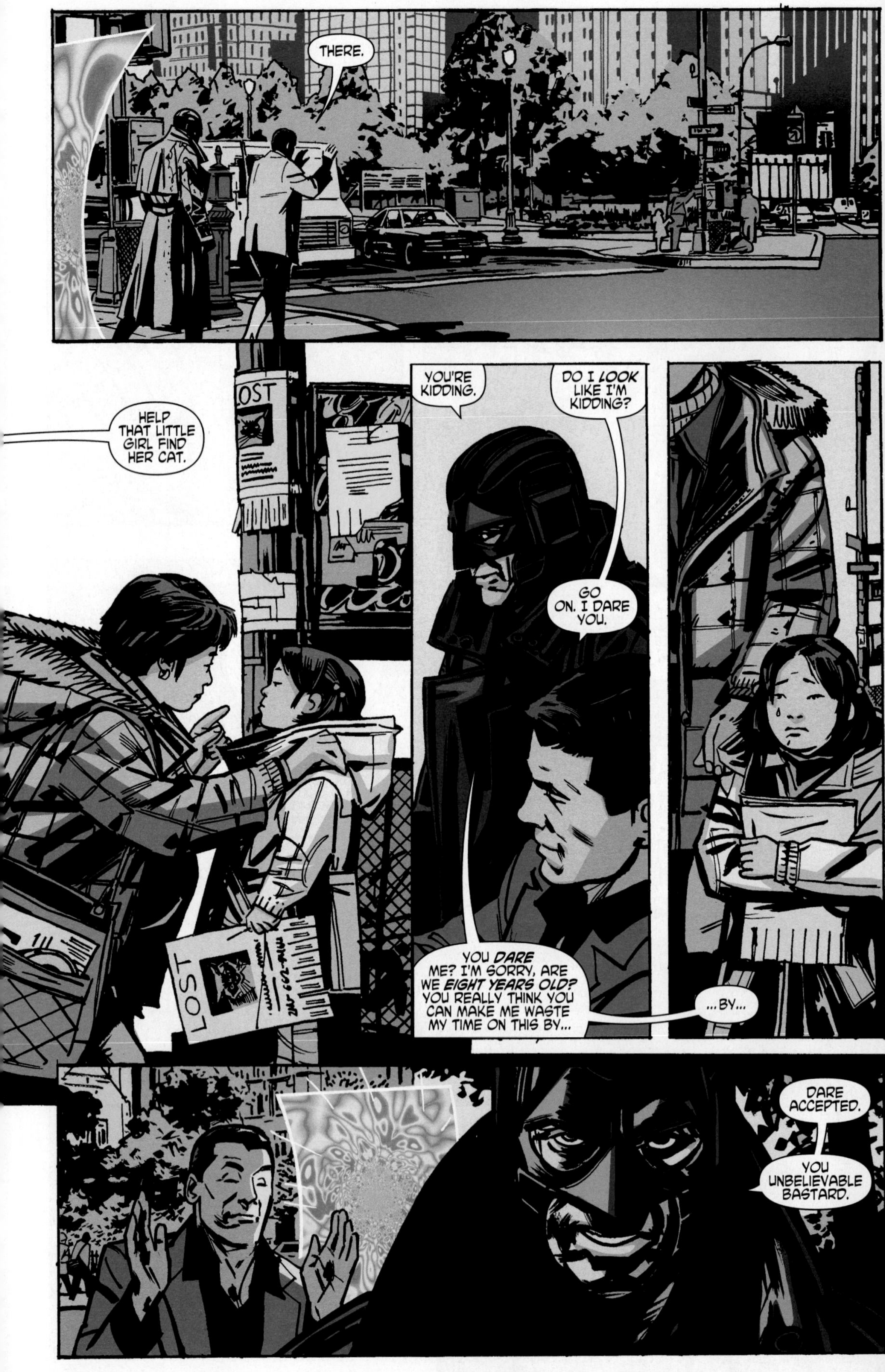
THERE.
HELP THAT LITTLE GIRL FIND HER CAT.
LOST
YOU'RE KIDDING.
DO I *LOOK* LIKE I'M KIDDING?
GO ON. I DARE YOU.
YOU *DARE* ME? I'M SORRY, ARE WE *EIGHT YEARS OLD?* YOU REALLY THINK YOU CAN MAKE ME WASTE MY TIME ON THIS BY...
...BY...
LOST
DARE ACCEPTED.
YOU UNBELIEVABLE BASTARD.

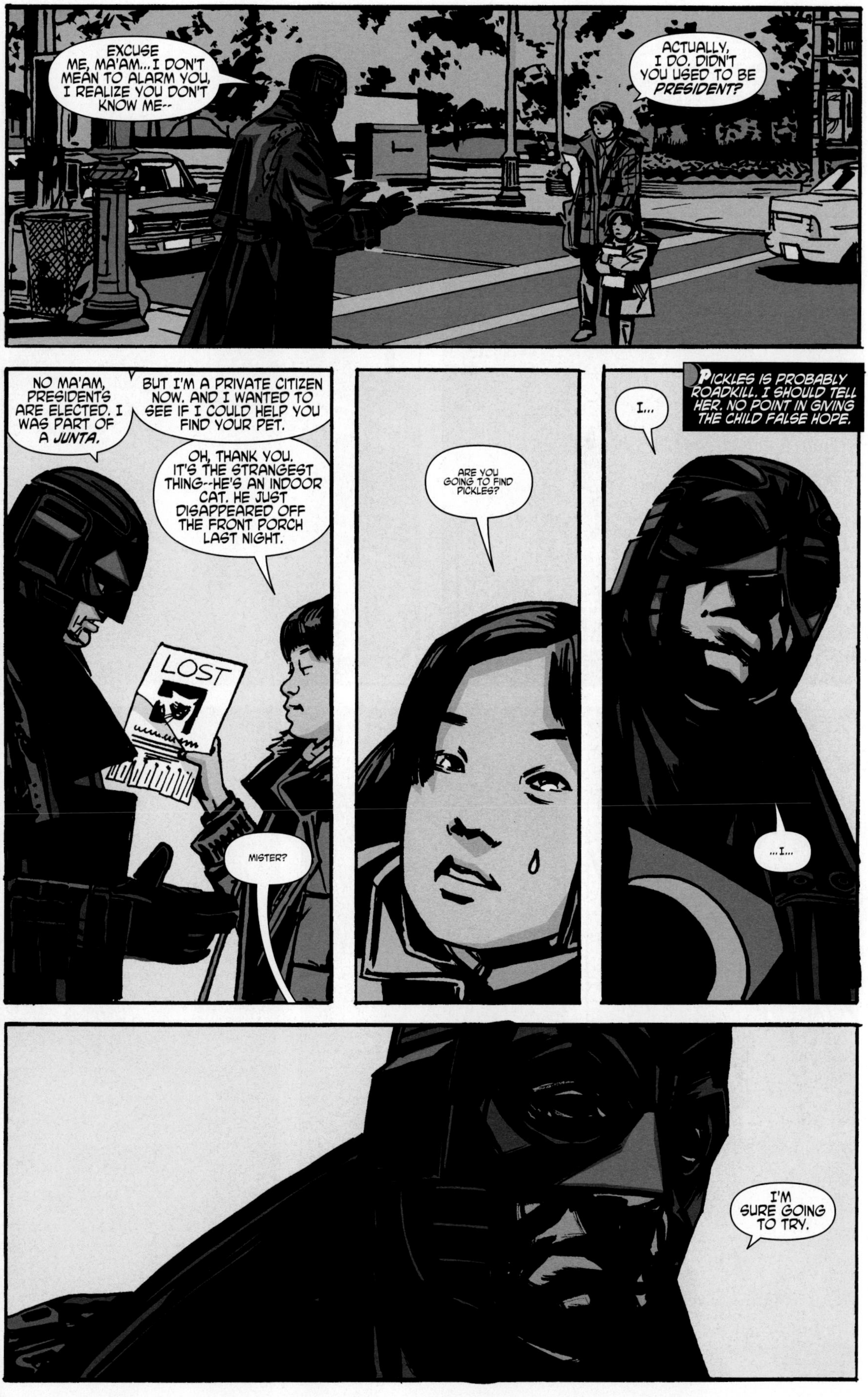
EXCUSE ME, MA'AM... I DON'T MEAN TO ALARM YOU, I REALIZE YOU DON'T KNOW ME--
ACTUALLY, I DO. DIDN'T YOU USED TO BE *PRESIDENT?*
NO MA'AM, PRESIDENTS ARE ELECTED. I WAS PART OF A *JUNTA.*
BUT I'M A PRIVATE CITIZEN NOW. AND I WANTED TO SEE IF I COULD HELP YOU FIND YOUR PET.
OH, THANK YOU. IT'S THE STRANGEST THING--HE'S AN INDOOR CAT. HE JUST DISAPPEARED OFF THE FRONT PORCH LAST NIGHT.
LOST
MISTER?
ARE YOU GOING TO FIND PICKLES?
PICKLES IS PROBABLY ROADKILL. I SHOULD TELL HER. NO POINT IN GIVING THE CHILD FALSE HOPE.
I...
...I...
I'M SURE GOING TO TRY.

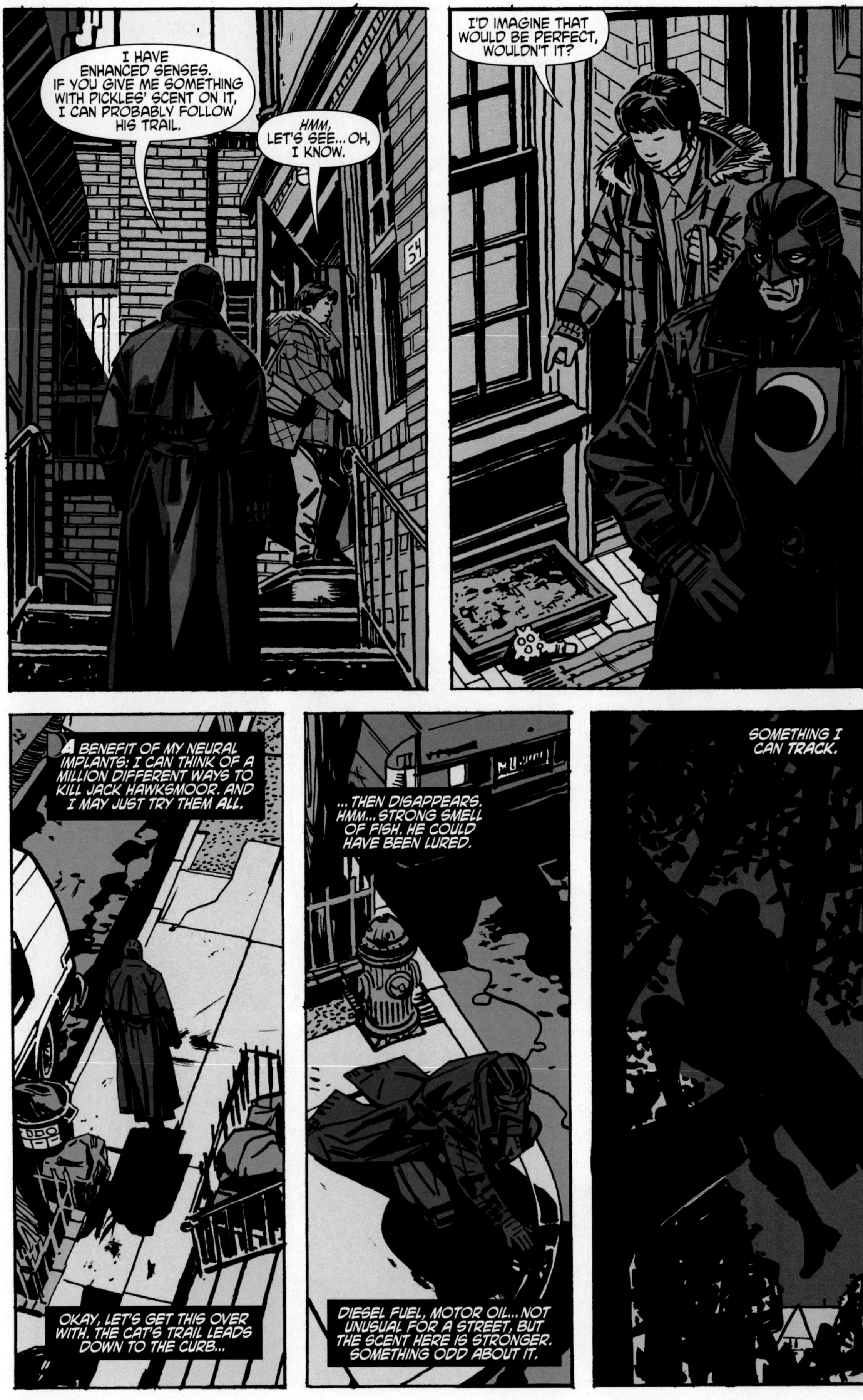
I HAVE ENHANCED SENSES. IF YOU GIVE ME SOMETHING WITH PICKLES' SCENT ON IT, I CAN PROBABLY FOLLOW HIS TRAIL.
HMM, LET'S SEE... OH, I KNOW.
I'D IMAGINE THAT WOULD BE PERFECT, WOULDN'T IT?
A BENEFIT OF MY NEURAL IMPLANTS: I CAN THINK OF A MILLION DIFFERENT WAYS TO KILL JACK HAWKSMOOR. AND I MAY JUST TRY THEM ALL.
OKAY, LET'S GET THIS OVER WITH. THE CAT'S TRAIL LEADS DOWN TO THE CURB...
...THEN DISAPPEARS. HMM... STRONG SMELL OF FISH. HE COULD HAVE BEEN LURED.
DIESEL FUEL, MOTOR OIL... NOT UNUSUAL FOR A STREET, BUT THE SCENT HERE IS STRONGER. SOMETHING ODD ABOUT IT.
SOMETHING I CAN TRACK.

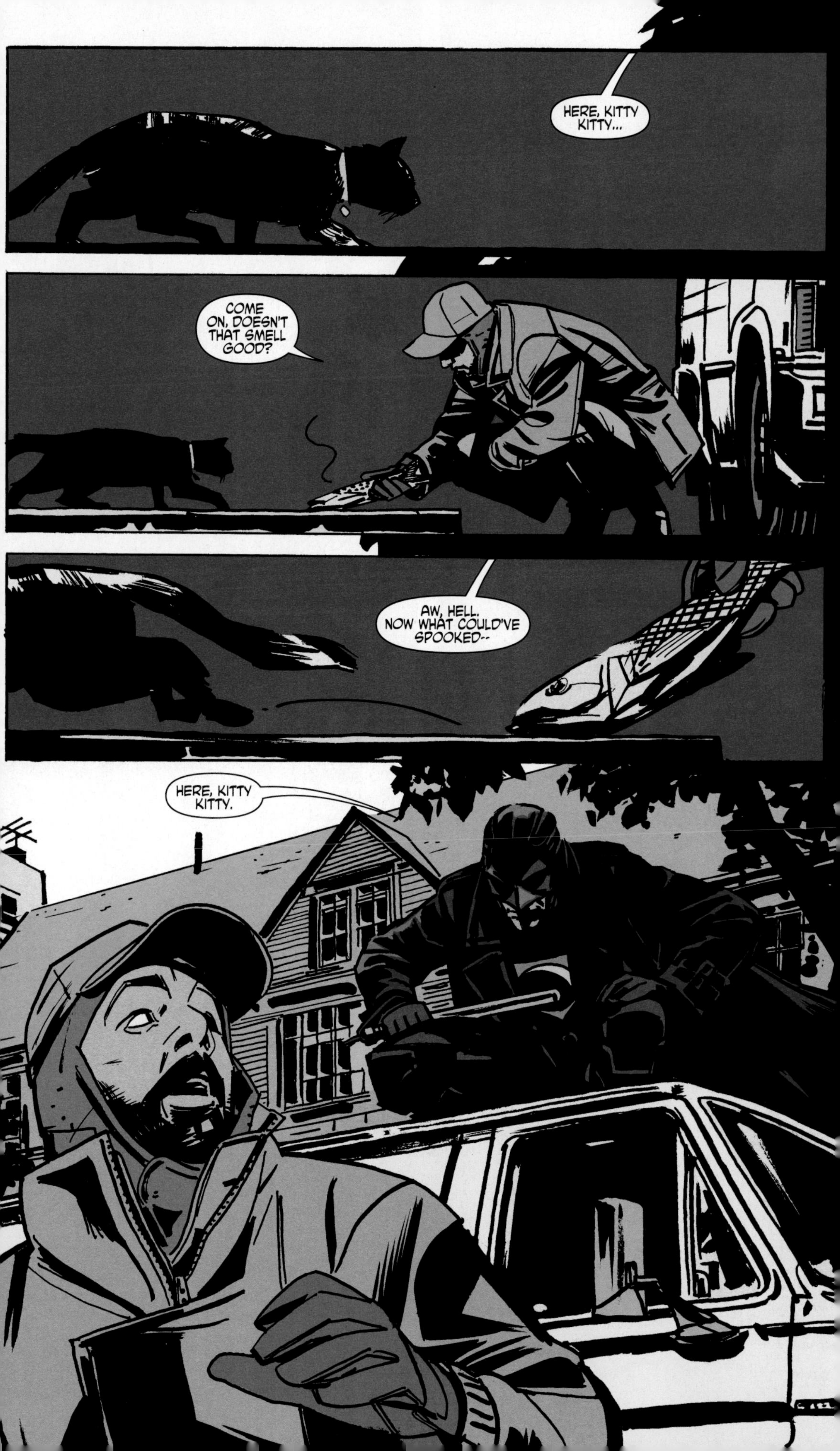
HERE, KITTY KITTY...
COME ON, DOESN'T THAT SMELL GOOD?
AW, HELL. NOW WHAT COULD'VE SPOOKED--
HERE, KITTY KITTY.

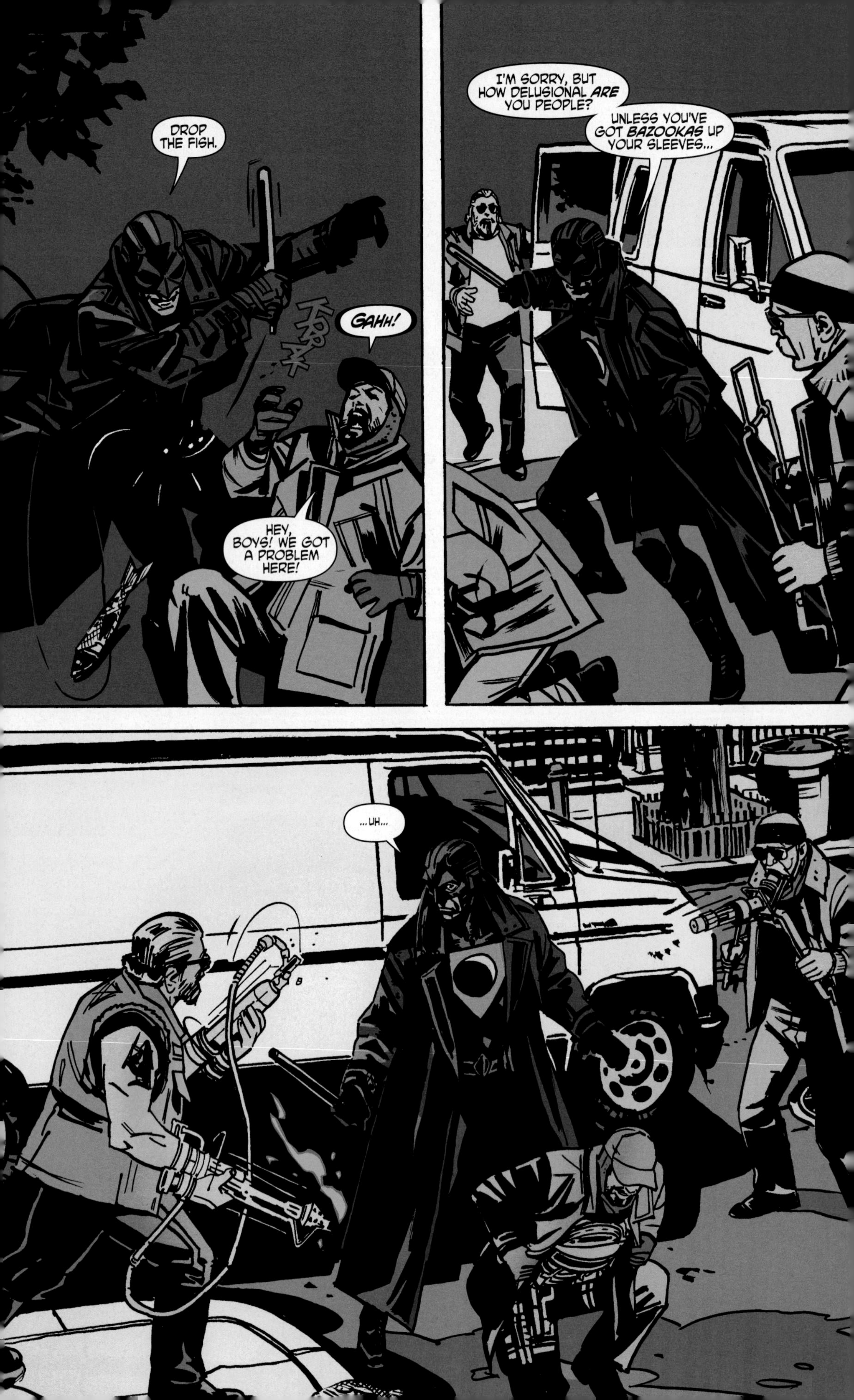
DROP THE FISH.
KRAK
GAHH!
HEY, BOYS! WE GOT A PROBLEM HERE!
I'M SORRY, BUT HOW DELUSIONAL *ARE* YOU PEOPLE?
UNLESS YOU'VE GOT *BAZOOKAS* UP YOUR SLEEVES...
...UH...

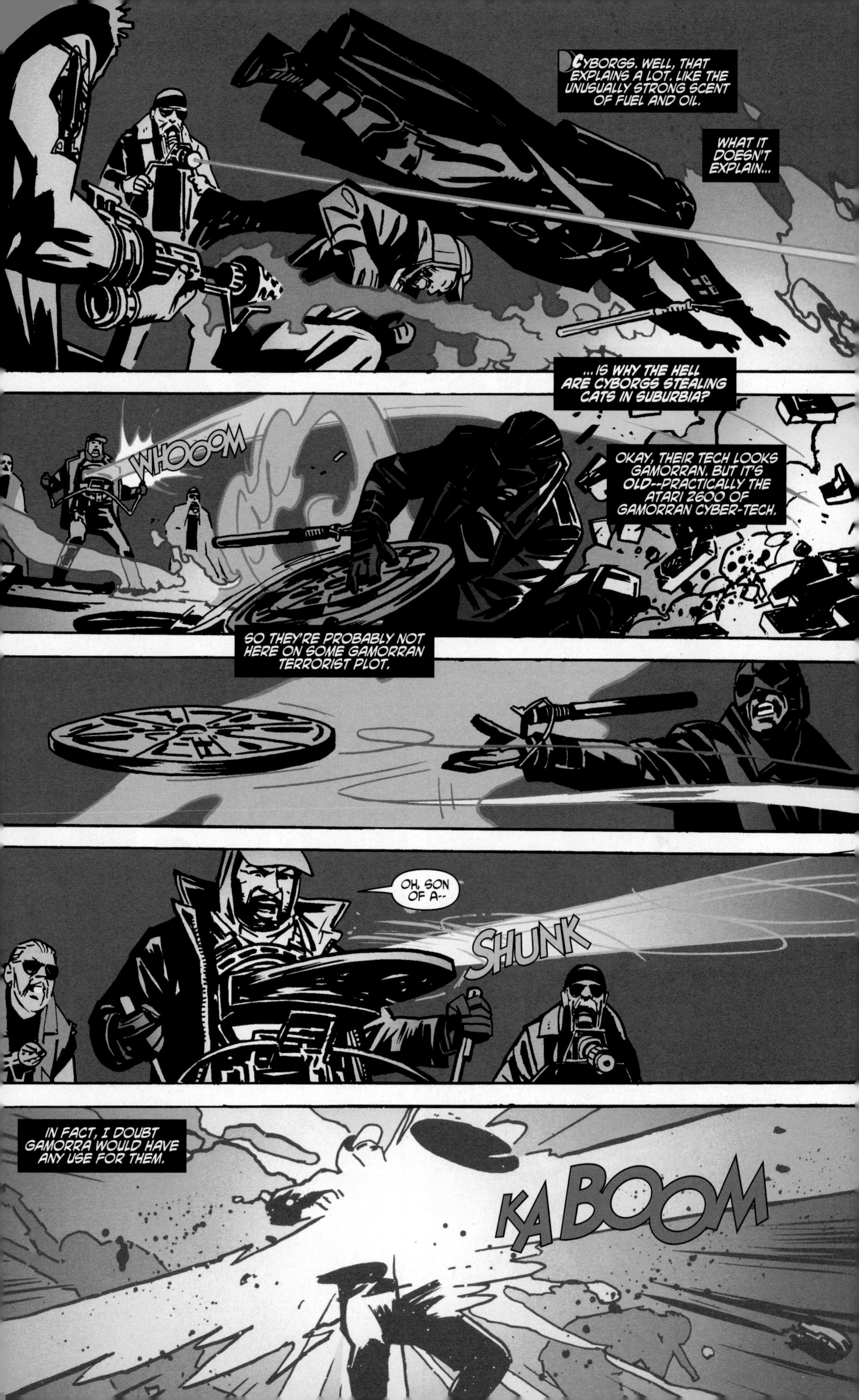
CYBORGS. WELL, THAT EXPLAINS A LOT. LIKE THE UNUSUALLY STRONG SCENT OF FUEL AND OIL.
WHAT IT DOESN'T EXPLAIN...
...IS WHY THE HELL ARE CYBORGS STEALING CATS IN SUBURBIA?
WHOOOM
OKAY, THEIR TECH LOOKS GAMORRAN. BUT IT'S OLD--PRACTICALLY THE ATARI 2600 OF GAMORRAN CYBER-TECH.
SO THEY'RE PROBABLY NOT HERE ON SOME GAMORRAN TERRORIST PLOT.
OH, SON OF A--
SHUNK
IN FACT, I DOUBT GAMORRA WOULD HAVE ANY USE FOR THEM.
KABOOM

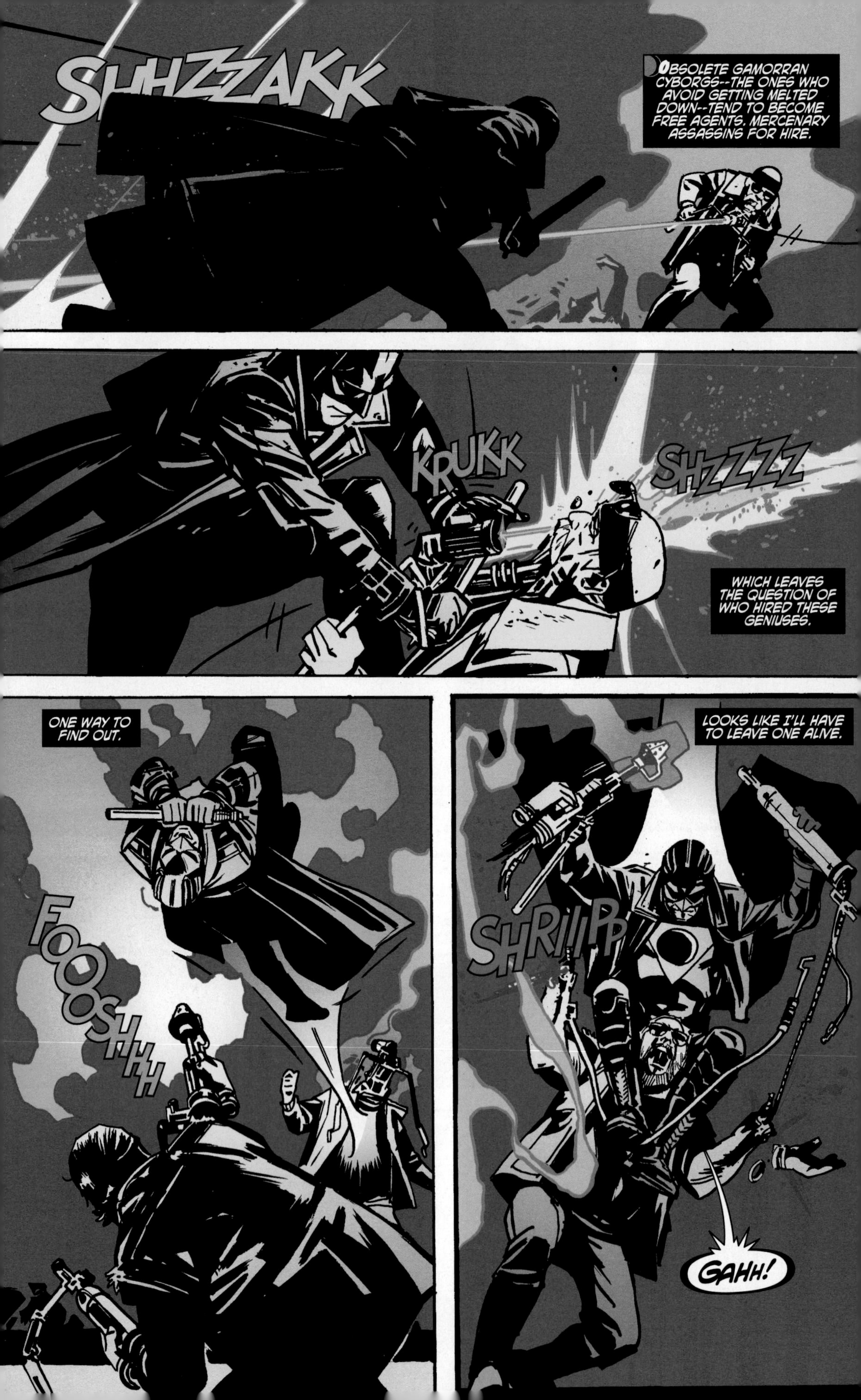
SHHZZZAKK
OBSOLETE GAMORRAN CYBORGS--THE ONES WHO AVOID GETTING MELTED DOWN--TEND TO BECOME FREE AGENTS. MERCENARY ASSASSINS FOR HIRE.
KRUKK
SHZZZZ
WHICH LEAVES THE QUESTION OF WHO HIRED THESE GENIUSES.
ONE WAY TO FIND OUT.
FOOOSHHHH
LOOKS LIKE I'LL HAVE TO LEAVE ONE ALIVE.
SHRIIPP
GAHH!

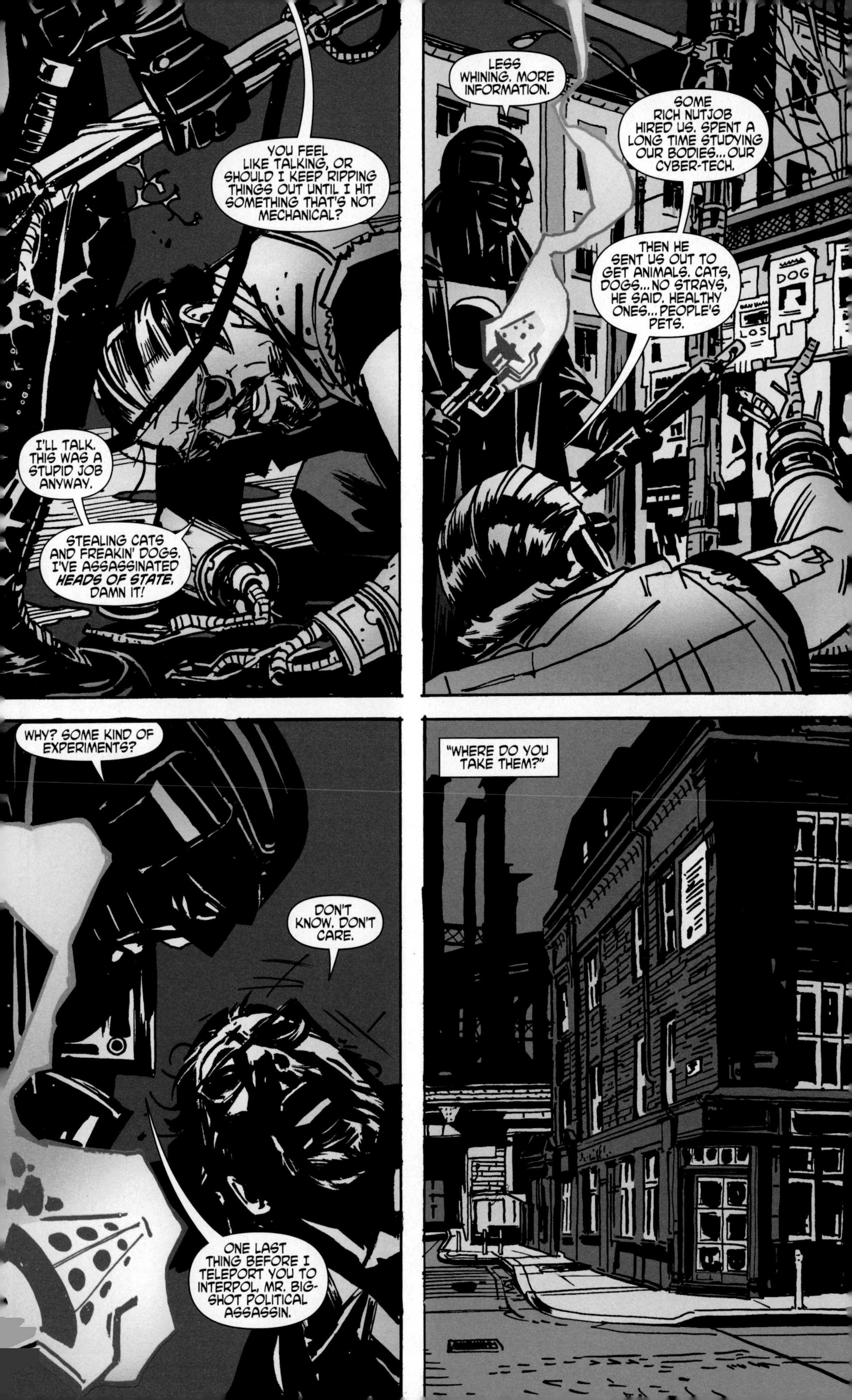
YOU FEEL LIKE TALKING, OR SHOULD I KEEP RIPPING THINGS OUT UNTIL I HIT SOMETHING THAT'S NOT MECHANICAL?
I'LL TALK. THIS WAS A STUPID JOB ANYWAY.
STEALING CATS AND FREAKIN' DOGS. I'VE ASSASSINATED *HEADS OF STATE*, DAMN IT!
LESS WHINING. MORE INFORMATION.
SOME RICH NUTJOB HIRED US. SPENT A LONG TIME STUDYING OUR BODIES...OUR CYBER-TECH.
THEN HE SENT US OUT TO GET ANIMALS. CATS, DOGS...NO STRAYS, HE SAID. HEALTHY ONES...PEOPLE'S PETS.
DOG
LOS
WHY? SOME KIND OF EXPERIMENTS?
DON'T KNOW. DON'T CARE.
ONE LAST THING BEFORE I TELEPORT YOU TO INTERPOL, MR. BIG-SHOT POLITICAL ASSASSIN.
"WHERE DO YOU TAKE THEM?"

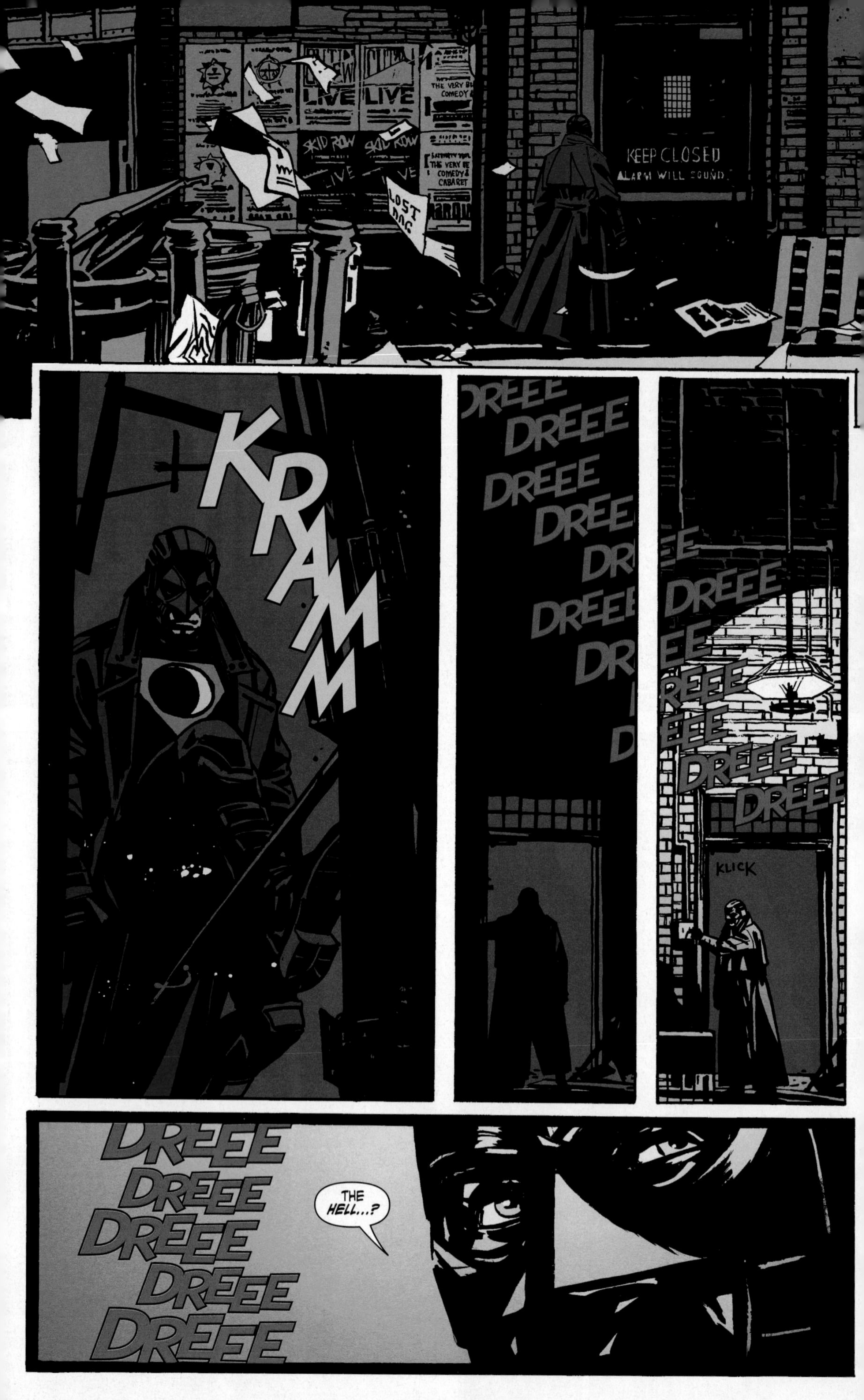
KEEP CLOSED
ALARM WILL SOUND
KRAMM
DREEE DREEE DREEE DREEE
DREEE DREEE DREEE
KLICK
DREEE DREEE DREEE DREEE DREEE
THE HELL...?

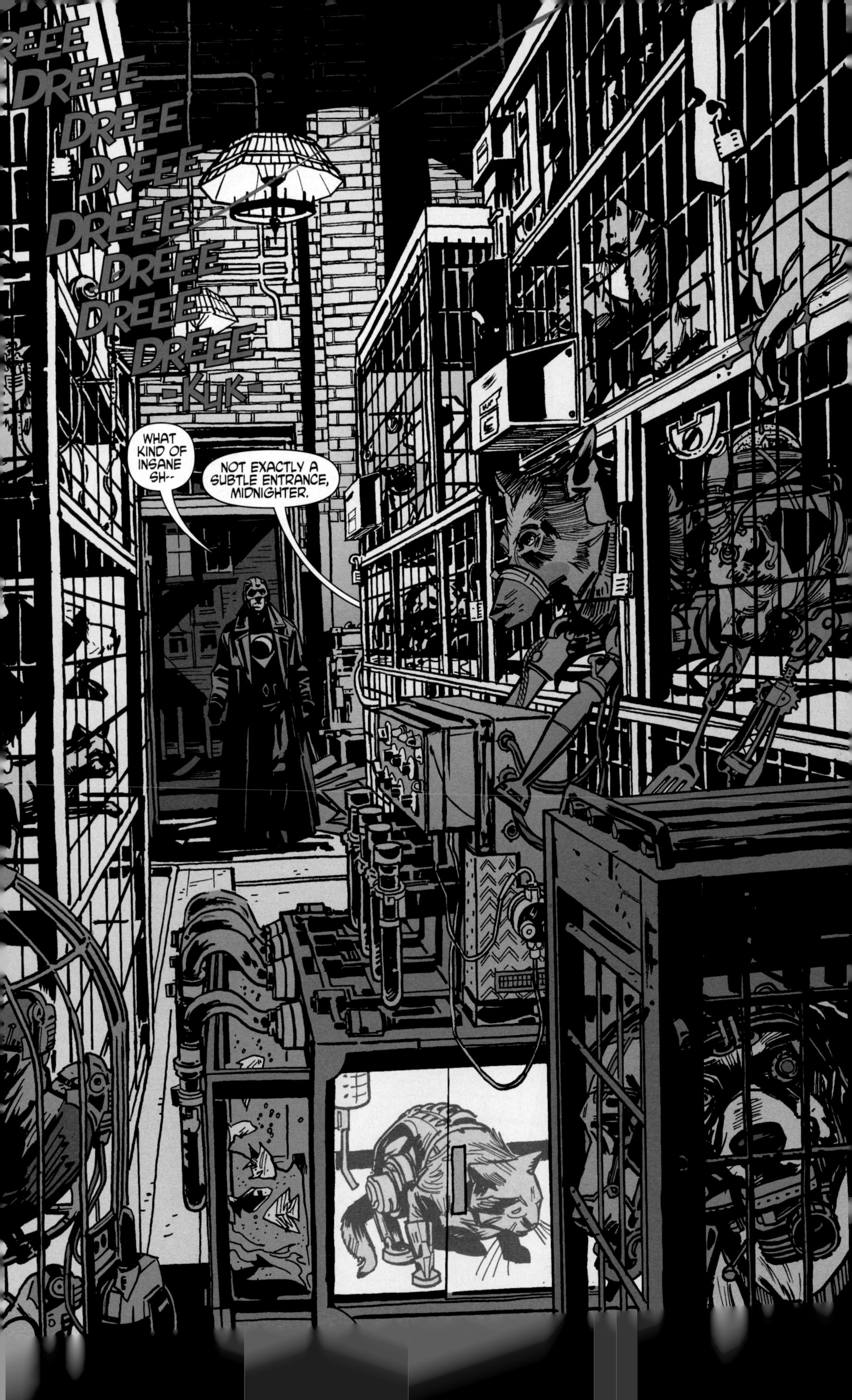
DREEE DREEE DREEE DREEE DREEE DREEE DREEE DREEE
-KLIK-
WHAT KIND OF INSANE SH--
NOT EXACTLY A SUBTLE ENTRANCE, MIDNIGHTER.

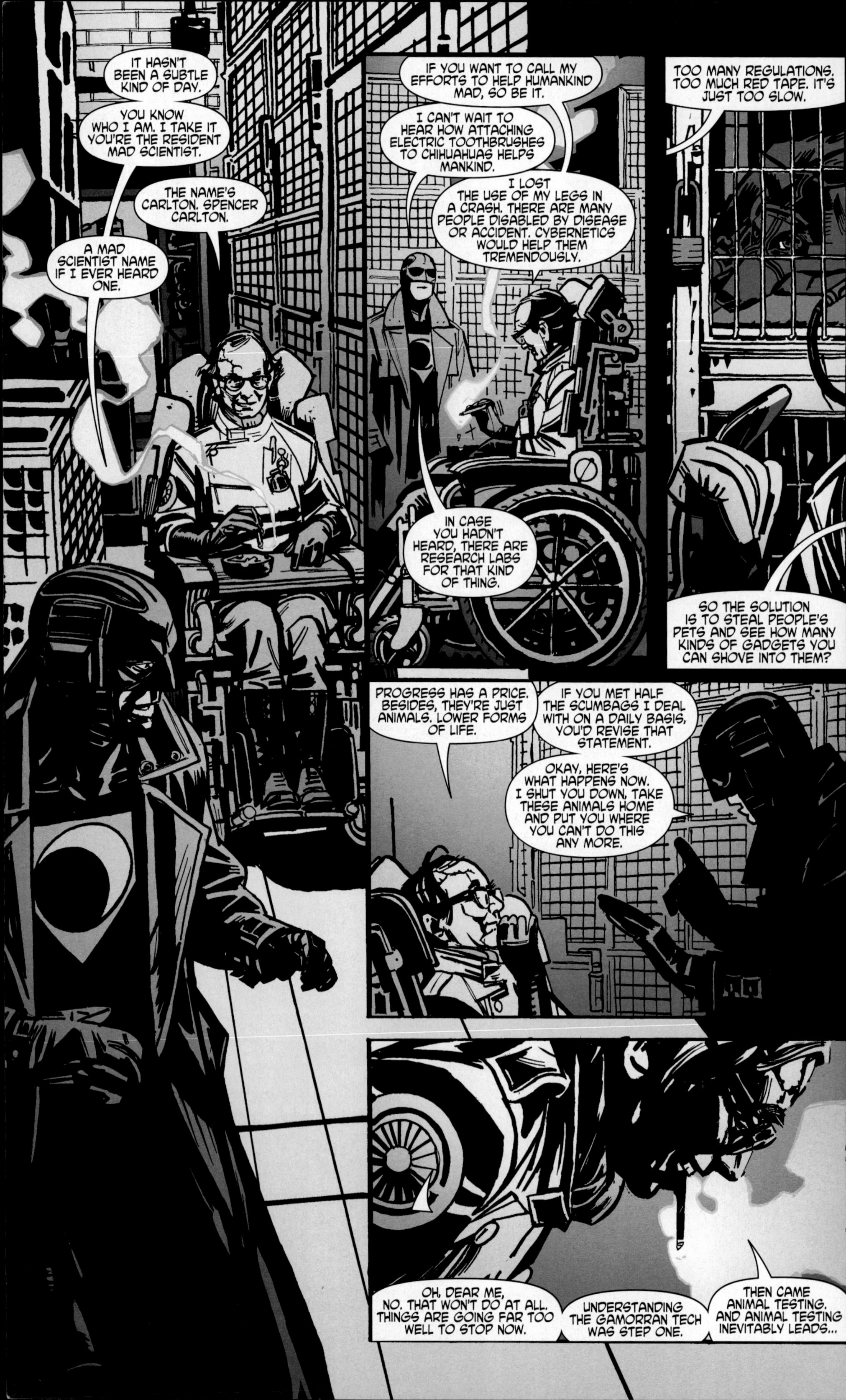

IT HASN'T BEEN A SUBTLE KIND OF DAY.
YOU KNOW WHO I AM. I TAKE IT YOU'RE THE RESIDENT MAD SCIENTIST.
THE NAME'S CARLTON. SPENCER CARLTON.
A MAD SCIENTIST NAME IF I EVER HEARD ONE.
IF YOU WANT TO CALL MY EFFORTS TO HELP HUMANKIND MAD, SO BE IT.
I CAN'T WAIT TO HEAR HOW ATTACHING ELECTRIC TOOTHBRUSHES TO CHIHUAHUAS HELPS MANKIND.
I LOST THE USE OF MY LEGS IN A CRASH. THERE ARE MANY PEOPLE DISABLED BY DISEASE OR ACCIDENT. CYBERNETICS WOULD HELP THEM TREMENDOUSLY.
IN CASE YOU HADN'T HEARD, THERE ARE RESEARCH LABS FOR THAT KIND OF THING.
TOO MANY REGULATIONS. TOO MUCH RED TAPE. IT'S JUST TOO SLOW.
SO THE SOLUTION IS TO STEAL PEOPLE'S PETS AND SEE HOW MANY KINDS OF GADGETS YOU CAN SHOVE INTO THEM?
PROGRESS HAS A PRICE. BESIDES, THEY'RE JUST ANIMALS. LOWER FORMS OF LIFE.
IF YOU MET HALF THE SCUMBAGS I DEAL WITH ON A DAILY BASIS, YOU'D REVISE THAT STATEMENT.
OKAY, HERE'S WHAT HAPPENS NOW. I SHUT YOU DOWN, TAKE THESE ANIMALS HOME AND PUT YOU WHERE YOU CAN'T DO THIS ANY MORE.
OH, DEAR ME, NO. THAT WON'T DO AT ALL. THINGS ARE GOING FAR TOO WELL TO STOP NOW.
UNDERSTANDING THE GAMORRAN TECH WAS STEP ONE.
THEN CAME ANIMAL TESTING. AND ANIMAL TESTING INEVITABLY LEADS...

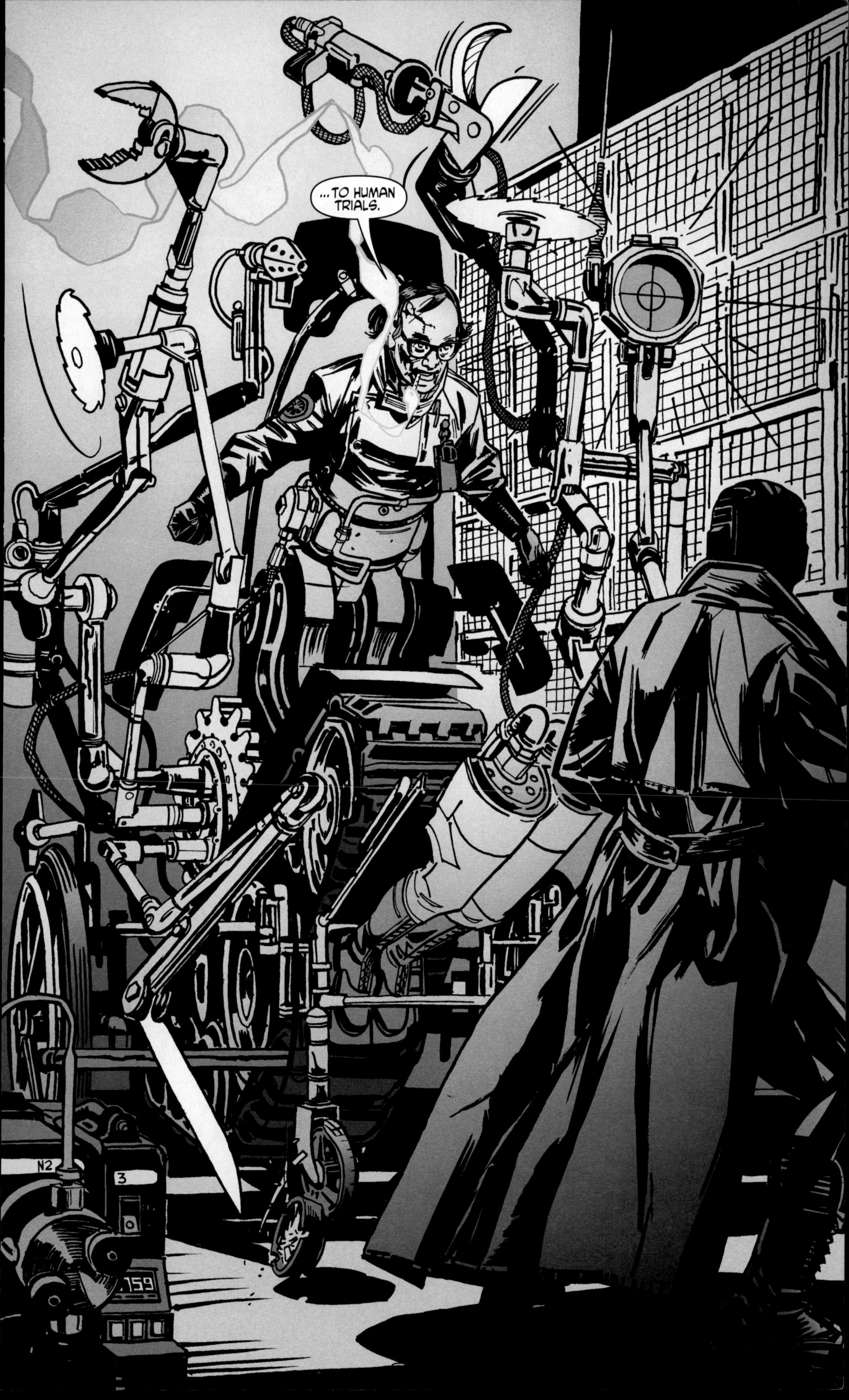
...TO HUMAN TRIALS.
N2
3

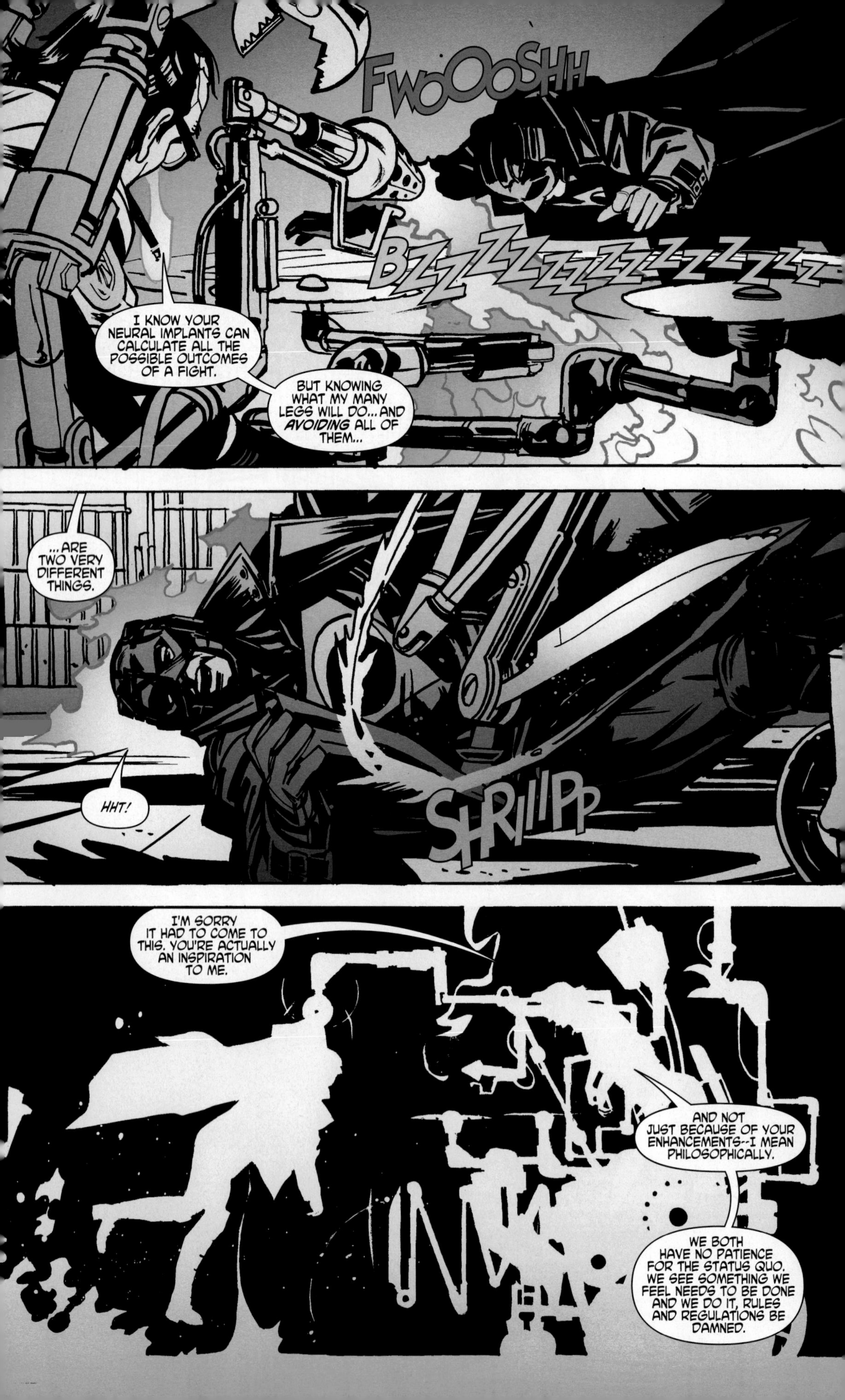
FWOOOOSHH
BZZZZZZZZZZZZZZZZZ
I KNOW YOUR NEURAL IMPLANTS CAN CALCULATE ALL THE POSSIBLE OUTCOMES OF A FIGHT.
BUT KNOWING WHAT MY MANY LEGS WILL DO... AND *AVOIDING* ALL OF THEM...
...ARE TWO VERY DIFFERENT THINGS.
HHT!
SHRIIIPP
I'M SORRY IT HAD TO COME TO THIS. YOU'RE ACTUALLY AN INSPIRATION TO ME.
AND NOT JUST BECAUSE OF YOUR ENHANCEMENTS--I MEAN PHILOSOPHICALLY.
WE BOTH HAVE NO PATIENCE FOR THE STATUS QUO. WE SEE SOMETHING WE FEEL NEEDS TO BE DONE AND WE DO IT, RULES AND REGULATIONS BE DAMNED.

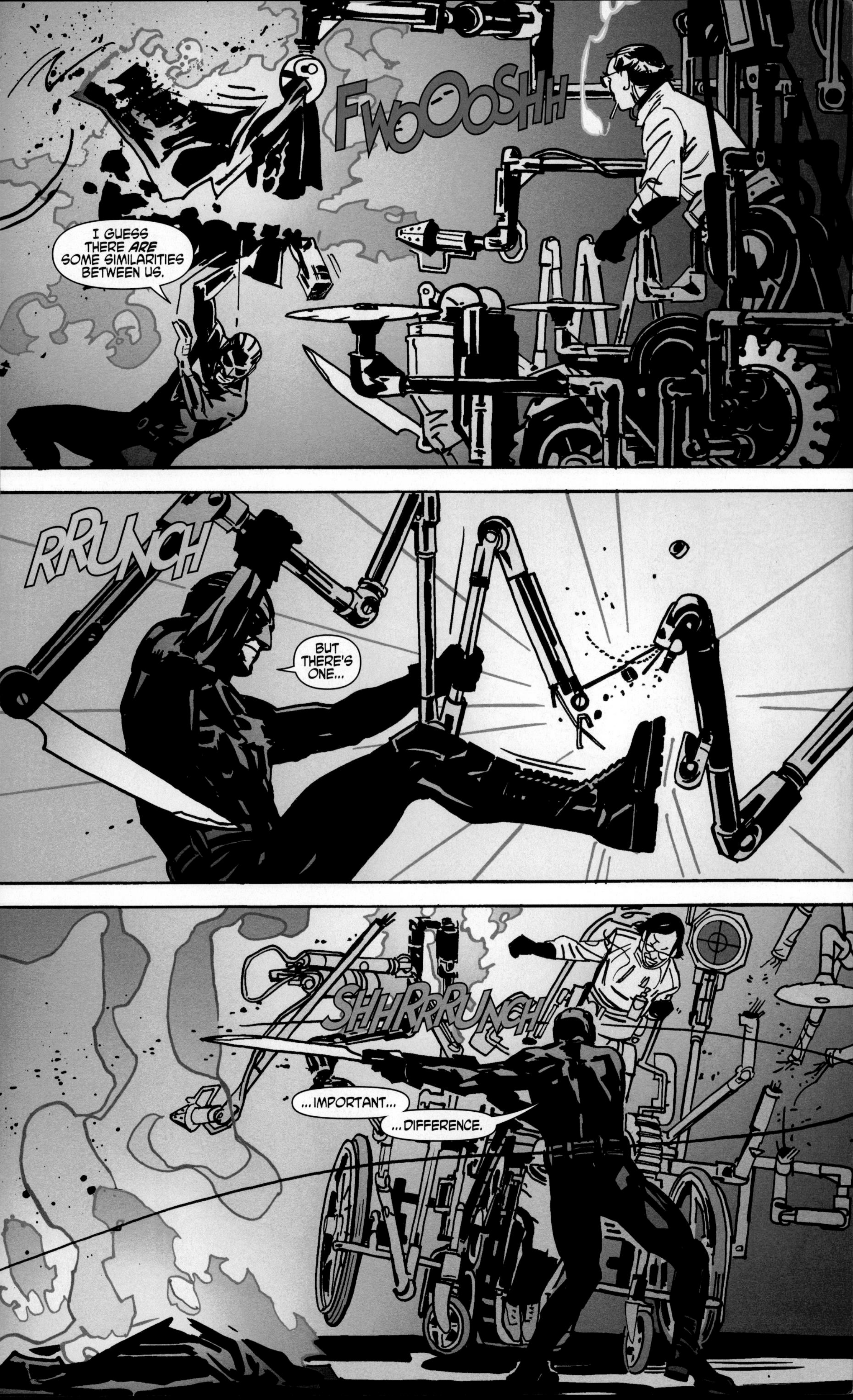
FWOOOSHH
I GUESS THERE ARE SOME SIMILARITIES BETWEEN US.
RRUNCH
BUT THERE'S ONE...
SHHRRRUNCH!
...IMPORTANT...
...DIFFERENCE.

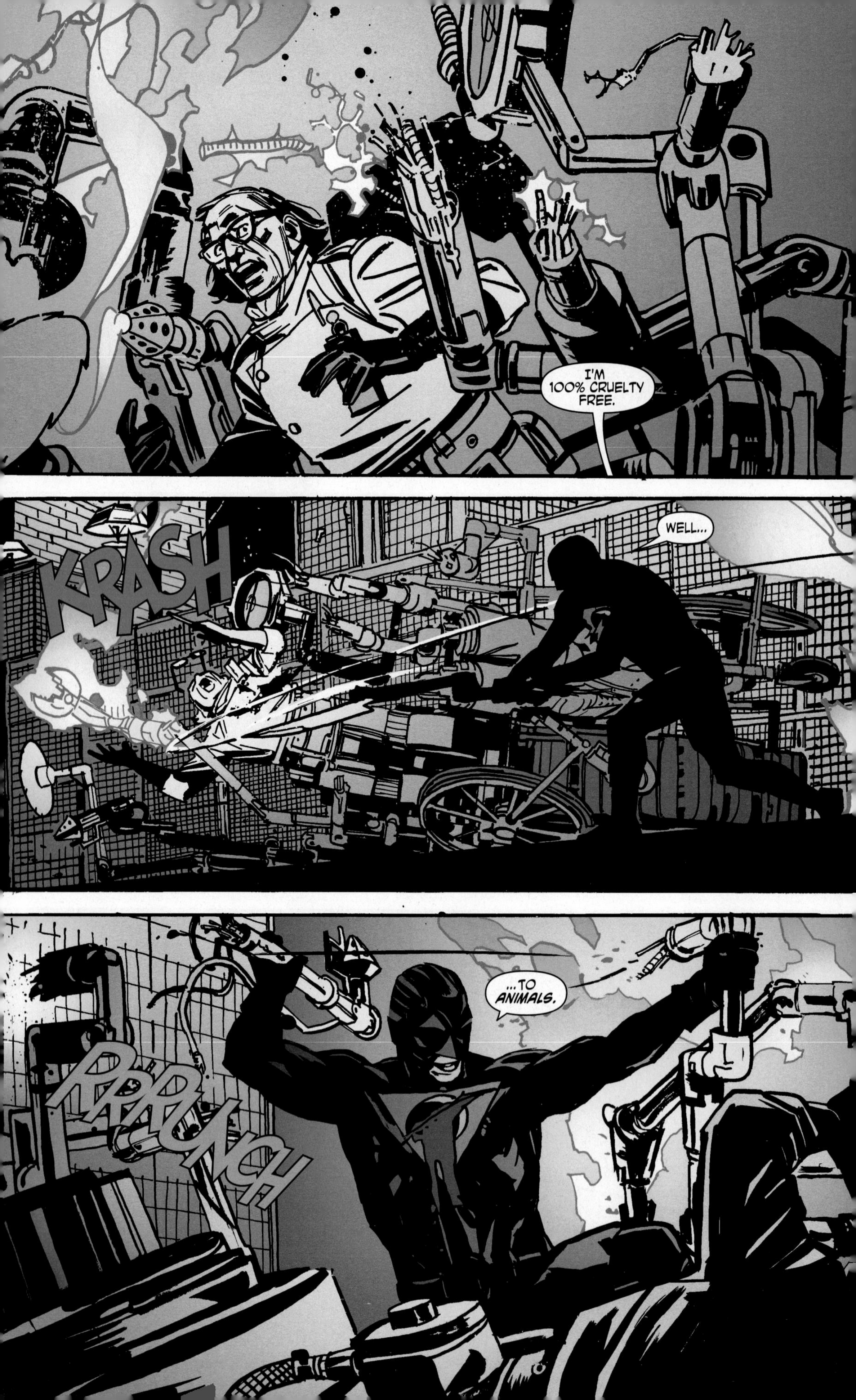
I'M 100% CRUELTY FREE.
KRASH
WELL...
...TO ANIMALS.
RRRUNCH

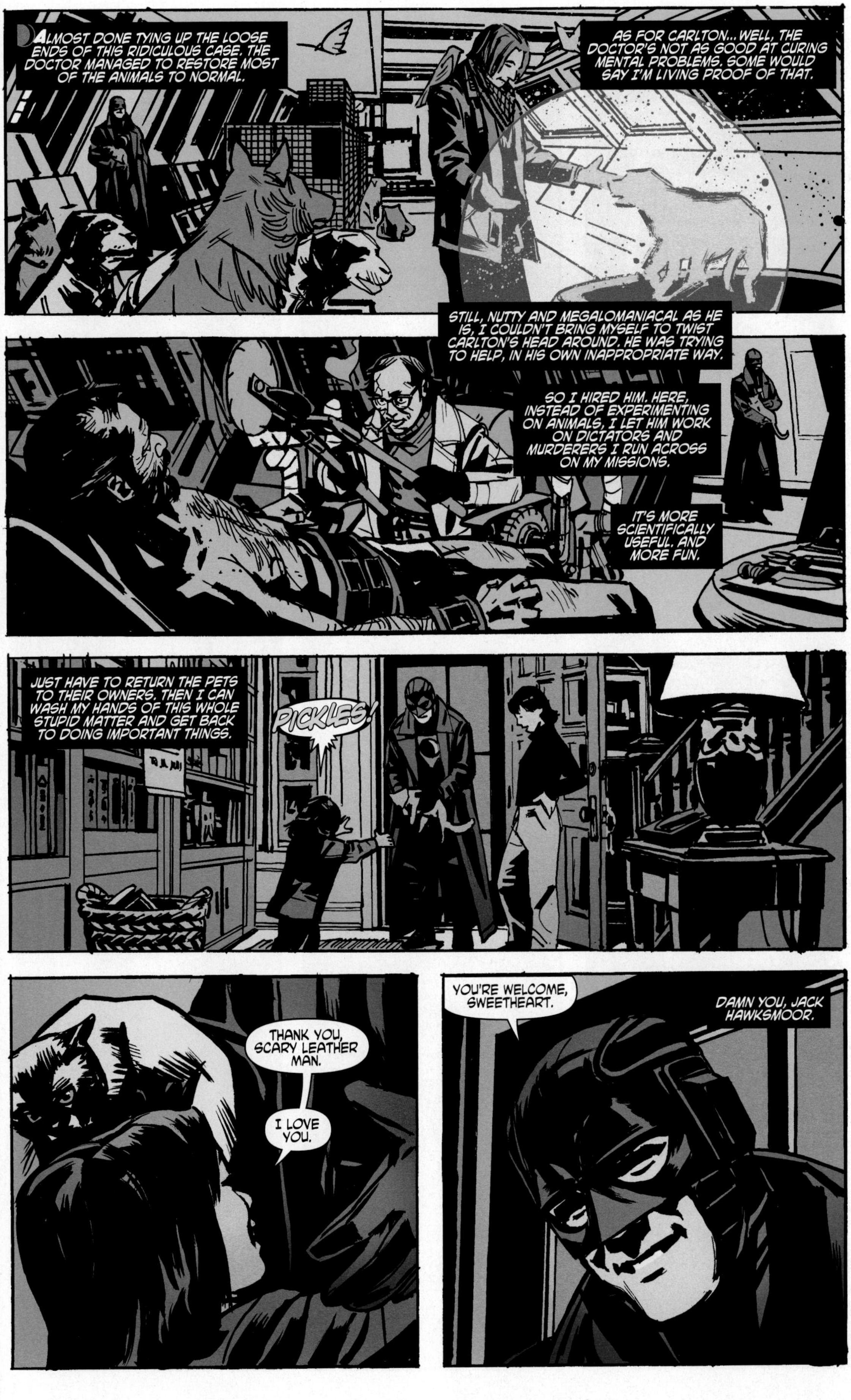
ALMOST DONE TYING UP THE LOOSE ENDS OF THIS RIDICULOUS CASE. THE DOCTOR MANAGED TO RESTORE MOST OF THE ANIMALS TO NORMAL.
AS FOR CARLTON... WELL, THE DOCTOR'S NOT AS GOOD AT CURING MENTAL PROBLEMS. SOME WOULD SAY I'M LIVING PROOF OF THAT.
STILL, NUTTY AND MEGALOMANIACAL AS HE IS, I COULDN'T BRING MYSELF TO TWIST CARLTON'S HEAD AROUND. HE WAS TRYING TO HELP, IN HIS OWN INAPPROPRIATE WAY.
SO I HIRED HIM. HERE, INSTEAD OF EXPERIMENTING ON ANIMALS, I LET HIM WORK ON DICTATORS AND MURDERERS I RUN ACROSS ON MY MISSIONS.
IT'S MORE SCIENTIFICALLY USEFUL. AND MORE FUN.
JUST HAVE TO RETURN THE PETS TO THEIR OWNERS. THEN I CAN WASH MY HANDS OF THIS WHOLE STUPID MATTER AND GET BACK TO DOING IMPORTANT THINGS.
PICKLES!
THANK YOU, SCARY LEATHER MAN.
I LOVE YOU.
YOU'RE WELCOME, SWEETHEART.
DAMN YOU, JACK HAWKSMOOR.

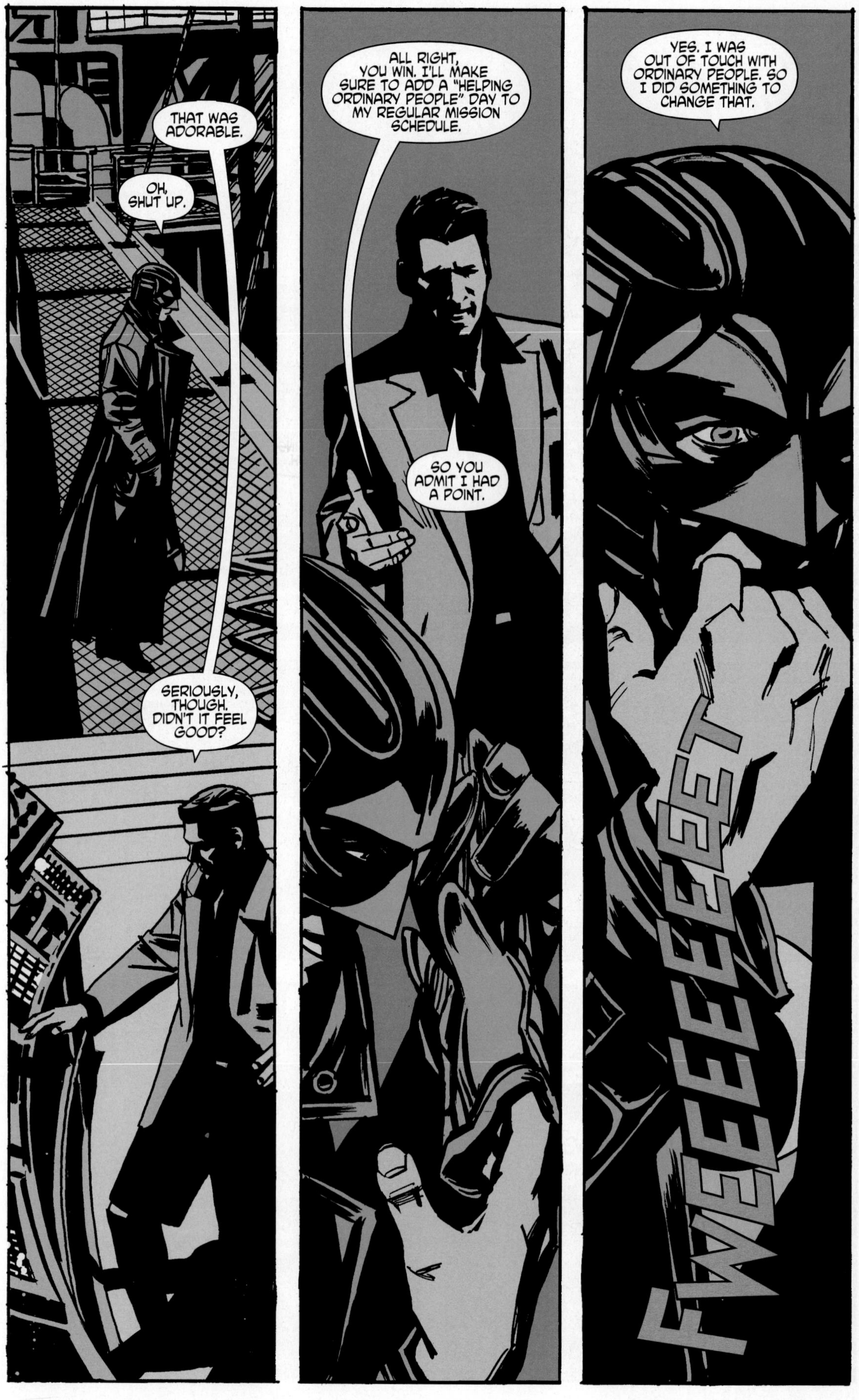
THAT WAS ADORABLE.
OH, SHUT UP.
SERIOUSLY, THOUGH. DIDN'T IT FEEL GOOD?
ALL RIGHT, YOU WIN. I'LL MAKE SURE TO ADD A "HELPING ORDINARY PEOPLE" DAY TO MY REGULAR MISSION SCHEDULE.
SO YOU ADMIT I HAD A POINT.
YES. I WAS OUT OF TOUCH WITH ORDINARY PEOPLE. SO I DID SOMETHING TO CHANGE THAT.
FWEEEEEEET

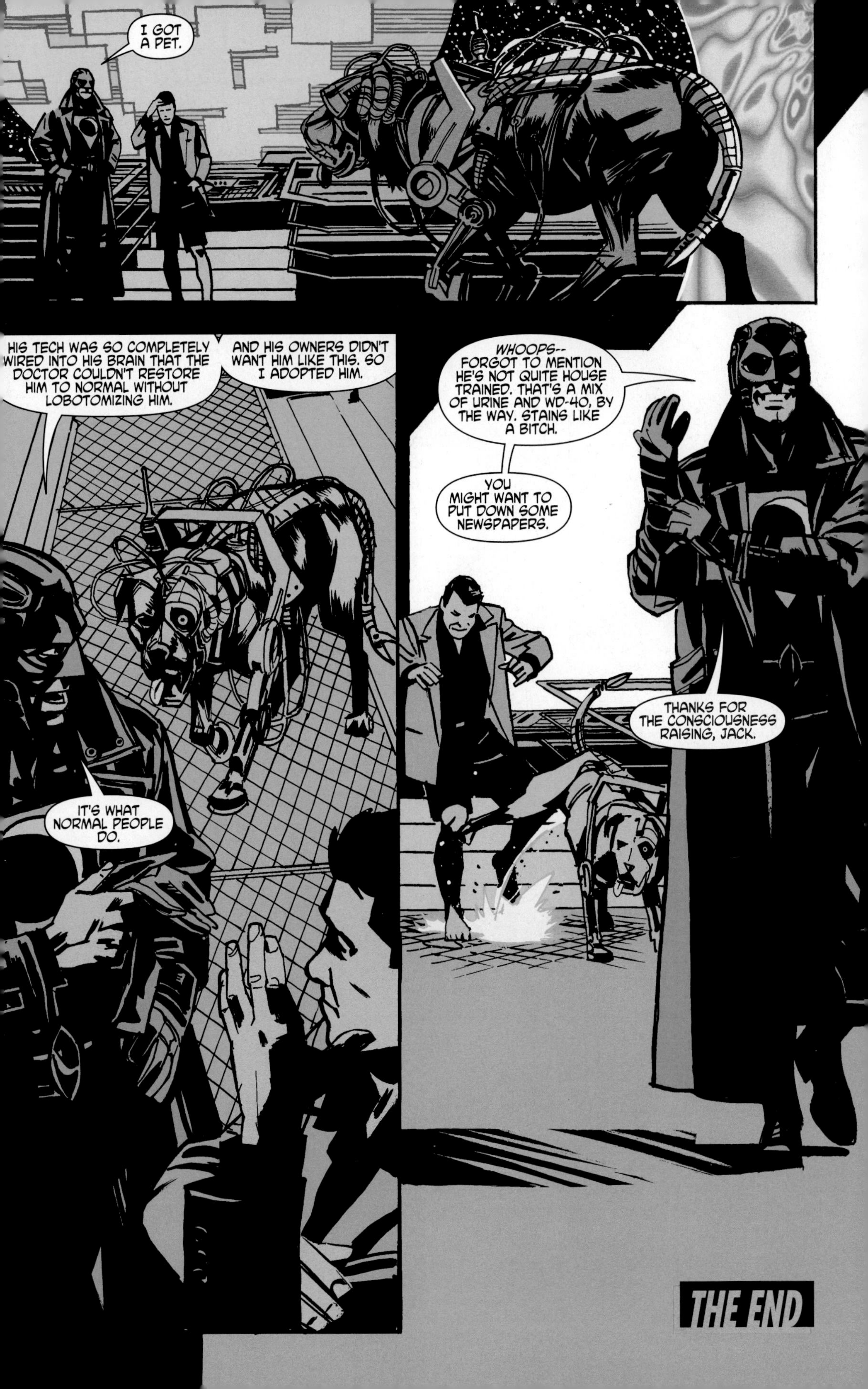
I GOT A PET.
HIS TECH WAS SO COMPLETELY WIRED INTO HIS BRAIN THAT THE DOCTOR COULDN'T RESTORE HIM TO NORMAL WITHOUT LOBOTOMIZING HIM.
AND HIS OWNERS DIDN'T WANT HIM LIKE THIS. SO I ADOPTED HIM.
IT'S WHAT NORMAL PEOPLE DO.
WHOOPS-- FORGOT TO MENTION HE'S NOT QUITE HOUSE TRAINED. THAT'S A MIX OF URINE AND WD-40, BY THE WAY. STAINS LIKE A BITCH.
YOU MIGHT WANT TO PUT DOWN SOME NEWSPAPERS.
THANKS FOR THE CONSCIOUSNESS RAISING, JACK.
THE END

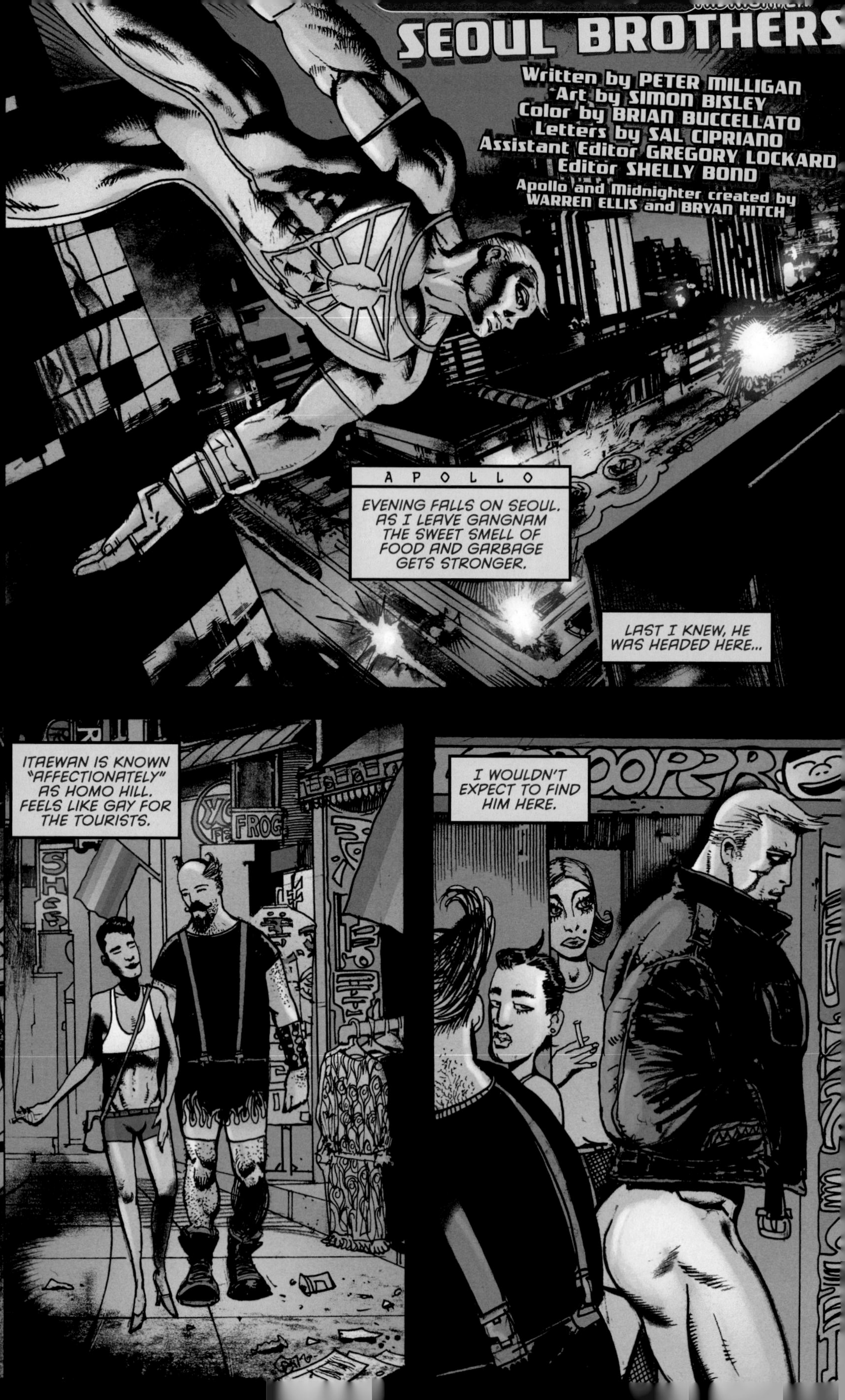
SEOUL BROTHERS
Written by PETER MILLIGAN
Art by SIMON BISLEY
Color by BRIAN BUCCELLATO
Letters by SAL CIPRIANO
Assistant Editor GREGORY LOCKARD
Editor SHELLY BOND
Apollo and Midnighter created by WARREN ELLIS and BRYAN HITCH
APOLLO
EVENING FALLS ON SEOUL. AS I LEAVE GANGNAM THE SWEET SMELL OF FOOD AND GARBAGE GETS STRONGER.
LAST I KNEW, HE WAS HEADED HERE...
ITAEWAN IS KNOWN "AFFECTIONATELY" AS HOMO HILL. FEELS LIKE GAY FOR THE TOURISTS.
I WOULDN'T EXPECT TO FIND HIM HERE.

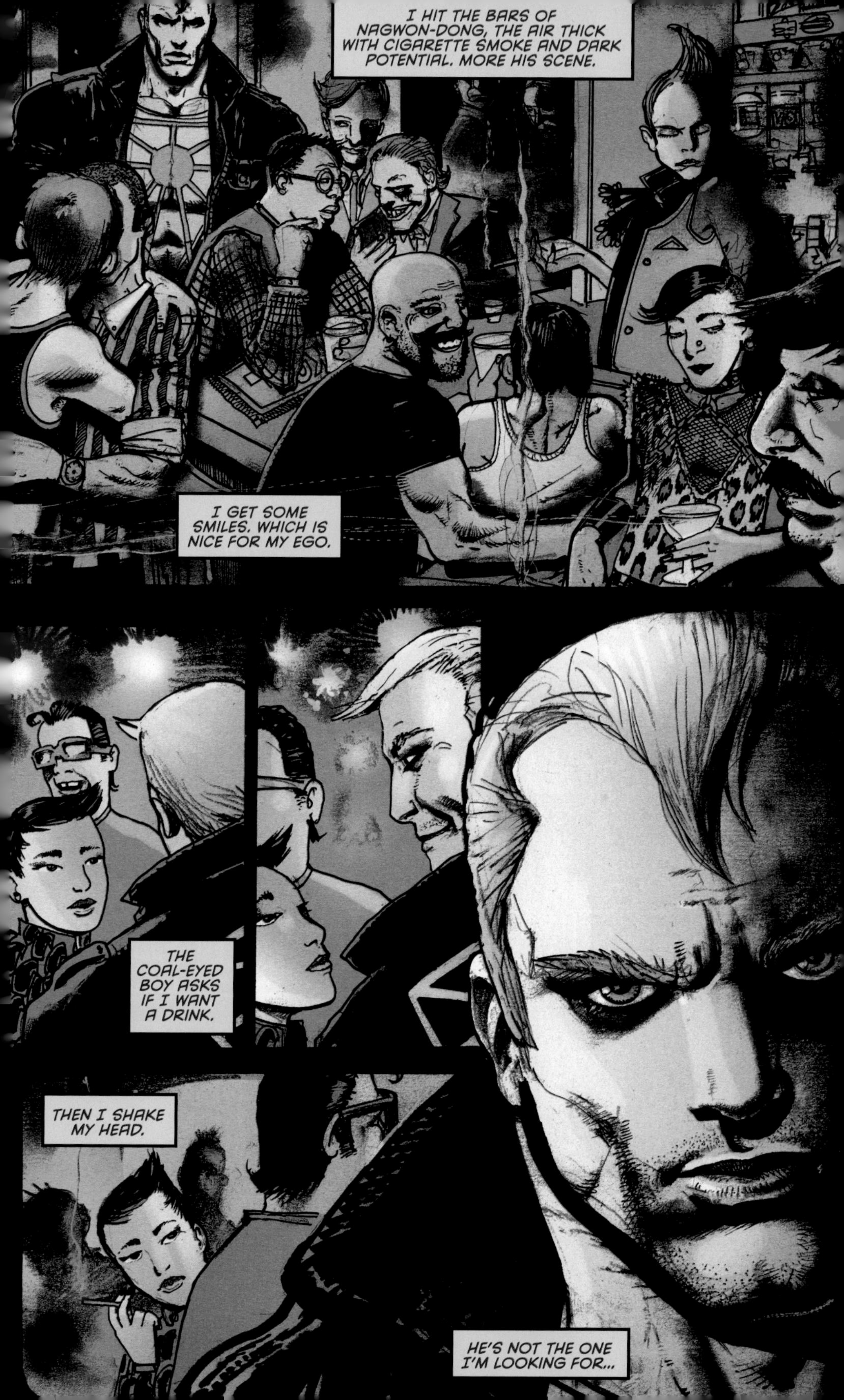
I HIT THE BARS OF NAGWON-DONG, THE AIR THICK WITH CIGARETTE SMOKE AND DARK POTENTIAL. MORE HIS SCENE.
I GET SOME SMILES. WHICH IS NICE FOR MY EGO.
THE COAL-EYED BOY ASKS IF I WANT A DRINK.
THEN I SHAKE MY HEAD.
HE'S NOT THE ONE I'M LOOKING FOR...

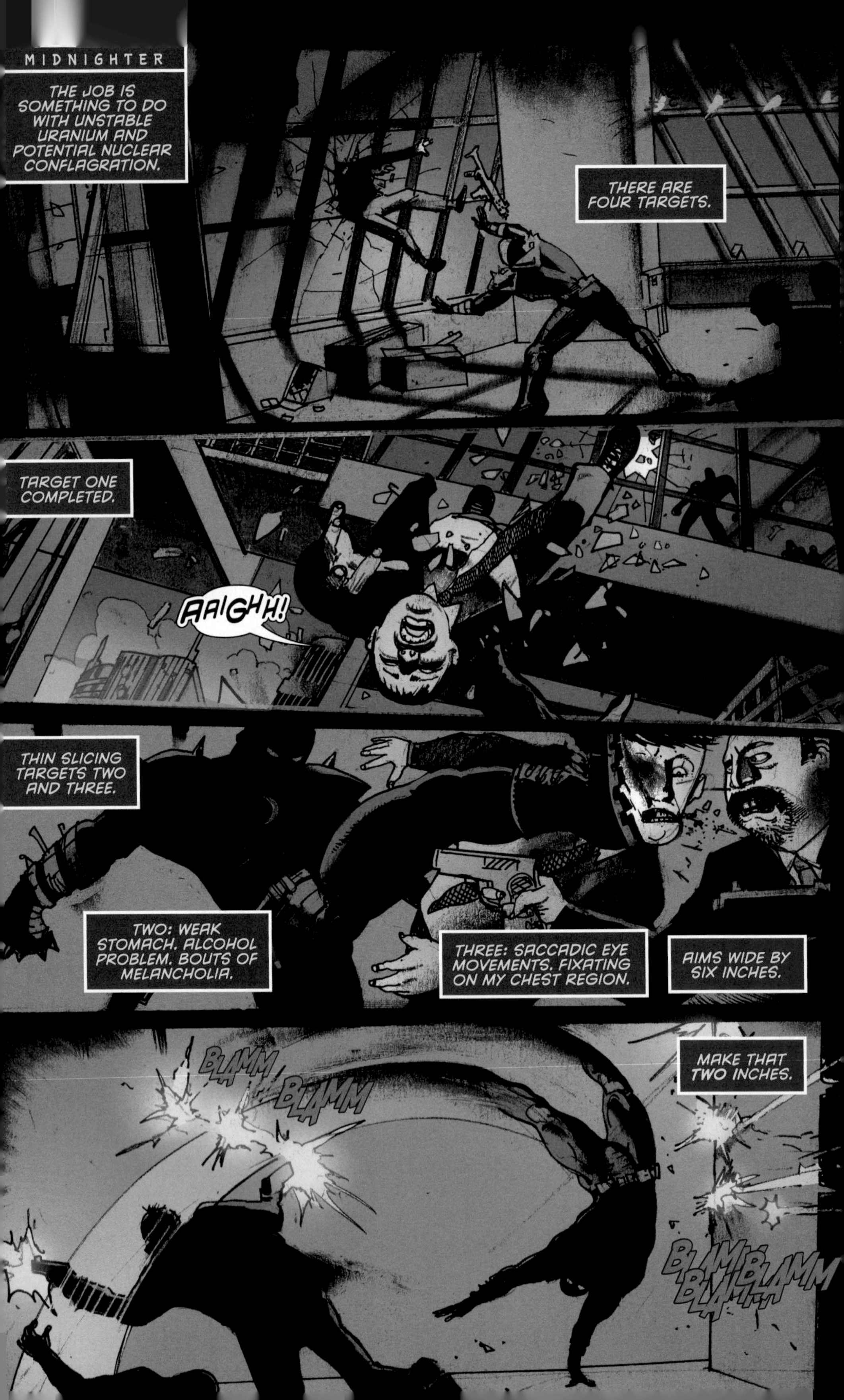
MIDNIGHTER
THE JOB IS SOMETHING TO DO WITH UNSTABLE URANIUM AND POTENTIAL NUCLEAR CONFLAGRATION.
THERE ARE FOUR TARGETS.
TARGET ONE COMPLETED.
AAIGHH!
THIN SLICING TARGETS TWO AND THREE.
TWO: WEAK STOMACH. ALCOHOL PROBLEM. BOUTS OF MELANCHOLIA.
THREE: SACCADIC EYE MOVEMENTS. FIXATING ON MY CHEST REGION.
AIMS WIDE BY SIX INCHES.
BLAMM
BLAMM
MAKE THAT TWO INCHES.
BLAM BLAMM
BLAM

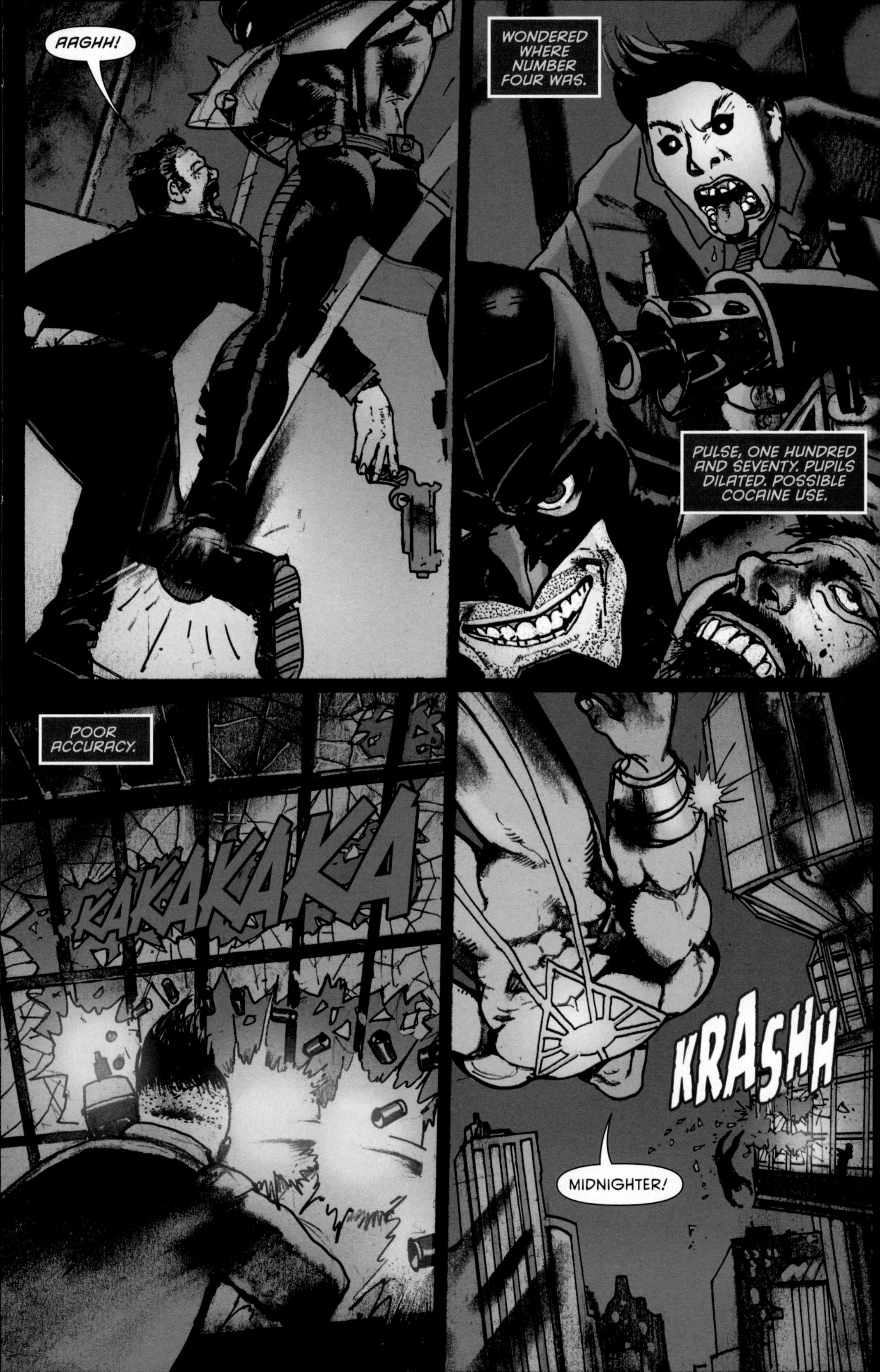
AAGHH!
WONDERED WHERE NUMBER FOUR WAS.
PULSE, ONE HUNDRED AND SEVENTY. PUPILS DILATED. POSSIBLE COCAINE USE.
POOR ACCURACY.
KAKAKAKAKA
KRASHH
MIDNIGHTER!

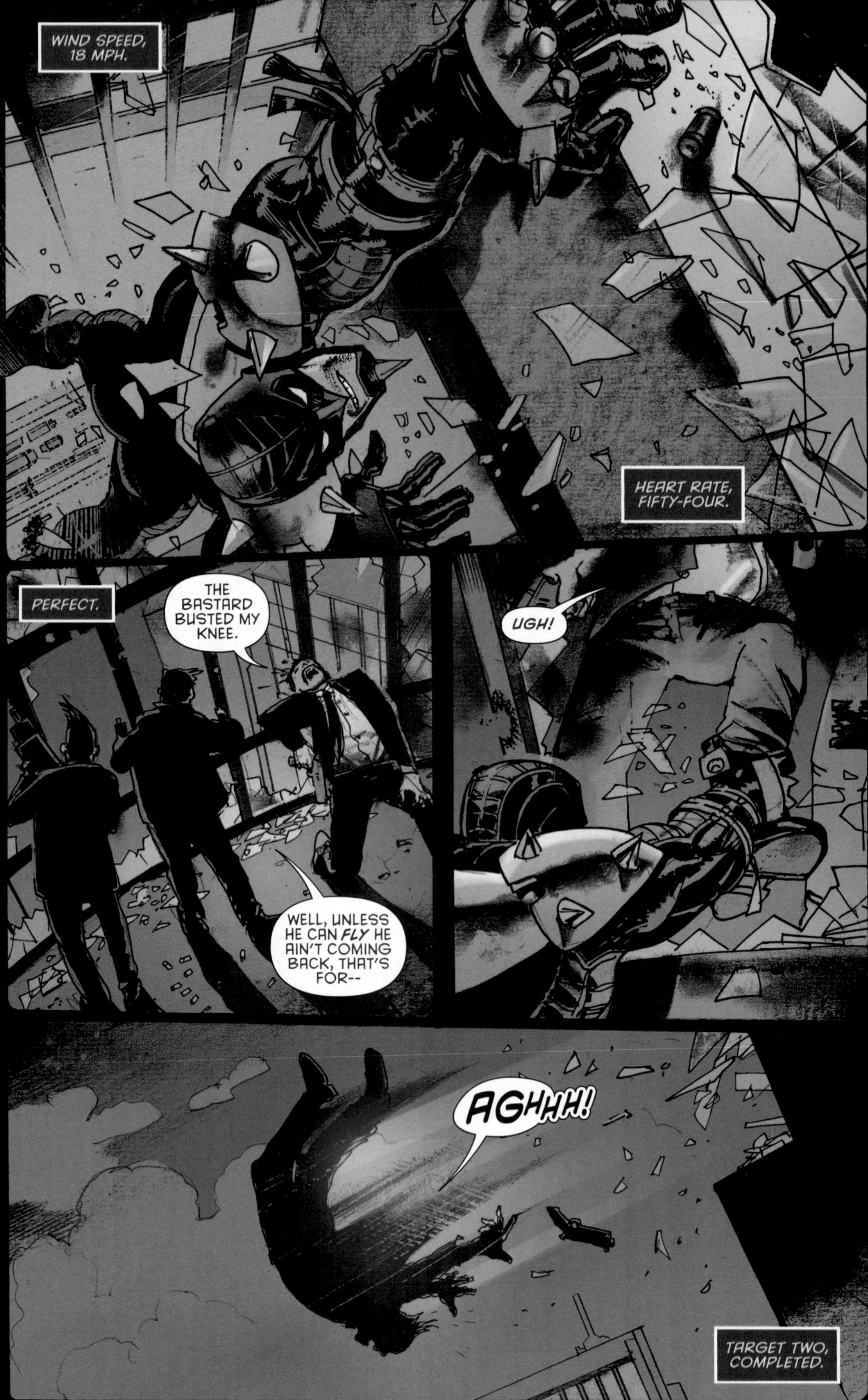
WIND SPEED, 18 MPH.
HEART RATE, FIFTY-FOUR.
PERFECT.
THE BASTARD BUSTED MY KNEE.
WELL, UNLESS HE CAN FLY HE AIN'T COMING BACK, THAT'S FOR--
UGH!
AGHHH!
TARGET TWO, COMPLETED.

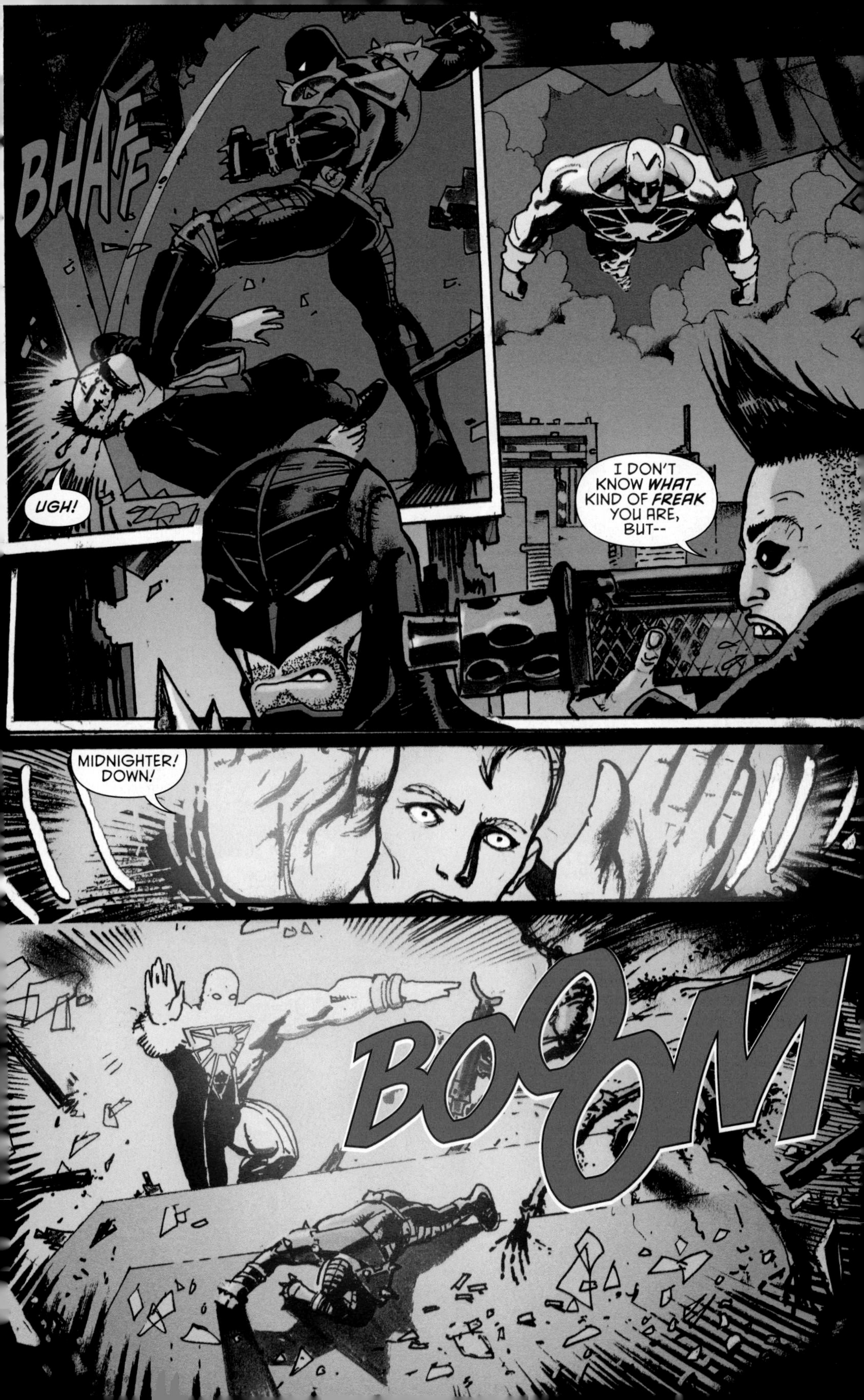
BHAF
UGH!
I DON'T KNOW WHAT KIND OF FREAK YOU ARE, BUT--
MIDNIGHTER! DOWN!
BOOOM

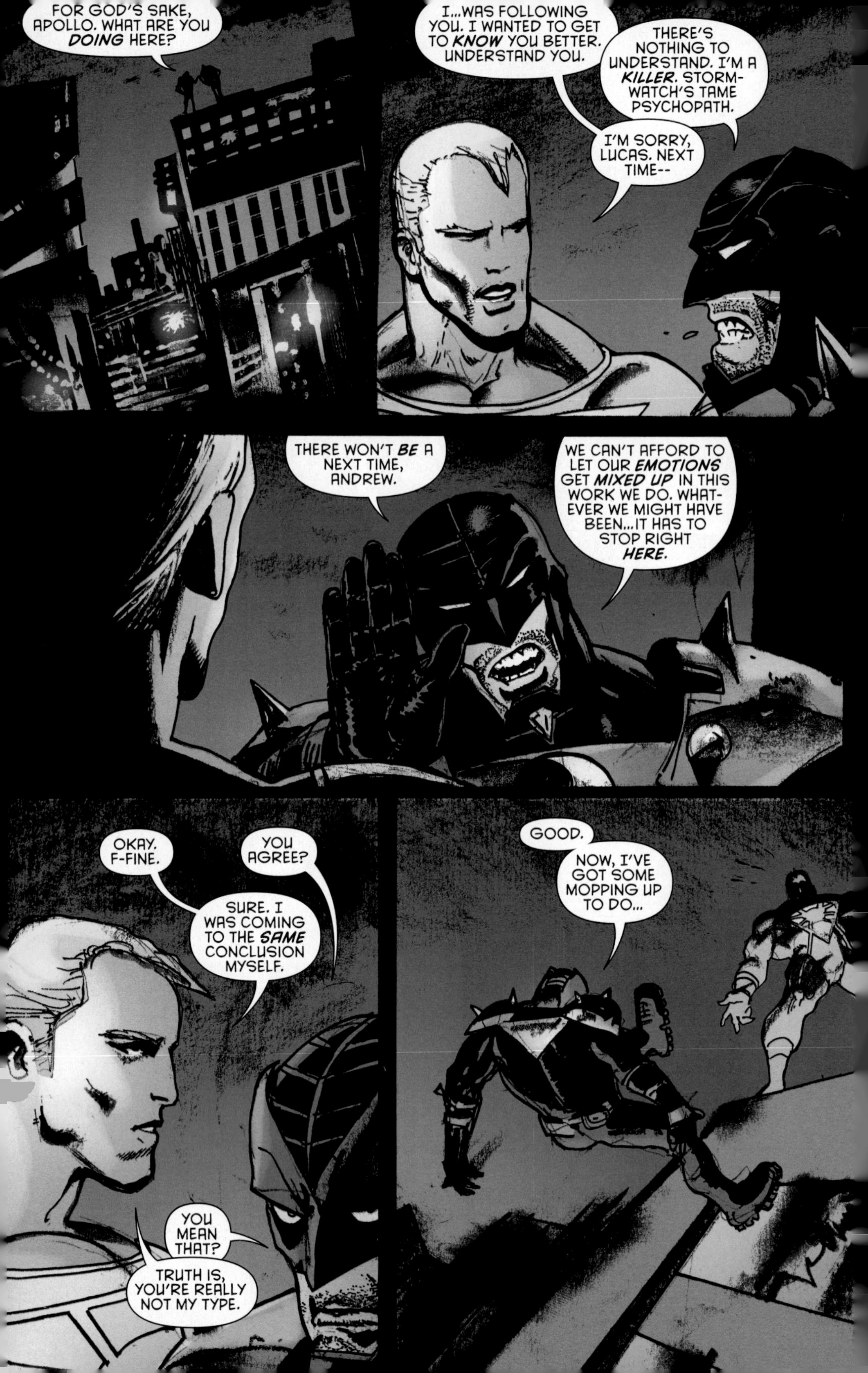

FOR GOD'S SAKE, APOLLO. WHAT ARE YOU DOING HERE?
I...WAS FOLLOWING YOU. I WANTED TO GET TO KNOW YOU BETTER. UNDERSTAND YOU.
THERE'S NOTHING TO UNDERSTAND. I'M A KILLER. STORM-WATCH'S TAME PSYCHOPATH.
I'M SORRY, LUCAS. NEXT TIME--
THERE WON'T BE A NEXT TIME, ANDREW.
WE CAN'T AFFORD TO LET OUR EMOTIONS GET MIXED UP IN THIS WORK WE DO. WHAT-EVER WE MIGHT HAVE BEEN...IT HAS TO STOP RIGHT HERE.
OKAY. F-FINE.
YOU AGREE?
SURE. I WAS COMING TO THE SAME CONCLUSION MYSELF.
YOU MEAN THAT?
TRUTH IS, YOU'RE REALLY NOT MY TYPE.
GOOD.
NOW, I'VE GOT SOME MOPPING UP TO DO...

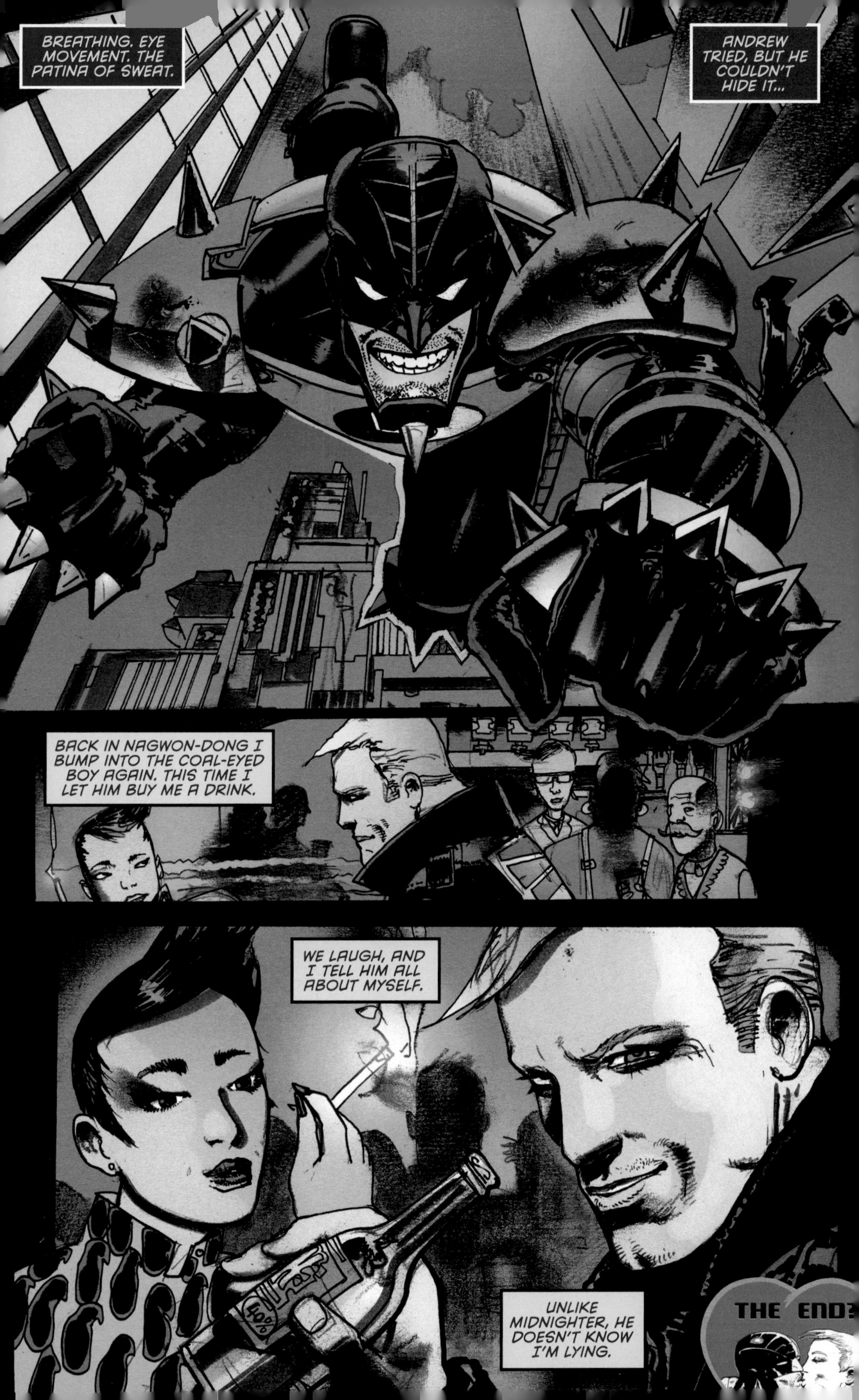
BREATHING. EYE MOVEMENT. THE PATINA OF SWEAT.
ANDREW TRIED, BUT HE COULDN'T HIDE IT...
BACK IN NAGWON-DONG I BUMP INTO THE COAL-EYED BOY AGAIN. THIS TIME I LET HIM BUY ME A DRINK.
WE LAUGH, AND I TELL HIM ALL ABOUT MYSELF.
UNLIKE MIDNIGHTER, HE DOESN'T KNOW I'M LYING.
THE END?

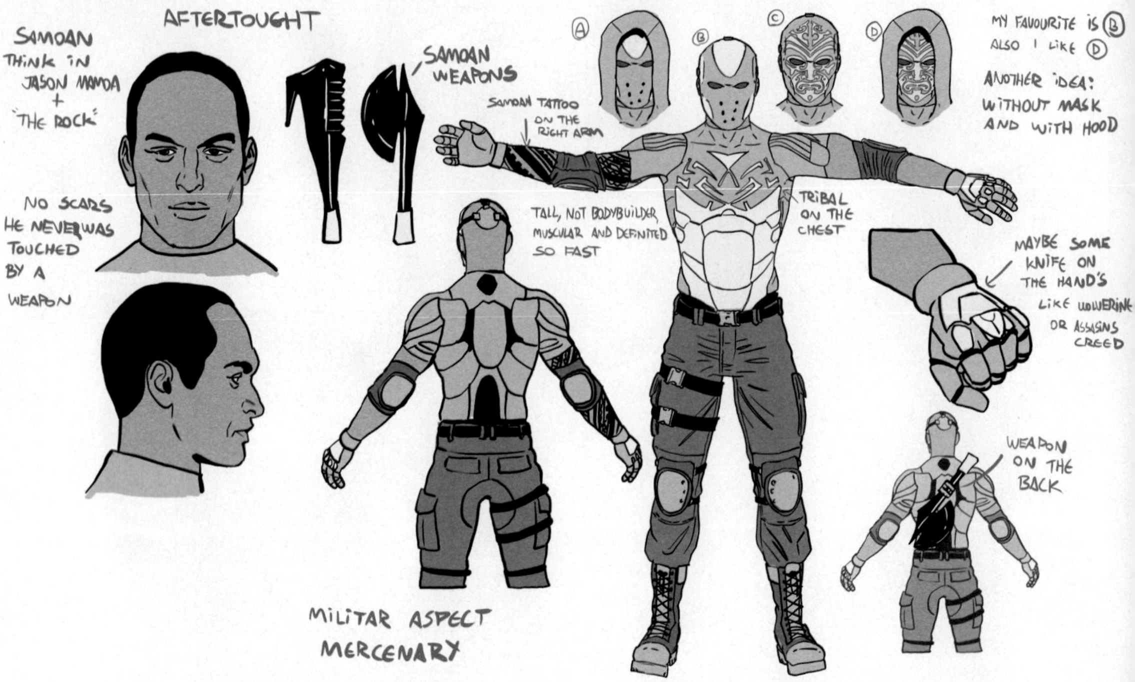
AFTERTOUGHT
SAMOAN
THINK IN
JASON MAMOA
+
"THE ROCK"
NO SCARS
HE NEVER WAS
TOUCHED
BY A
WEAPON
SAMOAN
WEAPONS
A
B
C
D
SAMOAN TATTOO
ON THE
RIGHT ARM
TALL, NOT BODYBUILDER,
MUSCULAR AND DEFINITED
SO FAST
TRIBAL
ON THE
CHEST
MY FAVOURITE IS B
ALSO I LIKE D
ANOTHER IDEA:
WITHOUT MASK
AND WITH HOOD
MAYBE SOME
KNIFE ON
THE HAND'S
LIKE WOLVERINE
OR ASSASINS
CREED
WEAPON
ON THE
BACK
MILITAR ASPECT
MERCENARY

2

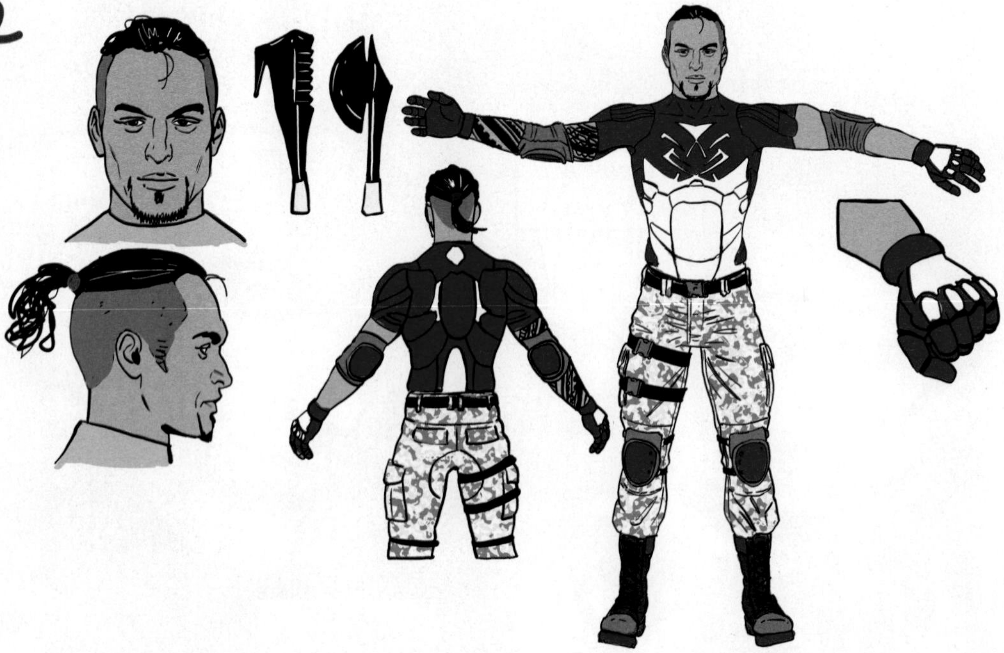

UNIFIED

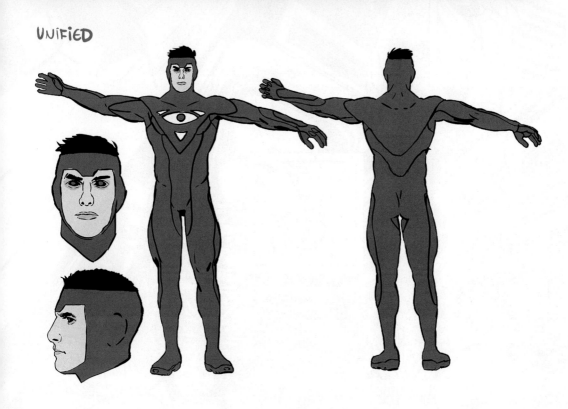

PROMETHEUS N52

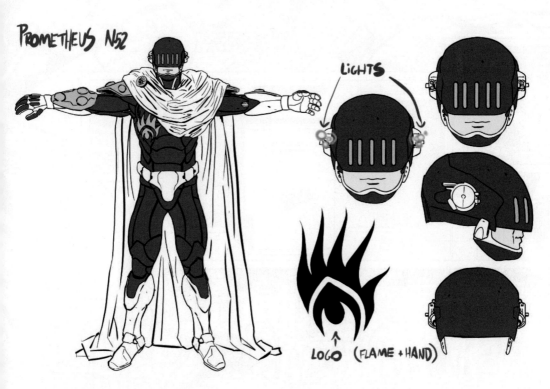

LIGHTS

LOGO (FLAME + HAND)

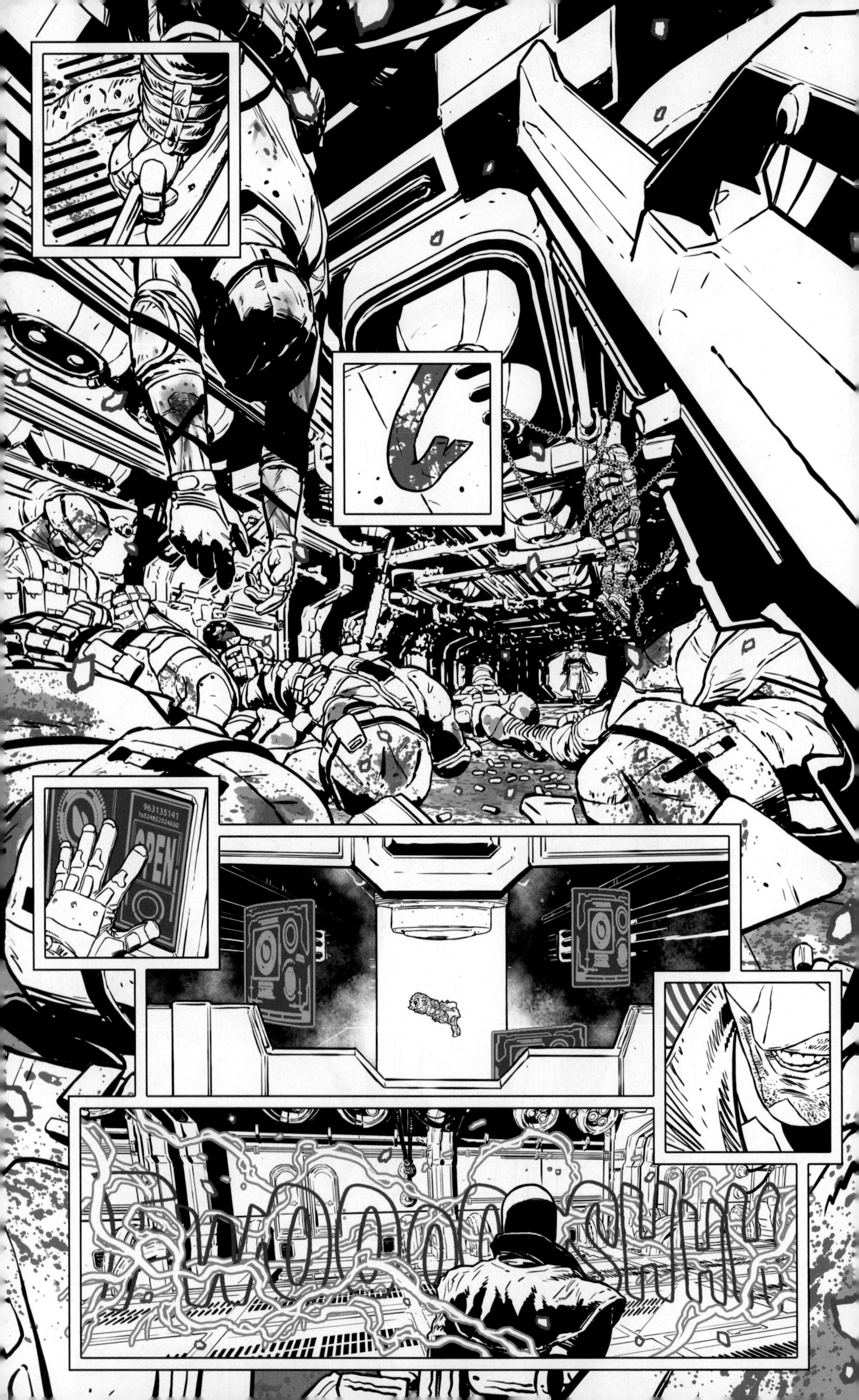
963135141
16524852024030
OPEN

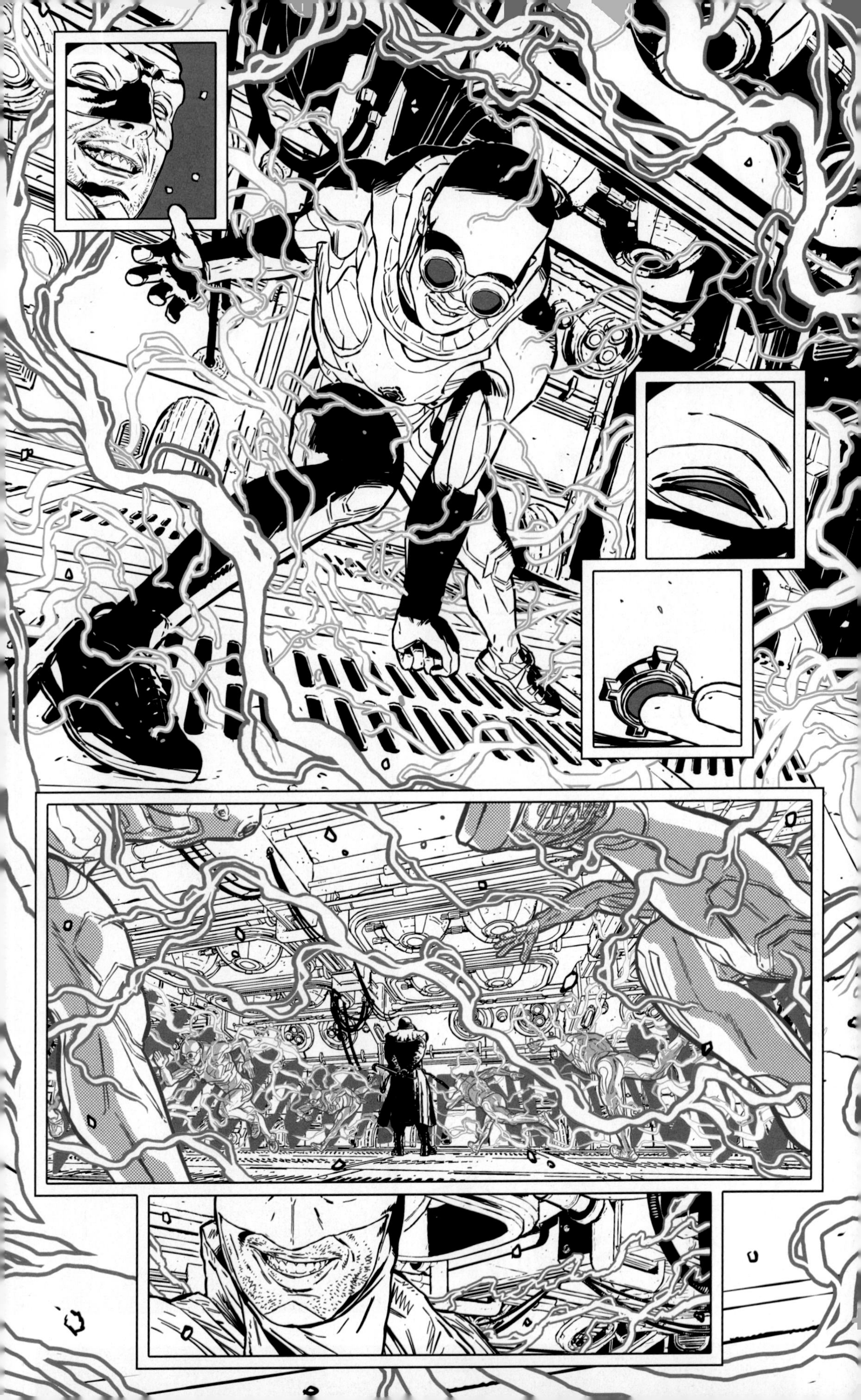

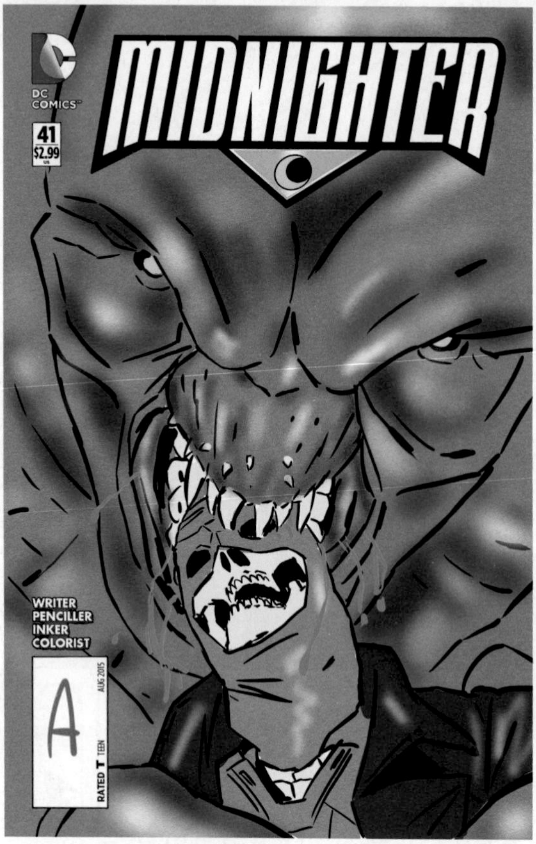
DC COMICS
MIDNIGHTER
41
$2.99
US
WRITER
PENCILLER
INKER
COLORIST
A
AUG 2015
RATED T TEEN
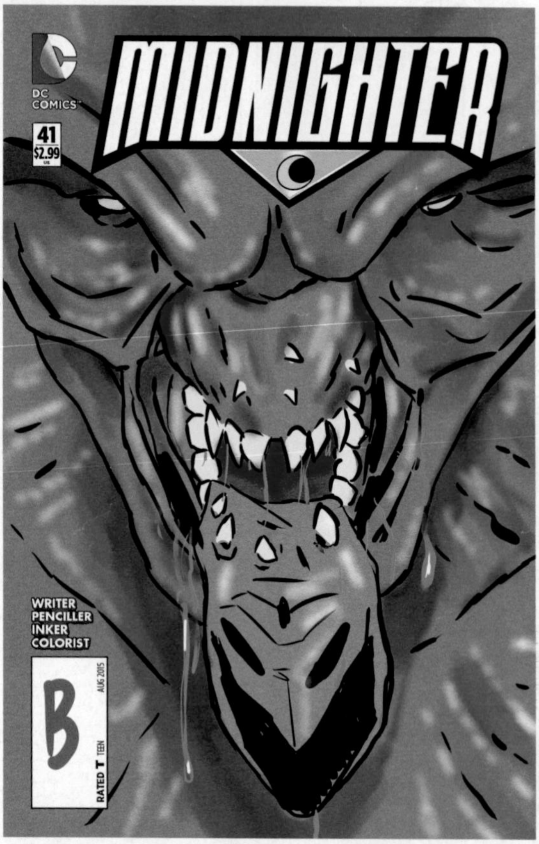
DC COMICS
MIDNIGHTER
41
$2.99
US
WRITER
PENCILLER
INKER
COLORIST
B
AUG 2015
RATED T TEEN
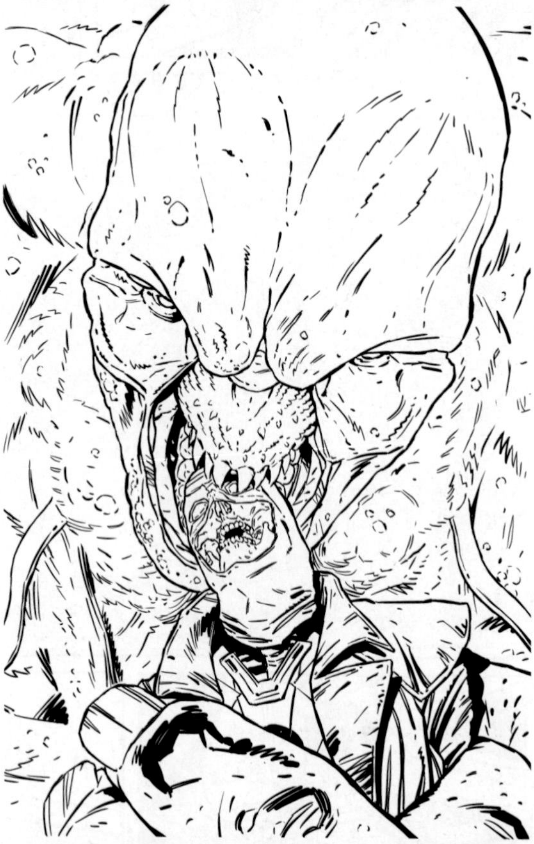
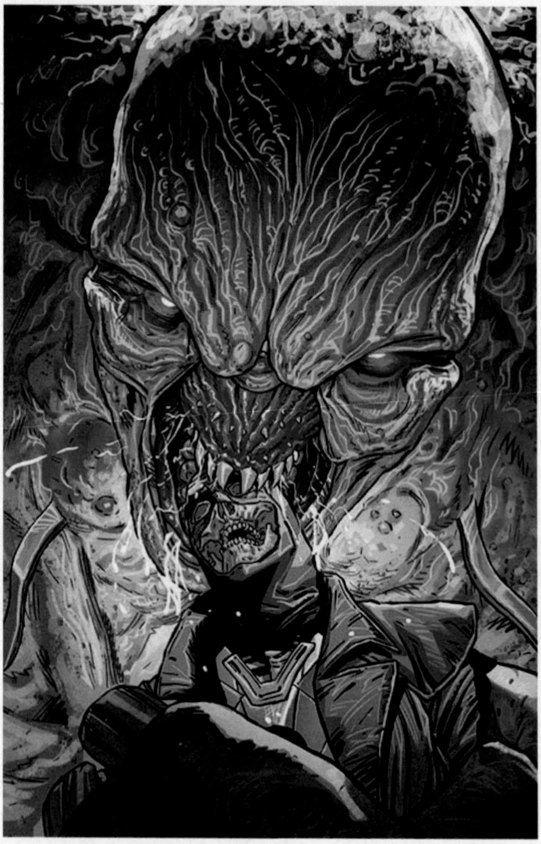